PotemkinPress

OKSANA BULGAKOWA
SERGEI EISENSTEIN. A BIOGRAPHY
translated by Anne Dwyer

PotemkinPress

First published 1998 in German.

Copyright © 1998, 2001 by PotemkinPress
Berlin · San Francisco

Bulgakowa, Oksana
SERGEI EISENSTEIN. A BIOGRAPHY
Translated from German by Anne Dwyer
Cover design and layout by impulsio.com

Library of Congress Cataloging-in-Publication Data

Bulgakowa, Oksana.
  [Sergej Eisenstein. English]
  Sergei Eisenstein : a biography / Oksana Bulgakowa ; translated by Anne Dwyer.
    p. cm.
Includes bibliographical references and index.
  ISBN 3-9804989-8-0 (pbk) — ISBN 3-9804989-9-9 (hbk)
  1. Eisenstein, Sergei, 1898-1948. 2. Motion picture producers and directors—
Soviet Union—Biography. I. Title.
  PN1998.3.E34 B86213 2001
  791.43'0233'092—dc21   2002001694

PRINTED IN THE UNITED STATES OF AMERICA

www.PotemkinPress.com

A NOTE ON TRANSLITERATION

In the text of this biography Russian names and places are transliterated in accordance with a slightly adapted version of J. Thomas Shaw's "Transliteration System II" (J. Thomas Shaw, *The Transliteration of Modern Russian for English-Language Publications*, New York, 1979). The conventional English spellings of well-known names (such as Eisenstein or Meyerhold) are used even when these differ from the transliteration guidelines. However, the endnotes and bibliography adhere strictly to the Library of Congress system of transliteration. Thus, for example, Eisenstein is spelled 'Eizenshtein' in all citations of Russian-language sources.

CONTENTS

To touch or not to touch ....?

Not a mummy's boy.
Not an urchin.
Just a boy.
A boy aged twelve.
Obedient, polite, clicking his heels.
A typical boy from Riga.
A boy from a good family.
That's how I was aged twelve.
And that's how I was when my hair turned grey.
At twenty-seven, the boy from Riga became a celebrity.
For the only time in his life, his hand shook as the boy from Riga signed his name—on a contract in Hollywood worth $3,000 a week.
In 1939, the boy from Riga was snowed under with cuttings from American newspapers saying that ALEXANDER NEVSKY was given a screening in the White House, at Franklin Delano Roosevelt's special request.
1941 saw the first edition of the American Film Index come out: a conspectus of the first forty years of cinema. According to the foreword, it turned out that the boy from Riga came fourth in terms of the amount of column-inches devoted to him. First was Chaplin, then Griffith; but our boy from Riga came straight after Mary Pickford, who was in third place.
You might think it about time to start feeling like a grown-up. Because all this time my country was lavish with medals, orders and titles.
But the boy from Riga is still twelve, as before.

Sergei Eisenstein, 1946[1]

THE NOVEL OF A NARCISSIST

Eisenstein's biography falls comfortably into the pattern of a conventional Bildungsroman. A bourgeois family is shattered by the father's tyranny and the mother's neurotic love affairs. The only son's path in life is predetermined before his birth: he is expected to become an architect like his father. But the Revolution gets in the way of these plans, robbing his father of his general's rank, his mother of her fortune, and giving the son the freedom to make his own decisions. The boy opposes his father, who is driven into exile by the Revolution. The boy thus experiences the Revolution as his own personal liberation and becomes a director. At 27, he is known as a Revolutionary artist around the world. At 50, he dies as a celebrated but banned academic...

The reception of this Revolutionary artist, who has long since become a classic, has been somewhat ambiguous. Marie Seton, Eisenstein's first biographer, constructs his personality out of pre-programmed conflicts: the inherited complexes of mixed ancestry (Jewish father, Russian mother), the self-denial of a mystic surrounded by materialists. However, Eisenstein supplied Seton with many of the facts himself and had no qualms about including some of his own effective fabrications. Dominique Fernandez put full trust in these stories and discovered repressed homosexuality in his psychoanalytic study of Eisenstein's personality. When the Soviet avant-garde was rediscovered in the sixties, a generation of Westerners celebrated Eisenstein as a leftist artist. But at home, just after the 20th Party Congress, that same generation condemned the director as a conformist: like the Futurists in Italy, who celebrated and supported Fascism, Eisenstein had constructed a moving and thus questionable monument to the Stalinist era. This opinion is voiced by the prisoner X-123 in Alexander Solzhenitsyn's *The Life of Ivan Denisovich* (1962). Young Russian intellectuals today often declare Eisenstein's desire to influence consciousness by means of art to be a form of 'totalitarian poetics': art feeding the violence of the state.

Eisenstein wanted to preempt his biographers. In 1927, under the influence of Freud's essay on Leonardo da Vinci, he decided to write a psychoanalytic study of himself and called his (unwritten) book *My Art in Life*. In his autobiographical notes, begun only in 1943, he transforms himself into a fictional character out of an old-fashioned Bildungsroman, composed in the new style of 'automatic writing'. In retrospect he sketches his life as a goal-oriented, regular progression, purposefully shifts events in time and often conceals the truth. In fact Eisenstein's life was rich in unexpected turns and seductions: to become an architect or a specialist on Japan? to emigrate to Germany? to stay in the USA? or—like his friends Isaak Babel and Vsevolod Meyerhold—to be condemned to death by a special court? Eisenstein experienced all kinds of upheaval and conflict: between his bourgeois home and the existential model of the avant-garde artist; between the leftist avant-garde artist and his audience, the proletariat, whom the artist represents but who does not understand him. As a Soviet artist of the Left he encountered the European bohème and the Hollywood machine, he learned to live under Stalin—in a mix of prohibition, seduction, blackmail, fear, and conformity.

He feared his sexuality and repressed it in erotic drawings and jokes that shocked many of his contemporaries, as well as in his art. He conceived of his art, however, not as the sublimation of his sexuality, but of his sadism. Attractive young men must die violent deaths in his films. His handsome assistant Grisha must often play the role of the repulsive cynic, even of the murderer.

Eisenstein viewed himself as a child whose brutality was formed by emotional immaturity and sexual inhibitions.

Celebrated as a Revolutionary artist the world over, Eisenstein remained apolitical his whole life. This is the most astonishing discovery of this new attempt to trace the tracks of Eisenstein's life. Nonetheless, as a director, Eisenstein was extremely familiar with the struggle for power that went on behind the scenes.

In his art—for Eisenstein the true reality and only necessity—he hits upon the wounds of the century: violence and mass murder; the eroticism of the masses and the space this eroticism conquers; the fragmentation of perception; the longing for lost totality, experienced by Eisenstein as the Stalinist utopia of the 1930's.

Was Eisenstein homosexual? A Stalinist? A conformist? A dissident? He left no clear answers for his biographers. The answer lies somewhere between the lines of his diaries and letters, in his drafts to scripts, films, drawings, projects, and scientific research. Late in life Eisenstein viewed his research as his only possible means of salvation from the compromises he had consciously made with himself and his creativity.

CHILDHOOD AND YOUTH. THE BETRAYED FATHER
1898-1918

On February 2, 1898 in the Riga Cathedral a baby boy was baptized Sergei. The child had been born January 10 or January 23 (the latter according to the Gregorian calendar, which Russia adopted only in 1918). The priest Vladimir Pliss congratulated the boy's father, court councillor and civil engineer Mikhail Osipovich Eisenstein, and mother Yulia Ivanovna. The godparents had arrived from the capital St. Petersburg. They were Yulia's mother, the merchant's widow Iraida Matveevna Konetskaya, and Yulia's uncle Grigory Ivanovich.

Mikhail Eisenstein was a Jew from Germany who had converted to Christianity and who kept quiet about his ancestry. He had two brothers: Dmitry, an officer, died in 1904 near Mukden fighting in the Russo-Japanese War; Nikolai, a judge in Pskov, suffered from a severe psychological disorder and ended up in a mental institution. The family did not discuss the latter. Mikhail was a self-made man who modeled himself after Napoleon. He was born September 5, 1865 and graduated from the St. Petersburg Institute of Civil Engineering in 1893. From there he was sent to Riga to work in the Baltic State Property Administration. The city of Riga, built by the Teutonic Knights as a fort on the Baltic Sea, remained under German rule until the sixteenth century. For the next two centuries, Riga served as a bone of contention for Poland, Lithuania and Sweden. In the eighteenth century the city fell to Russia. At the turn of the twentieth century, Riga was home to a strange amalgam of peoples at the fringes of a mighty Empire: Jews enjoyed greater freedom here than in Russia proper, but both Jews and Latvians were oppressed by the new Russian colonial rulers, who had replaced the old colonizers, the Prussian Junkers.

Mikhail Eisenstein made a successful career for himself in Riga. In 1902, after only one additional year of study, he received a diploma from the Petersburg Archeological Institute—history was his second passion. He spent almost twenty years writing a book about the Baltic peoples, an achievement for which he was to be awarded noble rank in 1916, but the monarchy's collapse disrupted that plan. Soon he was named chief engineer for road construction in the Livonian province, then became an official city architect. He received the usual decorations—the St. Stanislav and St. Anna medals—and was awarded a higher rank. He was corpulent, went slightly bald at an early age, wore a Kaiser Wilhelm mustache, and enjoyed good food, silk ties, horses, and operettas—especially *Die Fledermaus*.

On February 2, 1897 Eisenstein married the 23-year-old Yulia Konetskaya, the daughter of affluent Petersburg merchants. A scandal erupted immediately after the wedding: Mikhail had presented himself as a baron, but it soon became obvious that his origins were murky at best. If he were really a Protestant Baltic German, then why had he converted to Russian Orthodoxy? The conversion more likely pointed towards a Jewish background.

Growing up, did Sergei Eisenstein know of his father's Jewish origins? Was he bothered by them? He remained silent on that account. Nonetheless, the Berlin Jewish Encyclopedia devoted an entry to Eisenstein in 1928. In 1930-31 Sergei was confronted with an anti-Semitic campaign directed against him in the United States. In 1939, after the pact between the Soviet Union and Nazi Germany, Eisenstein was amused that he, a Jew, had been awarded the contract to direct the allies' new national epic, Wagner's *Die Walküre*. Eisenstein never tried to cover up his Jewish background in later autobiographies and questionnaires. Instead, he hushed up his father's high rank and his mother's family wealth.

Yulia brought money, furniture, expensive porcelain and fancy silver into the marriage. She also had a taste for luxury, elegance and nice clothes tailored by Pavel Kitaev, a couturier for the royal family. She was attractive—petite, but round—with a disproportionately large head of curls and a high forehead—a trait her son inherited. The mother's family was immensely wealthy. They came from the city of Tikhvin in the north of Russia. Great-grandfather, so the story went, had come to Petersburg on foot, where he traded in wood and linen and quickly made a fortune with his business, the Neva cargo shipping company. The Konetskys had already come to wealth during the reign of Peter the Great. Most of their relatives now lived in St. Petersburg. The daughters received the usual high-society education: private school, piano lessons and foreign languages. Grandmother Iraida and her brothers-in-law ran the business after Grandfather's death. She was pious and surrounded herself with monks and pilgrims, and died on the steps of the Alexander Nevsky Monastery. The old aunts who lived in the family's house often took little Sergei to mass. Was Eisenstein's penchant for mysticism and superstition as much a product of his upbringing as was the ambition he inherited from his father?

Mikhail Osipovich strictly supervised the education of his only child and monitored the boy's friends and pastimes. The child learned how to dance and ride horses. The house where Eisenstein spent his childhood still stands today, at Nikolai Street 6. Apartment number seven was on the fifth floor. Three rooms looked out onto a street with a small park. Three smaller rooms had a view to the south, onto the back courtyard. The household was strictly regimented and included a servant and a cook, a chambermaid and a nanny. The Eisensteins received important guests. Their circle of acquaintances included high state officials, engineers and military men: the governor came to visit, as did the privy councillor Nikolai Zvegintsov; the son of city commandant General Ostap Bertels was one of Sergei's good friends; General Wenzel's daughters took dance lessons with little Seryozha; Josef Daragan, head of the Riga-Orlovsk railways, held balls for the children in his household. Receptions and visits to the opera were a set part of Eisenstein family life.

The exemplary marriage of Eisenstein's parents—the perfect combination of the husband's status and the wife's wealth—did not last long. Soon there were scenes of jealousy. His father fought duels and his mother attempted suicide. In order to consolidate the family, the Eisensteins traveled to France in 1906. They visited Paris and the Atlantic seashore. Social unrest in Riga and its surroundings gave additional incentive to leave the city. The Revolution disturbed the vacation calm of the Baltic coast. By traveling, the young Eisenstein was spared the sight of the government's bloody repression of the insurgents. Sergei visited the wax museum, Musée Grevin, instead, where the model torture chamber and scenes of execution particularly impressed him. On the Boulevard des Italiens he saw the first film of his life: *Les 400 farces du diable-*, a fairy play by Georges Méliès.

The trip did not save the marriage. In 1909 the Eisensteins were divorced on grounds of the mother's unfaithfulness. Interviews with the chambermaid and unpleasant rumors among the family's acquaintances accompanied the separation. Mikhail's cousin General Wenzel was exposed as Yulia's lover. Mama was oversexed, Eisenstein wrote years later, and Papa undersexed.[1]

At that time divorce was a radical step. Until 1903 a wife's adultery could be punished under the criminal code. In 1910 the Synod agreed to reform the marriage laws, but the question was not discussed in the Duma, Russia's parliament, until 1914. In Russian society—patriarchal even at the beginning of the twentieth century—a woman had no legal rights. She needed the permission of a man—either her husband or her father—to work or to change residence. Abortion was considered premeditated murder. Only 0.02% of women had access to higher education. Leo Tolstoy idealized the subordination of women and taught the nation about the destructive power of passion. As late as 1910, stable clichés about the erotic innocence of woman allowed politicians, doctors, and anthropologists to label prostitution a psycho-pathological phenomenon. Popular literature was the first to explore women's emancipation. Young writers heatedly defended free love as a new way of looking at life, as in, Mikhail Artsybashev's 1907 novel *Sanin*, a manifesto of the new movement.

Yulia Ivanovna moved to her mother's place in St. Petersburg at Tauride Street 9, but rented her own flat. She took the furniture, the silver, and the grand piano with her, thus relieving her child from piano lessons. The Eisenstein apartment was empty; you could ride a bicycle in it. The boy stayed with his father, since the courts had deemed his mother guilty. His father worked long hours and traveled, often to foreign countries. He always took an early summer trip to Paris, where he would indulge his weakness for bright ties and patent leather shoes. Latvian nanny Maria Elksene raised the child. At home the family spoke German, but Sergei also had both French and English governesses. Sergei's father, who had repressed his own culture and background, strove to be cosmopolitan.

In the earliest photographs the boy looks like a small English lord: blond curls, velvet suit, lace collar. He imagined himself as David Copperfield: safe and secure, but lonely. The hectic family life of his first eight years, the loss of his mother, and the inexorable will of his tyrannical father all contributed to a trauma that Sergei had difficulty overcoming. A sense of impotence (why did she leave me?) and a love-hate relationship with his mother remained. This emotional brew also shaped Sergei's relations with his father. Neither parent shielded the boy from upheaval; each eagerly informed him about the other's sins. Mother considered Father to be a thief and an imposter. Father called Mother a whore. But the divorce was still treated as an amicable separation, and the child was allowed to visit his mother. He usually spent Easter vacation with his mother and summers with his father on the Baltic coast.

In tender letters to Yulia, written on the backs of the German *Boys' Calendar*, Sergei reported on his reading (Dickens, Hugo's *Les Misérables*, Dumas père) and his grades. He would also cover the calendar sheets with drawings.

The parents' separation—two homes and two cultures—shaped the personality of this easily injured, but reticent person who avoided showing his feelings and suppressed his emotions. Not surprisingly, Samurai warriors, who exercised masterful control over their emotions, thrilled Eisenstein. But Russians, who have a radically different understanding of passion, always considered Eisenstein to be heartless, 'a cold, ironic person who thinks rationally and methodically, who has a brutal and dry imagination and is deeply egocentric, concentrated, and reserved.' This is how the director Valentin Tikhonovich described his then 22-year-old colleague.[3]

For all of Eisenstein's emotional self-control (later depressions and crying fits remained strictly private), people around him did notice his fascination with physical pain, with bodily and sexual abnormalities. The 12-year-old Eisenstein was treated to first strong impressions in these areas by reading Octave Mirbeau's *The Garden of Tortures*, de Sade's *Juliette*, and Leopold Sacher-Masoch's novel *Venus in Furs*. Their cruel eroticism attracted him. He was also enticed by an eerie Pathé film about an adulteress whose husband (a blacksmith) brands her lover with a prison mark: 'I remember it vividly: the bare shoulder . . . . the white smoke (or steam) rising from the burn.'[4] Eisenstein insisted in 1934 that his first biographer Ivan Axyonov put this picture on the cover of the book. The biography finally appeared in 1991—with a different cover.

Eisenstein had a complex-ridden attitude towards his own body. He appeared to be disproportional: his legs were too short, his hands too small, his head too big. His torso was at first extremely thin, then fairly fat later in life. Eisenstein always viewed himself as a clown. His first great passion was the circus, since it demonstrated the perfect body—lithe, nimble, and even magical. One pantomime that impressed him greatly as a child told the story of a lost body. That clown was able to run away from his own body, something Eisenstein had always wanted to do. He attended gymnastic lessons only under duress.

Eisenstein's Petersburg visits to the circus and his first encounter with the commedia dell'arte—the Nezlobin Company's guest performance of *Turandot*, directed by Fyodor Komissarzhevsky—ranked among his most powerful early experiences of art. Their version of eccentricity countered the naturalist cruelties of Eisenstein's other passion.

When Eisenstein was twelve, one of his Christmas presents was a book by François Auguste Mignet about the French Revolution. Could this book have kindled curiosity about the rebellion of the hungry in Sergei's world of abundance? The contrast was too simple: Christmas in a rich home versus *les misérables*. But this revolution had frozen into art, was set in copperplate engravings and cartoons. Eisenstein noticed the art. He was thrilled by Daumier's drawings and by Olaf Gulbransson's *Simplicissimus* style. One of his father's coworkers, the engineer Pavel Afrosimov, showed Sergei how to draw in an uninterrupted line. This technique felt like magic to Sergei: the drawing seemed to flow from his pencil tip. He enjoyed drawing and spent a lot of time at it. He especially liked the animal circus comic strips that he based on his own life. But in art class at school Eisenstein maintained only the equivalent of a 'C'-average. One of Sergei's favorite pastimes was home theater, a passion he shared with his Moscow friend Maxim Strauch. The two families regularly rented adjacent summerhouses on the Baltic Sea. Maxim told Sergei about the performance of *The Blue Bird* in Stanislavsky's Art Theater. They reenacted the play at home with Eisenstein in the role of Fire. They even wrote their own play, 'Twenty-three years in the life of an alcoholic', the plot for which they took from a comic strip in the magazine *Ogonek*, a supplement to *Birzhevaya gazeta* ('The Stock Market Paper'). Strauch played the alcoholic, and Eisenstein took care of all the other parts: the faithful wife, the unhappy children, the evil policeman, the robbed banker.

Their games ended in the fall. Eisenstein's father decided that Sergei should attend the *Realschule* located in the same street as their house. The *Gymnasium* education wasted too much time on Latin, a subject his son would not need at university. His father was uninterested in the psychological problems that a child of a high official of German-Jewish background might have at a school full of mostly lower-class Latvian children. The boy was supposed to learn to hold his own. But in school the son of the oppressor became a member of the oppressed and failed to make a single friend.

Sergei entered school on August 14, 1908 and finished on June 2, 1914. After graduation his mother wanted to take him on a grand educational tour—from Egypt to Greece, from Rome to Germany. But the war disrupted their holiday plans. Instead of traveling to Africa, they visited the depths of the Russian provinces: Volkhov, Ilmen, Novgorod. These are the locations of his later film *Alexander Nevsky*, a work that deals with a different German war, namely the Russian battle against the Teutonic Knights who had once founded Riga.

His father's loyalty to the Russian crown was not shaken by the war with Germany. Mikhail had always respected authority and had raised his son in the same spirit. Sergei was seized by anti-German sentiment and ridiculed the stupid foe in cartoons. Since he had graduated from *Realschule* instead of the more elite *Gymnasium*, Sergei had to attend an extra year of preparatory school in order to apply to university. He passed his final exams on May 1, 1915 with excellent grades. He received 'B's' only in Russian and drawing.

In March his father was promoted to state councillor, the equivalent of a general's rank. From now on he was addressed as 'Your Excellency.' In addition to his public responsibilities, Mikhail also accepted commissions from private citizens. He designed multi-storied apartment residences for the rich German inhabitants of the city, for Ladsing and von Tvardovsky. Most of the buildings, like those on Elizabeth Street, were located in the center of Riga. He created a whole street, the Albertstrasse, in the style of Viennese art nouveau with elaborate stucco ornamentation—dragons, masks, fake stairways, and statues. On several occasions, Mikhail took Sergei to the movies to watch a weekly special about his architectural achievements; he had designed more than fifty buildings in Riga. In spite of the domestic tyranny, the boy idealized Mikhail Osipovich. The father had unlimited influence over his son—this influence was founded on admiration, rather than fear. Not surprisingly, Sergei applied to study at Papa's Institute of Civil Engineering, which stood under the tsar's direct patronage. Sergei enrolled on July 25, 1915. He followed his father's well-trodden path and—moved to live with his mother in Petersburg, which had been renamed Petrograd at the beginning of the war. Anti-German sentiment erupted in several pogroms against the German population in that city too.

The boy from the provinces arrived in the capital, the elegant and calm heart of the Empire. He traded in one way of life—endurance, will, ambition, and paternal severity—for another, defined by his mother's sensibilities and carefree attitude. *La Nietzschéenne* by Daniel Lesueur, *The Demi-virgins* by Marcel Prévost and Sacher-Masoch's novels were on the reading list of the rich society lady with new and independent views. The only liberties that Yulia Ivanovna allowed herself in this rigid and misogynist society were of an erotic nature. She remained oblivious to politics and could afford not to work. She once tried to write a novel, but quickly abandoned the effort. In his mother's salon Sergei met the writer's widow Anna Grigorievna Dostoevskaya, art collectors, the Futurist theoretician Nikolai Kulbin, who took Sergei to the cabaret The Players' Rest, and the fashionable director Evreinov, who impressed Sergei with thick albums full of articles about himself.

His mother showed Sergei's drawings to the painter Nikolai Tyrsa, the art teacher of Eisenstein's cousin Nita Butovskaya. Sergei wanted to study painting and was thinking about transferring to the Academy of Fine Arts. But Tyrsa said that Eisenstein had no talent: the boy didn't *see*, but drew only with his head. After this conversation Eisenstein wrapped up his sketches and packed them away.

In his first year of university, Sergei had to pass coursework in physics, math, chemistry, geometry and architecture. His grades were mediocre, mostly 'C's' and 'D's'. His performance improved in his second year, when he excelled in geometry and theoretical mechanics. The beauty of the city overwhelmed him. It was a calculated sort of beauty, designed by Italians, Frenchmen, and Russians trained in Italy.

Theater became Sergei's true passion. This sensual, chaotic experience worked against the engineer's precision, against order. Eisenstein avidly followed the reviews of the Kamerny Theater in Moscow, where Alexander Tairov invited Futurist painters to create multilevel scaffolding and decorative scenery for highly stylized productions of exotic, decadent plays. Eisenstein saw all of Meyerhold's productions at the Alexandrinsky Theater. These were baroque classics with extravagant set designs, for example, Molière's *Don Juan* and Calderón's *The Constant Prince*. He collected newspaper clippings about the scandalous Nikolai Evreinov, who had declared the whole world to be a theater because he believed the basic human instinct was the drive towards transformation. He began designing costumes, masks, and sets for his own imaginary productions. Theater was his first real obsession—he did not smoke and avoided the bohemian student life of alcohol, women, and politics. Politics left him completely indifferent.

Eisenstein's orderly life, barely touched by the war, by court scandals, by strikes or social unrest, was rudely interrupted. Bread riots—caused by the collapse of food and fuel distribution—political demonstrations and strikes paralyzed the city in February 1917. The inhabitants of the Petrograd suburbs—workers and soldiers—flooded the elegant downtown streets and squares. There were political meetings in the barracks and factories. The streetcars stopped running, and there was shooting in the streets.

Eisenstein missed the outbreak of this second Russian Revolution. On February 25, 1917, two days before Tsar Nicholas II abdicated the throne, Eisenstein went to the theater to see Vsevolod Meyerhold's production of Lermontov's *Masquerade*. He compared *Masquerade* (not the collapse of the Empire) to a thunderclap that defined his vague intention to abandon his carrier as an architect and 'give himself' to art—to the theater.[5] But things turned out differently.

After the proclamation of the Republic, the students of the Institute (including Eisenstein) were recruited into the voluntary militia. They were to replace the old police force. After his fourth semester exams in May, Eisenstein was drafted into the army and sent to the Ensigns' Engineering School. However, Prince Georgy Lvov's new bourgeois government could do little to improve the lax army discipline that gave even the new recruits broad freedoms. Theaters no longer showed plays and were instead used for political meetings. The Circus Moderne was now regularly filled with masses listening to Leon Trotsky. The Tauride Palace, adjacent to Sergei's mother's apartment, housed the Soviet Central Executive. On July 3, 1917 workers and newly arrived sailors from Kronstadt set out from the Palace in an armed demonstration. The initiators of the march, the Bolsheviks, did not themselves know whether the workers would overthrow the government or whether they would demonstrate peacefully. Eisenstein watched from his window as the ranks of the marchers swelled. He did not see the riots on Nevsky Prospect (reenacted in his film *October*) where demonstrators were shot dead. This demonstration was the only political event that Eisenstein witnessed. He did not experience the terror against the Bolsheviks that raged the next day. The Party was declared illegal, and the Tauride Palace was surrounded. The inhabitants of that quarter had to stay at home, since it had become nearly impossible to move about the city. Eisenstein's reaction to the February Revolution was fundamentally artistic: he tried out his talents as a cartoonist. He was deeply hurt when Arkady Averchenko, the publisher of the well-known magazine *Satirikon*, rejected his drawings. Other papers (Sergei Khudekov's *Peterburgskaya gazeta* and Stanislav Propper's *Birzhevye vedomosti*) accepted his caricatures of Kerensky, which he signed 'Sir Gay.' The cartoons were never printed, but the student received a 25-ruble advance. He used his royalties to buy Georgy Lukomsky's history of classical theater.

In August Eisenstein was sent to Izhora with the Ensigns' School to build pontoon bridges. They returned to Petrograd in the fall.

In October 1917 Eisenstein saw his father for the last time. He visited him on the Baltic coast in Yurev (now Tartu), the city to which his father's office had been evacuated in 1916. Mikhail had met his new companion there, the young Elizaveta (Liza) Michelson. The three of them spent two evenings at the cinema.

Sergei was back in Petrograd when the Bolsheviks and about 25,000 armed workers stormed the Winter Palace and arrested the Provisional Government. Eisenstein was at home sorting his notes about eighteenth-century engravings. His aunt Anna Vasilievna Butovskaya had inherited a rich collection of engravings by Callot, della Bella, Hogarth and Goya from her late husband, a general. She had just begun to introduce her nephew to the intricacies of this material.

This revolution, later known as the October Revolution, was the second upheaval that Eisenstein failed to notice. But he was highly aware of the intoxication that broke out after the masses located the Palace wine cellar. Eisenstein made the most of this grotesque side of the coup in *October*. In his memoirs Eisenstein identified remarkable details as signs of the Revolution: Valentin Serov's portrait of the Tsar, impaled on the palace gate, a necklace of empty vodka bottles on the monument to Empress Catherine outside the Alexandrinsky Theater. As always, Eisenstein viewed the Revolution as set of artistic images—no matter how profane.

In January 1918 the Bolsheviks dissolved the Ensigns' Engineering School and Eisenstein returned to the Institute of Civil Engineering. Lectures were often canceled. He accepted a position in a new firm, which was led by a woman with a strange name, Minna Pinkerton. The only reason Eisenstein took the job was a promised business trip to London.

For the first time in his life Eisenstein had plenty of free time. He succumbed completely to the theater. He studied theater history and designed sets and costumes for *Hamlet*, Hauptmann's *The Weavers*, Molière's *The Scoundrel Scapin*, Tchaikovsky's *Queen of Spades*, Gozzi's *The Love of Three Oranges* and *The Green Bird*. His own dramatic sketches followed the fashion of the times: he wrote a satirical parody in the style of Evreinov's cabaret 'The Crooked Mirror' and a stylization of baroque theater imitating Evreinov's experiments in the Old Theater. He also wrote *Dawn of the Red Alarm*, an agitation mystery play about the factory owner Capitalistov and the workers Libertov, Egalitov and Fraternitov, which had clearly been influenced by Mayakovsky's *Mystery-Bouffe*.

On March 18, 1918 Eisenstein—like many of his fellow students—was drafted into the Red Army. Contrary to his later claims in various autobiographies and questionnaires, Eisenstein did not enlist voluntarily. There was simply no way for him to dodge the draft. His mother managed to arrange a position for him under a family friend in the Corps of Engineers, far away from the front.

While Trotsky was in Brest-Litovsk negotiating a separate peace with Germany, the Bolshevik government decided that since the old army was no longer battle-worthy, the new Red Guard should represent the single armed force of the country. This decision ran contrary to the original Bolshevik intention of founding a state without a police force or a standing army. In the spring of 1918 the situation became desperate. After the Treaty of Brest-Litovsk, German troops occupied Finland, Poland, the Baltic States, Ukraine, and the Crimea. British, American, and French troops landed in Murmansk. The Japanese attacked Siberia.

In February 1918 the Germans occupied Riga, and Eisenstein's link to his father was severed. When the Workers' Soviets briefly regained control of Riga in December, Mikhail Osipovich and Elizaveta Michelson emigrated to Germany. The beloved son was unable and, as he later wrote, unwilling to follow his father. He stayed in Russia with his mother and with the Reds. He gave his father up forever.

Eisenstein would later mock his father's buildings, which he had once so admired. He also made derisive comments about his father: 'Papa himself was a *lion de plâtre* [a plaster lion]. Vainglorious, petty, too stout, industrious, unlucky, broken—but still he wore his white gloves (on weekdays!) and his collars were perfectly starched.'[6] Was the stone lion in *The Battleship Potemkin*, which angrily rises after the revolt of the sailors (the 'tsar's children'), a portrait of Papa? Seryozha's revolt—the rebellion of a good, well-behaved boy against his father and his father's values—could not hide that some paternal values had left a deeper impression than Sergei wanted to admit even to himself. While Sergei easily gave up silk ties, horses, and starched collars, his deep respect for authority remained unshaken. He followed his mother's pattern by indulging only in small erotic freedoms: an erotic joke or drawing. His father's heritage survived in Sergei's cosmopolitan attitudes and his love for curved lines—Sergei merely replaced art nouveau with Baroque.

As a child Eisenstein had not been allowed to choose between his parents in either a legal or emotional sense. Even as an adult Eisenstein spoke 'in Mama's or Papa's voice,' as he called it. This phrase was not a metaphor (or was it?), but referred to a phenomenon resembling a prolonged stage of puberty: his voice was sometimes high and squeaky, sometimes low and gravelly. He often made his listeners laugh, so Eisenstein quickly had to give up his dream of becoming an actor. Later, in the twenties, he worked hard on his voice under the medical supervision of a Moscow doctor. He finally succeeded in replacing Mama's voice with a schooled baritone.

Eisenstein's separation from his father was made easier by a newly discovered supporting figure: Sigmund Freud. During his leave in the summer of 1918, Eisenstein read *Leonardo da Vinci and a Memory of his Childhood* in the streetcar. This was the first bit of psychoanalytic writing that had ever fallen into his hands. The reading captivated him so much that he failed to notice that a whole bottle of milk had fallen over and spilled onto his pants—a kind of intellectual ejaculation. Over the next few days, Eisenstein read every bit of Freud that he could get his hands on. This was not an insignificant amount of writing, since Freud's works had been well received in Russia. The essay on Leonardo describes a motherless and inhibited child who grows up with his father. Eisenstein read the story as an analysis of his own trauma, as a first explanation of his own dark sensations. He would later return to Freud's interpretation as a way to make sense of his own crises. In a 1929 Paris interview Eisenstein said that in 1918 he had immediately wanted to leave for Vienna and study with Freud.[7] However, war and Revolution stood in his way.

A YOUNG SOLDIER'S READING LIST.
FREEMASONS AND JAPAN
1918-1920

Eisenstein became a technical expert for the army and ended up in the Corps of Engineers of the Second Battalion, later the 18th Regiment of the Red Army. At this point there were still ongoing debates about the status of professional officers from the old army and whether they would be allowed to serve in the new force. But the Corps of Engineers consisted only of experienced military engineers, whose high level of professionalism thrilled the young soldier Eisenstein. Since there were no uniforms, Eisenstein continued wearing the white student's jacket with his institute's insignia. During the Civil War Eisenstein barely noticed the action at the front; he also did not experience the violence of the Revolution.

During the summer his detachment was stationed in Gatchina near Petrograd. The assignment felt like summer vacation. He could take the tram home and stock up on fresh laundry and new books. In June 1918 there was heavy fighting in the south, on the Volga near Tsaritsyn, and in the Ukraine: Eisenstein's regiment was traveling around the northeast. The nearby Polish Front (the Red Cavalry was fighting farther south) quieted down in July 1919. There was an informal cease-fire, since the Polish leader Józef Pilsudski was waiting to see how the southern battles against Anton Denikin's White Army would turn out.

Eisenstein did not even suffer the hunger and cold that reigned in Petrograd in 1919 and 1920. The city was deserted since the government had moved to Moscow in March 1918. He spent the war away from the action, in rural areas near the Russian-Lithuanian border: Pskov, Izhora, Voshega, Velikie Luki, Kholm, Dvinsk.

His detachment destroyed German defense systems—solid buildings with ventilation and windows that were protected from ground water. The German sites stood in stark contrast to the provisional Russian constructions that consisted of water-filled trenches. Eisenstein experienced the war as an encounter with the enemy's superior technology.

During frequent halts, Eisenstein read Schopenhauer, Maeterlinck, Oscar Wilde, Ibsen, and Otto Weininger's *Sex and Character* in the shade of his military wagon. This amounted to remarkably modernist reading for a soldier in an army of workers and peasants. He avidly took notes on books about Elizabethan theater, the Shakespearean stage, Kabuki. The sheer number of books that he lugged around was incredible. He read manifestos by proponents of a new, emancipated conception of theater. These included *On Theater* by Vsevolod Meyerhold, *Theater as Such* by Nikolai Evreinov, and *Revolution in the Theater* by the Munich author Georg Fuchs. All of these works had been published in 1908 and 1909. They asserted the art of *one personality*—that of the director. The authors viewed theater as the one true higher form of reality.

In May 1919 Eisenstein had begun to keep a journal. It was not yet a personal diary. He did not record his experiences, but only his thoughts on his reading—art was more important than life. He described the collective building of a bridge as a perfect mise-en-scène. He perceived reality as an artistic image, the Revolution as a dramatic act.

In his journal Eisenstein pondered changes in theater: intermissions should be abolished, since they disturbed the overall effect. He dreamed of using colored lights in the way Evreinov had in his production of Wilde's *Salome*. He tried to project everything he read into other areas. His mind became attuned to discovering parallels, reflections, and correspondences between painting, theater, literature, and philosophy. Of course, he dreamed of becoming a theater director himself.

In this violent period Eisenstein read Symbolist plays. The life of a soldier, the Revolution, the war and the working class seemed distant. Real everyday life remained absent from the journal, but appeared in letters to his mother. Here Eisenstein described the food, the circumstances under which he kept his underwear clean, and a toothache that plagued him for a month. In the meantime, his mother sold some of her possessions and included money with her letters full of well-intended advice on sexual hygiene. She suggested that he visit a brothel, but not without protection. This recommendation was probably a response to a letter in which he described how the Dvinsk prostitutes had been recruited for construction work. Eisenstein was ill prepared to deal with his mother's worries and insisted that she was overly concerned about his libido. He was still a virgin. His interest in sex was purely theoretical: one of his comrades impressed him with his substantial knowledge of the details of animal copulation.

In March 1919 Eisenstein arrived in Dvinsk (now Daugavpils), where he began to write the long play *The Comedy of Power or Queen Isabella*, but he dropped the project when he discovered Maeterlinck's *Princess Maleine*. Kleist's essay 'On Marionette Theater' impressed him greatly. He designed sets for Ben Jonson's *Bartholomew Fair* and Ibsen's *Peer Gynt*.

Eisenstein finally got to live out his passion for the theater in January 1920. His company had been stationed in Velikie Luki since the fall. There was a club in town where the Corps of Engineers organized amateur theater. They staged *The Double*, a comedy by Arkady Averchenko, the man who had once snubbed Eisenstein's drawings; and performed Nikolai Gogol's *The Gamblers*. Eisenstein's superior, the engineer Sergei Peich, played the main role; Eisenstein, the corps' construction leader, built the stage. In another club, the House of Enlightenment, Eisenstein attended lectures on the history of theater costumes. The lecturer had translated Edward Gordon Craig, knew Evreinov personally, and had performed in Evreinov's theater. However, when Eisenstein wrote his mother about the event, he forgot to mention the name of this well-connected person. In the House of Enlightenment Eisenstein also met the painter Konstantin Eliseev, who had studied with Nikolai Rerikh and worked as a stage designer and actor. Eisenstein knew of Eliseev's work for the Liteiny Theater in Petrograd and showed him his own theater sketches, which the older artist liked.

When Eliseev took over the direction of the front theater in the spring, he tried to arrange for Eisenstein to change units and join his Agitprop detachment. He succeeded only after the third try: Eisenstein's military superior Peich did not want to lose his construction leader and resisted Eliseev's demands. On July 17, 1920 Eisenstein wrote his mother that he had finally received the identification card that listed him as a set designer. His 'benefactor' Eliseev, a member of the Revolutionary Council, had gotten his way.[8]

In his new division, the Political Administration of the Western Front (with the silly abbreviation PUZAP), Eisenstein met Pavel Arensky, the son of the composer Anton Arensky. Like most men his age, Pavel had been drafted into the army. He was, however, declared unfit for service and worked as an instructor. This chance meeting deeply impacted Eisenstein's life.

Arensky was ten years Eisenstein's senior and came from a family of artists. He knew Moscow's theater elite, wrote mystery plays, and was willing to discuss every possible aspect of theater with the young and eager construction leader who still wore a student uniform.

In July 1920 Eisenstein and Arensky were transferred to Smolensk, and then a month later to Minsk, a city just abandoned by the Poles. Now Eisenstein was officially engaged as a set designer in a front theater with professional actors. He was thrilled. He wrote to his mother, 'Minsk, August 4, 1920, Hotel Livadia . . . . I didn't write from Smolensk . . . . life in a cattle car didn't prompt me to write joyful letters. But this is really Europe. For instance, they sell *lemons* on the free market (and only 350 rubles a piece!), potato flour (200!), rice (1,400!), almonds, prunes, walnuts, chocolate (from 600 for the 'homemade' German-Polish-military-cocoa-honey kind to 4,000 for a real Cailler!!!), ceramic dishes, suspenders, underwear (the ideal kind), rolls (200 a piece) etc. There is even a 'café' . . . . Everything is here except—except for money. But I should be able to earn a bunch on the side . . . . Three of us are living together in a hotel room reserved just for us. Me, the 'lover' Belsky and the 'neurasthenic' Phew-Kean . . . . Too bad that I don't have any money. (I got 3,000 today [his monthly wages were 3,600 rubles] and I already blew it on food. But I was smart enough to buy half a pound of soda). Chocolate and white rolls are just so seductive!'[9]

At that time buildings in the Empire-style were still standing in Minsk. The city had electricity and there were even magazines showing 1920 Paris summer fashions. Eisenstein made some extra money by painting agit-trains with Eliseev, a common way for artists to supplement their income. 'All sorts of priests, the Entente, idealized Red Army men, etc. For 3 days of work we got 3 food rations and 3 pounds of wheat flour each!' he wrote his mother on August 27.[10] He was embarrassed by her generous financial contributions. She would send him 20,000 or 30,000 rubles at a time. He would beg her not to sell everything and sent her 75 grams of real cocoa. The theater's next production was supposed to be *The Lower Depths* by Maxim Gorky, but the work fell behind schedule. Peace talks with Poland were being held in Riga. All the members of the front theater were given the option of moving on to Roslavl with the Army after the end of the war or staying in Minsk, where the People's Commissariat intended to start a theater.

Eliseev chose Minsk. Eisenstein made a different decision altogether, since he had become part of a new circle around Arensky that offered him new and enticing prospects. Arensky's crowd brought about a fateful turn in Eisenstein's life: the Freemason Arensky introduced Eisenstein to a forbidden Masonic lodge. But due to circumstance, Sergei became a member of yet another secret brotherhood. The archbishop of the Rosicrucian order came to Minsk to celebrate the induction ceremony. The bishop's worldly name was Boris Zubakin, and he earned his bread ration by lecturing in army clubs on various topics, including Henri Bergson's theory of laughter. The secret lodge usually met in barracks. Here Zubakin systematically introduced the new knights to the foundations of occultism, gave lectures on Rosicrucianism and its connection to Freemasonry, Russian secret lodges, Egyptian magicians, and the Cabbala. Now the Rosicrucians took the place of Father and Freud—Eisenstein had found yet another authority that offered higher knowledge and theatrical rituals.

In a letter to his mother on September 20, 1920 Eisenstein described the archbishop as a 'truly exceptional person.' 'He sees the astral body of each individual and reads hidden thoughts . . . . This is an overwhelming, gripping doctrine . . . . His knowledge is boundless.'[11] Eisenstein asked his mother not to tell anyone about his letter: the Rosicrucians and Freemasons were being persecuted. The Masonic order in Moscow, which Arensky later helped Sergei discover, attracted the special attention of the political police force Cheka because its founder, Apollon Karelin, also led the Anarcho-syndicalist (or Anarchist) movement. Karelin had become a member of a Masonic order during his French emigration. In 1917 he returned to Russia to found its eastern division. The Cheka suspected that the lodge acted as a cover for the forbidden Anarchist movement that had been crushed by the Bolsheviks in 1918.

Pavel Arensky introduced Eisenstein to a young couple, Vera and Leonid Nikitin. Leonid was a painter and also a member of the order. One evening Arensky shared some exciting news: he had learned that it was possible to get out of Minsk and to obtain an assignment to the Department of Oriental Languages at the General Staff Academy. All they needed was an invitation from the academy. Arensky's source of information was an old friend whom he had met at Scriabin's home, Professor Nikolai Popov-Tativa, the new dean of the Japanese department at the academy. Arensky immediately traveled to Moscow, where the dean welcomed him warmly and informed him that the applicants would have to take a language exam. Arensky brought back study materials and the three friends began to cram hieroglyphs. Two weeks later they arrived in Moscow to take the test. They paid for the trip in produce—with hundreds of eggs. After the exam Popov-Tativa generously sent all three young men invitations to study at the academy.

They planned to spend about two years learning Japanese; then they wanted to leave for Japan. Eisenstein dreamed of these travels and especially looked forward to studying Japanese theater. Minsk had definitely exceeded his expectations! He carefully prepared his mother for the adventurous turn his life had taken and suggested that they travel to Japan together. After all, Arensky was also planning to bring his wife and his mother along.

Yulia Ivanovna was horrified and called her son back to the institute in Petrograd. She had just received a certificate from the institute that would free Sergei from army service: on August 13 the Peoples' Commissariat had decided to demobilize university students.

Sergei begged his mother to understand: the temptations of *Moscow*, home of the Tairov Theater, and of *Japan* were too great. Only the acceptance into the General Staff's Academy allowed him to leave the front quickly and live in the capital city. Furthermore, the situation at the front had suddenly become critical at the end of September. The peace talks with Poland had fallen through. Encouraged by the success of Wrangel's White Army in the south, the Polish Army had chased Red Army troops from the outskirts of Warsaw. The front line was moving closer to Minsk. The city was hastily evacuated. On September 27 the three soldiers who had been ordered to leave for Moscow only barely squeezed onto a train packed with refugees. Somehow Eisenstein still managed to take along bags full of books. During a stopover in Vitebsk, he saw a city transformed by Kazimir Malevich's Suprematist painting: the brick facades had been whitewashed and painted with green circles, orange squares, and blue squares. These walls only hinted at the surprises awaiting Eisenstein in the Moscow art scene. Eisenstein did not even suspect that he was now traveling towards his own artistic career. He was preparing for a life of Japanese studies.

In his later memoirs, Eisenstein described his arrival in Moscow as an adventurous chain of lucky coincidences. In reality everything had been well planned. His decision turned out to be most advantageous. He received the coveted military ration. The students of the General Staff's Academy for Workers and Peasants were given two pounds of bread a day, though even the soldiers at the front were allotted only one and a half pounds. Although some of Eisenstein's relatives lived in Moscow (several were in the Cheka-prison), he decided to stay at the dormitory (a former hunters' club) across from the Kremlin. Eisenstein was even promised a new uniform. His studies only kept him busy about two hours a day. French and Japanese classes met three times a week. There was a small stipend, and he could have his laundry done for free. He could reach all the museums and theaters on foot because both his department at Vozdvizhenka Street 6 and the dormitory were located in the center of the city. Since the streetcars had all stopped running and there was a strictly enforced curfew, Eisenstein was lucky that his walk to any downtown location took less than half an hour. He spent most of his time in libraries reading volumes on art and every book on theater that he could find.

He often visited Arensky, who was staying in his first wife's apartment. Arensky's ex-wife had been living with the Art Theater director Valentin Smyshlyaev for the last two years. Smyshlyaev also directed productions at the Proletkult Theater and was so moved by Nikitin and Eisenstein's sketches that he offered to work with them. The opportunity was ideal, since the Proletkult Theater had just moved into a new building, the Hermitage Theater on Karetny Ryad.

Smyshlyaev's immediate trust did not come out of the blue. He was one of Karelin's confidants and an active member of the same secret order as Arensky and Nikitin. Mikhail Chekhov, the neurotic star of the studio at the Moscow Art Theater, and the young Yury Zavadsky (who was rehearsing the part of the prince in *Turandot* at Vakhtangov's theater) were also members of the lodge. They now met in Smyshlyaev's Moscow apartment, and Eisenstein was allowed entry into their secret society.

Almost all of the Freemasons and Rosicrucians were condemned and executed in 1937 and 1938. Arensky and Boris Zubakin were arrested several times in the twenties. Nikitin and Zavadsky were arrested in 1930, though

Zavadsky was released after Stanislavsky intervened in his favor. Smyshlyaev avoided arrest by dying of a heart attack in 1936; the warrant had already been signed. Eisenstein escaped the fate of his friends and colleagues, and made only mocking comments about his Freemason and Rosicrucian brothers in his 1946 memoirs. He described one former friend as a 'gigantic Russian aristo-crat with a German surname, degenerate and a former anarchist' and Arensky as 'a failure—the son of a second-rate Russian composer.' 'I alone,' he wrote, 'remained in possession of my wits.'[12]

At one time, however, this order had given Eisenstein quick access to the Moscow theater elite, to the people who made his artistic development pos-sible. Within two weeks of his arrival in Moscow the soldier Eisenstein, who had absolutely no experience in professional theater, was hired as a theater's chief stage designer. This is even more remarkable in light of the Proletkult's scrutiny of its employees' social origins. The Proletkult leadership trusted Smyshlyaev completely. His stepfather, Fyodor Blagonravov, was a close friend and comrade of the Proletkult chief Pavel Lebedev-Polyansky.

Even in the light of all the changes brought about by the Revolution, Eisenstein's career jump-start was exceptional in the relatively closed world of the Moscow art scene.

Eisenstein's living situation unexpectedly improved when he ran into Maxim Strauch, his friend from summer vacations on the Baltic Sea, at the Tairov Theater one evening. Eisenstein usually bought three theater tickets during the day, which he would sell at a higher price shortly before the show. This way the poor student managed to go to the theater almost for free. On that evening, he first feared that Strauch was a policeman coming to arrest him. But the misunderstanding was quickly cleared up, and the childhood friends rejoiced over their unexpected encounter. Since Strauch was about to go to Siberia for a month, he offered Eisenstein a room in his six-room apart-ment—his father was a wealthy physician—so the room would not be given to someone else in his absence. Large apartments that were considered under-inhabited were often split up quickly and irreversibly. (The new housing policy was called 'compression' or 'uplotnenie.') Getting a trustworthy acquaintance from a good family to move in was a safe way to prevent the housing authori-ties from assigning your apartment space to complete strangers. Eisenstein's mother used the same approach in Petrograd. She asked Sergei's godfather Uncle Grigory and his wife to move in with her. ('Just please lock up my books!' her son admonished in his letters). So Eisenstein moved to Chistye Prudy Bou-levard 23, apartment 2. The apartment was fairly far from the Vozdvizhenka, but the location was very quiet. The distance from downtown soon decreased as well, since all eight streetcar lines began operating again on December 1.

This one room remained his Moscow address until 1935.

In his classes Eisenstein diligently studied Japanese and Chinese hieroglyphs. He read Zola, Barbey d'Aurevilly, and Baudelaire in French. His mother had a winter coat sewn for him and sent him money for boots. She repeatedly begged her son to return to Petrograd and reminded him of his studies at the Institute of Civil Engineering. In his letters Eisenstein made excuses. He could not leave Moscow—the Japanese courses were so intense that he could impossibly miss a single class. Was this a pretext? A mere two weeks after his arrival, Eisenstein became a member of the Proletkult Theater's company. As stage designer he had to supervise the work of all the workshops. Suddenly everything assaulted him at once. He had to take his first exam in Japanese (an eight-page translation) and prepare his first professional theater production, Smyshlyaev's *The Mexican*. Eisenstein could not handle both. He had to choose between Japanese and the theater. The decision was made for him. At the beginning of December a special commission found a formal mistake in Eisenstein's application to the academy: Eisenstein was not officially a member of the army, so he could not study at the General Staff Academy. Eisenstein had to leave. This was a hard blow, since Eisenstein lived off of the academy. The stipend was meager (4,800 to 5,800 rubles), but the academy gave its students coveted military rations: camel meat, soap, salt, sugar, four cartons of cigarettes a month, 'Soviet coffee', almost two liters of kerosene and a pound of butter.

The Proletkult promised Eisenstein similar rations, but they could not arrange them immediately, so Eisenstein spent some time without any food cards. He lived from the seven and a half pounds of old meat he kept on his balcony for the winter. Bread was hard to come by.

At first Eisenstein was insulted by the expulsion. He wanted to continue his studies by auditing classes with Arensky and Nikitin at the Lazarevsky Institute for Oriental Languages. After all, he had already memorized 1500 words, 150 characters, and just as many sentences. He promised his mother to return to Petrograd if his plans for the Lazarevsky Institute did not work out. But the theater production took up all of his time.

On December 31 he received a letter (forwarded by his mother) from Elizaveta Michelson in Berlin informing him of his father's death. Eisenstein should know, Miss Michelson wrote, that his father had designated Sergei his single heir. The money had already been deposited in a Berlin bank. He would have to take care of the Riga apartment himself. Eisenstein entrusted this task to his Riga nanny Maria Elksene, who conscientiously did what needed to be done. In her long letter Elizaveta described in detail how his father had passed away on the first of July. He had been living in several German cities, most recently in Berlin, and had died of a stroke in a small guesthouse at Unter den Linden 62-63. Elizaveta had buried him at the Russian cemetery in Tegel. According to Mikhail's wishes, she had put a picture of Sergei as a schoolboy and an icon from home in his coffin. 'I ordered the best wreath in your name. In spite of significant material privations, your father was doing well financially. A brilliant future and grand projects awaited him. When he died, he was carrying 10,000 Marks in cash.'[13] Liza arranged for the upkeep of the gravesite, but she had to sell Mikhail Osipovich's Amati violin to cover the costs. Miss Michelson, whom Eisenstein's father had never married, wrote the same letter three times, on October 3, 21, and 31, 1920. She did not receive an answer from Eisenstein until March 15, 1922. She then mailed him pictures of the funeral and of the grave.

Eisenstein read this belated news as a sign. He had decided to work in the theater and to become an artist on the day that he heard of his father's death.

At that time Eisenstein was working on a Hymn of the Rosicrucians with Arensky, who had just transferred to the Hindi department. Eisenstein was also writing an adaptation of E. T. A. Hoffmann's mystical work *The Golden Pot*. He had succumbed to mysticism completely and was designing Cubist decorations for *The Mexican*.

Proletkult finally started giving Eisenstein food rations, so he was able to celebrate Christmas 1920 with milk pudding.

On December 31 Eisenstein wrote in his journal: 'The coherence of all parts of the performance, the plastic correspondence of rhythm and image—for all the contrasts of the theatrical approach (in my sense) and life itself—ultimately has a deeply mystical foundation that symbolizes the oneness of the rhythm of the Universe. Not for nothing do I experience a kind of *vertige* [vertigo] when I imagine the perfectly organized theatrical act moving in an uninterrupted rhythm; I feel like I am losing consciousness . . . . I experience a similar sensation when I contemplate the deep night sky or the stars during a solitary nighttime walk.'[14]

ANARCHISTS IN MEXICO.
MEYERHOLD – THE SECOND FATHER
1920-1923

That fall the Proletkult leadership announced a competition for the best revolutionary play. The announcement was printed on October 20, 1920 in the newspaper *Kommunistichesky trud*. On the same page the editors suggested some prose works that might be dramatized, including short stories from Jack London's collection *The People of the Abyss*. In the upper left hand corner there was also a notice in bold print, 'Communism in Mexico'. Did Smyshlyaev come up with the idea to combine Jack London and Mexico? Or was it his coauthor Boris Arvatov, theoretical brain of Vladimir Tatlin's laboratory, who lectured in Proletkult on art history? The two authors joined forces to write a play for the competition. They chose Jack London's short story 'The Mexican', which had more to do with boxing than with revolution. By the beginning of November a first draft of the play was ready. The theater agreed to the production, and Smyshlyaev assigned the set design to Eisenstein and Nikitin.

The plot of the play was simple. Mexican Anarchist revolutionaries need money for weapons, so a boy climbs into the boxing ring in order to win it. The first episode takes place among the Anarchists, the second in the office of the boxing manager, and the third is the boxing match. The play ends with the rebellion.

Eisenstein was enthusiastic and worked hard to make hundreds of designs for three sets and sixty-three costumes. Nikitin's expertise compensated for Eisenstein's lack of practical experience with stage machinery. They finished a model of the set and all the costume designs by the beginning of January. The sketches were very geometrical, but painted in grotesquely bright colors, a bow to the taste of the Russian provinces. The competing boxing managers were stylized to look like spheres and squares. Eisenstein put them in costumes with big green, white, blue, and yellow checks and stripes. These clothes and masks with hanging red noses were reminiscent of Cubist circus clowns.

Smyshlyaev was very precise in his work. He came from Stanislavsky's naturalist school of acting and was oriented towards psychological nuance. This approach was radically different from Eisenstein's tendency towards the playful eccentricity of the commedia dell'arte or the Futurist circus. Conflict with the director was inevitable, but erupted late: since work on *The Mexican* was in full swing, they had no time for large-scale artistic debates. The first performances were set for March 10, 11, 13, so Eisenstein and Nikitin spent their nights painting. 'Our idiot-ideologues,' Eisenstein wrote his mother after the premiere, 'are at the height of bliss. This is the first production that hasn't flopped. What's more: it's even entertaining! There are colossal mistakes in the directorial work, which I predicted a month ago. Since my opinions differ completely from Smyshlyaev's (he is a terrible amateur in this regard), I stayed away from the directing. But my costumes blew everybody away . . . . I share the laurels for the sets with Nikitin. They are too bright (I noticed this little defect first!). But by next month we'll soften the colors a little . . . . so the sets don't swallow up my costumes.'[15]

One major directorial idea can be attributed to Eisenstein. Smyshlyaev spent so much time rehearsing the second act that he gave the actors creative license with the third act (the fight). In the third act the most important action (the fight itself) occurred off-stage, and the actors mimed the audience's response. Eisenstein suggested moving the ring into the audience and letting the actors box for real—real blows to sweaty bodies, with a real knock-out. The theatrical illusion was replaced by the real tension of a match. The effect on the audience was thus intensified in a new and different way. This idea broke one of the basic laws of theater—the separation of theater and life. But Eisenstein aimed to question precisely this distinction. With this innovation, the director Eisenstein was born. While his set designs remained heavily influenced by the brightly colored Cubist decorations of the Tairov Theater, this theatrical solution represented a new idea, which he would later modify and develop. In the rebellion scene he made use of special lighting effects. A spotlight chaotically roamed the dark stage so that the silhouettes of the three actors in different poses appeared as a large mass of people. Both solutions— the fight and the light's three-dimensional graphic effect—exceeded the limits of Cubism. 'All the rest,' Eisenstein wrote his mother in the same letter, 'was ruined by the 'internalized' representation, which Smyshlyaev demanded according to the Stanislavsky system. He was incapable of understanding the beauty of shaping mise-en-scène and movement rhythmically.'

The Mexican, a play about an anarchist rebellion, was premiered during the bloody repression of the revolt of 27,000 armed sailors in Kronstadt. The first reviews were delayed until April, so as not to awaken unnecessary associations. Henri Barbusse's enthusiastic article, first published in *Clarté*, was translated into Russian and republished in the Proletkult paper *Gorn* ('Horn') one year later. Barbusse highlighted the boxing scene as the 'symbolic replacement of class warfare with all the frenzy of Symbolism.'[16] Eisenstein clipped all the reviews and underlined the sentences that mentioned *his* innovation, though it was always attributed to Smyshlyaev. The critical attention spurred his ambition, but he did not let his eagerness show.

In comparison to his soldier and student days, the set designer Eisenstein suddenly had a lot of money. He was paid overtime for rehearsals, so he earned 92,000 rubles in January and later made 250,000 rubles a month. But the Proletkult could not get him any food ration cards. A lunch on the 'free market' cost around 2,000 to 3,000 rubles, firewood sold for around 70,000 rubles, and bread was virtually non-existent. Eisenstein had to report as a soldier in order to receive bread rations. Bread hunts cost him nerves and time. But his ascetic everyday life was orderly. Every Thursday he would go to the city baths; Kuzminichna, the Strauch family's housekeeper, washed his clothes and cooked buckwheat and cabbage soup for him. That way he was able to spend most of his money on books, his old passion. He bought English editions of Shakespeare and Ben Jonson and purchased a two-volume set of 'Italian Renaissance novellas'.

After three months of working day and night, Eisenstein was stressed. He decided that after *The Mexican* finished its run, he would begin studies at the Stroganov School for Applied Art. The school had been renamed VKhUTEMAS—Higher Artistic Technical Workshops—and had just become the seat of Constructivism. The radical innovators Vladimir Tatlin, Alexander Rodchenko and Boris Arvatov had pushed out the old avant-garde artist Vasily Kandinsky. They had won the battle for the school in a highly charged debate. The victors rejected abstract, non-representational art and embraced art's programmatic social mission. Eisenstein went to the school twice a week to audit lectures on theater and art history. He also discovered Dalcroze gymnastics, the new program of the Proletkult's Ton-Plasso Studio. He reserved eight hours a week for these exercises. 'I never would have thought that galloping to music, tossing my legs up, or running rhythmically could so improve my mood,' he wrote his mother on February 13, 1921.[17]

New productions awaited him. The Proletkult had just accepted a play by Valerian Pletnyov about the workers' uprisings in the Lena gold mines in 1911, which had ended in a massacre. All summer long Eisenstein and Nikitin worked on a new set that resembled their designs for *The Mexican*. Their set hardly suited the naturalistic, proletarian, and rather boring tragedy. The premiere took place on October 11, 1921 but the play did not even last until spring in the theater's repertoire. 'All of these pipes, cubes and circles painted purple and green, the actors' masks and other Futurist oddities might have interested the theater specialists during the premiere, but they are incomprehensible and useless for the Proletariat. The actors in fur coats, striped in all the colors of the rainbow, and the gray-brown-raspberry-colored circles that were supposed to represent Siberian nature may have pleased the Futurists who attended the show, but they had nothing to tell the heart and mind of the worker,' judged one reviewer.[18]

Eisenstein was twenty-three years old. He still had to revise *The Mexican* and design one more production. Then it was time for summer vacation. He had to make a decision: should he move to Moscow for good or should he return to his mother in Petrograd? Should he apply to the Technical College at the Theater Department, or should he study at the VKhUTEMAS art school? Or should he go on vacation and travel to Dagestan or Turkestan to stock up on food supplies? Many Moscow intellectuals took these kinds of trips. Eisenstein was uncertain.

He dreamed of independent work as a director, of a production of E. T. A. Hoffmann's *The Golden Pot*, but his dramatization did not pass the censor at Glavrepertkom. A second Hoffmann play, *Master Martin the Cooper and his Journeymen*, was forbidden by the censor in the spring of 1922, even though the production was ready to go on stage. (The 'Mexican' trio again collaborated on this project: Eisenstein and Nikitin designed the set and costumes; Smyshlyaev directed.)

Eisenstein invested a lot of energy in this effort and coauthored two versions of the play with Arensky. After the Proletkult's rejection, they considered performing the play in the Art Theater studio of their lodge brother Mikhail Chekhov ('Now that would be something new!' Eisenstein wrote his mother[19]), but the play failed to pass censorship—both in 1922 and on later attempts.

In his journal Eisenstein wrote down thoughts about a new theater that would embody the old occult scheme 'Body-Soul-Spirit' as a triangle: body and soul would form its base, its apex was the spirit. Rhythmic sensations would bring about spiritual fulfillment. Eisenstein even made *The Mexican* fit this scheme. Instead of working on E. T. A. Hoffmann, Eisenstein had to design a set for *Dawn of the Proletkult*, a production based on the verses of proletarian poets that honored the fiftieth anniversary of the Paris Commune. He found the production 'revolting'. It was performed only once, on May 21, 1921.

Designing sets at the Proletkult Theater for bad, orthodox proletarian plays began to bore Eisenstein. He even considered returning to the Petrograd institute if things were to continue in the same vein. 'This is impossible,' he wrote his mother January 4, 1921 'since there are two specific trends here that I *physically* cannot stand: first, *art proletaire quand-même* and second, the 'Stanislavsky system'. If I get my own studio here, I will stay. If not, I'm leaving.'[20]

He gradually lost his friends. Arensky, a student of Hindi at the Lazarevsky Institute, had succumbed to Buddhist mysticism. Nikitin was busy with Japanese and studied in Aristarkh Lentulov's studio at VKhUTEMAS. After going back and forth between Moscow and Petrograd for a year, Eisenstein decided in May 1921 that he would stay in Moscow for good. He finally dropped the idea of ever returning to architecture.

The Proletkult Theater with its pitiful agitation plays bored Eisenstein terribly. His conflict with Smyshlyaev and Smyshlyaev's artistic ambitions reached a new peak. When the Proletkult troupe left for their summer tour, Eisenstein decided to bow out and to go study theater.

Eisenstein knew that in spite of all the books he had read, he still lacked practical experience. The Technical Theater College that he applied to in June had just been reorganized as 'Higher Workshops in Directing' (GVYRM). The program was led by Vsevolod Meyerhold, the living legend of innovative theater in Russia.

Eisenstein had studied Meyerhold's productions for years. He had secretly attended rehearsals of *Mystery-Bouffe* in May 1921, but was sent away as an 'unauthorized person'. As Meyerhold's student, he now had the right to participate. Eisenstein was lucky, since Meyerhold had withdrawn from his R.S.F.S.R. Theater in March 1921. Meyerhold's temporary retirement was partially caused by the introduction of NEP, the New Economic Policy, which guaranteed state support only for the former imperial theaters. They had been renamed 'academic' and included the Bolshoi, Maly, Alexandrinsky, and Mariinsky. The only independent company still receiving state subsidies was Stanislavsky's and Nemirovich-Danchenko's Art Theater. When Meyerhold's ensemble was forced to merge with the more traditional Nezlobin troupe, the radical theater innovator declared that his house was now closed. Meyerhold stopped directing for almost a year—he now had plenty of time for his new school, GVYRM.

After his radical turns from Symbolism to Baroque, from commedia dell'arte to political theater, from a dandy in a top hat to a Communist in a leather jacket, Meyerhold now entered a new stage of development. He was working on a new system of acting—biomechanics—and understood his school to be a 'laboratory of Theater Constructivism'. Eisenstein passed the entrance exams on September 13, 1921. His assignment was to draw a mise-en-scène 'six pursue one'. In addition to Meyerhold (who was wearing big military boots on his feet, a rough scarf around his neck, and a red fez on his head), the entrance committee consisted of the school's director Ivan Axyonov, and Meyerhold's assistants, the Georgian Valery Bebutov and the Buryat Valery Inkizhinov. Axyonov was a bald man with a long red beard who also worked as a translator and was a member of the Futurist group 'Centrifuge'. Inkizhinov was to star in Pudovkin's 1928 film *Storm over Asia* and earn fame for his role as the descendant of Genghis Khan.

At the examination Eisenstein met the younger Sergei Yutkevich, a painter influenced by Cubism. Yutkevich was born in Petersburg in 1904. His father was an engineer who specialized in bridge building. The only son received an excellent education at a private *Gymnasium* and later studied at several art schools and with Alexandra Ekster, the costume and set designer at the Tairov Theater. Yutkevich loved the theater and the circus, attended the same shows as Eisenstein, and knew the same clowns. The two men soon became close friends.

Meyerhold's school was on the first floor of a small city villa on Novinsky Boulevard that used to house a *Gymnasium*. He lived on the second floor of the house with his family. The school consisted of one classroom and one assembly hall. The students included future film and theater directors Nikolai Ekk and Grigory Roshal, Vasily Fyodorov and Vladimir Lutse, actors Igor Ilyinsky, Maria Babanova, Vasily Orlov and Mikhail Zharov, Meyerhold's daughter Irina, as well as the critic Khrisanf Khersonsky. There were only two subjects of study: biomechanics and directing. Meyerhold's wife Zinaida Raikh, who had previously been married to the poet Sergei Esenin, and Valery Inkizhinov taught biomechanics—a system that dealt with the analytical construction of movement in space. Nikolai Bernstein, who expanded biomechanics into a scientific discipline, also gave lectures on the subject. His research paved the way for later work in the physiology of movement and cybernetics. At that time Bernstein was in the process of founding a biomechanics laboratory at the Central Institute for Labor (TsIT), which was run by the poet Alexei Gastev.

Meyerhold rejected systems of acting that made use of the actor's inner life as harmful to the actor's psyche. He considered movement to be the expression of emotion materialized in motor functions. In Meyerhold's system, the body was not subject to mysterious forces; its motor functions could be explained with help of a new science, reflexology. Like the behaviorists, Meyerhold believed that the psyche was ruled by strict causality. A reaction, or reflex, followed every stimulus. Instead of viewing a reflex as the consequence of an emotion, he viewed an emotion as the consequence of a reflex: we don't cry because we are sad; we are sad because we cry. Following this logic, actors could achieve a necessary emotional state by making the correct reflexive movements. The body's dynamics should develop in the conflict between drive and inhibition, between the movement of the body as a whole and the movement of its limbs. Biomechanics were supposed to lay bare the construction of the theatrical role and the technique of acting. The stage remained empty. The actors performed without make-up in their production clothes. Every movement in this free universal space was isolated and perfected like an acrobatic trick.

In the spring of 1922 this new system of acting was introduced to the public in a production of *The Magnanimous Cuckold*, an erotic farce by the Belgian author Fernand Crommelynck. Axyonov had translated and adapted the play. The GVYRM students sat in on every rehearsal and played the parts of the heroine's lovers. Eisenstein was thrilled by the principles of biomechanics. This was a new school of expressive movement, conceived as a Russian response to European expressive dance and to American 'Taylorism' on stage. The production's set design and costumes horrified Eisenstein. He placed the blame on the 'old maid' of Constructivism, Lyubov Popova. But in Meyerhold, his teacher, Eisenstein had found a new father figure—another beloved tyrant.

In his classes Meyerhold wanted to devise an analytical and systematic way to teach directing. The birth of ideas had to be grasped in a single formula. The chaotic master was excited by schemes and diagrams. He planned to use his students, whom he called lab assistants, to write a theater encyclopedia and to develop a new system for the notation of movement. He designated Eisenstein the leader of the encyclopedia team: he should adapt Japanese theater terminology and write an article on expressive movement.

In 1934 Eisenstein would continue the project that Meyerhold gave up after only one year in his own directing classes. Systematic thinking had never been Meyerhold's forte—he excelled instead in spontaneity, improvisation, and play.

Bored with drawing vectors, rings, and squares, Eisenstein and Yutkevich would prod Meyerhold to tell them stories after class. They asked about his production of Alexander Blok's symbolist play *The Fairground Booth* or how he worked in Paris on D'Annunzio's *Pisanella* with Ida Rubinstein. This story hour became the school where the great director's secrets came to light.

'Godlike. Incomparable . . . . I was to worship him the rest of my life.'[21] Eisenstein wrote in his memoirs twenty-five years later. Meyerhold was the embodiment *par excellence* of the principles of theater. He glittered and sparkled, was always transforming himself—a theater *magician*. Eisenstein adored him and sought to be close to him. This desire was unexpectedly fulfilled with help from Irina, Meyerhold's daughter from his first marriage. Irina taught biomechanics in the school and had fallen in love with Eisenstein. During his time at GVYRM, she was considered to be Sergei's fiancée. Irina looked like a female version of her father. She was tall, slender, had short cropped hair—an androgynous being. Eisenstein was received as an 'almost-son-in-law' in the Meyerhold household, was invited to dinner and treated as a part of the family. Meyerhold even went to see *The Mexican* with the other students and praised the production.

Irina and Sergei's romance followed the plot of the thick German books that blue-eyed girls get for Christmas, joked the observer Axyonov, where the declaration of love always comes in the second volume.[22] But the declaration was omitted from this novel. After two years the engagement petered out.

Eisenstein was a diligent student, but he suffered only defeat in the new school. He was supposed to design a set for Ludwig Tieck's *Puss-In-Boots*, and continued the experiment he had begun in *The Mexican* of spatially blurring the boundaries of life and art. The space of the real audience in front of the stage was mirrored in an imaginary space behind the stage. In this way the figures on the stage would have to lead a double life, addressing both real and the imaginary spectators. At the school, stage design was taught by Lyubov Popova. She had recently abolished the term 'set' and replaced it with 'scenic construction', where she emphasized dynamic elements such as wheels or steps. She had done away with all decorative elements and any hint of illusionistic representation. She considered Eisenstein's work to be fairly traditional and therefore bad.

In the meantime Meyerhold was supposed to produce a play for the Nezlobin Company. He chose *Heartbreak House* by George Bernard Shaw and assigned Eisenstein as his set designer. Eisenstein built a model that repeated his spiral-shaped design for Tieck's play. Lyubov Popova again criticized him: it was the old three-dimensional decorative solution. Eisenstein was written off as a traditionalist. He modified his construction and turned it into a collage of steel cable, trapeze, and rings that Nezlobin's actors would never be able to use. The play was never staged. Eisenstein saved his design for later. Another assignment, a dramatization of *The Count of Monte Cristo*, also went to waste.

The school's director Axyonov became Eisenstein's friend. They shared a passion for Elizabethan theater, for Ben Jonson and Shakespeare. That the witty, cynical, well-read Axyonov was an active Cheka agent, an informer on Moscow's artistic community, did not trouble Eisenstein. After all, Eisenstein was not yet a full member of that artistic crowd.

He spent a whole day running after *the* fashionable director of the season, Nikolai Foregger, who had opened an eccentric Futurist Music Hall on New Year's Eve 1921. But Eisenstein was too scared to speak to him. Eisenstein trusted his journal with this scene only years after the event. By then Foregger had been forgotten and Eisenstein had achieved world fame.

He gave up the dream of Japan. On March 8 he wrote his mother, 'Japan is finally crushed: the political situation.'[23] Eisenstein was not officially demobilized until 1922, an event which worsened his material situation. There was no stipend and the food rations for students were extremely modest. Eisenstein needed to earn money. He agreed to split work assignments with Yutkevich. Yutkevich was friends with Nikolai Foregger, so the latter hired Yutkevich as set designer. Yutkevich offered Eisenstein the chance to design the costumes. To repay the favor, Eisenstein suggested that Yutkevich help out in the

Proletkult Theater. Eisenstein was in charge of designing the set for Valentin Tikhonovich, one of the ensemble's new directors, who was rehearsing *Macbeth*.

Foregger parodied Moscow theaters and produced modern revues. For their project, Eisenstein and Yutkevich imitated Pablo Picasso's Cubist design for *The Parade*. Adolphe Appia's multilevel stage stood model for *Macbeth*.

Foregger was successful, and his new set designers got good press. Their efforts for Foregger and Tikhonovich stood in direct opposition to Popova's principles of 'scenic construction.' At the school they were considered to have fallen from grace. Meyerhold had always been envious of the success of others; this personality trait caused some tension between him and Eisenstein.

In April, after the premiere of *The Magnanimous Cuckold*, Yutkevich and Eisenstein traveled to Petrograd. Many things came together: Eisenstein's visit home, Foregger's guest performance, and a new encounter. Yutkevich introduced Eisenstein to his childhood friend Grigory Kozintsev. Kozintsev had just proclaimed the new art movement Eccentrism, which he sought to establish somewhere between Futurism and Dada. He had opened a new school, the Factory of the Eccentric Actor (FEKS), with the Odessan Leonid Trauberg. Kozintsev had just turned seventeen. His brother-in-law and cousin Ilya Ehrenburg was then living in Berlin, where he published the international magazine *Veshch-Objet-Gegenstand* in three languages. Kozintsev assured the two Muscovites that all of Europe would soon know of FEKS through that magazine. He generously made Yutkevich and Eisenstein the offer of directing at his 'factory'. Kozintsev himself was rehearsing *Hamlet* and *The Wedding (Not Based on Gogol)*. Eisenstein and Yutkevich wrote *Columbine's Garter*, a libretto in the style of Foregger's parodies. In 1910 Meyerhold had directed *Columbine's Scarf*, based on a pantomime by Ernst von Dohnanyi and Arthur Schnitzler. Three years later Tairov answered with the production *Pierette's Veil*. Eisenstein and Yutkevich wanted to take on those two rival leaders of the new Soviet theater, so they parodied both versions in their play. They defined its genre as the 'invention of scenic attractions'. Like a roller coaster or a devil's wheel, each number was supposed to have a physiological effect on its viewers and make them hold their breath. Pierrot, a poet, was addicted to morphine. Harlequin, an industrialist, produced garters. The action was set in Paris and took place exclusively on vertical ropes. Old Paris appeared as an Americanized metropolis with bars, jazz, and American dances. Columbine's mother took the shape of a restaurant vending machine. Her fat thighs were wrapped in pink and fenced in by a glass case. They looked like an imitation of a Westphalian ham. Glasses full of apéritifs stood on a counter that was attached to her bosom. However, Eisenstein and Yutkevich did not want to produce the play at FEKS, but in a real theater, on Foregger's stage. Foregger would not allow it. His theater had only one director, namely Foregger himself.

After the summer break Eisenstein assisted Meyerhold in the production of *The Death of Tarelkin*. His relations with his 'almost-father-in-law' were rapidly deteriorating. Meyerhold now reacted to Eisenstein irritably. But his discontent had nothing to do with Sergei and Irina's relationship. He accused Eisenstein of treachery and claimed that Eisenstein had shared the school's secrets with Foregger and the Proletkult, enabling other people to steal his discoveries.

During a seminar meeting Zinaida Raikh stared at Eisenstein for a long time, then tore a piece of paper from a poster that was lying on the table and wrote Eisenstein a message: 'Seryozha! I like you. I adore your talent and originality. My opinion: leave M[eyerhol]d, just as M-d left Stanislavsky back then. You're ready. My advice: break off your studies here. Smart and magnanimous. In principle I'm your enemy, though I have most tender feelings for you.'[24] Eisenstein did not have any other choice. Late November 1922, shortly after the opening night of *The Death of Tarelkin*, he left the school. He went away without understanding Meyerhold's change of heart. Not until 1928, when Stefan Zweig told him about scenes of jealousy and expulsion in the Freud circle, did Eisenstein recognize his teacher's psychological pattern. He believed that Meyerhold reproduced his own break with Stanislavsky in his relationships with students.

Meyerhold was pathologically intolerant, not only in respect to rivals like Tairov, but also towards his students. Those who continued to work in theater, such as Nikolai Okhlopkov and Vasily Fyodorov, particularly bothered him. 'I am afraid of all of you,' Meyerhold supposedly said on the first day of classes, 'therefore I hate you.' The patriarchal atmosphere of the run-down villa on Novinsky Boulevard housed a tyrant's (Meyerhold's) suspicion towards all who tried to make their own way. Those accused of desecrating the master's teachings would be disowned and exiled. This is how Eisenstein would later describe the school.

Eisenstein confided the extent of his hurt feelings only to his diary, a new personal diary that he had begun to keep January 16, 1923 following Irina's advice. She had been advised to keep a journal by Meyerhold. Eisenstein recorded not only the events of the day, but also described incidents that had taken place weeks or months earlier.

In his notes Eisenstein ruthlessly called Meyerhold to account, but not until 1926-27. In that year Meyerhold's *Inspector General* competed with Eisenstein's *Battleship Potemkin* as *the* Moscow art event of the season. Eisenstein picked out every sign of Meyerhold's feebleness and noted signs of senility and vanity in his former demigod. He found the *Inspector General* to be erotic, but *impotent*, like a 'hot, but flaccid penis'.[25] That expression was borrowed from the sharp-tongued Isaak Babel, Sergei's new close friend. Eisenstein now considered Meyerhold a miserable teacher: 'Purely impressionist empiricism. No net result. M[eyerhold]'s 'Saturnalism': he devours his children and disowns the ones that don't finish their studies if they show the slightest inkling of independence. M. created neither a school, nor a collective. I came to him with a lot of experience and he spent a winter telling anecdotes.'[26]

On November 23, 1928 Eisenstein read an article about the 'cinefication' of Meyerhold's theater[27] and made a list of the things Meyerhold had stolen from him, Eisenstein. He even considered biomechanics to be *his own* invention.

Eisenstein had to live out the break with his attractive, strong second father and the beginning of his own independence in his diary. His devastating rhetoric danced around the theme of Meyerhold's impotence. His love-hate relationship with Meyerhold repeated the psychological pattern of his relationship with his own 'undersexed' father. This relationship, too, was fraught with ambivalence. He compared his schooling with Meyerhold to Hell, but he likened the separation to the fall from Paradise.[28] 'Is this my own greedy self-obsession? Or just an Oedipus-complex—the worship of authority, the attainment of equal status, the debunking of the authority—independent of that phenomenon's actual worth?' he asked himself later. He wanted to understand his own pattern of behavior and his question sounds more like an answer.[29]

But in his memoirs, written in old age at a time when Meyerhold had been destroyed, consigned to oblivion, and declared a non-person by the system of terror, Eisenstein noted that he was, 'not worthy even to untie the sandals' on Meyerhold's feet, and that he was ready, 'in reverence to brush his lips against the prints left in the dust by the firm tread of his stooping teacher.'[30]

Eisenstein dedicated his first independent theatrical production to Meyerhold. Otherwise he spent a life striving to be Meyerhold's opposite. He tried to be gentle with his assistants, not sneaky and rough. But he lovingly demanded total devotion.

Eisenstein experienced his break with Meyerhold dramatically. He did not give up at once, but rejoined the school six months later, only to be expelled January 6, 1924 for failing to perform required work. Still, he had prepared his departure well and made plans for the future. In September the Proletkult came to blows with Smyshlyaev over the production of a new play by Pletnyov, *On the Abyss.* Smyshlyaev abandoned the Proletkult Theater, which left the theater scrambling for a replacement. The Proletkult theater department was also starting up an itinerant troupe.

Eisenstein was offered the leadership of the group. The temporary address of his own first theater was Vozdvizhenka 16.

THE WISE MAN. THE SUFFERINGS OF YOUNG S.
1923

The best way for Eisenstein to overcome the trauma of expulsion was to start his own school, where he himself would occupy the place of the beloved tyrant. The institution that would allow him to develop as an artist seemed structurally complex. To date Eisenstein had worked at the Proletkult as a mere set designer, always with his friends, his brothers from the order. Now he was alone, in a leading position, and had to deal with the institution's bureaucracy. The Proletkult had lost its independence when Eisenstein took up work on *The Mexican* in December 1920 and now stood under the direct supervision of the People's Commissariat for Enlightenment. This decision had been Lenin's initiative, since he saw an unacceptable deviation from Marxism in the theories of the Proletkult ideologue Alexander Bogdanov. This scientist, economist, physician and novelist tried to replace Lenin's theory of knowledge with modern epistemological philosophy. He proposed treating physical, biological, and human sciences as systems of relationships governed by the same organizational principle. His notion that culture would play a central role in building Communism was attacked, and Lenin personally formulated a resolution that was published in *Pravda* on December 1, 1920: 'The Proletkults are being overrun by hostile petty bourgeois elements . . . . Their leadership has been taken over by Futurists and Decadents, those who subscribe to an idealistic philosophy counter to Marxism, and finally simply losers from the ranks of bourgeois journalism and philosophy. Behind the mask of proletarian culture, workers are being offered bourgeois opinions in the realm of philosophy (Machism) and *silly, depraved, degenerate* tastes in the realm of art (Futurism).' Lenin was clearly targeting Bogdanov for attack; he had been conducting polemics against Bogdanov's philosophical views since 1905. Bogdanov and Lebedev-Polyansky, Smyshlyaev's patron, objected to the decision, but the Proletkult plenary session would not support them. They were forced to resign. Valerian Pletnyov, a worker and professional revolutionary, was elected chairman of the Proletkult Central Committee. Pletnyov later became the organization's leading publicist and dramatist.

Eisenstein was uninterested in these high level machinations, and he only discovered Marxism later in life. He had to deal with Pletnyov mainly as a playwright and as his immediate supervisor. This was not easy, since both men soon discovered their artistic and personal incompatibility.

At first Eisenstein worked mostly with Boris Arvatov. They developed a program of new social-theatrical ceremonies that fit into Pletnyov's policy of socially-engaged theater. However, Arvatov and Eisenstein embraced an even more radical program than Pletnyov. Arvatov conceived of theater as a laboratory for a new way of life, which could be modeled on the stage and would then be transposed into reality. Subjects to be tested and demonstrated included improvised 'kinetic constructions': meetings, banquets, tribunals, gatherings, athletic events, cafeterias, parties, processions, funerals, parades, carnivals, election campaigns, and factory work. Through Arvatov Eisenstein became acquainted with Sergei Tretyakov, a Futurist who had come to Moscow in the fall of 1922 and had remained an active part of the artistic scene ever since.

Tretyakov was also from Latvia, had lived in Riga since 1907, and even shared Eisenstein's name and patronymic—Sergei Mikhailovich. He was a member of the Proletkult Central Committee and led workshops on newspaper writing and applied rhetoric. His mind was cool and rational, and his words were straightforward and radical. Tretyakov had spent many years in China and the Far East. Now he lived with actors, directors, and musicians in the Proletkult dormitory and promoted his ideas of an artistic and disciplined communal life. Tretyakov co-founded the Left Front of Art with other Moscow Futurists and Cubo-Futurists. The group included the poets Vladimir Mayakovsky, Boris Pasternak, and Boris Kushnir, the theoreticians Osip Brik and Arvatov, and the Constructivists Alexander Rodchenko and Anton Lavinsky. Literary critics and linguists from the Formalist circle, including Viktor Shklovsky, Yury Tynyanov, and Viktor Vinogradov, also joined forces with the Left Front. The unaligned prose writers Isaak Babel and Artyom Vesyoly stood in close contact with the group. In 1923 they began publishing their own journal *LEF*.

These former Futurists, who now considered themselves production artists, replaced the Freemasons for Eisenstein. Arvatov and Tretyakov quickly became the group's leading ideologues. Once again Eisenstein had entered a select all-male circle. Lili Brik, Mayakovsky's lover and Osip Brik's wife, was the only woman in the crowd. Their orientation was radically different from that of Eisenstein's earlier acquaintances. While Zubakin, Arensky and Smyshlyaev viewed art as a mediator between life and higher spheres, the LEF artists wanted art to be fully absorbed into life. In the current transitional phase art was to function as an experimental school: theater would teach people how to move; literature would teach them how to express themselves; photography how to see; film how to think. For this reason, LEF members called themselves life-builders. Eisenstein was still only a beginner. The old mystic and the new production artist could not coexist. In his very first independent production Eisenstein made fun of theosophy. Though Lenin's resolution had decried Futurism as degenerate art, harmful to the proletariat, Eisenstein chose to direct plays by the former Futurist Sergei Tretyakov. In this manner, Eisenstein could put into practice the Left Front's art politics in the Proletkult Theater. The contradictions between the two platforms would not lead to open conflict until later.

When Eisenstein became the head of the itinerant troupe in October 1922, a group of nineteen young people was put under his direction. Most of them had already acted in *The Mexican.* Now they were his pupils. They included his friend and landlord Maxim Strauch, Strauch's wife Judith Glizer, Grigory Alexandrov, Ivan Pyrev, Alexander Antonov, Mikhail Gomorov, Alexander Lyovshin, Ivan Kravchunovksy, and Vera Yanukova.

Eisenstein replaced Smyshlyaev's Stanislavsky-based system with biomechanics, taught by Inkizhinov. He also sent his students to a riding school to study trick riding like circus artists. Neither Eisenstein nor his students quite knew how these skills would come in handy, but their acrobatic ability proved essential to their later work on *The Battleship Potemkin.* Mornings were reserved for instruction. Rehearsals began after lunch and often lasted until midnight. 'Courtesy is the best means of exploitation' was Eisenstein's motto. He was the same age as his students. Together they learned to tap dance, played volleyball, snuck into movie theaters without tickets; but 'nobody in his wildest dream thought about addressing him in the familiar 'ty' form,' said one of his students.[31] Eisenstein taught his students and learned from the process himself. He completed an intensive seminar with Lev Kuleshov in another craft altogether—in film. Kuleshov, a very eccentric figure, taught classes in the Proletkult from January 1922 to March 1923. He had begun his film career as a set designer, first working for the exquisite silent film director Evgeny Bauer. Just as Kuleshov turned eighteen, Bauer died and the Revolution erupted. Kuleshov understood the Revolution as a radical break with the old way of life. He thought that the psychological attire and the mentality of nineteenth-century Russians had been changed radically. Art nouveau interior design, ladies with big hats, men in tuxedos, dark passions, irrational fate—all of this seemed to have been swept away. The new man rationally rebuilt society and nature and viewed life, art, and his own person as perfectly organized entities. Psyche was ruled by causality (stimulus-reaction), the irrational had been locked out. Tuxedos and top hats were exchanged for leather jackets and pilot's caps, the *flâneur's* stroll was replaced by an energetic gait, and acrobatics took the place of lasciviousness. Only two months passed between Kuleshov's last job for Bauer and his own debut as a director, but the difference was that of a lifetime. Kuleshov discovered a new cinema and a new way of living and called it 'American'. Americanism stood for the excitement of technology, tempo, and energy, for a pragmatic and ironic mind. Kuleshov wanted to reform the slow Russian film with action, dynamism, and eccentricity. Movement was to be shortened and shown only in the most thrilling phase. Kuleshov called his new images 'American shots'. Once the moment had been captured, the succession of long, static, deep focus shots would flow into a dynamic montage of short, flat, rhythmic fragments. The film should be structured completely around effective stereotypes: criminal intrigue and chase scenes, masks of evildoers and vamps surrounded by modern props—trains, airplanes, cars, telephones. Kuleshov wore a leather jacket, rode a motorcycle and would later race cars. He conceived of film as a magician's art. On the screen he could create a space that did not exist in reality. He could assemble a 'perfect body' from the 'parts' of other people. He discovered that when watching a film the viewers themselves produced the meaning of the action. This could turn a sequence of two unrelated images into a wonderful play of montage. Someone might shoot a gun in the first image; a person would fall over in the second. The audience believed that the man had just been shot, even if the first image had been filmed in Alaska and the second in Jamaica. A man stared into space. Kuleshov played with the shots that followed this image: the face—a child, the face—a coffin, the face—a woman. In these different combinations the audience tended to interpret the same facial expression as tenderness, grief, and lust. This basic property of film montage was dubbed the Kuleshov-effect.

In 1921, when Meyerhold opened his directing school, Kuleshov put together a group of young people to prove that he could turn them all into great film actors. He chose the chemist Vsevolod Pudovkin, the boxer Boris Barnet, Alexandra Khokhlova (granddaughter of the art collector Sergei Tretyakov), and the tap dancer Leonid Obolensky. He trained them according to his own system—he wanted them to become 'models' (*naturshchiki*) that moved perfectly and could express any emotion in their movements. Film stock was scarce, so they produced 'films without film', a simulation of the cinema on the stage. Black velvet screens imitated the frame of each shot, and light spots created the impression of close-ups. The dramatic effect of each sketch was expressed through body language—like in the movies.

Eisenstein heard of this new school, which had just been barred from the state film program, from Leonid Obolensky, Eisenstein's partner in *The Magnanimous Cuckold*. When Obolensky described the Kuleshov-effect, Eisenstein was thrilled: this would mean that anything could be put together in any order, even backwards. Each segment would mean something different in a new combination!

Eisenstein generously let Kuleshov use his stage in the Proletkult Theater (after his disagreement with the film college, Kuleshov was out of practice space) and received lessons from the film director in return. He also followed the progress of the 'films without film'. Through Kuleshov, Eisenstein met Kuleshov's students, who would soon be the leading film directors of Soviet Russia. He also became acquainted with Esfir Shub and her husband Alexei Gan. Shub cut Soviet versions of foreign films for the Film Committee. Her husband was a graphic artist, and had just started a new film magazine, *Kino-fot*. Gan supported yet another cinema innovator, Dziga Vertov, the founder of the Cine-Eye (*Kinoki*) group. While Kuleshov decidedly reformed the feature film, Vertov went one step further. He took a stance against artists who 'nego-tiated' between camera and life and stood up against writers and actors. He demanded the creation of pure cinema, unpolluted by literature, painting, music, or theater. He conceived of cinema as dynamic geometry, a succession of dots, lines, planes, and volumes, as movement of pure form in an organized space that consciously made use of rhythm. Thanks to the patronage of a child-hood friend, the journalist Mikhail Koltsov, Vertov was named the director of the new Soviet weekly newsreel *Cine-Pravda*, the film version of *Pravda*.

Vertov's cameramen, whom he called 'Cine-Eyes', now had to tame the chaos of visual impressions. Dynamic geometry was no longer declared filmic material. Instead, Vertov was now concerned with 'life caught unawares'. Thus, *Cine-Pravda* received the status of absolute film truth.

Vertov and Kuleshov were rivals. Eisenstein only got to know the group around one of them closely and wasted little thought on the other side. At this point the intrigues of the film world still seemed remote, and he was busy with his own ensemble.

Eisenstein had been working on his first production since March 6. The model for his text montage was a play by Alexander Ostrovsky, the founder of Russian naturalist theater. It was the 100th anniversary of Ostrovsky's birth, and the Commissar of Enlightenment Anatoly Lunacharsky had called on the theater establishment to reflect on the tradition of the great playwright and director. Meyerhold began rehearsing Ostrovsky's *The Forest* in February 1923. Eisenstein decided to compete secretly with his teacher and chose the play *Enough Simplicity for Every Wise Man*, shortened to *The Wise Man*. The play had been written in 1868 and dealt with a young man's career. An influential pa-tron first promotes the man, but then drops him—Sergei may have experi-enced the plot as a reflection of his own life. On April 2 Eisenstein's troupe performed one scene from the play at the Bolshoi Theater celebration of the 25th anniversary of Meyerhold's stage debut. Eisenstein did not really try to settle accounts with his old patron in the play. Sergei Tretyakov had written a new text and transposed the plot to the Russian émigré milieu in Paris.

Eisenstein conceived of the play a as comedy of masks hidden in the disguise of naturalist theater. The characters—tsarist officials and Moscow merchants—appeared as political clowns. The audience was expected to associate them with the French general Joffre or Italian Fascists. One groom metamorphosed into three officers of Wrangel's White Army. In order to deal with the multiplicity of grooms in Tretyakov's play, Ostrovsky's priest mutated into a mullah officiating at a Muslim wedding. The puns and allusions of *The Wise Man* were barely comprehensible even to the audience of the time. One of the hero's names, Mamilyukov-Prolivnoy, referred to the leader of the Constitutional Democrats, Pavel Milyukov. Milyukov had demanded the Russian annexation of the Turkish straits (*proliv* in Russian, hence *Prolivnoy*). The production was christened a 'leftist salon of political crossword puzzles'. Ostrovsky's text was spiked with recent political jokes and sung to the tunes of old favorites, *Rigoletto* arias, and romances popularized by the singer Alexander Vertinsky.

The characters were dressed in electric clown suits. A man wearing a bra with electric lamps played the role of the mother—the bra's red lights lit up in moments of passion. The villain Alexandrov wore a black mask with green lights next to his eyes.

The play was premiered on April 26 and May 6 in the former villa of the merchant Savva Morozov on Vozdvizhenka Street. A green circus carpet with red cloth around the edges covered the floor of the hall. A rope stretched downward from a box seat in the first circle to the carpet on the floor—this was one performance space. There was a trapeze and a large box into which the actors could disappear (a stage 'exit'), in order to then reappear on the ropes or in the box seats. One actor sat in a ring dangling from the middle of the ceiling and imitated a parrot. A small curtain hanging from two circus masts served as a film screen.

Under the influence of his new friends, Eisenstein decided to incorporate a piece of film into his first theater production. The piece was called *Glumov's Diary*. Eisenstein wanted to shoot the film in the manner of the beloved American series *The Exploits of Elaine* or *The Iron Claw* starring the actress Pearl White. Pearl was catapulted to fame after the 1914 series *The Perils of Pauline*. These 20 episodes introduced a dynamic and athletic young heiress who, at the end of each part, had to survive either a plummeting hot-air balloon or a raging fire only to face new, more perilous adventures in the next. Mikhail Boitler, the brother of the well-known film comic Arkady Boitler, had opened his own movie theater on Malaya Dimitrovka number six. (The government had recently allowed some private businesses to reopen). Boitler showed these old series from 1915-16 and let Eisenstein and his ensemble in for free.

The film's content was supposed to parody the Pathé weekly newsreel.

Eisenstein asked the Film Committee for support. Dziga Vertov was sent to assist him. The two men came into conflict on April 19, the very first day of filming. Maxim Strauch and Ivan Pyrev were standing around in clown suits, and Grigory Alexandrov was climbing up the villa's turret wearing a black mask. He was about to mimic Harry Piel, a German film star famous for his thrilling stunts, and jump into a moving car. Vertov, who had just announced his 'life caught unawares' program, which rejected the old film tricks and film-theater, thought the scene was silly. His cameraman Alexander Lemberg was worried that the shot would be too dangerous. They left the scene. The next day the cameraman Boris Frantsisson shot the ten-minute episode without any ado. From that time on, a strange animosity, even enmity, developed between Eisenstein and Vertov. They engaged in sharp polemics even though both men were considered members of the Left Front.

At the end of the film reel, the director Eisenstein (the filmed director) stepped in front of the audience. He tipped his cap and released the mighty curls that adorned his head like a halo. He bowed to the production poster, where the three words 'plenty for everyone' jumped into focus.

The performance resembled a circus act, a complex kinetic formation that included life-threatening stunts like tightrope walking. The press debated whether eccentricity was an ur-proletarian art form and whether this form of theater could develop the proletariat's consciousness.

Eisenstein conceived of theater as a method of attacking the audience's psyche. As in *The Mexican*, Eisenstein rejected the illusion of art. The work of his circus artist actors was real: anger was represented by a leap backwards, a surge of passion involved climbing the highest circus pole. The production combined different stimuli: tricks, sounds, a spot of color, a smell or a salvo of fireworks from under an audience member's seat. All of these stimuli were considered to be of equal value: a drum roll could have the same effect as Romeo's monologue or the color of a prima donna's tights. The director called one such effectual unit an 'attraction'. The way the attractions were combined was more significant then each individual 'trick'. Eisenstein arranged his production as a classical case of conditioning—he wanted to train and develop proletarian conditioned reflexes.

In May 1923 Eisenstein published a theoretical explanation of the performance, the manifesto 'The Montage of Attractions', in *LEF*, the magazine of the Left Front. The editors printed this text next to a manifesto by Dziga Vertov. Eisenstein believed that he had gone one step farther than his theater colleagues. Meyerhold and Foregger both experimented with a similar free montage of stunts, scenes, songs, and film fragments, but they had not yet grasped the theoretical significance of their experience. Viktor Shklovsky and other theoreticians of the Formalist school would analyze the principles of combination and recombination in these formal experiments, just as they examined more traditional literary works. Eisenstein was not interested in the *composition* of a play, but in its *effect*. He believed formal analysis needed to be accompanied by psychological studies—Eisenstein understood theater to be a form of psychological violence.

'Attraction .... is any aggressive moment in theatre, i.e. any element of it that subjects the audience to emotional or psychological influence, verified by experience and mathematically calculated to produce specific emotional shocks in the spectator in their proper order within the whole. These shocks provide the only opportunity of perceiving the ideological aspect of what is being shown, the final ideological conclusion.'[32]

Eisenstein did not want to share this discovery with anybody. On December 9, 1923 he wrote in his diary: 'I won't let anybody get a glimpse of my cards before Tretyakov's premiere. The attraction is *my* invention. It's good to have a theoretician on hand, but I'm afraid the credit will go to him.'[33]

Arvatov welcomed *The Wise Man* as an example of class warfare against the bourgeois academic theaters and against the bourgeois way of life.[34] Axyonov also wrote a programmatic review—about Constructivism's victory on stage.[35] The performance became an event in Moscow. On June 8, 1923 Eisenstein noted with satisfaction, 'with *The Wise Man* I have destroyed Foregger completely.'[36] 'My *Forest*,' the surprised Meyerhold commented, 'was absolutely naïve in comparison.'[37]

After the premiere Eisenstein worked with Pletnyov on a detective play, *Patatras*, but the preparations ground to a halt. He wrote an original play with Alexandrov, *Garland's Heirs*, but produced a different one that had been written by Tretyakov. In September and October he started rehearsing *Can You Hear Me, Moscow?*, an agitation play with naturalistic effects that responded to the revolutionary situation in Germany. The Proletkult planned to perform the piece at a train station in order to strengthen class hatred among volunteer soldiers who were departing for Hamburg and Berlin to bring about the World Revolution. In fact, the first performance took place on the anniversary of the Revolution, November 7, 1923, at the Operetta Theater. The play was not merely an operetta substitute—the former theater now housed the Party's City Committee.

There was *one* trick in the performance that had all of Moscow talking: the Count and his mistress made their stage entrance on a camel's back. Lyubov Popova went to the theater just to see the animal. Esfir Shub and Alexei Gan were thrilled by the performance and forgave Eisenstein his 'children's circus'—their opinion of *The Wise Man*.

Konstantin Miklashevsky, Russia's leading expert on the commedia dell'arte, praised the production to the skies. Miklashevsky was also Evreinov's friend and an aesthete through and through. Eisenstein again evaluated his own work in terms of his rivalry with Meyerhold. On December 16, 1923 he noted in his diary that Meyerhold now praised him everywhere as his own student (that explained why Eisenstein was so good), but that he was terribly annoyed and supposedly told Tretyakov, 'I dragged this Eisenstein into directing by his ears, and now he's snatching up all the good plays.'[38]

On December 20, 1923 Eisenstein wrote his mother, 'Moscow is the most melodramatic melodrama ever—there is death, heroism, etc. Even more noise than in The Wise Man. In addition to all the formal innovations, we somehow hit the mark. The newspaper Izvestiya wrote: 'This is already the new theater which we are still awaiting from Meyerhold.'"[39]

Meyerhold soon invited Eisenstein's successful writer Tretyakov to work for his theater. First Tretyakov adapted works by other writers, such as translations of dramas by the Frenchman Marcel Martuinet or Alexander Pushkin's erotic poem Gavriiliada, but he soon started writing original plays for Meyerhold.

In 1923 Eisenstein refreshed The Mexican, but the performance did not enjoy the same success as Smyshlyaev's sensational premiere.

Eisenstein's mother was not entirely satisfied with her son's way of life. She still worried about his career, perhaps because she herself was not doing very well. She now worked on and off, but changed jobs frequently. She did not have very many things left to sell and was worried about her financial future. Her son insisted that he was doing very well: 'I get 90 million in the Proletkult, 160 for lectures and 480 for seminars. That means that I make at least 840 million a month. Seems to me that my work in theater is more than just fun and games..!'[40] He had plenty of clothes: on October 10, 1922 a package from Miss Michelson arrived from Berlin with his father's things and the death certificate. Eisenstein had the pants, jackets and vests retailored. On November 11, 1922 he described his life to his mother: 'I receive 800 million a month; I had the clothes altered; I am happy with my work. Mornings and evenings I eat a bloody steak and a bowl of meat soup; I drink two cups of cocoa with two French rolls. I can afford to buy apples, grapes, even chocolate, almost every day. At work I eat cheese rolls. We have condensed milk every day. I conscientiously drink my Phisine Inosite.'[41] This sounded almost like a bourgeois life-style. Eisenstein was beginning to grow fat, so he attended dance classes twice a week. But he had to limit his physical activity because of a congenital heart defect. He began to take medication to strengthen his heart muscles at a young age.

Eisenstein became famous, and his first love affairs were not long in com-ing. His mother wanted to move from Petrograd to live with her boy in Mos-cow, but Eisenstein went to great efforts to keep her at a distance. Detailed letters to her were one thing, but when she was around she meddled in his life and wanted to control everything. His mother's hysterical claims to domi-nance strengthened Eisenstein's distrust, even fear, of women.

The twenties were a time of open promiscuity, free love, and new ideas of marriage. Alexandra Kollontai propagated these ideas, and Vladimir Mayakovsky, Lili Brik and Osip Brik demonstratively lived out the new mor-als in their open *ménage à trois*. Eisenstein remained celibate. His first youthful passion, Nataliya Pushkina, 'a lovely little girl with bad teeth,'[42] as he later described her in his memoirs, preferred an engineer. Her older sister Maria Zhdan-Pushkina, a ballerina whom Eisenstein had first met in 1918 in Dvinsk and then saw again in Moscow, married another man in 1921. Eisenstein gave the bride away at the wedding. In the meantime Irina Meyerhold left for Petrograd. In 1923 Eisenstein finally experienced his first romantic drama. He found himself torn between two women. Both were his students. Vera Yanukova, the daughter of the theater's dresser, dreamed of becoming the pro-letarian Sarah Bernhardt. The same was true for Ida (Judith) Glizer, Maxim Strauch's wife. Yanukova was an expressive dancer who was also trained in Dalcrozian eurhythmics. She had a perfect figure, green eyes, ash blonde hair and an erotic aura. She was the star of *The Wise Man*. 'The way Eisenstein dressed her! Silk and ostrich feathers!' Judith Glizer recalled. 'But most important was the way he undressed her! She suddenly lost her dress in the most serious moments and she was left standing in black tights! With a top hat! She looked like a foreign little statue!'[43] Eisenstein sent her into an obscene and breath-taking acrobatic number: during a 'surge of passion' she climbed up a 6-foot pole that emanated from Alexander Antonov's belly. During each performance Eisenstein became terrified that she might fall, and he would have to leave the room. He would wait in the foyer until she had jumped off the pole and the audience roared with applause.

Their romance did not amount to much. Eisenstein had problems with women and consulted his mother on his failure. Vera Yanukova was surrounded by admir-ers and did not wait for Eisenstein. She was later involved with many—some thought too many—famous and powerful men. The list included the North Pole pilot Mikhail Vodopyanov, the actors and directors Alexei Diky, Nikolai Okhlopkov, and even Erwin Piscator, who came to Moscow in 1931 to direct *The Revolt of the Fishermen*. Piscator gave Yanukova the part intended for Lotte Lenya.

While Vera gave up quickly, Agniya Kasatkina, whom Eisenstein called 'the blonde girl with the Dostoevskian name' (he was probably confusing her with Aglaya in *The Idiot*), became actively involved in Eisenstein's intimate life. She invited Aron Zalkind, a well-known psychologist and psychoanalyst, to a performance of *The Wise Man* and forced Eisenstein to meet him: she wanted Zalkind to heal Eisenstein. Eisenstein met with this flamboyant character from the Moscow psychoanalytic scene on several occasions. Zalkind was strongly influenced by Alfred Adler and treated the neuroses of Red Commissars. Zalkind did not advocate the liberation of the drive. Instead he preached the twelve commandments of proletarian sexual life: the proletariat's energy should not be distracted from its historical mission by spending itself in sex. He advocated abstinence and taught that members of the working class should become actively involved in the intimate life of their friends and relatives if necessary. Eisenstein attended several sessions. Zalkind may have been a bad match for Eisenstein, but Eisenstein never commented on Zalkind's modifications of psychoanalytic theory.

Eisenstein's involvement with Zalkind hardly changed his relations with Agniya. But she was the first woman who tried to become intimate with Eisenstein. Later Eisenstein wrote about her in English (a language less intimate than his native Russian), 'Agniya the first I slept with.'[44]

Agniya even corresponded with Yulia Ivanovna and expressed the conviction that she and Eisenstein could have a joint future. When Eisenstein withdrew and dashed her hopes she tried to poison herself. She survived and later married a high-ranking Party official. Eisenstein ran into Agniya and her child several times, since they lived in the same house as his later girlfriend Elizaveta Telesheva.

These experiences made Eisenstein deeply insecure. He could not immediately grasp his own sexuality. Since he had difficulties with women, he thought he might be homosexual or bisexual. Grigory (Grisha) Alexandrov, an attractive young man with blue eyes, golden hair, a muscular body and a charming smile, was promoted from his student status and became Eisenstein's devoted assistant. He modeled his life after Sherlock Holmes, the 'steel superman' from Conan Doyle's stories and infected Eisenstein with his animal joy of life. Eisenstein believed that his actor and assistant had achieved total suppression of reflexes and had become an ideal 'marionette.'[45] Grisha came from a working-class family in the Urals, grew up in Ekaterinburg, and started acting in theaters when he was nine years old. His love of life and his masterful way of spinning tall tales charmed the people around him. He was always able to explain very complex things in terms of something simple, a talent Eisenstein admired. Grisha was successful with everyone—with women, old men, children, policemen, and later with millionaires. But he was neither an erotic adventurer nor an erotic double of his teacher. At that time, he enjoyed a strictly monogamous marriage with Olga Ivanova, an actress of the Proletkult ensemble, and was completely devoted to Eisenstein.

Years later Eisenstein would return to his relationships with Agniya, Vera, and Grisha in his diary. He would try to analyze them—at least partly because his relationships with women repeated the same pattern over and over again. Agniya had left her boyfriend Arvatov for Eisenstein. The sensitive Arvatov fell seriously ill with a psychological disorder in the mid-twenties. Doctors identified a war injury (not his love life) as the cause of Arvatov's illness, but Eisenstein rejected the diagnosis and blamed himself. Arvatov appeared in Eisenstein's dreams, where he would pursue Eisenstein on a white stallion; this vision would regularly stir up Eisenstein.[46] Events took a similar course with another couple close to Eisenstein. 'January 3, 1927. Alexei Gan has gone mad. Alcohol. The psychological trauma—jealous of Esfir Shub because of me. Because I dominate her *par excellence* both erotically and morally. Gannushkin is Esfir's psychiatrist. Arvatov—Kasatkina. I'm involved again. Who will be next, who's next?'[47]

Two Constructivists went insane because of Eisenstein, or so Eisenstein thought. They lost their minds over women who desired Eisenstein, but whom Eisenstein never touched. Most important for Eisenstein was the power he held over the women. That alone satisfied him. It could even amuse him.

But Eisenstein still worried about his lack of erotic excitement. Was his state pathological? He found relief not in his conversations with Zalkind, but in Freud's interpretation of Leonardo da Vinci's sexuality. This model helped Eisenstein understand himself. He discovered an astonishing parallel to his own sexuality and viewed himself as a Russian Leonardo, in the Freudian sense of course. This analysis freed him from the shame and anxiety about his impotence or homosexuality. Like Leonardo, he stood above his sexual desires and could sublimate them in art.

If he did have a sexual abnormality, it was that of a bisexual androgyne, whose cult was celebrated in Russia at the beginning of the century among the Symbolists. This image, a constant motif of his homoerotic sketches, flattered Eisenstein. He lived out his sexual fantasies in these drawings and in obscene jokes.

Serious and classical—just as Freud would suggest—Eisenstein practiced the cult of creative sublimation.

THE JUMP INTO FILM: THE STRIKE
1924

Eisenstein spent all of December 1923 working on the new play *Gas Masks*. The story was taken from the newspapers, but Tretyakov transformed it into a production melodrama published in *LEF*: A pipe burst at the gasworks. Due to the factory director's negligence, there are not enough gas masks to go around. The workers have to take care of the accident without the masks, and the director's son dies in an effort to save the plant. His pregnant wife promises to name her child 'Gas Mask'. Maxim Strauch played the director; Boris Yurtsev—the red-haired clown in *The Wise Man*—was given the heroic part of the director's son. The play was reminiscent of projects planned by the Laboratory for Modeling New Behavioral Norms that Eisenstein and Arvatov had conceived while working on *The Mexican*. Eisenstein staged the performance in the workshop of the Moscow gasworks.

The decision to play in the gasworks was not purely programmatic. The Proletkult had lost its own performance space. As a part of NEP-policy, the Proletkult had to move out of the Hermitage Theater, and turn over the space to the Operetta Theater. Offenbach's *La Belle Hélène* simply attracted larger audiences and brought in more money than Pletnyov's plays. The Proletkult was assigned a poorly equipped room far from the center of town in the gypsy restaurant Yar, but the theater rejected this new home. After the performance of *The Wise Man* in a small room on Vozdvizhenka Street, Eisenstein was left without a space for rehearsal and performance. The Vozdvizhenka building had just been occupied by the Secretariat of the Party Central Committee. In 1925 VOKS, a new Society for Cultural Ties with Foreign Countries, moved into the building. Eisenstein now had to move from club to club, but *The Wise Man* needed a lot of equipment—ropes, trapeze, rings—requiring precise installation. Otherwise the show would be too dangerous for the performers. They simply could not take this production from one hall to the next, as they had originally planned. They performed *Can You Hear Me, Moscow?* in the building that housed the Party City Committee, but only on days when no meetings or demonstrations were scheduled. In other words, they performed less frequently than they wanted. For the most part, daily instruction was canceled. This state of affairs was another consequence of NEP, since state support for theaters had been cut and the halls were given away to private entrepreneurs. Even Foregger had to first commercialize and then close his theater. In short, Eisenstein's decision to perform at the gasworks was largely a pragmatic one.

In 1923 Meyerhold staged *The Earth Rampant*, his first collaboration with

Tretyakov, in the Kiev factory 'Arsenal'. *The Earth Rampant* was Tretyakov's 're-montage' of a play by Marcel Martinet. Meyerhold, however, only gave a one-time guest performance in the factory and then moved the show to a conventional theater. Eisenstein transformed the spatial constraints into programmatic art. His team built a small, wooden Constructivist set with stairs and several platforms in the gaswork's machine room. Their efforts looked rather pathetic next to the real turbo-generators. A small amphitheater was constructed for the audience. The actors wore worker's uniforms. Eisenstein made use of real factory noises—rivet hammers, pneumatic ratchets, iron saws. One year earlier the Proletkult-composer Arseny Avramov had attempted a similar project in his *Symphony of Factory Sirens and Train Whistles.* Eisenstein calculated the finale in such a way that the performance would end when the shift began. The arriving workers would replace the actors at the machinery. The premiere took place on February 29, 1924, four months after *Can You Hear Me, Moscow?*

Gas Masks also failed to attract a working-class audience. The art crowd showed up only for the first two performances (with free tickets). The actors played the third show in front of an empty hall. Nobody even bothered to stage a fourth.

In theory, this result was not supposed to worry its makers. According to the Left Front—the 'life-builders'—art would go extinct. But Eisenstein did not recover emotionally from this fiasco for some time. He was crushed by his real experience of the performance: the factory lived one life, the theater another. Mayakovsky and *LEF* had supported the production, but the critics made fun of its 'prehistoric, naïve naturalism'.[48] *Gas Masks* flopped and catapulted its director into another art form—into film.

By the end of March, one month after the disaster, Eisenstein was sitting at Esfir Shub's side in the editing room of the Film Committee. The committee's job was to rid foreign films of bourgeois ideology before they reached the Soviet audience. Shub was then editing Fritz Lang's two-part *Dr. Mabuse the Gambler* into a one-part film. Eisenstein eagerly assisted her and wrote the new ideologically tinged intertitles himself. Doctor Mabuse, a demonic tyrant, hypnotist, and psychoanalyst, was unveiled as the embodiment of the decadent West. The new film title was *Gilded Rot*. Eisenstein was looking for work in film and placed his hopes on Esfir Shub. He had already approached the Film Committee unsuccessfully a year earlier. Chances of actually making a film were minimal. While Russia still produced 334 films a year before the 1917 Revolution, only 28 were shot in 1923. Of those, only five were made in Moscow. The industry lacked everything: electricity, film stock, foreign technology, and specialists. Many qualified people—producers, directors, cameramen, outfitters, actors, technicians—had emigrated. Embargoes prevented Russia from purchasing film stock. Only after the Treaty of Rapallo was film stock again imported from Germany. The few productions that were not agitation reels continued the pre-Revolutionary film tradition. They were built on an anachronism, on the achievements of Russian *nineteenth-century* culture—Leo Tolstoy's great novels, the *peredvizhniki* artists' realist paintings, the naturalist psychological acting style of Stanislavsky and Nemirovich-Danchenko's Art Theater. The film industry picked up these bits and presented them as the art of the *twentieth century*. This translated into a slow narrative tempo and mostly static shots; directors avoided montage so as not to disturb psychological transitions in the acting; abundant props that were supposed to evoke a certain *milieu* created the atmosphere of an antique store. The old film lived on. In 1922 Alexander Panteleev directed *Infinite Sorrow*, a tried and true Russian melodrama. He had previously been known as the director of the first Soviet agitation film, *Miracle Maker* (1919). The plot of his new movie was simple. A young man with little money suffers from tuberculosis; his young, pretty wife is seduced by a rich friend on a yacht; the man commits suicide; the wife loses her mind at the graveside. None of this pointed either towards Soviet reality or towards a new art form. The historical film indulged in the genre of allegory and was oriented towards a fatalist philosophy of history. Revolutionary upheaval was interpreted as the work of mystical forces, even as the arrival of the Antichrist. When the assignment came in 1921 to shoot a film about the real famine on the Volga, the director Vladimir Gardin chose to film the Symbolist, very abstract play *King Hunger* by Leonid Andreev.

Kuleshov was still directing exercises on the stage and occasionally received 17 or 19 meters of film stock for his montage experiments. But Kuleshov did not believe that Russian everyday life could be photogenic. There were too few modern, dynamic objects like cars, trains, or bridges. Vertov dreamt of a new film liberated from the ballast of old art forms, but was only able to shoot the weekly *Cine-Pravda*.

In 1924 the stagnant film industry slowly started moving again. In February film people and influential journalists like Mikhail Koltsov and Nikolai Lebedev joined forces and founded the Association of Revolutionary Cinematography, or ARK. This group became a powerful public voice. In their founding declaration, published in *Pravda* on February 27, the group declared that although seven years had passed since the October Revolution, there was still no Soviet cinematography. Eisenstein's name was among the signatures, though as of yet Eisenstein had nothing to do with film. ARK demanded radical change and state subsidies. The 13th Party Congress reacted in May: a resolution declared the weak state department Goskino ineffective. Goskino had been founded only two years earlier with a 500,000 ruble starting budget and currently had only 3,000 rubles to its name (calculated according to the 1924 currency reform). In its place, the Party promised to create Sovkino, an institution that was granted monopoly status and 4 million rubles in subsidies. Trotsky called for cinema as an alternative to 'church and vodka' in a programmatic article in the June 12 issue of *Pravda.*[49]

1924 was a boom year for film. The production of Goskino alone increased from 5 to 25 films. The country as a whole produced 76 films, in comparison with 28 movies the previous year. Prominent directors—Yakov Protazanov, Vyacheslav Viskovsky, Pyotr Chardynin—returned from emigration. Kuleshov and Vertov were able to shoot their first full-length films, *The Extraordinary Adventures of Mr. West in the Land of the Bolsheviks* and *The Cine-Eye*. There were even first commercial successes, such as Ivan Perestiani's *The Little Red Devils*, a 'revolutionary western'.

Proletkult had founded Proletkino, its own cinema organization, in 1923. Proletkino published a journal and ran a small film studio. The influential Proletkult ideologue Platon Kerzhentsev had already formulated his conception of the new proletarian film in his essay 'Class struggle and cinema'. He claimed that the proletariat needed neither Dostoevsky nor Pinkerton in its films. People needed to see the history-making masses themselves; only film could do this job.[50]

Eisenstein was thrilled by the montage possibilities of the medium and by his own first practical taste of editing someone else's film. He pushed the Proletkult leadership, i.e. his boss Pletnyov, to produce a film as well. Pletnyov could write the script, Eisenstein would direct, and his students could act. He easily sold the idea to the dynamic Pletnyov.

In true Proletkult spirit, Eisenstein conceived the film as a mass action. He also followed LEF's program and envisioned the movie as a production scenario, a film textbook for the world proletariat. The film would teach workers how to organize and carry out rebellions, demonstrations, strikes, and revolution. His students collected facts and Strauch took notes on the 1922 book *The Technique of the Bolshevik Underground*, a work in two thick volumes. Eisenstein and Pletnyov came up with a plan for a series in eight parts, called *Towards the Dictatorship*. They would illustrate the history of the Russian workers' movement from the first underground printing press to the October Revolution.

There was no way to produce the film at Proletkino. Dmitry Bassalygo was working on a similar piece, the six-part *From Sparks—Flames* on the Russian textile workers' struggle for liberation. So Eisenstein took his project to Goskino. This time he arrived at an opportune moment. The film industry was in transition, and Eisenstein knew all about the new reforms. Boris Mikhin, to whom Eisenstein had turned for permission to shoot *Glumov's Diary*, had just reopened the studio of Alexander Khanzhonkov, Russia's biggest film producer. He needed new people to cope with the rapid increase in production. The eccentric young man with a high-pitched voice and hair standing out at all ends came just at the right time. Mikhin chose to produce *The Strike*, the fifth episode in Eisenstein's eight-part project. They came to an agreement on April 1.

Until June, Alexandrov and Ivan Kravchunovsky followed Eisenstein's orders and wrote the scenario in pencil in two school notebooks. They included all sorts of juicy *guignol* moments. One worker was to be sliced in half by a machine; another fell into a cauldron of boiling steel. The montage sequences savored contrasts. The death in the cauldron was to be cut against a woman bathing in champagne. An ox-eye was floating in the soup that some workers were eating; that eye was to dissolve into the eye of the capitalist looking into the camera through his monocle. Pletnyov tamed the writers' fantasy and tried to assign a concrete historical event to each scene. When the screenplay was finished, the Proletkult refused to give Eisenstein up to Goskino. He was still their employee. Mikhin suggested a compromise: the film would be made as a Proletkult-Goskino coproduction. Pletnyov, Eisenstein, Alexandrov and Kravchunovsky were listed as the collective authors.

With the exception of Mikhin, Goskino was not very excited about hiring Eisenstein. He was enthusiastic and had some successful theater productions under his belt, but he knew nothing about film. They made Eisenstein shoot a few test scenes. The shots turned out to be less than convincing, even though Mikhin had sent the group his most experienced cameraman, Eduard Tisse. Now Mikhin had to fight not only with Proletkult, but also with his own leadership at Goskino. After two chaotic days of shooting, they demanded Eisenstein's dismissal. Mikhin and Tisse had to sign a declaration in which they promised to carry full personal financial responsibility for a possible fiasco. Goskino ordered Mikhin to be on site every day and appointed Kirill Shutko to be Eisenstein's advisor.

They started shooting in Kolomenskoe, in a factory that made train cars; then they moved on to the courtyard of the film factory on Zhitnaya Street. Next they shot the pond near the Simonov Monastery, the forest in Serebryany Bor, and the paupers' cemetery in Luzhniki. Eisenstein was suspicious and egocentric—not an easy partner. He made a scene whenever his demands failed to be met. He refused to recognize Mikhin as his patron. For Eisenstein, Mikhin was just the Goskino supervisor who cheated him and cut corners at every turn. Eisenstein demanded 1,000 extras for the demonstration scene. Mikhin tried to explain that 1,000 were unnecessary—500 would fill the picture nicely.

A fight erupted between Eisenstein and Mikhin. In the end Mikhin lied to Eisenstein and passed off 500 extras for 1,000. In order to save money on another mass scene, Mikhin suggested that Eisenstein film a real workers' meeting as the beginning of the strike—the studio invited Trotsky to come speak and filled the factory premises with the masses. But Eisenstein had a new demand the very next day: he needed a large toad. By the time the toad had been caught, the sun had already set. Days like this exasperated even Mikhin. But Mikhin would later admit that demands that seemed capricious on the set were actually dictated by the director's iron will. Eisenstein had an all too precise vision of each shot and would tolerate no compromises.

The work on the set devoured all of Eisenstein's time and energy. He did nothing other than work on the film. All summer long the team spent every day shooting and took no breaks. They finished filming in October and cut the film in the fall. The movie was ready by late 1924. The Goskino directors were so impressed that Mikhin was not called to account for Eisenstein's work habits: the director had not been able to meet deadlines and had not used the film stock efficiently. But the inexperienced filmmaker had succeeded in capturing the Revolution as a *cinematic*, dynamic, and tragic event. The film shots could bear comparison to Constructivist painting and photography; the actors' eccentricity rivaled Meyerhold's theater. However, the film's unusual juxtaposition of images and its brutality—a child was torn away from its mother and hurled down a flight of stairs (only Erich von Stroheim had dared to show anything like it)—achieved an unprecedented, deeply shocking effect. Eisenstein's radical montage was *the* innovation. Instead of the usual 40-60 seams per film reel, there were 379. A scene lasting about five minutes now contained 100 shots ranging in length from 15 frames to 1.5 meters. The new arrival was an astute observer of film. He had grasped and restructured the possibilities of the medium. He turned the comic staple of the 'wet gardener' into a brutal massacre, the garden hose into a deadly weapon. Cossacks rode down stairs on their horses, and Eisenstein made their complex circus ballet look dramatic. The finale surprised its viewers the most: Eisenstein jumped from shots of an ox being slaughtered to the massacre. At first, the audience did not grasp the metaphor. Many viewers thought that the massacre was taking place in the slaughterhouse. Others guessed that hungry strikers were storming the slaughterhouse.

Eisenstein organized his cinematic 'montage of attractions' as a sequence of programmed shocks to his audience. He declared art to be a means of directing human experience; his film put the audience through a meat grinder. Montage allowed Eisenstein, a 'film-engineer' versed in control of human reflexes, to create a combination of stimuli, which, connected arbitrarily, would train social reflexes (such as class hatred and class solidarity). He had attempted to achieve a similar effect in the theater, but after this first experience with film, he discovered that he could apply his system more effectively in cinema. The audience reacted more quickly to images—thanks to their greater level of abstraction—than to a physical performance. The cinematic image also awakened more associations than real action on stage. Through montage he could now combine the gunning down of a demonstration (a fictional representation, mostly in long shots) with the authentic slaughter of an ox (broken up into fragments, closing in with each shot, ending with a close-up of the ox's wide-open eye). The physiological horror experienced in light of the real slaughter (and real death) was thus transposed onto the scene of the human massacre—no human actor could create the same gruesome total effect. The impact was not based on the logical comparison of the slaughterhouse to the massacre. Instead, the transfer of emotional impact from one scene to the other served the ideological message of the film, which culminated in the final title: 'Proletarians! Remember!'

Had Eisenstein, the apolitical man from a bourgeois family, the man who had failed to perceive the political dimensions of the Revolution or the Civil War, suddenly become a Marxist? Was this step into film more than a kink in his biography? His environs—not the Freemasons and Rosicrucians, but Meyerhold and the Left Front—were highly politicized. However, he had been most influenced by their call to modernize art, a task they called the artistic 'Revolution'. Eisenstein's dramatic productions were socially engaged, but even their author Sergei Tretyakov evaluated Eisenstein's work as formal experimentation. Eisenstein had not yet become engrossed with Bolshevik ideology. The decision not to emigrate and to stay with the Reds was mostly a private issue. His new situation freed him from pressure to succeed at a bourgeois career in engineering—the life his father had wanted him to lead. His mother could hardly stop the uncontrolled zigzag career moves that took Eisenstein from Japanese studies to art. Eisenstein experienced the proletarian Revolution as his own personal liberation. His first film catapulted him to the status of a socially engaged artist, but he had recently written his mother that he found proletarian art to be boring, even revolting. The new medium offered the unexpected possibility of creating something truly original in the realm of the proletarian mass film. His experiments were far removed from all three approaches to cinema of which Eisenstein was aware at that time: the psychological naturalism of traditional Russian cinema, commercially successful Hollywood movies, and highly stylized German Expressionism.

The new medium fascinated Eisenstein for a number of reasons. The radical avant-garde approach to art—deformation, fragmentation, dynamism, discontinuity, simultaneity, penetration of space and time—now became technically grounded. The camera could deform and segment reality, then reassemble it in every possible way. It could speed up or slow down the passage of time. Film was the modern Futurist art form *par excellence*. Film gave Eisenstein total freedom to play with stimuli, space, time, causality, the human body, rhythm. There was yet another lure to cinema—Eisenstein not only discovered the film director's power over time and space, but his power over real human beings. Thousands of people obeyed him *in unison*. City traffic and factory production could be stopped on *his* command. The masses may have gathered at the factory to listen to Trotsky, but they really belonged to him and to *his* film. These claims to power—if his theory of attractions were accurate—would soon be expanded. Not only the masses *in front* of his camera, but millions of viewers around the world would soon jump, scream out, and cry according to *his* plan, *his* montage of attractions.

Under the given circumstances the masses in front of the camera were dressed as Russian proletarians, not as Roman or Babylonian warriors à la D. W. Griffith's *Intolerance*, Eisenstein's American model. Their actions unfolded in the spaces of industrial modernity: in factories, on bridges, in the city. The plot was the historic fate of an oppressed class. For its effect the film could draw on the solidarity of the oppressed. The material (imagined masses, imitated by the crowd of extras in front of the camera), the experiment of manipulating the masses in the audience and the Futurist possibilities of film finally turned Eisenstein into a Bolshevik. The medium absorbed Eisenstein's subjective preferences. For all of the collective elements of the film—the subject, the makers, the addressee—*he* remained the author and became a demigod.

It was hardly a coincidence that Eisenstein's first experiment ended with a huge scandal about the copyrights to *The Strike*. Who was the author of this impressive work? The conflict had begun to build up during the work on the film. Pletnyov demanded written and oral progress reports from his subordinate. He was annoyed that Eisenstein had not finished by the agreed deadline. Eisenstein found this treatment to be humiliating and broke off their agreement.

The press first announced the film as a collective effort of Pletnyov and Eisenstein. But that summer film journals published photographs of Eisenstein on the set and referred to him as the single author and director. In an interview Eisenstein blamed the film's delays on Proletkult officials who had repeatedly distracted him from the editing process. He had had to save the film from corrections by the Proletkult leadership, who understood nothing about the film's composition. He demonstratively thanked his film supervisor Mikhin: 'The Proletkult never showed this kind of understanding for my work.'[51] His innovations in *The Mexican* had been attributed to Smyshlyaev; during work on *The Wise Man* he had been afraid that Tretyakov would reap the laurels. Now he was sure of his strength and originality and refused to accept Pletnyov's pretensions to joint authorship, since he had hardly used Pletnyov's script at all.

For a month the newspapers *Kino* and *Kinonedelya* published open letters by the two rivals. Pletnyov accused Eisenstein of Formalism, 'Trickism', and of a dubious element of 'Freudian origin'. Eisenstein replied that the Proletkult leadership (i.e. Pletnyov) supported a petty bourgeois realistic theater with plot and atmospheric setting that amounted to a 'rightist deviation'.[52] In his letters (not all of them were published) Eisenstein tried to clarify the differences between the two art forms for himself, since he now had to make up his mind. 'Theater that does not dissolve itself will be crushed like an archaic horse-drawn carriage—on the one hand by film, a more technically perfect bus, on the other hand by the marching Pioneers, the builders of the new life. They will no longer need that bourgeois institution.'[53] On February 24, 1927 Eisenstein wrote in his diary, 'I did not want to do theater in the Proletkult; I wanted to design new standards to solve experimental problems—Agit-revues (*The Wise Man*) or political agitation (*Can You Hear Me, Moscow?*). The Proletkult wanted to use my laboratory to cook jam and to make sappy theater (Pletnyov plays).'[54]

Eisenstein told the press that he had left the Proletkult because it was too far 'right'. Pletnyov made a correction: *he* had fired Eisenstein: 'It should be noted that S. M. Eisenstein, in his latest appearances and in his general attitude towards the Proletkult, has created a situation that makes his further presence in the Proletkult impossible. He has been severed from employment at the Proletkult.'[55] Pletnyov offered Eisenstein's position to Grigory Roshal.

This break received so much publicity because a larger battle stood behind the issue: the Left Front was fighting the rightist Proletkult. The Eisenstein case came at an opportune moment for all.

Eisenstein tried to hush up his dismissal or at least to play it down. Secretly, however, he was worried about his future. He asked his old acquaintance Konstantin Eliseev, who had recently moved from Minsk to Moscow, to find him employment as a cartoonist for the satirical paper *Red Pepper*, where Eliseev worked. Eliseev had already begun to get excited about the future of Soviet political cartoons, but then Meyerhold generously made his own theater available to his former student. Eisenstein could choose to stage either *The Inspector General*, *Woe from Wit*, or *Hamlet*. These were all plays that Meyerhold had reserved for himself. They also talked about staging Crommelynck's *Golden Tripe* using Axyonov's adaptation. But Eisenstein's break with the Proletkult turned out to be his final farewell to the theater. After some hesitation he turned down

Meyerhold's offer and decided that film was the only acceptable line of work.[56]

Eisenstein knew how to find his way in conflict situations. He never would have broken so thoroughly with the Proletkult without some form of insurance. He now dared to take this step because he had found a strong new patron, Kirill Shutko, his advisor during *The Strike*, whom he called his savior in the Proletkult affair. During the first studio screening of *The Strike* in March, Shutko led the discussion that followed the film. Shutko, an influential Bolshevik and member of several committees and editorial boards, was ecstatic. He immediately 'adopted' Eisenstein, and declared himself Eisenstein's patron, protector, and friend. In his youth Shutko had studied acting, and had worked for Meyerhold. Then he went underground for the Bolsheviks. Now he belonged to the Central Committee's department of agitation and propaganda.

Eisenstein could well use this high-ranked patron since his position was shaky after *The Strike*'s April premiere. The critics loved him, but the film bosses were against his film. The approval of the latter was crucial for a film director, especially for a newcomer. Even Mayakovsky, in spite of his power and influence, had failed to get his most important script *How Are You?* past the film administration. Sovkino, like the already dissolved Goskino, could produce only a very few films. Young talents had to have influential patrons. Eisenstein saw all this from a very pragmatic perspective. Without Pletnyov's help he never would have been able to produce *The Strike*. Now Shutko seemed more useful.

The Strike received good press even before its public premiere. Khrisanf Khersonsky's review in *Izvestiya* on March 11 and Mikhail Koltsov's enthusiastic reception in *Pravda* on March 14 were only the beginning. ARK chairman Nikolai Lebedev wrote: 'This is a major event for Soviet, Russian, and world cinematography . . . . In the richness and boldness of his fantasy, his mastery over actors and props, in the originality of the images, the rhythm of movement, and the perfection of montage, Eisenstein surpasses not only our local 'Griffiths' on Zhitnaya Street [Goskino's studio address], but even outdoes Hollywood's famous David Wark Griffith . . . . This is the first talented, original international and proletarian film.'[57] Eisenstein's directorial colleagues were of a different opinion. Kuleshov remained silent. Vertov called Eisenstein a failed imitation and accused him of plagiarism in an open discussion at ARK. Vertov claimed that Eisenstein had borrowed everything from him: montage structure, composition, title design. But Eisenstein had added decadent, artificial theater tricks, poses of silent ecstasy, and masks from the 'dummy theater'.[58] Even the slaughterhouse scene had been stolen from his *Cine-Eye*.

Eisenstein found these accusations extremely insulting and struck back in the ARK paper with the essay 'The Problem of the Materialist Approach to Form.'

Their polemics, which were concerned exclusively with their understanding of art, were conducted in a harsh and denunciatory manner. The labels that they tried to stick to each other were normally used in political battles against the opposition. Vertov called Eisenstein a 'deviationist'; Eisenstein accused Vertov of being an opportunist and Menshevik who engaged in impressionist 'art for art's sake' without thinking of how to influence the proletariat with his work.[59] Foreign reception of their films inadvertently stoked the debate. At the 1925 Exhibition of Art and Industry in Paris, *The Strike* was awarded the gold medal, and *Cine-Eye* took home silver.

Arvatov tried to reconcile the two LEF-members and told them they were behaving like 'intellectual artists' who still thought in the old categories of individual creation. Their work was really not that different.[60] Malevich and Shklovsky also became involved in the polemic. Shklovsky thought that *The Strike*'s success was a failure, a 'chamber success' that had never reached a real audience.[61]

The press and the film distributors took different positions in their evaluation of *The Strike*. After *The Strike* opened in the theaters, the distributors began a campaign against the film in the newspapers. They argued that Eisenstein had spent too much money, used up too much film stock, and brought in too little profit. The audience wanted a plot, something this film lacked. But the movie cost twice as much to make as a Kuleshov movie and four times as much as a picture by the old film hand Czéslaw Sabinski. *The Strike* made so little money that it ran only for a short while and was quickly replaced by *The Thief of Bagdad* starring Douglas Fairbanks.

The expressive force of *The Strike* has not faded even today, but at that time the film must have had the impact of a bomb. The film had nothing to do with Russian cinema, but was heavily influenced by Meyerhold's theater and by Russian Constructivism. *The Strike* was a child of the Left Front.

In spite of all the uproar, Goskino offered Eisenstein a one-year contract as a director. He signed the document on April 14, 1925. The contract guaranteed him 600 rubles a month; for work on the set and business travel he was to receive twice that sum. Eisenstein began sending his mother 15 rubles a month. (The currency reform in 1924 eliminated the millions of rubles from everyday speech.)

While shooting *The Strike* Eisenstein got to know Eduard Tisse, a quiet, determined man who was a strong athlete and a completely reliable cameraman. Tisse was from Estonia; his real name was Nikolaitis. His experience in film was much greater than Eisenstein's: he had been making movies since 1914. He first worked as a cameraman at the front, which prepared him for work in the field. Tisse introduced Eisenstein to cinema in a practical way: he unscrewed the camera and showed Eisenstein how the mechanism worked. He owned his own camera, an Eclair.

At that time Eisenstein and his assistant Grisha would run around in shirts sewn from wool blankets. Eduard always wore a plaid suit, a shirt with a starched collar, and polished yellow shoes. Under his influence Eisenstein and Grisha abandoned their wool shirts for plaid jackets.

Eisenstein turned down Goskino's suggestion to film the other episodes of *Towards the Dictatorship* in collaboration with the Proletkult. This would have been impossible anyway after Eisenstein's dismissal.

He declared that his next film would be *The Red Cavalry*, which he conceived as a film of the masses. Isaak Babel was discussed as a possible scriptwriter. Expert consultants were to include the Army commanders Semyon Budyonny and Klimenty Voroshilov. These two men were considered the film's initiators. In December 1924 Eisenstein wrote a script with Grigory Alexandrov and Yakov Bliokh, a former Commissar in the Red Cavalry, for the Moscow office of the Leningrad studio Sevzapkino. But the studio did not have enough money to finance this mammoth production. There was talk of making a movie for Gostorg, the Soviet foreign trade organization, about the import and export of furs. Dziga Vertov directed this movie in 1926 and called it *A Sixth Part of the World*.

Once again, things turned out differently.

THREE MONTHS AND A LIFETIME:
THE BATTLESHIP POTEMKIN
1925

On March 17, 1925 the Central Executive Committee decided that Eisenstein would make a film celebrating the twentieth anniversary of the 1905 Revolution. The committee was headed by Anatoly Lunacharsky, the People's Commissar for Enlightenment; members included Malevich, Meyerhold, Pletnyov, Shutko, the Central Committee member Leonid Krasin, and the First Secretary of the Party's Moscow City Committee, Vasily Mikhailov. The scenario was written by Nina Agadzhanova, Kirill Shutko's wife. The committee planned to unfold a panorama of the most important events of 1905: the Russo-Japanese War, the 'Bloody Sunday' massacre of St. Petersburg workers on January 9, the proclamation of the tsar's manifesto promising civil liberties and a parliament, the general strike, the armed insurrection in Moscow, and battles at the barricades. Both Pletnyov and Agadzhanova were suggested as scriptwriters, but they quickly settled on Nina: neither Pletnyov nor Eisenstein wanted to attempt another collaboration.

The film was only one moment in the anniversary's elaborate schedule of events. During his upcoming trip to Europe, Meyerhold was supposed to call on Prokofiev and commission a symphony. Malevich was in charge of the visuals. The Committee assumed that only one of the film's episodes could be ready by the deadline. Work on the film could be continued later and grow into a series that culminated in the events of 1917.

The Committee's decision—pushed by Kirill Shutko—was a huge break for the young director. He had received the most important state commission of the year—the anniversary film. The only condition was that he finish one of the episodes by December 20. The 'Cavalry' project was put on the back burner.

In an interview about the planned project, Eisenstein declared: 'The film *The Year 1905* will be as grand as the German *Nibelungen*.' He planned to shoot in Moscow, Leningrad, Odessa, Sevastopol, Tiflis, Baku, Batumi, in Turkestan and Siberia, in the Caucasus, near Tambov and in the region of Ivanovo-Voznesensk—in short all over the Soviet Union. He said that the masses would be his hero and there would be no plot. Powerful scenes of massacres were on his mind: the fire in the Tomsk Opera and pogroms against the Jews. He planned underwater shots of the wrecked ships of the Russian fleet near Tsushima. 'The images will rework real material in an expressionistic way.'[62] The press announced that the film would be 'an event'.[63]

The first take was filmed by March 19. Eisenstein shot the eccentric strike

56

of the undertakers. He faced a great adventure: traveling across the country enticed him as much as the enormous scope of the work he faced. Now the entire fleet and the whole army would follow his command.

That summer, Eisenstein, Nina, and Grisha reworked the screenplay at the Shutkos' dacha in Nemchinovka near Moscow. Eisenstein's eccentric fantasies—general strikes among lifeguards, icon painters, and chambermaids—were dampened by Nina's experience. She was an old underground fighter and had been a member of the Party since 1907. After the Revolution she became excited about film. She and her husband had coauthored a script for an adventure film based on her work in the underground, which they called *Behind White Lines*.[64]

The Shutkos shared the dacha with their old friend Kazimir Malevich (whose wife owned the house). Eisenstein thus became acquainted with this stubborn and very independent thinker. At that time Malevich was experimenting with the basic elements of visual art—space, color, line, surface. He called his doctrine the 'theory of the additional element', referring to the dynamic that led to the deformation of old forms. His graphic analyses of classic paintings had a lasting effect on Eisenstein. Their influence can be detected in Eisenstein's thinking long after Malevich's research institute had been closed.

At first Eisenstein traveled daily from Moscow to Nemchinovka. Then he moved into Shutko and Malevich's dacha. Alexandrov and Babel followed suit. Eisenstein wanted to work with them on parallel projects. He would dictate the script *The Year 1905* to Grisha in the morning and reserve his afternoons for Babel. Eisenstein intended to make a film based on Babel's Odessa story *Benya Krik*. The studio's director also saw the possibility of shooting two films at once during the team's stay in Odessa. But in the end nothing came of this plan.

To earn some money Alexandrov and Eisenstein quickly put together a screenplay for an erotic *guignol* under the pseudonym Taras Nemchinov. The last name came from the screenplay's place of origin. Taras was chosen because Eisenstein wanted Grisha to give that name to his new baby boy. But Grisha named his boy Douglas (as in Fairbanks), later the boy was called Vasya. The script's title was promising: *The Bazaar of Lust*. They sold it to the Proletkino studio and Valery Inkizhinov was discussed as a possible director. In style their screenplay followed the model of German films that enlightened the public about prostitution and sexually transmitted diseases, but the two authors had added a dose of crude social criticism. A pregnant girl is taunted, stoned and raped in the village, while a lustful estate proprietress amuses herself with her grooms. The country's excesses were complemented by moral perversions in the city: seduced chambermaids, gigolos, and orgies in the bordello. During the war Russian prostitutes had infected most of the German army with syphilis. The script's final title was, "Don't fight against prostitution! Fight against the society that produced it!" The screenplay was never made into a film.

In the meantime Goskino had figured out that *The Year 1905* would require 250 days of shooting and 20,000 extras. They calculated that the project could not be completed until August 1926—in other words, in one year. In August 1925 Eisenstein traveled to the old capital with a new name: Petrograd had been renamed Leningrad in 1924 after Lenin's death. They shot one episode with 700 extras. There was insufficient sunlight and the light technicians needed so much energy that the city's electricity occasionally had to be turned off. Work on the set was organized in a military fashion; the team even made use of the Marines' searchlights.

Since Tisse was busy shooting the film *Jewish Luck* with Alexei Granovsky, Eisenstein worked with Alexander Levitsky, an experienced cameraman. Unfortunately, Levitsky was afraid of heights and disliked having to climb on rooftops to shoot the film. The weather was terrible: it rained incessantly for a month. In order to save the project, the studio director Mikhail Kapchinsky advised Eisenstein to shoot the Black Sea episode first. At least they would have more sun there. The work in Leningrad was interrupted, and the team left for Odessa. They arrived August 24.

The sun finally decided which episode of *The Year 1905* would be finished by the anniversary committee meeting on December 20: it was the mutiny of the Battleship Prince Potemkin of Tauris. Of the 820 scenes listed in Nina Agadzhanova's scenario, Eisenstein used only 43.

In late September Tretyakov also came to Odessa to supervise the work. He was employed at Goskino's studio as a consultant. He had just returned from China, where he had spent a year teaching Russian at Beijing University. While Tretyakov wrote the intertitles and Eisenstein studied the facts and rewrote the script, the crew sat around idly for a whole month. Eisenstein was hesitant. Odessa was covered in a blanket of fog, not the right weather for making a film. Levitsky turned down the offer to stay on the project and recommended his co-cameraman, the Baltic German Alexander Stanke. Stanke was a lighting specialist who was strongly influenced by German Expressionism and had made a few films in Berlin in the past. Eisenstein did not trust him and sent Alexandrov to Moscow to get Tisse. Tisse arrived in Odessa on September 23. He was willing to shoot in the fog.

On September 28 Eisenstein finally returned to the set. The parts were split up among the inhabitants of Odessa and Eisenstein's Proletkult students. Alexander Antonov played the sailor Vakulinchuk; Grisha Alexandrov took over the role of an officer who was too eager to please his superior and in the end died a pitiful death. They also persuaded the film director Vladimir Barsky, who was in Odessa shooting his own film, to play the captain of the ship.

Eisenstein came up with the idea to film the massacre of the peaceful demonstrators on the port steps. Strauch later claimed that a drawing by a French eyewitness had provided the inspiration. But perhaps another Russian film was in the back of Eisenstein's mind: Vladimir Gardin had already filmed a massacre on the same steps in the 1923 film *The Specter is Haunting Europe*.

They spent two weeks shooting the 120 Odessa Steps. There were no accidents during the dangerous mass flight down the stairs. The shooting demanded acrobatic stunts from the cameraman: 10% of the material was shot without a tripod; to film the scene, the camera team sat on a plank that slid down the slope on wooden rails, supported only by a few ropes. Sometimes Tisse was chained to a rope and would fall down. Then the assistants would have to catch the cameraman and his camera. A 35-member brass band played at all times to keep the extras happy. Eisenstein's assistants, the 'iron five' (all in striped shirts), had the masses under complete control. They all lived together in the hotel—a sort of male commune. The only woman to have come along was Grisha's wife Olga. When they were done in Odessa, they traveled to Sevastopol to finishing shooting with the Marines. They were given full reign over Potemkin's twin ship, 'The Twelve Apostles'. Unfortunately the battleship was packed with mines. The crew was not allowed to smoke and, most importantly, had to remember that rule in order not to go up in smoke! Such were the circumstances under which the mutiny on the ship was filmed. Marines played the parts of the sailors and responded to their captain's whistle *in unison*. As they filmed on the rocking boat, six men often had to hold up Tisse and his camera; at times they were completely covered by waves. They spent a month working on the 'meat scene'—the scene lasted only a minute on screen. Finally they filmed the mutiny itself. Eisenstein took over the role of the priest during the priest's dangerous jump overboard. His trained assistants doubled as sailors for the acrobatic leaps into the cold water.

Eisenstein, Alexandrov, Strauch and Tisse took a day off and drove to the Crimea. They visited the palace of the former governor in Alupka and shot the stone lions on the palace staircase as a souvenir. They had no idea how the footage might come in handy.

On November 23 Eisenstein returned to Moscow with 4,500 meters of film in his luggage. The crew shot a few more scenes with a model of the battleship in the Sandunov city baths. Eisenstein took the long shots—the battleship's encounter with the squadron—from an old newsreel. He spent three weeks in the Film Committee's editing room on Gnezdnikovsky Alley putting together the film.

In the meantime Alexandrov and Tisse were shooting the finale—the encounter with the squadron—without Eisenstein. The director had left them exact sketches of the scene's composition. The Marines' support was guaranteed by a direct order from Mikhail Frunze, People's Commissar for Army and Fleet. Grisha sent his teacher detailed reports on their progress.

This course of events—Eisenstein's long inactivity and reluctance to start shooting, then his prolonged absence—set off rumors that Tisse had actually shot the film. But nobody could doubt who had cut it.

On December 21 the film was shown to the anniversary committee as planned. Eisenstein intended to end the screening with a sensation. During the last shot, when the bow of the ship approaches the camera and appears to cut the picture in two, Eisenstein wanted to tear the screen in two and reveal real Potemkin sailors sitting on the stage.

As Tisse delivered the first reels to the theater, Eisenstein was still pasting the final bits in the editing room. One by one Alexandrov drove the reels to the theater on his motorcycle.[65] The raw cut consisted of 1280 takes, which translated into at least 1280 'dangerous' seams.

At first the Bolshoi Theater orchestra refused to accompany the picture. The musicians wondered what kind of music would go well with 'rotten meat'. Finally one conductor compiled a medley of Beethoven's *Egmont* and Tchaikovsky's *Francesca da Rimini*.

This film about a mutiny on a ship of the tsarist fleet was divided into five acts—just like a classical tragedy. Eisenstein analyzed the film's composition ten, fifteen, twenty years later and marveled at its improvised perfection. Only in retrospect did the film seem so clear and calculated, as if it had intentionally followed the laws of Gestalt theory or the rules of the 'golden section'. While working on *Potemkin* Eisenstein had been more interested in the nature of affect and the associated behavioral patterns that would determine the desired effect and replace the attraction. This train of thought was heavily influenced by Eisenstein's new acquaintances, the psychologists Alexander Luria and Lev Vygotsky, whom he had met through Zalkind. Both men were members of the Russian Psychoanalytic Society and worked at the Moscow Psychological Institute. Luria corresponded with Freud and had opened a laboratory to study conflict, Vygotsky had written a treatise on affect in Spinoza and Descartes. He gave Eisenstein his dissertation *Psychology of Art*, in which he analyzed catharsis as an ambivalent affective reaction. He used the composition of literary works as his material. Eisenstein read this text very carefully.

The immediate effect of Eisenstein's film was so overwhelming that at first its rhythmic perfection was overlooked. Eisenstein painted a highly ambivalent picture of the Revolution: violence gives birth to more violence and starts a chain reaction. Mutiny is triggered by spoiled meat in the soup. First the sailors are forced to eat the soup. When thirty sailors refuse, they are to be shot as mutineers. During their execution the mood tips and all officers are killed in place of the rebels. After a short moment of mourning, the violence spreads again and sucks in the entire population of the city. The whole city gathers at the funeral of one of the sailors, who becomes the holy sacrifice that unites them all: children, infants, women, cripples, anti-Semites, revolutionaries, fishmongers, and students—those who had supported the rebellion and those who had not; everybody is united.

The massacre on the port steps lasts six minutes. The mass—a chaotic body—is confronted with the organized machine of state force; this force is unstoppable. Then the captured battleship responds and fires on the General Staff. Following the shot Eisenstein included a montage of three stone figures—one sleeping lion, one lion who has just woken up, one lion ready to pounce. The images follow each other so closely that it produces an illusion of motion and triggers a slew of associations. Originally Eisenstein had wanted to show a statue from the Odessa Opera at this point. The montage-induced moving lion confused viewers and made them insecure: was this an expression of the revolutionaries' anger or the disgust of reactionary forces? Simpler than that, Eisenstein would say later, the lions realized the idiomatic expression 'and the stones roared',[66] because it had been impossible to further intensify emotions using human material.

When the Admiral's squadron refuses to open fire against the mutinous battleship, the solidarity of the oppressed temporarily stops the flow of violence. Unbearable tension builds up as the audience wonders whether someone will fire the first shot. The absence of the expected blood bath in the finale unleashed a cathartic relief unrivaled by any Hollywood happy ending. Though Eisenstein had measured his own work against *The Nibelungen*, he had succeeded in juxtaposing Fritz Lang's static, ornamental mass scenes with the chaotic body of the masses. Eisenstein's dynamics were infinitely more complex and dramatic than the geometric UFA-ballet. Eisenstein had not only created the most impressive picture of revolutionary martyrdom. He had also shown that political art could be moving and still remain art.

After the preview in the Bolshoi Theater, the regular premiere took place on January 18, 1926 in the Metropol and Khudozhestvenny movie theaters. Both theaters were decorated to look like battleships, the employees and the attending camera team were dressed like Marines. The distributors, theater owners, film critics and officials wondered if this revolutionary film could compete with Hollywood. In the cinemas *Potemkin* was measured against *Robin Hood* starring Douglas Fairbanks. Film papers and magazines printed attendance figures as a duel between the USSR and the USA. During the first week

Potemkin drew an audience of 29,458, but *Robin Hood* attracted only 21,282 view-ers. In another theater 39,405 people went to see *Potemkin* and only 33,960 bought tickets for *Robin Hood*.

The film's production cost 100,000 rubles, an average sum. That same year 1926 another historical film, Alexander Ivanovsky's *The Decembrists*, was four times as expensive to make. The distributors put a lot of effort into advertise-ment. Alexander Rodchenko and Anton Lavinsky made six posters; two books came on the market when the film was released. The scenario was printed in the same book as Tisse's reports on the adventurous filming methods. The second book, *Eisenstein*, was published as part of a series on popular stars; Viktor Shklovsky had written the text.

The provinces were reluctant to distribute the film. In retrospect it is al-most impossible to judge whether the film was a success. In his 1928 book *Cinema in the West and at Home*, Lunacharsky started the rumor that *Potemkin* had been a failure. He claimed that the domestic flop of *Potemkin* had been hushed up and that the film only re-entered the Russian theaters after its euphoric reception in Germany. In fact the situation was more complicated. In Mos-cow, the Theater on the Arbat was granted a monopoly on the distribution rights; there were too few prints for the countryside, since Soviet Russia was unable to import enough film stock to make mass copies of the film. In late 1926 there were entire regions where *The Battleship Potemkin* had not yet been shown. The city of Odessa didn't get to see the film until 1927!

The press reviews were euphoric, but Eisenstein's colleagues judged the film more harshly. The ARK discussion did not beat around the bush. Kuleshov gave Eisenstein a 'C' in montage. Gan dismissed Tisse's work as saccharine and Eisenstein's efforts as eclectic. Eisenstein had not focused on the processes, as a true Constructivist should. Instead he had whipped up emotions as in a real kitsch-film. The director Abram Room denied *Potemkin* any artistic merit, since the film did not deal with the lives of individual human beings.

Eisenstein was not afraid of his new 'nightingale-lyricism' and he knew that he had radically developed Kuleshov's principles of montage and move-ment. The space of each shot was segmented in a Cubist manner, the narrative was not efficient, and time had been drawn out, but all this created a new effect that Eisenstein wanted to study scientifically. The experiences of the *grand guignol* and Pavlov's reflex theory made their way into Eisenstein's new ideas on film's effectiveness. He decided that cinema was all about violence and technology.

The Battleship Potemkin quickly found its devotees abroad. On January 21, three days after the Moscow premiere, there was a closed showing in Berlin's Großer Schauspielhaus in honor of the anniversary of Lenin's death. Willi

Münzenberg, the media mogul of the workers' press, immediately recognized the film's potential. When he found out that the German company Lloyd had just signed an agreement to import 25 Russian movies, but had turned down *Potemkin*, he offered to start a new company under the auspices of his International Workers' Aid that would distribute the film in the West. Münzenberg's new 'Prometheus Film GmbH' quickly signed a contract with Sovkino.

On March 18, 1926 Eisenstein and Tisse traveled to Berlin to study new cinema technology and to attend the German premiere of *The Battleship Potemkin*. They stayed at the Hotel Hessler, Kantstraße 165-166. Egon Erwin Kisch had given Eisenstein six letters of recommendation for Berlin.

Dmitry Maryanov, Albert Einstein's son-in-law and an employee of the Soviet trade mission in Berlin, ran a 'red' salon of sorts. Maryanov put Eisenstein in contact with Berlin artistic circles, took him to the UFA studios in Tempelhof and Babelsberg, and introduced him to film celebrities.

Eisenstein visited Fritz Lang on the *Metropolis* set in Staaken, where the episode 'Eternal Gardens' was being filmed. Eisenstein discussed the advantages of the 'unchained' camera with the cameramen Karl Freund and Gunther Rittau. Thea von Harbou, Lang's wife and author of the scenario, explained the film's central concept. Lang, Eisenstein wrote in his travel notes, resembled a Kuleshov who had been well fed over a long period of time. *Metropolis*, a vision of a city in the year 2000, inspired Eisenstein to a movie about a glass tower. Everything would be fully transparent; changing positions and visual perspectives would create the plot.

The Glass House was intended as a polemical response not only to Lang's film, but also to Bruno Taut and Mies van der Rohe's glass architecture. Van der Rohe proposed to build a glass tower on Berlin's Friedrichstraße in 1921. Eisenstein envisioned his own glass palace as an architectonic image of America. He thought an American author like Upton Sinclair might write the screenplay. In his notes Eisenstein referred to the project both by its English and German titles; he would alternate between *Das Glashaus* and *The Glass House*.

He also observed F.W. Murnau's work in *Faust* and met Emil Jannings, the German actor whom he admired most. But these two film giants paid hardly any attention to Eisenstein.

Maria Andreeva, Maxim Gorky's wife and head of the film division of the Soviet trade mission in Berlin, hired Edmund Meisel to write the musical score for *Potemkin*. Meisel had collaborated with his close friend Erwin Piscator and with Brecht, he was known for his experiments with jazz and noise-music. Eisenstein discussed the film music with him: he wanted rhythm, rhythm, and more rhythm. Meisel was not allowed to wax melodic, especially during the confrontation with the squadron.

All of these encounters were still hesitant, since Eisenstein was completely unknown. Almost nobody had seen his film.

Berlin deeply impressed Eisenstein as a city. He particularly liked the music halls and the city lights at night. He met with Elizaveta Michelson, who encouraged him to apply for German orphan's benefits, since he should qualify. Eisenstein made an effort to get a duplicate copy of his father's death certificate. However, his application was rejected on the grounds that he, the son of the Baltic German Mikhail Eisenstein, had served in the Russian Army.

He also visited friends and relatives of his mother who had emigrated to Berlin. He bought 'Victoria'-brand stockings for his mother and purchased a gramophone for himself.

Eisenstein had come to Berlin for the premiere of his film. However, the Army Ministry thwarted his plans. The Ministry had become alarmed and ordered a closed showing for Admiral Zenker and Generaloberst Hans von Seeckt, who recommended that the film be forbidden by the 2nd Chamber of Film Censorship on grounds that it might threaten public order.

The Soviet trade mission arranged for Eisenstein to meet with the influential critic Alfred Kerr. His approval was to be crucial during the Film Censorship's review on April 10. Kerr and Erwin Piscator belonged to the censorship committee's group of experts. Eisenstein believed that he had Kerr to thank for the film passing the German censor with only 14 cuts—or 29 meters of lost film. The film's credits listed Piel Jutzi, a Prometheus employee, as the German editor of the film, but Eisenstein made the cuts himself.

The Army leadership still forbade soldiers from watching *Potemkin*. After a month in Berlin, Sovkino called Eisenstein and Tisse back to Moscow. They had already stayed two weeks longer than intended, and hard currency was in short supply. They left for home on April 26 and missed the April 29 premiere.

The ambassador Nikolai Krestinsky sent Eisenstein a telegram on April 27 asking him to return to Berlin by plane, but the flight was canceled because of bad weather. Eisenstein had to experience his fame from afar.

The Berlin premiere took place in the Apollo, a former music hall, because the owners of the big movie theaters were reluctant to show the film. There had been a new attempt to forbid the screening, but the left press led a vehement protest against the renewed censorship.

The film surpassed anything Berlin had ever seen, including UFA-spectacles and American star films. This was a bloody film, a murderous film from Moscow, the height of brutality—'Soviet-Jewish propaganda' came the reaction from the right. It was the duty of every police chief in Europe to prevent people from entering theaters that showed the movie. On the other hand, Berlin's great cultural figures acknowledged that the film had left an unusual, lasting ('exciting, rousing') effect. Soon German writers—Bertolt Brecht, Lion Feuchtwanger, Gustav Regler—would mirror this effect in their poems and novels. Naturally this aesthetic fell on fruitful ground in certain Berlin circles: this was the age of Dada, Bauhaus photography, experiments with abstract films by Walter Ruttmann, Viking Eggeling, and Hans Richter. But the event *Potemkin* transcended these movements. *Die Rote Fahne* and *Das neue Rußland* attributed the '*Potemkin*-effect' to its ideology.[67] But it soon became clear that *Potemkin*'s attraction went beyond ideological barriers and infected more than the proletariat. The film's success in bourgeois Western circles took the Russian filmmakers by complete surprise.

The film projected a new understanding of cinema, a different image of Russia and a different type of hero. In *Potemkin* the Revolution was tied to violence. This violence—pogrom, ruin, mutiny, mass destruction—was the subject of the new Russian cinema. And still the apocalyptic images breathed the euphoria of a new beginning; the excitement was contagious. The new aesthetic puzzled people; they could not quite locate the cause of its hypnotic effect. Kerr thought that its success lay in Russian culture—Dostoevsky, Stanislavsky, 'frenzies, passions, the abyss'.[68] Yet in the masses, in their collective body, there was not a single Tolstoyan peasant or Dostoevskian hero to be found. Eisenstein had cast the film with original types and with actors from his troupe. Nonetheless, one reviewer curiously ascribed the film's success to the familiar dramatic art of the Moscow Art Theater.[69]

Herbert Jhering called *Potemkin* a 'people's film'. There was no equivalent in Germany, he claimed, since 'we are politically, spiritually, and artistically torn'. His juxtaposition of *Potemkin*, the *Iliad* and the *Nibelungen* proved to be prophetic.[70] Goebbels demanded a National Socialist *Potemkin* in 1934.[71]

The *Vossische Zeitung* likened the film to UFA's large historical productions, but wrote that in comparison the latter were mere pastoral plays.[72] Oskar A. H. Schmitz denied the film any artistic merit when he measured it against bourgeois novels, since the individual was completely absent. Walter Benjamin replied by offering the most surprising and most accurate comparison of all: American slapstick. Like *Potemkin*, that 'grotesque film' had discovered a new formula that marked progress in art and moved in step with the technological Revolution.[73]

A growing awareness of this progress and Eisenstein's reflection of the connection between space and collective fate, which would so define the twentieth century, transported *Potemkin* beyond old ideas of what art was, what cinema could do, and what made up the 'Russian soul'. Montage not only intensified movement, but also bared the mechanism of the social machine.

Film became the medium that helped achieve a total view of the development of society and history. This discovery was important not only for the new Russian cinema, but also for international art, including art in Germany. Montage influenced the development of Piscator's concept of theater and of film in the Weimar Republic.

Earlier Russian films had never exceed a maximum distribution of five cop-ies. Soon there were 45, then 50, then 67 prints of *Potemkin* in circulation to meet Germany's great demand. The film brought Prometheus a profit of one million Reichsmark.[74]

Mary Pickford and Douglas Fairbanks saw *Potemkin* in their own private matinée—Meisel conducted the orchestra for just the two of them. Prometheus used their enthusiasm in its advertising campaign. Both stars professed that watching *Potemkin* had been the most profound experience of their lives.

Potemkin ran in Vienna, Geneva, Stockholm, and Paris. Marcel L'Herbier suggested that Eisenstein receive the Nobel Prize. Charlie Chaplin called *Potemkin* the best film of all time. It was banned in Italy, Spain, Belgium, Den-mark, Norway, and the Baltic Republics. *Potemkin* catapulted Russian films out of their marginal status in world cinema, but only made $108,000 for the Soviet Union. This modest sum was excused by the Soviet film distributors' lack of experience.

The history of *Potemkin*'s creation seems full of coincidences, but every co-incidence was well thought-out and carefully planned. This also holds true for the six most famous minutes of film history: the massacre on the Odessa Steps. Eisenstein spent three months working on *Potemkin*; he earned praise for it his whole life.

In one fell swoop—with one film—the 27-year-old Eisenstein became a world-famous director.

The *Potemkin* negative was sold to Germany in 1926, since Soviet Russia did not have the means to make a duplicate copy. All domestic prints of the film were worn out, so today—as is the case with all of Eisenstein's films—no authentic copy of the original director's cut remains. The Soviet Film Archive Gosfilmofond purchased the original negative from the German Reich Film Archive in 1940—a bizarre consequence of the Molotov-Ribbentrop Pact. This negative became the source for the film's restoration in 1960 and contains all the cuts that the Berlin censorship imposed on the film in March 1926.

THE MORNING AFTER FAME
1926-1928

Back in Moscow, Eisenstein planned another project with Tretyakov, a film about China. In 1927 Tretyakov had compiled his own travel notes on the Middle Kingdom Zhonghua in the volume *Chzhungo*. They intended to use this text as a starting point. The premiere of Tretyakov's successful play *Roar, China!* in the Meyerhold Theater coincided with the release of *Potemkin*. While Eisenstein was in Berlin, Tretyakov wrote the libretto for a trilogy. The first part, 'The Yellow Peril', told the story of a girl who had been sold into prostitution. The second episode, 'The Blue Express', described an attack on a train by Chinese rebels. The third part, 'Roar, China!' dealt with the battle against the imperial 'paper tiger'. Social analysis was disguised as an adventure tale: a poor fisherman first becomes a bandit, then a revolutionary; his daughter becomes a prostitute and then ends up as the Emperor's concubine. Eisenstein and Tretyakov wanted to travel to China, where they would shoot a number of educational films on the side: on theater and painting, the village and the factory, religion and family. They applied for 250,000 rubles for the project from Sovkino, thinking that sum would suffice. But after several months the committee turned them down, since hard currency was in short supply and the situation in China was unstable after the defeat of the People's Army.

Eisenstein was hurt and wanted to leave the state-run studio. He wrote a letter to Moisei Aleinikov, who ran the last relatively independent film company in Moscow, Mezhrabprom-Rus. Though the group was financed by the International Workers' Aid and the German Communist Party, the real base was an old artists' cooperative. Mezhrabprom-Rus was better equipped technically than any other studio in Soviet Russia. The German connection also provided access to hard currency. The studio was in the process of organizing a film expedition to China and even had the funds to finance it. The highly diplomatic Aleinikov responded to Eisenstein: 'Your offer is extremely flattering, and I would be honored to accept it. However, it would be a piece of political tactlessness.' His studio was a thorn in the eyes of too many people. Aleinikov feared that the attitude of Party authorities would change radically if 'they find out that we are sucking the blood of the state studio.' Aleinikov was right. Did he already know more than the applicant?[75]

Eisenstein had to replace the exoticism of China with that of the Russian village. This inspiration came from Joseph Stalin, as did the title *The General Line*, based on Stalin's recent eponymous directive. The film was to show the transformation of the countryside according to Stalin's plan. But the Party line changed constantly. In 1926 the slogan had been 'Cooperative'.

The assignment was part of a cultural campaign that was just getting started. After Sergei Esenin, 'the last village poet', committed suicide in December 1925, there was a mysterious wave of suicides that affected more than just the 'hysterical' female section of the population. In June 1926 several young Komsomol members, who were all part of a secret society at VKhUTEMAS, took their own lives. This was particularly worrisome, since the art school was considered a stronghold of rational, Americanized artist-engineers. Where did the resignation and pessimism come from? The Party thought Esenin, whose poetry had a magical effect on people, to be the epitome of the most negative aspects of the so-called Russian national character. He embodied anarchism, a catastrophic lack of emotional discipline, alcoholism, and sexual chaos. His doubts about the possibility of rural Russia's social transformation, which were based on his knowledge of the national character, were read as a glorification of the backwardness of rural life. Only Trotsky emphasized Esenin's positive role: the poet's desperate surges of passion spoke of a time in the future; in Esenin's person, the Revolution had given a voice to the Russian peasant. But Stalin and Nikolai Bukharin disagreed. In 'The Foundations of Leninism' (April 1924) Stalin coined a formula that stayed in the air: he demanded the combination of Russian Revolutionary enthusiasm and American efficiency. At the Moscow Komsomol Congress in February 1926 Bukharin spoke of the necessity to rationalize one's lifestyle and to behave in a utilitarian way in everyday life. Esenin's poetry idealized the opposite as 'truly Russian' and 'truly peasant-like'. Therefore his poetry was dangerous.

The politicians were not just fighting about a poet. In the end they were debating what the desired ideal of Russia would be. Since Esenin's despair circulated in huge editions, the Party had to offer another image to the lost collective soul.

A young film director, a Constructivist director-engineer ('of human souls') had to reshape the image of the Russian village in transition as a utopia that was close at hand. The creator of this utopia was Stalin himself. Eisenstein was to film the Americanization of the countryside at a symbolic location: Esenin's home village Konstantinovo near Ryazan. In this context *The General Line* became more than a topical movie about Stalinist collectivization. The film was intended as a call to Russia to break out of the national stereotypes of anarchism and mysticism. The age-old forms of the Russian village were to be replaced by a new community. The transition was to be demonstrated on the lives of the poor. Eisenstein committed Andrei Burov, a Constructivist architect, to build a set in the style of Le Corbusier's buildings. It would be a modern, real Futurist farm in the village of Konstaninovo.

Eisenstein spent the month of May 1926 collecting material and read journals and newspapers with titles like *The Dairy Industry* or *The Day Laborer*. He
wrote the script and prepared shots from June to August 1926, as the Esenin
campaign was becoming increasingly political. He conceived of his village picture as an erotic comedy, a sensuous film in the style of Zola's novel *Earth*. He
wanted to test his hypothesis that any random object could provoke ecstasy.
His trip to Berlin had encouraged him to think in international terms. He felt
equal to the film greats who had previously enjoyed mythic status: Chaplin,
Griffith, Lang, Murnau. He planned to develop film into a world medium and
world language.

Soon the first pilgrims came to Moscow to see him. Mary Pickford and
Douglas Fairbanks arrived July 21, 1926. They had come not only as celebrated
stars, but also as business people. They were the bosses of United Artists, a
company they had started with Griffith and Chaplin, and wanted to invite the
new star to direct in Hollywood. Eisenstein showed them the old Kremlin
and offered them his project about new forms of architecture, life, and art—
The Glass House. Pickford was surprised by her host's youth, but commented
that 'genius has no age'. Eisenstein quipped that she had made that pronounce-
ment only after she discovered he could be her grandson. After his trip to Berlin the 28-year-old Eisenstein had had his head shaved in the style of
Mayakovsky, Tretyakov, and Rodchenko, which made him look even younger
than he was.

The film industry was going through a tense period. There were mass arrests from April to September 1926, especially among the old school film workers. They came for Alexander Khanzhonkov and for Eisenstein's former coauthor Yakov Bliokh. Eisenstein's diary entries sound callous: 'Khanzhonkov has
a progressive form of paralysis. They arrested him in his wheelchair. I imagined how they would roll him to the interrogations. And if it comes to an execution? . . . They shoot the man in his wheelchair, the chair begins to roll'[76]—a variant
of the baby carriage on the Odessa steps. Eisenstein was aware of his brutal imagination: 'Dec. 12, 1927. If something is good, I say it is brutally good.'[77]

He himself felt safe in these insecure times. In June 1926 Eisenstein applied for the recognition of his copyright to *The Battleship Potemkin*, a step that
would give him one percent of the film's worldwide earnings. A special Sovkino
committee processed his application. The committee decided that in principal neither directors nor cameramen had legal claims to a film's copyright, but
that since Eisenstein's montage list could be considered a literary source for
the film, the director could be officially recognized as the author of the movie.

The work on the village picture was already threatened in September, since
a committee led by Mikhail Kalinin and Nikolai Podvoisky decided that the

tenth anniversary of the October Revolution needed a 'major film'. The only
director who came into question was Eisenstein. The committee rejected the
second candidate, Lev Kuleshov, a decision that greatly hurt the older director. They suggested John Reed's *10 Days that Shook the World* as the basis for the
script. The Central Committee's decision was confirmed by a special film committee that included Dziga Vertov. Vertov was commissioned to make the
major documentary film for the occasion.

Eisenstein thought he could finish the village picture first. *The General Line*
was to tell the story of a poor, oppressed day worker who starts a dairy cooperative and soon becomes the first female tractor driver. Instead of casting a
professional actress, he gave the part to a peasant woman who played herself.
Evdokiya was even from the village of Konstantinovo. A problem arose when
she kept turning away from the camera. One day the police came to get her—
it turned out that she was a notorious criminal. Then Eisenstein chose Marfa
Lapkina. She was his anti-star—bony and haggard, with a sunken syphilitic
nose and a prominent mouth—anything but a beauty. There was nothing 'Russian' in her face, none of the Madonna-aura that surrounded the peasant women
in Venetsyanov's Romantic paintings depicting round-faced, harmonious, vo-
luptuous, flaxen-haired Slavic Venuses.

Eisenstein wanted to present the old village as crude, erotic slapstick. The
new community would be a Constructivist utopia—both would be ironically
defamiliarized. Eisenstein was most interested in testing his ecstasy hypothesis on different kinds of material—pagan, mythic, erotic and animal-like, religious, Constructivist. Could a simple machine in action (a milk separator,
for example) create an effect that was just as ecstatic as the final scene of
Potemkin?

He combined Freud and Constructivism: machines should experience orgasm, and animals should copulate in the manner of mythical beasts. He took
motifs from classical painting—the rape of Europa (his choice for the film
poster), and the Russian naturalists' beloved landscapes. His camera cut them
into the most unusual eccentric angles, literally sawing the pictures apart. He
wanted the montage to follow the syncopated rhythms of American jazz. An
alien from Mars could hardly have made a more defamiliarizing movie about
the Russian village.

The press documented the work on the set in detail. The newspapers promised that the film would be ready by November 7, 1926—in time for the big
anniversary.

But Eisenstein made slow progress. Because of rainy weather he had only
been able to film six or seven days in a month and a half. The film crew followed the sun and traveled south, to Rostov on the Don, the Kuban, Baku, to

the Persian border in the Mugan Steppe. But the weather was bad everywhere.

In the meantime Moscow demanded Eisenstein's return, but he did not let himself be bothered in the distant steppes. He started to keep a diary again and worked intensely on his theory of montage. He read Engels' *Dialectics of Nature*, recently published in Russian, *The Problem of Verse Language* by Tynyanov, and Leonid Sabaneev's books on Alexander Scriabin's theory of new music. Overtones, dialectics, and structural analysis of verse furthered the development of Eisenstein's own thoughts on film montage. Isaak Babel visited him on the set. Eisenstein admired this brilliant storyteller, especially his oral improvisations and *bon mots*. He often jotted down Babel's anecdotes in his diary and felt an affinity for Babel's erotic, fresh sense of humor. The diary includes an essay on Babel by Abram Lezhnev, since Eisenstein recognized his own style in Babel's writing. Eisenstein once said that his own sentence construction reminded him of a bad translation from German; Lezhnev likened Babel's stylistic idiosyncrasies to an 'imitated' translation from French.

Moscow urged Eisenstein to make a decision. On October 5, he agreed to direct the film for the October celebration, but work on *The General Line* was not interrupted until December. Then Eisenstein dedicated himself completely to the new project. Sovkino sent various materials compiled by the historian Alexei Efimov to the Mugan Steppe: books, other librettos about the Revolution, an outline of the most important revolutionary events. The collection included memoirs by Revolutionaries as well as White Guardsmen and Monarchists, for example Vasily Shulgin's *Days*. The main political department of the Central Committee had put its stamp of approval on this reading list.

One of the first films about the October Revolution came out in Great Britain in 1920, a gripping trashy movie called *The Land of Mystery*. Leonid Krasin, then the diplomatic representative in London, immediately brought the film back to Moscow and rounded up all the People's Commissars to watch the movie. Lenin and his wife Nadezhda Krupskaya also attended the screening. Since that event, the Soviet Union had tried to counter the film with its own pictures of the Revolution. The last days of the Romanovs were all the rage in film studios everywhere, especially in Hollywood. In 1927 the theme was huge all around the world. The new state project that had been reserved for Eisenstein was again the biggest commission of the year. The powers that were expected Eisenstein to show Lenin—this was almost an order. He jotted down a first sketch of the film on the train back to Moscow. In January 1927 he began to work on the script with Alexandrov. The script was critically discussed a number of times and they had to make changes. The committee demanded that Eisenstein give up his grandiose plan to include all the victories of Trotsky's Red Army and told him to limit himself to the Petrograd uprising. None of the actual film episodes resembled their screenplay descriptions—the script mostly listed well-known events and possible set locations. Since *The Bazaar of Lust* Eisenstein had stopped writing down his own scripts and instead dictated them to his assistant Grisha. Eisenstein would develop an idea, Grisha would write it down, then they would discuss Grisha's notes and modify them.

While the committee examined the screenplay, Eisenstein cut the village picture. On February 26, 1927 he showed the first versions to his friends Babel, Shklovsky, Tretyakov, Shutko, Shub, Kozintsev, and Trauberg. They were all greatly impressed by the physiological effect of the film. Someone remarked that it was a color film in black and white. The press was already announcing that the (unseen) film was ready and—brilliant.

On February 28 the *October* screenplay came back with comments from the censor's office Glavrepertkom; they changed the script again. When an American correspondent asked Eisenstein who was writing the screenplay to his *October* film, he answered without a moment's hesitation: 'the Party',[78] to which, incidentally, he never belonged. Paralleling the history of the Revolution, Eisenstein began to write his own life history. He polemically entitled the drafts *My Art in Life*, an inversion of Stanislavsky's 1926 autobiography *My Life in Art*. Eisenstein believed that he would be able to write a *psychoanalytic* book about himself and the origins of his ideas in the style of a 'diary of an immature girl'.[79] Though he soon dropped the autobiography, the project appears highly programmatic in the context of the ordered historical panorama.

On March 8 the screenplay finally passed censorship. A mere five days later, on March 12, the crew left for Leningrad. The evening before the departure Esfir Shub showed Eisenstein documentary footage that she had found of the events. In Leningrad Eisenstein did not stay with his mother, but lived with the camera crew in a hotel.

He visited the historical locations with the commanders of the rebellion, Nikolai Podvoisky and Vladimir Antonov-Ovseenko. Tisse had brought a new Bell and Howell camera and a set of new lenses from Germany. He had been sent abroad with the express purpose of buying equipment for the film.

They started shooting in April. The press announced *the* cinema event of the year. Everybody expected a second *Potemkin*. Eisenstein kept a journal of the work on the set and immediately had it typed out for later publication.

October was a mammoth production—just like the most famous Hollywood movies. Its budget was twenty times higher than that of an average movie. Estimated at 500,000 rubles, the final costs ran up to almost 800,000. Eisenstein clipped articles about Cecil B. DeMille's enormous production *The Ten Commandments* from German film magazines and glued them in his journal. *That* was the movie to which he aspired to compare his own project. He wanted just as many extras and the same kind of directorial omnipotence. He was the Soviet DeMille! The West still had to draw on the Bible for a story, but here there was a Revolution with Lenin in the role of Christ. The film was to become even more ostentatious than *The Ten Commandments*.

During the work on *October* Eisenstein became acquainted with the entire inner circle of power. He had a special contract and was paid more than any other director in the country. He received 550 rubles a month plus 550 rubles in special compensation. Sovkino had to get special permission to pay Eisenstein this sum, which greatly exceeded the salaries of high Party functionaries. The other directing star Pudovkin only earned 600 rubles a month, even though he was employed by Mezhrabprom, which could afford to pay higher salaries than the state companies.

No Hollywood-style sets were built for the film—Eisenstein was allowed to shoot in the Winter Palace itself! The work was bound to damage the historic buildings—too much light, a high risk of fire. Long after the film was completed, people complained that the actual storming of the palace had caused less damage than the film.

Eisenstein calculated that he would need 50,000 to 60,000 extras. There were notices in the Leningrad papers—Eisenstein did not want to hire actors. Instead he planned to find doubles of all the politicians of the time, such as Alexander Kerensky or Nikolai Chkheidze. The hunt for a good Lenin took some time. Members of Lenin's family, his sister Maria Ulyanova and his widow Krupskaya, participated in the search.

One of Eisenstein's Proletkult friends told him that his own father, a worker in the Urals, looked a lot like Lenin and had even played Lenin on the stage of the Maly Theater.

This man, Vasily Nikandrov, finally embodied Lenin in Eisenstein's *October*. His proletarian origins were as significant as the physical resemblance; the similarity was so uncanny that Eisenstein would have loved to film Nikandrov in front of the wooden mausoleum on Red Square and send the material to the Institute for Party History with the question of when the footage was taken. But Nikandrov whispered to Eisenstein that he would have preferred to play Kerensky or the tsar.

On April 12 people who had participated in the real rebellion read through the script and added some details. Alexandrov rewrote the screenplay one more time; Strauch collected costumes, props and distinctive faces.

In order to gather huge masses of people in front of the camera, Eisenstein shot the 1927 May Parade with its 6,000 people and passed it off as the 1917 July demonstration. He only had to change the slogans. That spring and summer they filmed in the Winter Palace and in Smolny. To fill the hall for night shots, the Party city committee ordered city officials to come to 'work' at night as extras.

The director's journal, April 13, 1927, reads: 'The Winter Palace is exotic . . . . this is unbelievably rich cinematic material. Muir&Merrilees.[80] The ground floor. The basement. Heating. Rooms for servants. Its own electric station. Wine cellars. Reception rooms. Private rooms. Floor and roof! One bedroom is worth 300 icons and 200 porcelain Easter eggs. A bedroom that no contemporary psyche could stand. It's unbearable . . .'[81] Everywhere else the objects of the past had all but disappeared, but the palace looked like the prop room in a film studio, like a 'museum of the past'. Eisenstein discovered the perversion and absurdity of power in the perversion of the seized items. These items could be used to shape the revolution that would lead to the liberation from this absurd world of objects. For Eisenstein the path towards dominance over things lay in signs. Filming at original historical sites with doubles and advisors who had stormed the palace ten years earlier, Eisenstein began thinking in terms of a deeply symbolic film that would destroy all symbolism as a form of ridiculous fetishism. He conceived and directed every event as a metaphorical act. He had the soldiers conquer the palace as they would take a woman—in the tsarina's bedroom.

As of June 13, the team spent ten days filming the storming of the Winter Palace: 90 arc lights turned night into day. Again, electricity was turned off in the city to guarantee the necessary 20,000 amperes. The takes were carried out like military operations with the help of the army. Five thousand extras arrived night after night under orders from the city committee. Cameras were mounted on roofs and columns and hung over portals. Eisenstein's assistants made their way around the set on motorcycles while Eisenstein directed the mass ballet through his megaphone. Even though Podvoisky, the leader of the real rebellion, advised Eisenstein every day on the set, Eisenstein defied historical reality and had the workers' brigades storm the main portal of the palace rather than the side entrance. This became the canonical representation of the event in all later images. Eisenstein's still shots decorated Revolutionary museums across the country as 'historical photographs' for many years.

Under the watchful eyes of the mounted militia, the city population admired the event as a grandiose spectacle. Eisenstein enjoyed this attention: the city he had first visited as a small boy now lay at his feet. He had all the opportunities offered by a large production; he moved the masses and shaped history even better than Evreinov had in his 1920 mass action, which Eisenstein read about in the papers when his corps was stationed in Velikie Luki.

On August 7 they filmed the raised bridge; in late August they shot Lenin's arrival. The team still needed to film the 'wild division'. In order to assemble enough exotic faces in front of the camera, the film staff mobilized all Caucasians (who controlled the city's shoe-shining business). A lot of newspaper *feuilletons* reported on this fact, since all the shoe-shiners disappeared from the streets for a few days.

On September 12 Eisenstein finished the work in Leningrad. His staff traveled to Moscow, where they the monument to Alexander III was being rebuilt out of cardboard and plaster. Eisenstein filmed the dismantling of the monument, inspired by photographs of the statue's destruction in 1918. The last shots were made on October 11.

Eisenstein was dissatisfied with the rushes. In letters to Alexandrov, who was still redoing a few scenes in Leningrad, he wrote that almost everything was poorly illuminated. In comparison to *The General Line* the shots looked like a child's game and he would have to throw out a lot of them on technical grounds. Eisenstein spent most of September sitting in the editing room with 49,000 meters of footage that was supposed to become a 2000-meter film by October 14, so that there would be time to make mass prints. He was expected to provide an anniversary film—the October Revolution was to shake the world for a second time. Films by Pudovkin, Shub, and Barnet were to run alongside *October*.

Eisenstein took endocrine stimulants to survive the incessant day and night work. He began his shift in the evening, so he could stay awake 48 hours without sleeping. But his omnipotence soon became impotence: Eisenstein was working so much that he temporarily went blind. On November 1 the newspaper *Vechernyaya Moskva* reported that Eisenstein had fallen ill and would be unable to finish the film on time. The doctors diagnosed complete exhaustion and ordered bed rest in a dark room.

Other problems were accumulating on the side. Eisenstein had gone well over budget, especially with the film stock. To top it all off, there was a major row. On the morning of November 7, 1927, the day the film was to be shown in the Bolshoi Theater, Trotsky's opposition took to the streets of Moscow and Leningrad. Alexandrov later wrote in his memoirs that Stalin came to the editing room personally around four in the afternoon. He asked if Trotsky was in the film and demanded to see those scenes. Stalin told them about the opposition. Eisenstein is said to have cut out all the episodes that showed Trotsky.[82]

Many consider Stalin's personal visit to the editing room to be Alexandrov's invention, but it cannot be denied that an order from above forced Eisenstein to remove Trotsky from the movie. This episode stood within the context of the larger Kremlin debate on the 'distribution of the arts and artists'. While Trotsky met with Esenin to discuss problems of literature over tea, while Bukharin backed the poetry of Boris Pasternak and Osip Mandelstam, the pragmatic politician Stalin chose the new medium of film. In his estimation, film was nothing other than an illusion, but the illusion 'dictated its laws to life'.[83]

Stalin, the General Secretary of the Party, had quickly taken note of the young, world-famous director who could show brutality without flinching and knew how to direct impressive massacres. From now on Stalin would try to influence Eisenstein's development.

A similar affinity could have developed between Eisenstein and Trotsky, since they shared a common interest in Pavlov and in psychoanalysis, but these two never collaborated. *Potemkin* began with a quotation from Trotsky, but that intertitle was primarily a tribute to the journalism of the day. When the Trotsky line was later replaced with a Lenin quote, it did not change the film at all. Trotsky simply disappeared from the screen and from the history of the October uprising. This piece of news was immediately reported in the German press. Eisenstein did not consider this order an infringement of his artistic freedom, but later American and European colleagues such as Upton Sinclair would not believe him.

On November 7 only two films were shown in the Bolshoi Theater: Pudovkin's *The End of St. Petersburg* and Barnet's *Moscow in October*. Eisenstein's half-finished picture ran in a branch of the Bolshoi, then called the Experimental Theater. Only a few episodes were shown in this screening: the storming of the Winter Palace, Lenin's appearance at the 2nd Congress of the Soviets and the arrest of Kerensky's government.

Eisenstein added the final editing touches in December and January. He formally asked Sovkino for 45 extra days for the first part ('Peace to the Cottages') and 15 for the second ('War on the Palaces') and requested a few more days for retakes. His wishes were denied; the film was to be shortened into one part.

Eisenstein still had to spend several days in bed, but he was in the editing room on New Year's Eve. On January 14 he showed the first version to some friends. On January 23, 1928 he made a diary entry at 1 p.m.: 'I turned 30 today and *October* is one year old. At 9 p.m. I'm staking my all. *Va banque*. I'm showing my film to the government, the Central Committee, and the Central Control Committee. It's all or nothing.'[84] All was not lost. The film was received favorably. Krupskaya asked Eisenstein if she should publicize her opinion and give the film a sort of public license—Mayakovsky had promised to throw rotten eggs at the screen if Eisenstein were to include a 'fake Lenin'. Eisenstein was flattered, but ultimately dissatisfied with her article. Krupskaya praised *October* as the art of the future that reflected the life of the masses, but she criticized Eisenstein's incomprehensible symbolism, the overwhelming presence of the baroque art of the ruling classes, and the obscene nature of many of the shots. She interpreted them as a concession to petty bourgeois taste.[85]

Eisenstein became ever more familiar with the high and mighty, and was soon close to the top echelons of power. He would phone the head of the propaganda department Alexander Krinitsky, his Sovkino advocate Podvoisky, and Fyodor Raskolnikov to ask for their impressions. But his film, intended to strengthen the myth of the October Revolution, had not become an icon of dead and living heroes of history. Of course he had created mass scenes that were probably more impressive than the actual events, but Eisenstein's new canonical representation of *the* founding moment of Soviet history is not the core of the film. The real heart of film lies in Eisenstein's intellectual montage games. Their metaphors—at times transparent, at times obscure—and their obscene visual jokes dismantle the myth of history itself. Medals awarded for 'service to the Fatherland' pile up as mounds of worthless trash. Kerensky takes forever to climb the staircase of power, but when the doors to the throne room open, he steps—thanks to Eisenstein's cut—into the back end of a mechanical peacock.

The film came into being on the editing table. This is where the dramatic decisions were made. Eisenstein wanted to write a book on the origins of his montage ideas. The book would include descriptions of scenes that were never shot and those that had been filmed, but were edited out of the final version. He was in an euphoric, 'Dionysian' mood—he had never worked so productively. He felt like a genius, for in this film he had not only grasped history, but had mastered the film medium itself: he had gone beyond the basic phenomenon of film, namely the illusion of movement. He no longer needed that illusion, since he could create movement in a different manner. To this end he used montage of extremely short, static shots of statues and things. Montage made these static objects dynamic and triggered the movement of *thought*. This discovery gave him a sense of total freedom. He now could control not only reflexes and emotions, but even dialectical thinking. He had invented a new language that visualized thought—this was his world mission. He called his new theory—largely developed in a psychedelic delirium—'intellectual film'.

In the essay 'Our October' Eisenstein wrote that he would have needed ten more days to truly finish the film, ten days that would have truly shaken the world. But his opposition to those responsible in Sovkino did not suffice. The film had to be shown on the eve of the Party Conference on Cinema on March 14, 1928. This conference, which lasted for most of the week, was to decide what the next decade of Soviet film would look like. None of the participants, including Eisenstein, realized its importance.

As with the release of *Potemkin*, the publicity campaign for *October* decided to organize a contest between the new Eisenstein film and a foreign movie. This time it was *Variety*, E. A. Dupont's 'bourgeois hit, erotic through and through'. Eisenstein was extremely annoyed. During *October*'s second week theaters began showing the comedy *Blitzzug der Liebe* ('Love Express') with Ossi Oswalda, even though Sovkino had promised to hold back that film. The audience stayed away from *October*. The critics were divided. Everyone had expected a second *Potemkin*! Only a few realized that *October* had intentionally been made to be something absolutely new and different.

Eisenstein's diary entries are first contemptuous and then insulted. Very few people knew how to take the movie. Even more: his experiments with film language were dismissed as aestheticism. Even Eisenstein's friends started a campaign with the slogan '*October* needs to be re-cut!' Worse yet, this was Esfir Shub's demand! Left Front circles reacted strongly, even violently.

The third issue of *Novy Lef* published a collage of 'worst quotations' from negative reviews of the film. The following issue contained LEF's own sharp critique. Osip Brik wrote that the rise and fall of fast-earned genius was a well-known tale. Eisenstein's story was just one more of the kind. He had misunderstood both the Revolution and the rules of film language. Shklovsky entitled his review 'The Reasons for Failure'. Eisenstein had not robbed things of their magic, but had become their slave. Brik asked: 'Can the consequences of the October Revolution really all be reflected in a trembling chandelier?'[86] Fifty years later Shklovsky would admit that he had only understood the film as an old man, after he had been allowed to travel to the West and experience the consumer age. Eisenstein's *October* had been way ahead of them all, since it was a film about the end of things.[87] At the time Eisenstein's LEF friends called *October* a historical lie, a serious ideological error, and a total artistic failure. Eisenstein subsequently left the group in March and refused to accept offers of reconciliation. The fateful meeting took place in Tretyakov's apartment. As a sign of his break with LEF, Eisenstein immediately signed the manifesto of another group of Moscow Constructivists. The group was called October (like his film) and consisted mostly of architects and graphic artists, among them the Vesnin Brothers and Gustav Klutsis. This signature was the extent of Eisenstein's activity in the group. He filled several notebooks of his journal with arguments against the opinions of Brik, Tretyakov, and Shklovsky. He could not grasp why they could or would not understand his discoveries—he genuinely thought his new ideas were brilliant. He had to accept their rejection as a fact. Tretyakov supported Eisenstein as a friend, but artistically misunderstood him completely.

Diary entry, February 13, 1928: 'I should have thought about pathetic hate earlier. I mean Tretyakov's pathos, the result of his particular nature. An old maid will damn all expressions of healthy sexuality as perversion. Tretyakov is a lot like that. And he immediately disguises his impotence as a social platform.'[88]

Who still understood him? His students? Amazed foreigners?

On April 2 the film was shown in Berlin; this time the Germans saw the full-length, uncensored version. Egon Erwin Kisch wrote the German titles; Meisel, once again, composed the score. Eisenstein hoped for a repeat of his *Potemkin* triumph, but the film's unique nature was lost on his Berlin audience as well. Meisel's wife, who was in love with Eisenstein, wrote of a great success, but Eisenstein interpreted this as a well-meant exaggeration. What kind of success could there be if *October* had only run one day!? But Eisenstein failed to register that the film had been released in eleven large theaters simultaneously—the distributors had simply miscalculated. The critics wrote of a 'failed monster-film'. The film flopped—just as *The Strike* had been a failure in Berlin the year before.

Eisenstein was offended and disgruntled about the cool reception of his new opus, which he himself valued more than *Potemkin*. Perhaps the following diary entry, written in German, is connected to the disaster. 'April 6, 1928. I am once again very, very sick. Hysteria. Madness. All of Moscow is talking about my illness! My unconscious, wild, pathological hubris. Terrible inferiority complex that will probably drive me insane.'[89]

Emotional tension and physical stress threw Eisenstein into a deep psychological crisis. He immediately went to see three different doctors—the school psychologist Professor Speshnev, the psychoanalyst Zalkind, and the internist Dr. Kramer. 'Maybe God does exist? Speshnev found nothing. Zalkind—psychoanalysis. We decided not to risk the liquidation of my neurosis. So as not to threaten my talent. Kramer prescribed glycerophosphate.'[90]

Though Eisenstein avoided Zalkind's psychoanalysis, in 1928 he attended a few sessions of hypnosis with Yury Kannabikh, the personal doctor of Adolf Ioffe. Ioffe was a friend of Trotsky who committed suicide in 1927. Kannabikh, the last president of the Russian Psychoanalytic Society, would again treat Eisenstein in the thirties.

Eisenstein feared for his sanity. His fear did not come from nowhere—his uncle Nikolai Osipovich had gone mad. Would his inheritance catch up with him? 'June 3, 1928. I'll call Zalkind again. *It won't hurt to try. Youth! Physically I'm okay, but psychologically? Will I be creatively ill, erotically healthy, or indifferent?*'[91]

In his diary he psychoanalyzed Pudovkin, his most serious competitor in terms of fame. He blamed Pudovkin and his anniversary film *The End of St. Petersburg* for the failure of his own work. 'Pudovkin killed my *October*.'[92] Eisenstein spent all winter wondering whether Pudovkin was a neurotic or a neurasthenic. He assigned the following roles to the troika of the Russian Renaissance: he himself was Leonardo da Vinci; Pudovkin played Raphael; and Alexander Dovzhenko, who had joined them in 1930, was generously given the part of Michelangelo.[93]

Only in April 1928 did Eisenstein begin intense self-analysis. He often returned to his father and his father's tyranny: 'Riga—a symbol of oppression. Riga, oh my undoing! The greedy, Freudian, and the beastly—banned and oppressed. That is why I have been erring so recklessly in the distance. A mixture of reserve and smut . . . . Riga as trauma. I consider all my oddities to be mistakes. Sin.'[94] He would make these entries in German, which became the language of his intimate diaries. However, he repeatedly reminded himself not to get too personal and would include teasing remarks, 'I'd like to see the man who will analyze and edit my diaries after my death.'[95]

'A director has to break through his inhibitions. It would be castration to anaesthetize (master) his weaknesses.' He glued an essay by Dr. V. Vinogradov on the creativity of the mentally ill into his diary. 'Just don't get better! Riga tamed the beast. Let the beast out! Long live the beast..! After 30 days. Genius is neurosis. There is a shift in my psyche. I no longer understand *mon cas* [my case]. I have to go see Zalkind. June 9, 1928. My notes have taken on a repulsively clinical character. I need to keep a separate journal, so my theoretical observations don't get mixed up with scraps of my illness.'[96] Most likely some event brought his homosexuality to the surface—he had already discovered this aspect of his sexuality as an adolescent in Riga, but had suppressed it for many years. His writing was full of detailed notes from a treatise on homosexuality and included an analysis of Socrates' and John the Baptist's homosexual orientation. In Eisenstein's assessment, the latter had been in love with Jesus. 'John' was a favorite figure in Eisenstein's drawings, fellatio was another recurring theme.

In an interview with the American paper *New Masses* Eisenstein said: 'Had it not been for Leonardo da Vinci, Marx, Lenin, Freud and the movies, I would in all probability have been another Oscar Wilde.'[97] An aesthete and a homosexual?

In May he was sent to the Caucasian town Gagra to recover. Grisha accompanied him and shared his hotel room. There Eisenstein read James Joyce's *Ulysses* in the original, 'the Bible of the new cinema'.[98] Whenever he had trouble with the language, he would peek at the German translation, the 1927 Basel edition. His close friend Ivy Litvinova, an Englishwoman and the wife of the People's Commissar for Foreign Affairs, had acquired the book for him. *Ulysses* fascinated him, especially since the linguist Nikolai Marr had recently spurred his interest in language. Now his diaries included etymological exercises and what he called 'illicit linguistics'.[99] He sensed that he was standing at the threshold of a total upheaval in film. His feelings were affirmed by the new technology. On July 20, as Soviet Russia received the first reports of the grandiose success of sound film, he composed the manifesto 'Statement on Sound' with Alexandrov and Pudovkin. They advocated the discord of sound and visual image in order to recombine the two in new ways.[100] The reaction of many experienced film artists, including Charlie Chaplin, René Clair, and the theoretician Rudolf Arnheim, to sound film was clearly negative. They equated the end of silent film with the death of art itself. Art had been replaced by an illusionistic wax-figure museum full of speaking dolls. Eisenstein, however, understood sound and image to be stimulants of equal value: the new auditory stimulus would influence the other senses. Two separate stimuli—the visual and the acoustic—could either suppress or intensify each other. Sound could help the viewer to see, could give the image depth, and activate the reception of movement and rhythm. The image made the abstraction of sound more concrete, and made it meaningful. The counterpoint of image and sound could thus achieve a new level of totally simultaneous sensory perception. He demanded not a separate 'I see' or 'I hear', but 'I hear with my eyes' and 'I see with my ears' = 'I perceive'.[101] Eisenstein found examples of similar applications of sound in Japanese art. In the summer of 1928, the Kabuki Theater came to Moscow. That August Eisenstein wrote a review of the guest performance that had led him to discover a radical solution to the problems of sound film in an archaic form of theater. The article 'An Unexpected Juncture' described the fusion of film and theater, Europe and Japan, image and sound. The Kabuki had mastered complete equivalence of auditory and visual senses: 'Instead of *accompaniment* the Kabuki reveals the method of *transference*: the transference of the basic affective intention from one material to another, from one category of 'stimulant' to another.'[102]

The visit to the theater reminded Eisenstein of an American science fiction novel that he had once read. In the book, a character's auditory and optical nerves had been cross-switched like cables, so that he perceived light vibrations as sound and air tremors as colors.

He wrote a letter to Malevich asking the artist to participate in a discussion of sound film that he planned to lead in *Kino-front*, the journal of the Association of Revolutionary Cinematography. But Malevich declined—he thought the direction that film and film theory had taken was too naturalistic, too illustrative. He had little interest in the effects of synaesthesia.

Kabuki was also an erotic experience for Eisenstein. His intimate diary recalls how the actor Asari's kimono shimmered magically in the light of an unforgettable dawn. Joyce awakened his interest in *écriture automatique*, so Eisenstein tried himself in *automatic writing* in English! He imitated Molly Bloom's inner monologue, but gave it the title 'Valeska Gert on a global scale'. However, instead of creating a portrait of the German expressive dancer Valeska Gert, he slipped into the role of a woman and wrote, 'Dec. 14, 1928: In

bed. Grisha. Want to coïte. Lake of women. Melancholics. My head full of
dreck. No possibility of thinking. Splendid ideas and no hands. The greatest
idea – conflict between form and subject. The finest idea. Especially for printing effects. Those o but written out of my unhappiness. Silly. Idiotic. Erotic.
Hunger. Schizophrenic. Eclectic. Idiot again, Uspensky hanged himself. Why
not me. Bao, boo, boo'.[103]

Eisenstein did not consider his erotic experiences part of the 'Dionysian'
side of his personality. That designation was reserved for the intellectual work
that often made him toil through the night. He was attracted to famous characters who showed suppressed homosexuality—he read Honoré de Balzac's
biography and recognized himself. Like Balzac, he would spend nights at his
desk writing and drinking black coffee.

Around this time Eisenstein met a young film journalist, Pera Fogelman,
who could do much more than make excellent coffee. She went by the name of
Pera Atasheva, but Eisenstein called her Pearl after Pearl White, his favorite
actress in an American series. Pera had black hair and was small and round.
She spoke good English and had a sense of humor that thrilled Eisenstein. He
wrote her a letter from Yalta in which he told her that he had been reading
Joyce and that Joyce looked at the world the same way she did: through a
microscope on to a macrocosm.[104] She started working for the film section of
the Society for Cultural Ties with Foreign Countries (VOKS) in 1927 and joined
the staff of the publishing house Teakinopechat, which was headed by Kirill
Shutko. She also contributed to the journal *Sovetsky ekran*. She intended to travel
to the USA, but her plans did not work out. Her father was arrested in April
1928 on embezzlement charges, and she was not given a passport. In addition
her uncle, who was supposed to send her an invitation to America, suddenly
went broke.

Pera's relations with Eisenstein became ever closer. She offered to work as
his press agent and to manage his household. Eisenstein gave her his entire
income. Pera paid the cook, transferred money to Eisenstein's mother, and
took care of the rent (51 rubles a month) and the phone bill. She managed his
correspondence and sent photographs to foreign film magazines. She organized his manuscripts and typed his essays. Eisenstein was pathologically
unable to finish an article, so Pera would do it for him by boldly adding 'Long
live the World Proletariat!' to the final paragraph. Soon she became a second
mother to Eisenstein, although her claims to dominance were modest in comparison to those of Eisenstein's real mother. Pera was an ideal friend. She was
so devoted and submissive only because she loved Eisenstein dearly and accepted his weaknesses. She also accepted that the roles he assigned to her—house
manager, mother, buddy, nanny—had to exclude her feminine sexuality.

THE PILGRIMS. THE SEARCH FOR A WORLD LANGUAGE
1928-1929

In 1927 the Moscow newspaper *Kino* conducted a survey that identified the best and most popular film directors. Eisenstein ranked only fifth on the list. The winner was Abram Room; he had just directed the box office hit *Bed and Sofa*. The rest of the world was of a different opinion. More and more foreign guests showed up in Moscow to see Eisenstein. His unconventional way of thinking, impertinent sense of irony, surrealistic logic and linguistic ability attracted American and West European celebrities to his small room at Chistye Prudy (Clear Ponds). The room was stuffed full of books, and there were orange and black concentric circles painted on the ceiling. Eisenstein served tea and gooseberry cake at a table covered with a wax tablecloth. Only a very few of his foreign visitors noticed the old, expensive books that dated as far back as the 17th century, the Japanese engravings, or the etchings by Piranesi. They were usually surprised by his modest, even poor accommodations. But Eisenstein's bed did not support that general impression. Theodore Dreiser wrote that Eisenstein had the largest and most comfortable looking bed in Russia. Eisenstein admitted that he had bought the magnificent thing from an American farming commune near Moscow.[105] László Moholy-Nagy's Bauhaus students described the luxurious life that Erwin Piscator lived in Berlin; everyone knew of Piscator's lifestyle from a photo-reportage in the magazine *Dame*. Eisenstein did not seem impressed, though he knew to appreciate the St. Laurent water closet that had been installed in his mother's apartment.

In January 1927 the star photographer James Abbe came to visit Eisenstein; he had been sent by Lillian and Dorothy Gish. The actresses wanted to work with the Russian director. Eisenstein sent Abbe on to Pudovkin. Melodrama was not his specialty.

Russian film had become fashionable. Montage, called 'American' in Russia, was known as 'Russian montage' the world over. Soviet filmmakers learned of this fact from the Hollywood director Lewis Milestone, who was originally from a rich Jewish family in Odessa, had emigrated to the United States when he was 18, and was now visiting Moscow as a foreign tourist. Eisenstein was the most prominent representative of the montage school and international figures came to him for advice.

Henry Dana, an American professor, came to Moscow for six months to write a book on the new theater and consulted with Eisenstein. Louis Fischer, Moscow correspondent of the liberal New York weekly *The Nation*, conducted a lengthy interview with the director.[106] Fischer was married to a Russian,

Berta Markovna (Markoosha), who kept a salon in Moscow. Eisenstein occasionally went to parties at their house. Joseph (Joe) Freeman, another American and correspondent for the leftist paper *New Masses*, was working on the book *Voices of October*. Eisenstein helped him to write the chapter on film.

Eisenstein told Freeman that Tretyakov was writing his literary portrait, a short biography: 'I have urged him to include a chapter on Freud whose influence on me has been enormous. Without Freud, no sublimation; without sublimation, a mere aesthete like Oscar Wilde. Freud discovered the laws of individual conduct, as Marx discovered the laws of social development. I have consciously used my knowledge of Marx and Freud in the plays and movies I have directed in the past ten years.'[107]

Eisenstein also became acquainted with the French communist film critic Léon Moussinac, who, like Freeman, was working on a book about Soviet film. He wrote for the prestigious literary monthly *Mercure de France*, the daily newspaper *L'humanité*, and film magazines. At the 1925 Exhibition of Art and Industries in Paris, he introduced Eisenstein's *The Strike* to France. He arranged to show other Soviet films that had been banned commercially, including *The Battleship Potemkin*, in November 1926. In the summer of 1927 he founded a new kind of ciné-club, 'Les Amis de Spartacus', in order to create a mass cinema movement and promote even more Russian films.

Moussinac had come to Moscow to screen a new film by Jacques Feyder, *Visages d'enfants*. Eisenstein asked him detailed questions. He had had little exposure to European avant-garde film—such films were not distributed in Russia. One year earlier, Ilya Ehrenburg had brought back several reels of experimental films by René Clair, Fernand Léger, and Henri Chomette: *Entre'acte*, *Le ballet mécanique*, *Cinq minutes du cinéma pur*. Eisenstein had not been impressed. 'These are sheer enfantillage – children's playthings.'[108]

Around November 1927 the pilgrimages became more frequent. Many foreigners came to Moscow for the tenth anniversary of the October Revolution. Eisenstein showed them the raw version of *The General Line*, since he had not yet finished editing *October*. On November 7 Edmund Meisel came to conduct his *Potemkin* score and to discuss the music for *October* with Eisenstein. On November 12 the People's Commissariat for Foreign Affairs held a reception for the guests. At that event Eisenstein met German graphic artist and sculptor Käthe Kollwitz, the French politician and chief editor of *L'humanité* Paul Vaillant-Couturier, Mexican painter Diego Rivera, and expressionist writer Arthur Holitscher.

In December, the successful American novelist Sinclair Lewis came to see Eisenstein; in September 1928 Eisenstein received the famous architect Le Corbusier, who had been invited to design a building in Moscow. Andrei Burov, the set designer on the village picture, gave Le Corbusier a tour of the city. Eisenstein showed him several reels of *The General Line*, about 40 minutes of film. Le Corbusier was thrilled by the film and identified a likeness to Donatello. Eisenstein described their meeting in the press in the third person—first he gave this person his childhood name Rorik, later he signed the article V.S.: 'Le Corbusier is a great enthusiast and fan of film, which he considers—with ar-chitecture—to be the only modern art form: 'It seems to me that I think the same way in my work as Eisenstein does in his, when he creates his kind of cinematography."[109]

In late December Eisenstein met Valeska Gert. He had written her earlier. She was astonished: neither *Potemkin* nor his harsh name [Eisen = iron and Stein = stone] matched the letter, which could have been written by a 'rococo person—delicate, charming, elegant'.[110] Gert had come to Moscow for a guest performance and spoke of 'love almost at first sight'. Eisenstein began to write an essay about her. As usual, he never finished it.

That fall he met Stefan Zweig, who had come to Moscow for Tolstoy's centenary. Eisenstein did not write about their encounter until somewhat later: 'Dec. 31, 1928: Zweig was here. A great day.'[111] Eisenstein grilled him about Sigmund Freud. Zweig, who had already arranged for Salvador Dali and Romain Rolland to meet Freud, promised Eisenstein to schedule a meeting with the great Viennese, if only Eisenstein would travel. Upon Zweig's re-quest, Anna Freud sent Eisenstein a signed copy of her father's autobiography *Freud, an Autobiographical Study*. The book later disappeared from Eisenstein's library. The meeting never took place. Eisenstein was ill-prepared for his fame and he still took note of his rivals' successes with envy. Pudovkin had been invited to Berlin as a star—he was to play the lead in a German-Russian co-production of Tolstoy's *The Living Corpse*. However, Eisenstein also had offers to choose from.

As *October* was playing in the Berlin Tauentzienpalast, the theater's owner Ludwig Klopfer suggested that Eisenstein direct Tretyakov's play *I Want a Baby!* in Berlin. Heinz Saltenburg of the Lessing Theater sent Eisenstein a play by Alexei Tolstoy, which Piscator would later use in *Rasputin, the Romanovs, the War, and the People who Revolted*. In 1927 Eisenstein received an offer to stage a large-scale production about the Russian Revolution in the Berlin Sportpalast. Meisel wanted to write a score for *The General Line* with Eisenstein, and was intent on having Eisenstein cut the German version of the film himself. Willi Münzenberg also supported that plan.

Upton Sinclair wrote to his editor at Malik Press that the Prometheus Film Company was interested in his novel *King Coal* (1917/1918) and requested that Eisenstein be the director.

In early 1927 the invitation from United Artists arrived; Pickford and Fairbanks had kept their promise. In August 1928 the United Artists president, Joseph M. Schenk, came to Moscow to negotiate a possible contract with Eisenstein. Eisenstein discussed Schenk's offers with Dos Passos, who was also visiting him at the time. (Eisenstein had not yet read *Manhattan Transfer*, but out of politeness he told the author that he had.) Dos Passos thought Eisenstein should be very careful about *the timing* of his U.S. visit. At that time New York was awaiting the arrival of Boris Chukhnovsky, the man who had saved the Nobile Expedition—one celebrity should not steal the other's show.

Gossip surrounding Eisenstein's imminent departure was so intense that he had to refute the rumors in an open letter. Several artists had already failed to return from their summer 1928 travels abroad. These included Mikhail Chekhov and the film beauty Vera Malinovskaya. There was talk that Meyerhold had defected and that the director of the Jewish Theater Alexei Granovsky had decided to stay in Berlin after his guest performance. In the same breath the German press announced that Eisenstein was leaving too—for Hollywood.[112]

Eisenstein's letter, published in *Izvestiya* on November 29, 1928, was addressed to Lunacharsky, who added the introduction: 'Lately the trash heap of the White Guards has become excited over the flight abroad of several artists.' We are really going to Hollywood, Eisenstein wrote, but only to study their technology. He added that his talent did not allow him to film anywhere but on the rich and fertile Russian soil. In fact, Eisenstein was upset that he had been left waiting for his passport for over a year. He had had to turn down a number of enticing offers because he needed to complete *October* and his village picture first. He worked very intensely—he was simultaneously finishing two films and entering a new scientific-theoretical period in his life. Misunderstandings of his practical discoveries drove him to write a book on montage and the new sign language, film language. He drafted a first outline in March 1928 and reorganized the book several times—on October 8, 1928, March 2, 1929, and finally during the week of July 24-31, 1929.

The project was more than a manifesto or a polemical article—the literary forms in which he had previously expressed himself. By 1927 his rivals had already published books on film theory. The Formalists Tynyanov, Shklovsky and Eikhenbaum wrote *The Poetics of Cinema*; the director Semyon Timoshenko published a brochure on film montage; Pudovkin's 1926 book *Film Director and Film Material* had even already been translated into German. Kuleshov had announced his forthcoming volume *The Art of the Cinema: My Experience* that was to appear in stores in 1929. He had already signed a contract with an American publisher and was able to buy a Ford with his advance. His car joined Mayakovsky's Renault as one of the few private autos on the streets of Moscow.

In his book, Eisenstein would not elaborate the current course of cinema or offer a technical classification of montage techniques, as Timoshenko had. He refused to compose a traditional, even archaic list of 'my experiences' in Kuleshov's style. He did not want to write another how-to manual on script writing and film making à la Pudovkin. He intended to write not a two-dimensional, but rather a spherical book: his ideal reader would not just read one essay after another, but would instead perceive the whole book *simultaneously*. The essays were to be arranged in clusters, each oriented in a different direction, but circling around one common theme—the method of montage. Only the shape of a sphere could assure this mutual reversibility. 'But unfortunately . . . books aren't written like that. Even today we only have books like soap bubbles. Particularly on art.'[113] Eisenstein wrote in his diary on August 5, 1929. He wanted to dedicate the spherical book to the founder of the Munich school of expressive gymnastics Rudolf Bode, the philosopher Ludwig Klages, Meyerhold, Griffith's actor Richard Barthelmess, and to his own students.

Several segments of the ultimately unfinished book were completed, but remained unpublished (such as 'Intellectual Attraction'[114] or 'The Montage of Film Attractions'[115]); some were published only in French or English journals at the time; yet others were never developed ('John and Schopenhauer') or only barely begun ('Khlebnikov', 'Ioffe', 'Le Paire'). The spherical book was also supposed to contain several commissioned essays. These included introductions to Nikolai Kaufman's monograph on Japanese film[116] and to the Russian version of *Filmtrick* by the famous German cameraman Guido Seeber,[117] as well as Eisenstein's contribution to the catalogue of an exhibition of the working group 'Film und Foto', commissioned by El Lissitzky's wife Sophie Küppers. ('The Dramaturgy of Film Form', which Eisenstein wrote in German, did not arrive in time to be published—the postal service was too slow.) 'The Montage of Attractions', 'Perspectives', 'The Fourth Dimension in Cinema', and 'An Unexpected Juncture' were scattered among various journals and never published in a coherent edition.[118]

How much was lost!

This 'ball' of essays looked at montage through various systems—music, Japanese drama and hieroglyphs, linguistics, reflexology, dialectics. Eisenstein managed to shift perspectives and dimensions, an achievement that he found extremely important in the late 1920s. Ultimately Eisenstein cared not about montage, but about film language and the future of film as such. Eisenstein was searching for new perspectives, which he called intellectual montage.

The whole of 1928 and the first half of 1929 were marked by this intense theoretical activity. In order to push ahead the study of the new film sign language, Eisenstein developed a research project with the psychologists Luria and Vygotsky and the linguist Nikolai Marr. On March 31, 1928 Eisenstein wrote in his diary: 'This is the eve of a great discovery, a watershed in the area of film consciousness.'[119] Unlike theoreticians who searched for the ontology of film in the photographic image, Eisenstein used a linguistic paradigm to describe montage in analogy to language. He viewed montage as a system of discreet units whose meaning could be determined only by context. He read the writings of the physiologists Ivan Sechenov and Vladimir Bekhterev, the Marxist philosopher Georgy Plekhanov and the idealist George Berkeley, the Swiss linguist Ferdinand de Saussure and the young Russian philologist Mikhail Bakhtin in order to trace the path from thought to speech, from sound to writing, from image to sign. He strove to make the process productive for film theory. Eisenstein called himself a scientific dilettante with encyclopedic interests.

The diversity of these essays is astonishing; they seem to have been written by different authors. 'The Dramaturgy of Film Form' is strictly Constructivist in its approach. Here Eisenstein deals with the central problems of modernity—movement and stasis in the new medium of film, mimesis and its negation in avant-garde art. 'The Fourth Dimension in Cinema' revives metaphysical ideas of the correspondences between image, sound, light, and color. The essay is influenced by the idea of the *Gesamtkunstwerk* as conceived by Scriabin and the Russian Symbolists, the Romantics, and Theosophists such as Elena Blavatskaya.

At this time Eisenstein was also interested in Marxist philosophy. He discovered dialectics by reading Lenin's *Philosophical Notebooks* (1929) and Engels. His views on psychology also underwent a transformation—this was due to a massive public campaign as much as to private insights. Power struggles within the Party led to the victory of dialectics, which Lenin favored as the only valid scientific method and the law of natural revolution and insight, over materialism, which had now been written off as 'reductionist', 'mechanical', and 'vulgar'. The prominent philosopher and founder of the dialectic-materialist society Abram Deborin was violently attacked and labeled a Trotskyite. In 1929 he was condemned by a Party resolution for mechanical tendencies in his philosophy.

The same move was made in psychology. Konstantin Kornilov, the director of Luria and Vygotsky's institute, was exposed as a 'Menshevik idealist' and relieved of his post. A Party resolution ordered all natural sciences to follow dialectics. The Psychoanalytic Society came under fire as well. Luria and Vygotsky announced their withdrawal.

Eisenstein also took up dialectics in 1929, but interpreted them in his way—as the study of conflict. He appropriated metaphors by Engels and Lenin: both thought that cell division modeled the transformation of quantitative changes to qualitative changes. Eisenstein used this metaphor to illustrate the law of the unity of opposites in film montage. The shot (a cell, also understood as an image or depiction) accumulated conflicts of foreground and background, of lines, contours, volumes, spots of light, masses, direction of movement, lighting, of an event and its temporal depiction in slow motion or timelapse. Conflict 'tore apart' the image and was then replaced (or resolved) by the next shot. The coexistence of conflicting shots could (potentially) cause the conflict to explode into a new quality. However, this transformation of quantity into quality was defined not by visual, but by psychological or semantic parameters (either by ideas or by concepts and images).[120] The dialectic leap that occurred at the intersection of two material pictures was to lead into a non-material sphere.

Eisenstein's 'spherical' book project responded to the disintegration of science into separate fields of study, one of the consequences of modernity. Eisenstein analyzed film as a specialist, but acted like a universal scholar from a past century who was looking for totality. His book was a radical attempt to locate a non-existent unity that consisted of shifting from one level to the next, of reinterpreting the incompatible segments and using them in diverse ways. But he did not explain the peculiarity of his mentality from a Constructivist point of view. A palm reader had once analyzed Eisenstein's hand and discovered that there were no traces of Apollo, but that the Mount of Mercury was well-developed—a sign that Eisenstein was gifted in the art of combining.

Eisenstein believed he could publish his book outside the Soviet Union. The English journal *Close Up* was in the process of printing several of his essays. The journal was published in Switzerland by Kenneth MacPherson and his wealthy wife Winifred Bryher.[121] Eisenstein told MacPherson that he would take the manuscript abroad.

Eisenstein never finished this ambitious book project even though—as he wrote MacPherson—he considered it his 'most serious and basic' project to date.[122]

Diary, February 12, 1928: 'I am beginning to write a lyrical diary—the tragic Shklovsky says I should not write articles, but just publish materials towards my articles. But they don't understand me anyway.'[123] He was referring to his new concept of 'intellectual film'. Eisenstein thought that people needed to be taught to 'see' intellectual film just as they were taught how to read and write. He would give lectures and interviews on the subject in Western Europe and in the United States. At first Eisenstein would speak of this phenomenon in the future tense, then he switched to past tense. The only film project that realized this newfound principle and developed its methodology remained a sketch in his diaries: in March and April 1928 he planned to film *Capital*. He attempted to apply Joyce's associative inner monologue to Marx and to illustrate the dialectic of history. The historian Alexei Efimov, who also compiled a list of events for *October*, offered a supply of historical material for the new film project. More than ever before Eisenstein wished to demonstrate a new narrative logic that transcended 'stories' and 'anecdotes': a woman cooks soup—an everyday event that cannot be separated from world history. Eisenstein used the pepper in the soup to create a chain of associations: 'Pepper, Cayenne. Dreyfus. French chauvinism. That 'Figaro' in the hands of Krupp. War. In the harbor sank English ships.'[124] He also made a transition from the spirit-stove to oil: 'This will be the sphere of the concept-explanation, that is freed by the subject, from the primitive. Love—'like I love', or tiredness—'like a tired man'.'[125] He tried to talk about the project with his new, powerful friends: 'I saw Podvoisky yesterday. He is against *Capital*.'[126]

As Eisenstein delved into theoretical work, a field that afforded him immense creative growth, he also discovered another exciting, analytic activity: teaching. On May 12, 1928 he was given a post at the Film Institute, then called the Technical College for Film. He opened his directorial laboratory, a 'research workshop' (he borrowed this term from Meyerhold), where he wanted to uncover the secrets of art with his students. The first assignment was to read Zola's novels and to analyze how the French writer represented love, death, and ecstasy with different kinds of material. He planned to turn this research into an independent treatise on pathos from a reflexologist perspective. Instruction was the first step towards theory. He would often discuss a concept with his friends and students before he wrote it down. Atasheva and Obolensky became his 'guinea pigs' and assistants.

Meanwhile Eisenstein was supposed to finish a very specific film—the one that had been postponed for *October*—about Stalin's plan to reshape rural Russia. In late January Eisenstein announced that he would edit and add a soundtrack to *The General Line* in Germany. But on February 12, 1928 Alexander Krinitsky and Fyodor Raskolnikov viewed the rough cut. (Eisenstein later blacked out their names in his diary). The erotic, psychoanalytic grotesque had little to do with the dramatic situation in the countryside and had even less to do with the Party's expectations. How would he have to change the film?! 'K. and R. viewed *The General Line*. We will renew the film together and adapt it to the directives of the 15th Party Congress.'[127]

Eisenstein made the film before anybody knew what dramatic effects Stalin's General Line would have on the countryside. Eisenstein seems not to have perceived the changing reality all around him. Only occasionally do his judgments during this time hint at some clairvoyance: Friedrich Ermler, a friend and fellow director from Leningrad, told Eisenstein the plot of his new film, *A*

Fragment of Empire, in which a man loses his memory for ten years and wakes up in the present in a socialist paradise. Eisenstein made the following note: 'What terrible skepticism and pessimism of this time is displayed in the idealism of Ermler's story!'[128]

On June 20, 1928 Eisenstein returned to Konstantinovo for reshoots. Soon the team found a village near Penza called Nevezhka, where people still lived as they had under Ivan the Terrible. None of the inhabitants had ever seen a railroad or any industrial products. They had no idea what film was. He continued filming until fall, but had to interrupt work on location: Marfa Lapkina took time off to give birth.

Eisenstein was again supposed to finish the film by the November festivities, but he missed the deadline. According to a Sovkino announcement in the newspaper *Izvestiya*, the film was finally completed on January 31, 1929. The film passed the censorship on February 14; the big screening was to be on March 8, International Women's Day. Pomp and circumstance were planned for the premiere. There would be a giant milk separator and a tractor outside the Bolshoi Theater. Critics published euphoric reviews of the 'film of the era', sight unseen. Henri Barbusse and Theodore Dreiser spoke of the film in interviews.

But it all turned out differently. The first Five-Year-Plan was passed in April 1929. It envisioned the collectivization of agriculture and marked a sharp turn in policy. Twenty-five million peasants were to be dispossessed and resettled. After one year, this policy led to a catastrophe. Widespread famine caused the death of millions of peasants. Stalin had had his way: the Party had been militarized, the opposition had been banned. In 1929 Trotsky was shipped abroad after two years of internal exile. The group around Bukharin had lost the internal Party war over the reform of agriculture. In early April 1929 Stalin and the Central Committee viewed Eisenstein's film to see if it still conformed to the new policy. This is how Stalin's comments were later recorded: 'The film misses the fundamentals of the Party line. The village is shown as something unified and immovable. But it is the expression of a process, of class warfare. One wishes in the end to see Marfa Lapkina in a resort on the Crimea, in the tsar's former palace in Livadia; her lover, the tractor driver, should be seated on the tsar's throne.'[129]

Stalin was annoyed by the ambivalent representation of the village in transition. He had already proved how violently he could rage against those who doubted him in his attacks on Andrei Platonov, who had published 'Makar the Doubtful' in 1929. His anger was notorious.

After the screening, Stalin spoke to Eisenstein and Alexandrov. They received permission to go abroad for a lengthy period of time if Eisenstein would first rework the film. Stalin recommended that Eisenstein travel within Russia to film impressive images of success. He also needed to change the title. *The General Line* was outdated.

The euphoric press campaign stopped immediately. Even though several copies of the film had already been printed, Eisenstein agreed to make a new version. But he could not quite bring himself to include the happy end with the tractor driver on the throne—the image that Stalin seemed to have taken straight from *October*.

In April Eisenstein took his camera team to Shakhty and Rostov, where they visited a plant that made agricultural machinery. Then they traveled to the northern Caucasus. They spent a month on the road. By late June, Eisenstein had finished a new version with a different finale: hundreds of tractors rode around in circles on an endless field. A grandiose image and a clever move: tractors were *the* precursors of Stalin's industrialization. The biggest tractor factory was built in a town that was given Stalin's name in 1925. Eisenstein shot this sequence at the state farm 'Gigant', which was later also to be renamed 'Stalin'.

He wanted to leave the country as soon as possible and took off for Berlin before the film's premiere. The first showing took place on October 7, 1929, without Eisenstein and without any pomp. What is more, the film received damning reviews in advance. The first negative review was published in *Izvestiya* on August 23.

Young critics defended the film. Old, experienced reviewers attacked it and claimed that the Party was missing in the film. The satirists Ilya Ilf and Evgeny Petrov wrote a nasty *feuilleton* in the magazine *Chudak* under the pseudonym Don Busilio. The title of their piece was '1001 Villages'. Boris Alpers noticed that 'Lapkina's acting was shocking in its animal pathology and hysterical affectation'.[130]

The film ran parallel to *The Bargirl Tanka*, a mediocre children's agitational melodrama, a kind of Soviet equivalent to *Variety* or *Robin Hood*, films that had competed against Eisenstein's earlier movies. Sometimes the two movies would even be combined in the same showing. The film flopped in the absence of the director, who could not avoid learning of its failure. Friends sent Eisenstein detailed letters with reports and clipped reviews. His bitterness was quickly overshadowed by the rich impressions of his journey. Eisenstein's powerful friends had warned him in advance that the film would be panned. Krinitsky had phoned him to tell him how the reviews would turn out. He explained the political necessity of the critique and asked Eisenstein not to take the issue personally. They still trusted him completely.

Eisenstein left the Soviet Union at a time when trips abroad had become something special. Bulgakov, Pasternak and even Mayakovsky had been turned down for passports in 1929 and 1930. After Trotsky's deportation to Turkey in the summer of 1929, there was a wave of arrests and executions of 'the opposition'. Towards the end of the summer a campaign began against the writers Evgeny Zamyatin and Boris Pilnyak. They had both published their work abroad; the tone of the campaign was exceptionally harsh. The Formalist school was crushed in 1929; its members stopped publishing. The administration of the Art Theater was replaced, and several philologists were arrested or relieved of their posts. The Association of Proletarian Writers (RAPP) took the lead in these attacks.

Eisenstein had left the Soviet Union with Alexandrov and Tisse just a bit earlier, on August 19, 1929. They left with 25 dollars each, a fresh print of the film, which had been renamed *The Old and the New* at Stalin's behest, and an ambivalent assignment: 'Learn from the West and teach the West.'

THE JOURNEY
1929-1930

The official reason for the journey abroad was 'the study of sound film'. Since the Americans were most advanced in the area of sound, the trip was supposed to take the filmmakers to Hollywood. Eisenstein already had an invitation from Joseph M. Schenk in his pocket. There were rumors going around Moscow that Schenk, the son of Russian Jewish émigrés, was a distant relative on Eisenstein's mother's side of the family, and that was why Eisenstein was having so much luck. The travelers had to wait until they were in Berlin to apply for an American visa, since there was no American consulate in Moscow. The German entry visa was fairly easy to get. Eisenstein, Alexandrov and Tisse took off for Berlin. They had matching blue suits tailored just for the trip.

Their train derailed in Warsaw, but that barely delayed their arrival in Berlin, and on August 21 they stepped onto the platform at the Zoo station. They stopped off at the Marie-Luise guest house on Martin-Luther-Straße. Leonid Obolensky, an old friend from Kuleshov's workshop, was already staying there; he had also been sent to Germany to study sound film.

They spent several days watching American movies, most of them starring Al Jolson, a singing movie star and son of a rabbi from Russia. An employee of the Russian trade mission who tested films for future acquisition threw a party in the Hotel Esplanade for the Society of Friends of the New Russia. Reichskunstwart Dr. Redslob, Alexander Granach, Hans Richter and Alfred Döblin all gave speeches.

Richter was just about to leave for La Sarraz in Switzerland, where the Congress of Independent Filmmakers was gathering from September 3-7. He was one of the meeting's initiators. Dziga Vertov had been invited to represent Soviet Russia, but he had decided that he would rather continue filming in the Don Basin. Richter invited the guests to take Vertov's place. However, they were unable to get Swiss visas, since Switzerland did not maintain diplomatic relations with the Soviet Union. A coincidence came to the rescue. The Swiss entrepreneur Lazar Wechsler, son of Russian émigrés and owner of Praesens-Film (a *Potemkin* distributor), wanted to become known as the founder of Swiss national cinema. According to Wechsler's plans, Sergei Eisenstein would shoot the first Swiss film, and he would be the producer. He had already found a hot topic: abortion. When Wechsler heard of the problems that the Russians faced coming to La Sarraz, he offered to smuggle them into Switzerland in his car. He expected them to make his film in return. They left at once. At Eisenstein's request they stopped at the most famous German art museums: the Zwinger in Dresden and the Pinakothek in Munich.

The Swiss police spied out the Russians in the La Sarraz château. Instead of deporting them, the governor allowed them to stay—as long as they promised not to leave the château. The penalty for breaking the rule was up to three days of prison and a fine of 15 Francs. The governor was one of Eisenstein's fans, so he treated the Russians as artists and not as representatives of a hostile regime.

The château belonged to the aging patroness Madame Hélène de Mandrot. The previous year she had brought together almost all noteworthy avant-garde architects to found CIAM (Congres intérnational de l'architecture). This year she had turned her attention to film. Walter Ruttmann, Hans Richter, Enrico Prampolini, Béla Balázs, Alberto Cavalcanti and Ivor Montagu—directors, artists and critics—had all gathered to discuss means of producing and distributing non-commercial films in Europe. They also founded their own professional organization, but it would dissolve only two years later because of political disagreements.

Directors and critics watched the newest productions on a screen that was stretched over the château's medieval archways: *Un chien andalou* by Luis Buñuel and Salvador Dali, Carl Theodor Dreyer's *The Passion of Joan of Arc*, and Eisenstein's *The Old and the New*. The meeting was a sort of film festival ahead of its time. Ivor Montagu, an Englishman from a respected aristocratic family, had just turned 25 years old and had already worked for Alfred Hitchcock. He had also founded and now directed the London Film Society with Jacob Isaacs, who would later become professor of theater history at King's College. La Sarraz was Montagu's first chance to meet the Russians. He noted that Tisse and Alexandrov were young, slim, handsome, blond, and tanned. Eisenstein appeared older and stocky, with small feminine hands and an enormous head. But Eisenstein was always the center of attention, even in the circles of the European film avant-garde.

Before La Sarraz, Eisenstein had seen only a few films of this sort and had spoken of them with condescension. He thought they were nothing more than formal finger exercises in comparison to his own movies. He wanted to revolutionize not only the film medium, but also the world itself. Now he watched the abstract works by Richter and Ruttmann, Man Ray, and Viking Eggeling. He was most astonished by the Surrealism of *Un chien andalou*. He would later share his impressions with Jean Cocteau in Paris.

While Ruttman lectured on sound film Eisenstein spoke on mimesis in film. He had to place his films, which did not renounce the imitation of reality, in the context of the European avant-garde and defend his position. Four years earlier Kazimir Malevich had already told Eisenstein that his films were excessively naturalistic and could therefore never be put on a level with modern abstract art.[131] At home Eisenstein did not need to respond to this criticism. The effect of his revolutionary movies, their lack of plot, and his use of montage guaranteed their place in the avant-garde. But here he was confronted with abstract film. Was he perhaps a conservative artist?

In his lecture 'Imitation as Mastery',[132] Eisenstein developed a Platonic opposition between appearance and inner essence. How was cinema, a photographic art form that brought together essence and appearance on the visible surface of the material world, supposed to deal with this fissure? The desire to imitate, according to Eisenstein, comes from the longing for immortality that is materialized in art itself. Since art is rooted in a mythological consciousness which lacks the higher cerebral functions to differentiate between object and subject, between a thing and its representation, between man and nature, a form of 'cannibalism' develops in art: form is identical with the object; by imitating a phenomenon in a material immortal form, the phenomenon itself is also immortalized. The development of modern intellect has overcome this mythological, magical thinking, and all other art forms have outgrown the era of imitation. Only cinema has remained 'cannibalistic'. The 'visible man', the actor, is a remnant of that ancient form of thought. Film should take an example from architecture: Le Corbusier, Walter Gropius and Bruno Taut do not ape the proportions of the body, but examine the inner logic of its proportions. Among the crowd at La Sarraz, Eisenstein's defense of abstract film sounded like a diplomatic maneuver. Eisenstein told Hans Richter that he thought film art was still too primitive.

Béla Balázs listened to Eisenstein's elaboration and called him a 'hopeless Kantian dualist'.[133] Eisenstein took his own form of revenge. He made a film with the congress participants called *The Storm over La Sarraz*, a playful allegory about the struggle of independent film against commercial cinema. Knight Bluebeard (played by Jacob Isaacs), boss of a mighty film company, keeps watch over independent film, embodied by the journalist Janine Bouissounouse (a friend of Jean-Georges Auriol, the publisher of the Paris film journal *Revue du cinéma*), who is locked in chains. A young army of knights led by Léon Moussinac (alias D'Artagnan) comes to her rescue. Bluebeard's loyal servants, headed by Béla Balázs, put up fierce resistance. (This was possibly an allusion to an argument between Richter and Balázs over elite and mass film: Balázs vehemently defended the latter.) Finally a Japanese man wearing the mask of commercial film commits hara-kiri. This latter was the goal of the congress. Eisenstein himself played Don Quixote. In hindsight, that role looks like a carnivalesque precursor to Eisenstein's later battles against the windmills of Hollywood.

The film has been lost. For a long time there has been speculation that it may never have existed. Hans Richter claimed that the Russians were so poor that they could not have afforded any film stock and that, at Eisenstein's request, Tisse had used an empty cartridge. But that is probably not true. Japanese participants in the congress apparently took the film home to Japan, where it was screened in 1930.

The congress concluded on September 7. The Russians' journey continued through Basel, Lausanne, Bern, and Zurich. The three men needed money, so they shot the abortion film that Wechsler had ordered. *Frauennot—Frauenglück* ('Women's Misery—Women's Happiness') was an educational film with an entertaining plot that depicted the fates of several women: the wife of an unemployed worker despairs over her pregnancy; a saleswoman dies of an illegal abortion; a rich lady is able to afford a hospital procedure. They spent a week shooting at the gynecological clinic in Zurich, staying at Wechsler's house. Wechsler also accompanied them on sightseeing tours through Switzerland. Eisenstein was set on seeing a cesarean birth, and the group received permission to watch the operation. However, the surgical procedures as shown in the film did not consist of documentary footage, but were all staged.

Eisenstein later denied that he had directed this movie, although several on-scene photographs contradict his account. The film was attributed to Tisse, and Eisenstein was listed as the artistic supervisor. The Swiss cameraman Emil Berna later said that Eisenstein was present every morning for the close-ups. He would then spend his afternoons reading on the terrace of a hotel on the lake.

Eisenstein gave lectures in Zurich on September 10, 14, 16, and 17. This naturally came to the attention of the authorities, who expelled him on September 18. By September 19 Eisenstein was back in Berlin.

Albert Einstein's son-in-law Dmitry Maryanov took care of Eisenstein and arranged meetings with various celebrities. Eisenstein was looking for work and commissions. One morning he had breakfast with Luigi Pirandello, who had just been invited to work for Paramount. Eisenstein could still only dream of such luck. Another man present at the meeting was a good friend of the American billionaire Otto H. Kahn. Kahn was an art-collector and a generous donor to the Metropolitan Opera. He could potentially help Eisenstein establish a connection to Paramount, since he had financially invested in the company. Eisenstein had high hopes after this encounter.

He met Pirandello in an Italian restaurant, dined with Rabindranath Tagore's nephew in an Indian restaurant, met Dreiser's publisher Horace Liveright at the Adlon, ate sushi with the Japanese. He joined the Berlin art crowd—the expressionist playwright Ernst Toller, the Dada artist George Grosz, the creator of epic theater Erwin Piscator, the expressive dancer Valeska Gert—at the Romanisches Café, where he became a regular. Eisenstein had an insatiable hunger for impressions. Kenneth MacPherson, an attractive Englishman who had been publishing the film magazine *Close Up* with his wife's money since 1927, met Eisenstein just after the group's return to Berlin. Eisenstein drank hot chocolate with loads of cream and ate a pile of éclairs. They chatted about film theory and Eisenstein's articles in *Close Up*. They also discussed Eisenstein's book. MacPherson intended to make a film that would combine Eisenstein's montage theory and psychoanalysis. He wanted his lover, the poet Hilda Doolittle, and Paul Robeson to play the leads. He had just hired the young Berlin architect Hermann Henselmann to design a house to be built in Switzerland. The house would double as a set for the film. He invited Eisenstein to his home and introduced him to Hanns Sachs, the director of the Berlin Psycho-analytic Institute. Sachs had advised G. W. Pabst on the first psychoanalytic film *Secrets of the Soul* (Geheimnisse einer Seele, 1926) and had written an article on psy-choanalysis and film for *Close Up*. The article included an analysis of *Potemkin*.

Hanns Sachs invited Eisenstein to give a lecture in October at the Berlin Psychoanalytic Institute. Eisenstein chose 'expressive movement' as the sub-ject of his talk. He understood 'expressive movement' to be the realization of the conflict between the drive and the suppressive force of will. He interpreted this movement as a kind of Freudian parapraxis.

The institute's interior had been designed by Freud's son, an architect; the institute itself was financed by the illustrious Max Eitington, one of Freud's Russian students, who had made big money trading in Russian furs. Rumor had it that the money actually came from his brother Naum, who was in cahoots with the GPU. It later was alleged that Naum had organized several terrorist acts abroad. He was said to be behind the kidnapping of former White Army generals and Trotsky's murder. Naum was the commanding officer of Ramon Mercader, who bludgeoned Trotsky to death in 1940, and the lover of Ramon's mother. It is unclear whether Eisenstein met these people while he was in Berlin.

Eisenstein also visited Sachs' private practice in the Mommsenstraße. They discussed the death penalty and Sachs' thoughts about art. The psychoanalyst gave Eisenstein a copy of Sándor Ferenczi's *Thalassa: A Theory of Genitality*. Eisenstein later called it the most interesting psychoanalytic book he had ever read.

The Gestalt psychologist Kurt Lewin seems to have attended Eisenstein's lectures as well. This was exceptional, since the university's psychologists scoffed at psychoanalysis. The two schools had virtually no contact; Freud's name was taboo at the Psychological Institute. However, Kurt Lewin was known for his interest in psychoanalysis and the subject of the lectures in-trigued him. He was developing his own theory of behavior with his Russian assistants Bluma Zeigarnik and Tamara Dembo at the time. He would later call his work 'field theory'. Kurt Lewin was also an enthusiastic filmmaker who used a camera in his research. He filmed the expressions, affects, actions, and movements of his subjects, who were mostly children. He showed Eisenstein his films and invited the director to participate in making them—he wanted advice from a specialist. Alexander Luria had already recommended Eisenstein to Lewin in a letter—the two psychologists were friends. Lewin was so impressed by Eisenstein's talk that he immediately wrote him: 'Of course I spent a long time thinking about your lecture. You do know that I hold your theory of expression in higher esteem than any psychologist's work on the subject.'[134] He suggested that Eisenstein repeat his lecture at the Berlin Psychological Institute. Eisenstein also became acquainted with Wolfgang Köhler, the institute's director. When Luria heard about the invitation, he urged Eisenstein to accept, since the offer was an unbelievable honor for a Russian scholar, but they could not find time to arrange the talk.

Eisenstein's adventures in these circles remained hidden from the public. They also knew nothing of one of Eisenstein's other passions: in the company of Valeska Gert and the *Film-Kurier* critic Hans Feld, Eisenstein frequented gay, lesbian, and transvestite cafés in Berlin. They stopped by the famous club Eldorado, as well as other lesser-known establishments. To Feld's great amusement, Eisenstein bought a number of occult and pornographic books. That was not the way he had imagined a revolutionary artist! Valeska Gert, who played the part of Eisenstein's lover, was deeply disappointed by Eisenstein's reaction to her signs of affection. 'Your lack of instinct regarding women made you mistake my sympathy for something completely different,' she wrote in a letter, 'namely for horniness and interest in the *man* Eisenstein, and that's the way you treated me. Your false opinion about my attitude has a laming and torturous effect on me . . . . The amount of egotism you develop towards someone you are forced to perceive as more like you than anybody else is punishable. It's starting to make me freezing cold inside.'[135]

Schenk wrote to Eisenstein in Berlin and said he could not offer him a contract. The capacity of United Artists was limited by the stock market crash in September 1929 and by the film moguls' bitter competition over the transition to sound. The Russians needed to look for other opportunities. Their search for a connection to the film industry led Eisenstein to Mikhail Dubson, an employee of the Soviet trade mission who was shooting the film *Poison Gas* at 'Loewfilm'. The man behind the company was Arthur Loew, son of the late MGM-mogul Marcus Loew. Arthur was also the son-in-law of Paramount president Adolph Zukor. Russian actors Vera Baranovskaya (now an émigrée) and her husband Valery Inkizhinov, Eisenstein's biomechanics teacher at Meyerhold's school, had parts in the movie. Eisenstein went to the set at the Efa-studio and directed several scenes. But when the Berlin press announced his involvement, he denied that he had participated in the shooting. In mid-

October Eisenstein went to Babelsberg to meet Josef von Sternberg, who had a contract with Paramount. Sternberg had just been sent to Germany from Hollywood to direct a sound film, *The Blue Angel*. Eisenstein gave him a book by Malevich that had been published in German as part of the Bauhaus series. Sternberg showed Eisenstein several excerpts from his new movie. During a dinner Eisenstein watched two great actors, Emil Jannings and George Bancroft, try to steal each other's show. Since Eisenstein had already received a number of offers from advertising agencies, he spontaneously suggested shooting a beer commercial with the two stars. The plans never went beyond a dinner joke.

Liza Michelson also sought out Eisenstein, but he tried to avoid her and replied only after her fourth letter. Eisenstein felt that he was being watched. His suspicions proved to be well founded. He met the director Friedrich Ermler, who told him that some people in Moscow thought his trip had gone on too long without achieving the desired results.

Eisenstein kept looking for assignments and was strapped for cash. He received some money for the essays published in *Close Up* and earned some cash from lectures and performances. The Moscow print of his film helped him get these engagements. On October 18 he went to Hamburg to give a lecture and his first radio interview. Invitations to Holland and Belgium followed his Hamburg performance. On his way to Brussels, Eisenstein stopped in Cologne to see the cathedral.

In November Eisenstein traveled to London. Montagu kept the promise he had made in La Sarraz and arranged the invitation. Eisenstein was to attend a screening of *Potemkin* on November 10 and to give lectures at the Film Society. Hans Richter accompanied him; Grisha and Tisse stayed in Germany. Montagu had booked rooms in the luxury hotel West End, but neither Richter nor Eisenstein had a penny for tips, so they moved to the Lincoln Hall Hotel near Russell Square. The lectures were not the only reason for their journey. Meisel, who now lived in London, wanted to write the score for Eisenstein's *The Old and the New* and was negotiating with British International Pictures. In London, Eisenstein heard Meisel's music for the first time. The composer himself conducted, but Eisenstein was dissatisfied with the performance. Meisel stole the show and the applause. Eisenstein acted annoyed and said that Meisel had misunderstood the rhythm and covered up the film with his melodies. In addition, the print was incomplete and Meisel slowed the film down to match his music. Eisenstein was most incensed by this last violent alteration of his rhythm. Negotiations about a score for the new film came to naught.

One week later, on November 18, Eisenstein met George Bernard Shaw and told him of his admiration for *Arms and the Man*. Shaw immediately gave Eisenstein the rights to film the play, but he could offer no money for the production. The next day Eisenstein began his lecture series at the Film Society. The audience was full of young people who would later become important English film directors: Basil Wright (who eagerly took notes), John Grierson, Anthony Asquith. Other noteworthy listeners included Ivor Montagu, Thorold Dickinson, Herbert Marshall and Jacob Isaacs. Eisenstein spoke of Kabuki and hieroglyphs, Darwin and Toulouse-Lautrec, Arsène Lupin and James Joyce. He visited all the museums in London. He was most intrigued by Leonardo da Vinci's manuscripts.

On November 29 Eisenstein left London for Paris, where he met James Joyce the next day. The writer had already gone almost blind, but he asked Eisenstein to show him his films anyway. They spoke of the inner monologue and ways of filming *Ulysses*. Joyce thought only two directors could do the job: Eisenstein and Ruttmann.

Tisse and Alexandrov were waiting for Eisenstein in Paris. They could even afford a hotel, because they had just been paid to do the postproduction of *Women's Misery—Women's Happiness*. The movie was going to be edited in Paris. Although he disavowed his participation as director, Eisenstein never denied his involvement in the film's montage.

Eisenstein's friends Moussinac and the young critic Jean Mitry accompanied Eisenstein on his exploration of the city. He made a glum, melancholic impression on them. Perhaps appearances were misleading. Eisenstein himself thought that the city turned him into a salon lion; meanwhile he wrote that Paris salons 'lionized' him. Exclusive and fashionable photographers like Man Ray and André Kertész took his portrait. Germaine Krull and Buñuel's cameraman Eli Lotar were also given permission to take his picture. Man Ray earned money by photographing high-society ladies who visited his studio. Kertész was even allowed to immortalize the ladies in their villas. Eisenstein asked Kertész if he could come along and carry the tripod. He wanted to observe the ladies 'without their posery'.

Eisenstein continued his search for bizarre characters and famous people. He was both a gourmet and omnivore in everything. He had no free time either for his diary or for letters. He sent Pera and his mother postcards. His calendar was completely booked; a new celebrity awaited him each day.

On December 3 he returned to London. Hans Richter was filming the exercise *Everyday* with his film students, a project he would not complete until 1968. Eisenstein played the role of an English bobby and danced an eccentric dance in front of the camera. He traveled to Cambridge with Richter to speak on the psychology of art. He dined with the Russian physicist Pyotr Kapitsa and Kapitsa's English colleagues. The tranquillity of Cambridge so deeply impressed Eisenstein that he told Richter he would give up film to live and work there. He could imagine spending the rest of his life at the university, in the library among old books. Eisenstein was only 31.

On December 20 Eisenstein returned to Paris, where he stayed until early May with short interruptions (lectures in Holland and Berlin). He raced through much of France in an old car, a 1909 Hotchkiss that he bought for a laughable sum.

He feverishly looked for work, but the French and German film industries were stingy with offers. Small companies wanted to give him advertising jobs— the Western European version of the social assignments so familiar to him from home. In a letter to Atasheva he described them as a 'cascade of fantastic, suspect, beguiling offers'.[136] Nestlé wanted a commercial for condensed milk and tempted Eisenstein with a world trip through five continents. No other director, so the company's spokesperson said, had ever depicted milk in such an impressive manner. He was referring to the scene of the milk separator in *The Old and the New*. Another company tried to get him to make a movie for the centenary of Belgium's independence. A French firm asked him to film the biography of the English oil magnate and arms merchant Basil Zacharoff. This offer tempted Eisenstein. He wanted to meld Zacharoff, whose biography had been published in the United States as *The Mystery Man of Europe*, with the Swedish match king Ivan Kreuger and the banker Löwenstein, who had jumped out of an airplane window after the Black Friday crash. This composite character would be 'the man of darkness'. He had even found a title for these tragic heroes of the depression: *The Twilight of the Gods*. Eisenstein discussed filming a Zola novel with Gaumont; Societé générale du film was interested in a screen version of Albert Londres' novel *Le chemin de Buenos Aires* ('The Road to Buenos Aires'), but these negotiations failed. An offer arrived from Berlin to film the history of Eldorado according to Stefan Zweig's novel. A Venezuelan suggestion involved making a picture about Simon de Bolívar in South America; the Markus Company sent Eisenstein that libretto on March 21, 1930. Trotsky's son Lev Sedov met with Eisenstein in Paris and tried to convince him to liberate himself by becoming an Argentinean citizen. The opera singer Feodor Chaliapin, who was unable to sympathize with the Bolsheviks and left Russia in 1921, wanted to play Don Quixote; he even offered to finance the project himself, but he did not have enough money. The famous *diseuse* Yvette Guilbert dreamed of the role of Catherine the Great under Eisenstein's direction. She did not have any money either. In England, the film section of the British Chamber of Commerce wanted Eisenstein to make a film about Africa. Montagu conveyed this offer. Eisenstein declined—he thought the project had too much of a colonial tinge.

Eisenstein's funds grew tighter, and negotiations with the United States dragged on. In the meantime, Alexandrov got to know the pearl trader Léonhard Rosenthal. Rosenthal's girlfriend Mara Gris was a Russian émigrée who dreamed of becoming a film star. Rosenthal was willing to finance a short sound film, *Romance sentimentale*, to promote her. The film was very simple: Mara sings a romance at a white grand piano; the mood of the music is reflected in associative scenic images. This was Eisenstein's first opportunity to experiment with sound film, and he worked on the film with dedication. He described his work with sound montage in a letter to Pera. He wanted her to rewrite his ideas and publish them as an article: 'The sound is cut into the visual montage composition right 'on the [editing] table'. Film practitioners abroad used to consider this kind of sound montage to be impossible. *Romance sentimentale* has to some extent successfully realized our thoughts and experiments in the 'play with sound': we have written in or drawn in sound, increased and reduced the tempo; we have made the sound go backwards, regulated it in special ways and recorded sound to pre-exposed film. All of this produced remarkable results. Our work with sound deformation and the creation of new, previously non-existent sounds was successful and created an unusually strong physiological effect. This must be why our small experiment, the *Romance*, elicited such a stormy reaction. Whenever we lacked pre-recorded sounds, we drew and touched up the exposed film itself. This process created the necessary effect. In several spots, we scratched the film with a ruling pen— this is how we caused explosions, thunder, etc.'[137]

In Berlin, *Romance sentimentale* was shown in a double feature with *The Battleship Potemkin* and received only negative reviews. The film's reception was no better in France or in England. As he had done in the past, Eisenstein denied that he had anything to do with the film. In the German press, Hans Richter announced that claims of Eisenstein's participation were false. This caution was well planned: Eisenstein did not want to waste his fame on small change.

In early 1930 Eisenstein was introduced to the Paris art world. He became acquainted with James Joyce's first publisher Sylvia Beach, who ran a small bookshop. He also met Fernand Léger, a visual artist deeply influenced by industrial technology, the surrealist poet Robert Desnos, who had begun to write film scripts, and Jean Cocteau, who was then working on his first film *Le Sang d'un poète*. Cocteau gave him a copy of his book *Les enfants terribles* with the inscription, 'to the person who shocked me by showing me what I had only touched with the hands of a blind man.' The Futurist painter Enrico Prampolini, whom Eisenstein had met in La Sarraz, introduced him to Marinetti. The bloated Marinetti, one of the first Futurists and now an avowed Fascist, gave Eisenstein his newly printed book and wrote, 'for the great Futurist talent'. Eisenstein also got to know Viconte Charles de Noailles, who had just financed Buñuel and Dali's film *L'Âge d'or*. His wife was a descendant of the Marquis de Sade. Eisenstein's hopes that Noailles would also be his patron were in vain.

At this time, Eisenstein was living on the Boulevard Montparnasse in the Hotel des Etats-Unis. Léger introduced him to Man Ray's lover, the model Kiki.
She had been immortalized as the woman with the cello back; she lived in the Café
Dôme and in La Coupole. Kiki gave Eisenstein a copy of her memoirs and drew his
portrait, which was published on December 26, 1930 in the magazine *Pour Vous*.

Eisenstein had visited all the disreputable cafés in Berlin; in Paris he frequented Catholic book stores, collected religious souvenirs and drove to many
pilgrimage sites: Chartres, Reims, Amiens, Lisieux, Domremy, and Lourdes. 'I
am interested in the places of religious ecstasy,' he told Moussinac, who often
accompanied him.

In Paris he met the vice president of the French Psychoanalytic Society,
Dr. René Allendy, who was also the psychoanalyst of Anaïs Nin, Henry Miller,
and Antonin Artaud and a friend of Hanns Sachs. Allendy translated books
and articles from Russian under the pseudonym 'soudeba' (Russian for 'fate').
He wrote about the subconscious, dreams, and early forms of thinking for the
journal *L'Esprit nouveau*, which was edited by Amédée Ozenfant and Le
Corbusier. In 1927 he had already published an essay on the psychological values of the image in *L'Art cinématographique*. His book *Capitalisme et Sexualité* came
out in 1931. All these topics were on Eisenstein's mind during this period.
Eisenstein and Allendy discussed French mysticism and various manifestations of
ecstasy, including art. Eisenstein thought that art was a transitional stage that
would only be necessary until the social body had secured its biological paradise.
He wrote Magnus Hirschfeld that art was a 'biological necessity'.

In early January 1930 Eisenstein spent a short time in Holland. He was
welcomed by dozens of reporters at the Rotterdam airfield—they had mis-
taken him for Einstein. He visited the Van Gogh museum in Amsterdam and
gave two lectures. He also traveled to Zaandam to see the house of Peter I. On
January 20 he flew from Amsterdam back to Berlin. On January 22 he visited
Magnus Hirschfeld's institute. Hirschfeld was the first public defender of homosexuality in Germany. Eisenstein did not meet Hirschfeld but his assistant
and became involved in a discussion of open homosexuality and of Hegel's bisexu-
ality. Eisenstein was still not sure if his own sexual behavior was 'normal'.

The next day, his thirty-second birthday, Eisenstein raced from one meeting to another. He saw Hans Feld at eleven o'clock; met Balázs at two thirty to
talk about the titles for his village picture; chatted with Alfred Kerr, Montagu,
and Toller at three thirty; at six thirty he met Richter; at eight thirty Asta
Nielsen, the film star whose androgynous beauty and talent for tragedy had
enraptured European artists. She now lived with the Russian émigré and actor Grigory Khmara. Three days later Eisenstein had tea with Albert Einstein—
Maryanov had arranged the meeting. On January 29 he went to Brussels to

give a lecture and then returned to Paris.

On February 17 René Allendy organized a screening of *The Old and the New* at the Sorbonne, where he led a group in philosophical and scientific studies (today one might call his field 'interdisciplinary'). Two thousand people gathered to see the film, but the police interfered and forbade the screening. Eisenstein turned his introduction into a full-length lecture on intellectual film. The talk was followed by a discussion of the differences between capitalist and socialist film production, between a mass-film and an Eisenstein-film. Eisenstein also spoke of his project for *Capital*. His French was an amusing mixture of high style and argot, and he provoked a lively audience response. The evening ended in 'Le Bâteau ivre'. The next morning Eisenstein was awakened by the police. The event turned into a political scandal that had less to do with Eisenstein's performance than with an operation of the Soviet secret service. On January 26 GPU agents kidnapped General Alexander Kutepov, the leader of the Union of the Russian Military in Exile, in Paris. The kidnapping provoked a huge protest campaign in diplomatic and political circles. The protest was directed against the Soviet embassy, but came to include all Soviet citizens living in France. They were considered co-conspirators. An employee of the Soviet embassy, Georgy Berezovsky, who had just escaped from the guarded embassy under sensational circumstances and asked for political asylum, had divulged some of the intricacies of the affair. Eisenstein's visa expired against this backdrop, so his request for an extension was rejected. Eisenstein and his coworkers were now threatened with deportation. The police searched their hotel room; Eisenstein was taken to the police station and interrogated.

Once he was released, Eisenstein ran all over Paris from one celebrity to the next. All promised to use their connections to settle the matter. The threat of deportation was serious, since it could have dashed all of Eisenstein's hopes for Hollywood. Charismatic novelists André Malraux, Colette, Cocteau and film director Jean Painlevé, son of the former war minister, tried to help or at least cheer up Eisenstein. Cocteau gave him free tickets to his play *The Human Voice*, which had just premiered in the Comédie Française on February 14. Eisenstein took Paul Eluard along to the theater. Eluard caused a scandal and gave Eisenstein the proud feeling of having started a protest. Abel Gance, whom he visited the next day on the set to *End of the World*, promised to talk to two ministers about the visa. Colette met with the secretary to the foreign minister. On March 25 the premier received a petition signed by prominent artists and intellectuals. Cocteau turned to the actress Marie Marquet, who was generally assumed to be the lover of Premier Tardieu. On April 1 the visa was extended for four weeks, until April 26. The Soviet press made the most of the story and hailed the extension as the victory of democracy in France. A cartoon was printed in the government paper *Izvestiya* showing the director in confrontation with the bayonets and pistols of the French police—Eisenstein was dressed as a *Potemkin* sailor.

In order to recover from the stressful affair, Eisenstein drove south with the Moussinacs to their house on the Côte d'Azure. From there, they took short trips to St. Tropez and Cannes. The European bohème and a Soviet revolutionary artist—how did the two go together? Eisenstein led an ascetic lifestyle, but he knew about luxury. He was nonetheless astonished by the life the leftist radicals led in Europe. In Berlin he had been surprised by Toller's lower middle-class apartment and by Piscator's upper middle-class surroundings. But the French outdid the Germans: Vaillant-Couturier owned an island on the Côte d'Azure; Henri Barbusse had a villa in Cannes; there were better collections of Impressionists hanging in the waiting rooms of the 'scene' doctors than in museums. Eisenstein's French fans spoiled him: he was allowed to ride in their luxurious cars, Colette's stepson drove him through Paris in a Bugatti. He was picked up from the English ferry in a classy racecar, a 'Hispano Suiza'. He was invited out to lobster dinners, but he also had opportunities to observe the lives of people on the margins of society. This was exotic. He danced in the port bars of Marseilles and went to the funeral of a butcher from the red-light district.

His residence permit soon expired. None of his hopes had been fulfilled. Just as Eisenstein had begun to come to terms with the idea that he would not be able to shoot a film abroad, a phone call from Paris reached him on the Côte d'Azure. Jesse L. Lasky, Paramount's business manager, invited him to come to Hollywood. Eisenstein rushed off to Paris, where Lasky was waiting for him. On the train he read Blaise Cendrars' novel *Gold*, since Lasky had sent him a list of twenty titles as possible film topics. The list included Zola's *Germinal*, *The Revolt of the Angels* by Anatole France, *Manhattan Transfer* by Dos Passos, *R.U.R.* by Karel Capek, *The Tunnel* by Bernhard Kellermann, biographies of Al Capone and the abolitionist John Brown. In his memoirs Eisenstein wrote that he had also been offered a story about Indians who had been tortured by missionaries. He himself suggested Vicki Baum's novel *Grand Hotel*, H. G. Wells' *War of the Worlds*, Shaw's *The Devil's Disciple* and the Dreyfus affair. He told his American friend Joe Freeman that he wanted to film the story of the Wall Street crash, but he apparently did not share these plans with the Paramount bosses. In order to negotiate with Lasky, Eisenstein had to get permission from Sovkino. Once Moscow had given the go-ahead, Eisenstein signed a contract with Paramount on April 30 in the Paris luxury hotel George V. The contract had been prepared in New York and guaranteed Eisenstein complete freedom in his choice of subject matter. The document stated that he would spend six months in the United States and six months in the Soviet Union, so he could make a film at each location. If the first U.S. film had not been started within three months, the contract was to be terminated. During the preparatory period, Eisenstein was to receive $500 a week in addition to $400 for his assistants. Once the filming started, he would get $3,000 a week.

In an interview with a Paris journalist, Eisenstein assessed the situation positively: 'I am very happy to be able to make use of the great organization and the technical achievements that are available to film workers over there. Zukor is an energetic and very intelligent man who knows a lot about European film production. His generous understanding of film art surprised me very much.'[138]

In early May Valeska Gert came to Paris to give a concert. Eisenstein went to the Magic City Ball with her, where all the gays and transvestites of the city gathered. Members of high society joined in the fray. Afterwards they went to 'Bals musettes' on Rue de Lappe, where men did not take off their overcoats when dancing. 'At night Eisenstein came into my room after I had gone to bed. He sniffed at my clothes and touched my stockings, pants, and everything that was lying around; then he rushed out of the room. Maybe he was expecting me to rape him, but the idea didn't even occur to me.'[139]

The next day, May 6, 1930, Eisenstein and Tisse left on board the steamship *Europa*. Lasky accompanied them. Alexandrov stayed in Paris to finish *Romance sentimentale*. Looking back on the eight months he had spent in Europe (instead of the three months allowed by Sovkino—a complete bluff), Eisenstein said the four days on the *Europa* were like a dream. The insecurity, failures, crashes and fresh starts, the eternal search for money had ended. In Paris the men had been living off the money they begged from the hotel owner— 100 to 250 francs at a time. They had shared small rooms and slept on hard beds. Here, there were beds 'too soft de luxe', five bars, a social hall made for 800 people, black tie dinners, a ballroom, a casino, a pool. The Paramount contract was a 'dizzying feat in a major key' that followed despair, Schenk's empty promises, and Fairbanks' uncertainty. Only a month earlier Fairbanks had advised Eisenstein not to come to Hollywood. Once Fairbanks had heard of the negotiations with Lasky, he immediately sent his own offer. The contract was a victory. Eisenstein knew that 'in order to realize an idea, you need a material 'base.' Lasky supposedly told him: 'We're not going to make an average movie together.' Eisenstein wrote back to Moscow, 'I feel so small, like a newcomer. Another new beginning. A situation like before *Potemkin*. I can't go back. This affair has already cost too many nerves and too much blood.'[140] During the trip across the Atlantic, Lasky gave Eisenstein lessons in American customs and good manners. The rest of the time Eisenstein read the newly published novel *Lady Chatterly's Lover* by D. H. Lawrence.

AMERICA
1930

On May 12 they arrived in New York. They stayed first at the Hotel Astor on Times Square, then moved to the Savoy on Fifth Avenue. Eisenstein sent his mother and Pera postcards from the hotels and circled the window of his 18th floor room in the Savoy. Pera also got a postcard of the Paramount skyscraper in New York. On the back Eisenstein had proudly written: 'This is my office'.

Paramount had adapted to sound film before the other large studios. As of May 1929 the studio produced sound films only, which increased profits sevenfold. Adolph Zukor, who resided in the New York Plaza Hotel, had sent Lasky to Europe to recruit the singing star Maurice Chevalier. Other Europeans, including Ernst Lubitsch, Josef von Sternberg and Marlene Dietrich, had also signed contracts with Paramount. Eisenstein was the next prize. He was welcomed like royalty and assumed that he was receiving the same treatment as Lubitsch and Sternberg. He lived next door to Lubitsch in the hotel. Eisenstein admitted that it was a strange feeling to see the great man 'in flesh and blood'.

On May 17 Eisenstein gave a talk at the annual meeting of Paramount distributors in Atlantic City. He was overwhelmed by the experiences and engagements that the studio organized and that he arranged on his own. 'I am enjoying myself like a big kid here,' he wrote Pera, 'The city is crazy; this exceeds anything I have ever seen. My dream goes on.'[141]

The studio launched a publicity campaign that included press conferences, photo opportunities, and PR lunches. Eisenstein had to attend various high-society dinners that made their way into the gossip columns of the papers. Every performance was stressful. He had trouble enjoying his food, since he had to be entertaining even between his ice cream and his coffee. He was not allowed to act careless or 'Bolshevik', on Lasky's orders. His ice cream melted and his coffee grew cold, but Eisenstein remained cautious and charming. The press photos showed a well-dressed, conventional modern man: dark suit, shirt with a loose collar, striped tie, handkerchief always in his breast pocket. Eisenstein posed with the canine celebrity Rin-Tin-Tin (an effective press photo) and joked that he was testing Pavlov's reflexes on the dog. His jokes went over well with the media; he wrote his mother that he had been getting excellent press. Otherwise he spent his time 'splendidly'. He sent Pera comic strips that seemed to depict his life: Little Piggy on vacation.

The press also ironically alluded to the 'newly-arrived Messiah', and Eisenstein almost fell for the joke: the film star Rudolph Valentino, in Russia considered to be the incarnation of kitsch, had died unexpectedly in 1926. They told me, Eisenstein wrote Pera, that he had just finished watching *Potemkin*.[142]

On May 24 Eisenstein and Tisse went to Boston. They had been invited by Harvard professor Henry Dana, whom Eisenstein had met in Moscow. Dana was Henry W. Longfellow's great-nephew and lived in the poet's 18th-century house—George Washington's residence during the American Revolution. Eisenstein gave a lecture to the Department of Fine Arts at Harvard. He returned to New York on May 26 in order to conduct a seminar with John Dewey at Columbia University. Jay Leyda, Eisenstein's future student, was in the audience.

Eisenstein was still waiting for Grisha, who was taking forever to finish *Romance sentimentale*. Grisha sent a telegram to New York and told Eisenstein that the producer insisted on listing Eisenstein as the film's director. Eisenstein agreed.

In the meantime, Otto H. Kahn had invited them to his house. Eisenstein had never seen such wealth. The house was built like an Italian palazzo. Four paintings by Gainsborough hung in the dining room; a Rembrandt graced the fireplace. Their host remarked that 'only a Jew can paint a face with such subtlety'.[143] Eisenstein frequently encountered strange mixtures of anti-Semitism and philo-Semitism in America. Many of the film industry's bosses were Jewish; some were even Orthodox Jews. Several of them had come from the Russian Empire, for example Louis B. Mayer, Samuel Katzman, Joseph M. Schenk, Samuel Goldwyn, and the Warner brothers' parents.

After Alexandrov's arrival on June 5, the friends set off for Hollywood. It was a long journey full of surprises. First they took the train to Chicago, where they were welcomed by the Society for Cultural Relationships between the U.S.S.R. and America. Eisenstein complained to Agnes Jacques, the society's young executive secretary, that, just because he was Russian, everybody wanted to show him skyscrapers, bridges and factories. He would have felt much more comfortable dancing at the pier, where he could stuff himself with popcorn and cotton candy. He decided not to go to fancy restaurants in Chicago and set out on his own to discover American coffee shops. Agnes' brother, a doctor, introduced Eisenstein to the psychologist John Landesco, who took him to the suburb of Cicero to see the home of Al Capone's clan. Landesco may have also been responsible for arranging Eisenstein's lecture at the Institute of Criminology at the University of Chicago.

Eisenstein discovered that America was not only the land of skyscrapers and railroad lines, but that it was also patriarchal and rigid. Unlike Russians who had come to America before him—Gorky, Esenin, Mayakovsky—

Eisenstein was not bothered by 'uncultured American civilization'. He was clearly intrigued by the country's strange mixture of tradition and modernity, realism and superstition, by its preservation of the dwindling remnants of Europe and its grand leap into the future. The combination was topped off by the technical perfection that permeated everything from simple doorknobs to ice-making to film technology. Eisenstein was now able to find time to write letters; every one betrays his excitement. After a ten-day journey through the Great Plains and New Mexico, they arrived in Los Angeles on June 16. This was Hollywood!

By now the relations between the three men had become extremely tense. All the latent conflicts that had been developing in Europe erupted in full force. Alexandrov and Tisse spoke no foreign languages. Eisenstein served as their bridge of communication, but the whole world was interested only in him. Only his name appeared on the posters; the papers printed only his picture. Even the contract named only Eisenstein—he paid his assistants from his salary, which they perceived as an insult. They felt as if they were being kept like bellboys and servants, like the silent entourage of the king. Alexandrov vented his frustration; Tisse remained silent. Eisenstein wrote Pera and his mother for advice. Pera told Eisenstein that he had always liked being surrounded by slaves. Yulia Ivanovna wrote Grisha a soothing letter.

They had arrived in the USA shortly after the stock market crash. Economic crisis and massive social upheaval were plaguing the country. Herbert Hoover was president, and prohibition was in full swing. Hollywood nonetheless seemed to consist entirely of palmtrees, press agents, and stars. Ivor Montagu was already on site; he had come to Hollywood as a scriptwriter in early 1930. He had urged Paramount to hire Eisenstein and was now assigned a job as Eisenstein's English script-writing assistant.

They shared a house that they rented from the newspaper columnist Proctor (Ted) Cook. The house was in Beverly Hills, Coldwater Canyon, 9481 Readcrest Drive. Montagu had picked out the place: it was a very nice and comfortable snow-white cube in Spanish style on the slope of a hill. Montagu writes in his memoirs that money was tight and that his wife Hell received only $100 from Eisenstein as household money, but that seems unlikely. The $900 that Eisenstein received a week should have provided for a comfortable lifestyle. The renters were even able to hire the landlord's cook, who was of African-Irish-Indian descent.

The change in lifestyle after thirteen ascetic years at home and in cheap European hotels must have reminded Eisenstein of his childhood years, when he had been more closely acquainted with comfort, even luxury. At that time, nice things and good food were still normal and not exceptional. Now

Eisenstein could again afford to buy books. They also bought a used car. Montagu called it the shabbiest model ever driven by a great Hollywood director. Tisse usually sat behind the wheel.

While the three lived abroad, their families back home received financial support first from International Workers' Aid, then from Sovkino itself. Pera managed the money. She was in charge of giving Eisenstein's mother 100 rubles a month and Grisha and Tisse's wives 200 rubles each. Several Moscow acquaintances wanted to move into Eisenstein's room, but Eisenstein was adamantly opposed. He finally agreed to let the Dutch director Joris Ivens, who was spending some time in Moscow, stay there.

Montagu urged Eisenstein to choose his subject matter while the Paramount bosses were still interested. But Eisenstein hesitated; he was much too curious and wanted to see the country, its people and spaces. Six months seemed like a long time and life in Hollywood was too tempting. Eisenstein enjoyed the receptions and dances, the bizarre and famous people.

Eisenstein was introduced to Marlene Dietrich and Gary Cooper. He was intent on meeting the comedian Harold Lloyd, but the latter was in Florida. Gloria Swanson was traveling through Europe; Erich von Stroheim was out of town. Eisenstein visited Walt Disney in his studio. On June 20 the millionaire King Gillette invited them to a picnic at his hacienda. This is where Eisenstein met Upton Sinclair and Berthold and Salka Viertel. During the meal a beautiful woman asked Eisenstein why he had not prevented the murder of the tsar's family. Sinclair turned it all into a joke. But Eisenstein first felt the caution and then the hatred that his presence elicited in certain circles.

Paramount took care of Eisenstein's publicity—systematically, as if on command, the press began to write about Eisenstein and to publish photos of the director with stars, including Mickey Mouse. However, another type of press campaign was simultaneously launched against him. The assault was led by Major Frank Pease, who took various measures to defame Eisenstein. Pease sent Lasky letters and telegrams that were also published in the *Motion Picture Herald* and wrote a 24-page brochure with the title *Eisenstein, Messenger of Hell* that made its way through Hollywood. In this first 'monograph', Eisenstein was called a dangerous cosmopolitan Jew and blamed for all murders and violent acts committed by the Bolsheviks since the Revolution. After all, in his movie this sadist had even shown marine officers having their throats cut. Now the successful Paramount Jews had imported him to make propaganda films for American boys and girls: 'If your Jewish clergy and scholars haven't enough courage to tell you, and you yourself haven't enough brains to know better or enough loyalty toward this land, which has given you more than you ever had in history, to prevent your importing a cut-throat red dog like Eisenstein, then let me inform you that we are behind every effort to have him deported. We want no more red propaganda in this country. What are you trying to do, turn the American cinema into a communist cesspool?'[144]

Perhaps the major was crazy, but he managed to jump-start the Fish Committee, a precursor of the House Committee on Un-American Activities. Pease demanded of Senator Hamilton Fish and other congressmen that Eisenstein be expelled from the United States. He started collecting signatures for his petition to rid American film of the red threat.

Eisenstein sent the relevant news clippings to Moscow. Pera was supposed to turn them into an article and sign it with Eisenstein's pen name 'R.O.Rik'.

Paramount was under pressure and had to defend itself. The press campaign, which had been presenting Eisenstein as a famous director of films with mass impact, changed tactics. Now Eisenstein's exclusivity was put under the spotlight. Paramount had invited Eisenstein to the United States. to make *art*. Lasky announced the studio wanted to combine the Russian creative temperament with American high technology.[145] Paramount quickly released pictures of Eisenstein with Marlene Dietrich and Josef von Sternberg. The most was made of Eisenstein's friendship with Douglas Fairbanks, who for his part now tried to avoid Eisenstein.

Mr. Krumgold of Paramount's publicity department arranged a dinner in Eisenstein's honor at the Ambassador Hotel in Los Angeles and invited the international press. The three 'Roossians' were put on display to satisfy the media's curiosity. Eisenstein amused the columnists with puns and eccentric movements. After a dinner that Lubitsch gave for Eisenstein, the society pages described the director as a man with blue eyes, a nice mouth and pretty teeth that could grace any toothpaste advertisement. Paramount sold Eisenstein's name to the Hollywood audience, and Eisenstein played along. He soon grasped Hollywood's obvious and covert power relations and would later give the inexperienced Upton Sinclair advice that demonstrated his understanding of the system. All the Hollywood bosses were also players who put their money on stocks, horses, and stars. Eisenstein considered himself a stake in their game, which came with a calculated risk. But the role of the world-famous director, whose films had immediately conquered Europe, served Eisenstein poorly. There were situations in which he simply did not know how to react. How should he? He found Marlene Dietrich dull and Greta Garbo dumb because she asked him who Lenin was. At least this is the way Marie Seton tells the story.[146] In letters to Pera Eisenstein complained that he found it impossible to live with their interests: real estate, money, bridge, golf, gossip. He was plagued by loneliness. In Hollywood, much like in Moscow, approval for his projects was anything but guaranteed: 'It's all hanging by a thread. And seven Fridays a week, like at home at Sovkino.'[147] Eisenstein wrote the Moussinacs that, with the exception of Sternberg and Lubitsch, everyone in Hollywood was an idiot and suffered from unimaginable cretinism.[148] But Sternberg was at the bottom of the Hollywood hierarchy. Paul Kohner, an agent for Universal who had met Eisenstein in Berlin, encouraged his boss Carl Laemmle to arrange a lunch for Eisenstein with Uncle Carl's inner circle. Laemmle invited Eisenstein to make a big movie with him. His employees discreetly reminded him that Eisenstein was already under contract with Paramount. He asked Eisenstein if Trotsky could write a script on the intrigue in the Kremlin that could be turned into a decent movie.[149] (Alexandrov later wrote that Lasky even asked him to film a script by Trotsky![150]) Eisenstein did not know how to react. The question alone could bring about his undoing, both here and at home.

He spent a lot of time with people who wielded absolutely no influence in Hollywood. One of his best friends was Seymour Stern, a production assistant for Laemmle; he also enjoyed being around Stern's German girlfriend, the translator Christel Gang. After Stern had been fired from Laemmle's team, he started the ambitious film journal *Experimental Cinema*, in which he published a number of Eisenstein's articles. Eisenstein took long walks on the beach with Salka Viertel, who had not yet begun her Hollywood script-writing career. Greta Garbo would later ask her to write the screenplay *Queen Christina*, then *Anna Karenina* and *The Two-Faced Woman*. At this point Salka was already one of Garbo's confidantes and had become close friends with the family of B. P. Schulberg, Paramount's head of production. Eisenstein also corresponded with Paul Robeson and dreamed of making a film about the Haitian Revolution with Robeson in the lead. He visited the Russian Old Believer community in Los Angeles and drove to Death Valley in the Mojave Desert. In Douglas Fairbanks' Turkish baths Eisenstein met Charlie Chaplin.[151] He would visit him often—Chaplin's house became Eisenstein's second home. Eisenstein and Chaplin were similar in their 'gluttony' and desire to know about everything. Eisenstein tried to find an explanation in Chaplin's personality for his legendary success. He discovered the traits of a violent child, a sort of double of himself. Was this a wishful projection?

They played tennis almost every day (Chaplin had floodlights on the court), swam in the famous swimming pool built in the shape of Chaplin's bowler, and sailed on Chaplin's yacht. Eisenstein also bought a light pair of trousers and red suspenders; he thought he needed the outfit to play tennis. Eisenstein wanted Chaplin to introduce him to celebrities; he was especially keen on meeting the media giant Randolph Hearst, but Hearst was in Europe at the time. Instead he met two Spaniards: one of them was Luis Buñuel.

Eisenstein wondered why Chaplin took Hollywood's customs so seriously and led such a humorless life. He himself wanted to be the opposite of the traditional successful film artist. In this optimistic mood, which betrayed his ignorance about Hollywood's true nature, Eisenstein began writing screenplays for 'true' American films.

But what material should he use? He had immediately vetoed Wells and Shaw and never told Paramount about his idea to make a film about Haiti with Robeson. After long deliberations, he stuck with two stories, *The Glass House* and Blaise Cendrars' novel *Gold*. Eisenstein favored *The Glass House*, the story of a transparent skyscraper and the dark passions that it contains. He had conceived of the idea in Berlin in 1926 after talking to Fritz Lang and Thea von Harbou about *Metropolis*. Montagu preferred the novel about gold diggers and the fate of the Swiss adventurer John Sutter. Sutter had become unbelievably rich, but the discovery of gold on his land had brought him disaster. His life had ended tragically when his ranch land was destroyed by gold diggers. The novel had been published in 1925 and was translated into Russian just one year later. The Swiss Frenchman Cendrars, one of Guillaume Apollinaire's friends, confessed that he had written the novel under the influence of American Westerns.

Montagu did not have high hopes for *The Glass House* and Paramount appreciated the plan even less. The studio assigned the gangster movie scriptwriter Oliver Garrett to the job, but he too had no luck developing Eisenstein's idea. In 1926 Eisenstein had already hoped that Upton Sinclair might coauthor the script, but Sinclair was not asked for help. Eisenstein had trouble writing the script himself. He met with Chaplin's friend, a psychoanalyst, and spent large sums of money trying to understand what was keeping him from finishing the story. These psychoanalytic sessions upset Montagu, since he managed his money like a thrifty housewife. On June 17, 1930 Eisenstein wrote to Pera: 'I've spent ten days being depressed. Now I'm starting to get better. It seems that I may be liquidating a whole bunch of my neuroses forever. For three days I have sat through high-speed psychoanalysis with one of the most renowned doctors in the States (the editor of *Psychological Review*), my good friend Doctor Stragnell. Very interesting. We have uncovered 50% of my 'doubt' complex—this is of course my sore spot. We have been applying a scientific method—this isn't the usual quack treatment. The latest hysterical depression (during my present fortunate circumstances!) upset me so much that I decided to root out the guilty group of neuroses (without touching the others). My decision happened to coincide with Dr. Stragnell's arrival (sometimes I'm lucky). It's very interesting to see how my 'obsession of doubt' developed and who and what are guilty. Imagine Pearl! I will no longer need constant affirmation! To hell with it all! I will be able to do everything!'[152] Eisenstein's enthusiasm for psychoanalysis was also reflected in the screenplay he was writing.

In its first 1926-27 incarnation, *The Glass House* was conceived as an abstract film. The camera and an elevator played the main roles: the elevator acted as the materialized eye of the camera as it roamed between the different floors of the building. Unlike the building's blind inhabitants, the camera could move, change its position, and was able to 'see'. Inside, a husband was incapable of seeing his wife's lover, well-fed people could not see those who were starving. In other words, vision and the possibility of looking at things from different angles were the prerogatives of the mechanical camera. Eisenstein defined this genre as the 'comedy of the eye'. He planned to experiment with abolishing the sensation of hardness and weight and to blur the lines between up and down, inside and outside. He wanted light to dissolve the materiality of glass. In 1928, after his *October* crisis, Eisenstein changed the story and personalized the mechanical eye. He gave the gift of vision to a poet and transformed the 'comedy of the eye' into a 'drama of enlightenment'. In spite of the transparent walls of the building, human relationships remained opaque. Whenever the poet made these relationships transparent, a murder or suicide would occur. The gift of vision turned out to be dangerous, invariably leading to disaster.

Once in Hollywood, Eisenstein conceived of his idea as a three-way conflict between an old architect (the building's creator), a crazy poet, and a robot. The architect constructs the glass house and gives it to humanity. The poet opens people's eyes and perishes from his own gift. The robot, the perfect citizen of the new civilization, destroys the house. In the end it turns out the robot was the real architect all along.

In his project, Eisenstein dissolved the trinity of Zebaoth, Jesus the Son, and the Holy Ghost (the robot) and traced the trinity back to a duality that acquired autobiographical significance. Eisenstein's nickname at the time was 'Old Man': he himself was the failed architect who created a doubled oedipal self-portrait. He identified both with the architect and with the poet (the son who had rejected his father's creation). Eisenstein tellingly called *The Glass House* his own *private* mystery play. In Eisenstein's final version of the screenplay, the comedy of the eye and the drama of enlightenment were subsumed by the tragedy of two utopian dreamers. One was the architect who designed an ideal house, the other the poet who doubted the validity of that functional model.

Modernity has been fascinated with the idea of transparency. A transparent building would aid in the creation of transparent relationships and destroy the distinction between public and private. Walter Benjamin wrote: 'To live in a glass house is a revolutionary virtue *par excellence*. It is also an intoxication, a moral exhibitionism, that we badly need.'[153] The trait that Benjamin considered revolutionary became frightening in Evgeny Zamyatin's novel *We*, where the glass walls of a utopian city allowed for total surveillance. However, Eisenstein's project was not intended to be a film version of Zamyatin's novel, which was published in an English translation in 1925 and caused a huge scandal that led to the author's emigration from Soviet Russia.

Eisenstein's film concept was basically a complex examination of the utopias of glass architecture as they had been designed by Bruno Taut or the European Constructivists Le Corbusier and Mart Stam. Taut's circle 'Die gläserne Kette' ('The Glass Chain') believed that glass cathedrals would enable people to see in a new way and enjoy the cosmic play of nature. The Constructivists thought that glass walls would simplify communication and make social structures transparent. But Eisenstein's glass wall isolated people. The wall did not teach people to see, nor did it make the existing social hierarchy more harmonious. He made his heroes destroy the new visual space into which they had been placed. They were unable to participate in the 'spectacle of modern life' either as observers or as actors. The new glass house was torn apart by old passions that dominated the architecture. The final result was neither a cosmic spectacle nor regulated behavior. Instead, the Constructivist cosmogony was destroyed and transformed into a psychoanalytic drama of a son's rebellion against his father.

The Glass House took vision as its theme—both the perfect vision of the medium and also the voyeurism of man. Eisenstein returned to the ancient Plotinian tradition of inner vision by allowing only the poet to 'see'. He thereby destroyed his own film, since film was the medium of 'new vision' *par excellence*! If the film's plot was based on the danger of the new vision and on the value of inner enlightenment, then how was the medium itself supposed to be effective? It may have been inevitable that Eisenstein eventually abandoned the project.

While Eisenstein was struggling with *The Glass House*, Tisse studied film technology and Alexandrov hobnobbed at parties. Eisenstein finally gave up and devoted his time to *Sutter's Gold*, a compromise that Montagu had urged Eisenstein to make all along. In July, they traveled to Sacramento and San Francisco to gather inspiration from the actual place of events. They spent August working intensely on the script.

Work was organized like an assembly line. Paramount sent typists, translators, and huge supplies of paper. In the morning Eisenstein would go over an episode with Grisha, who would write down the idea, which was then translated and typed out. Montagu would then read through the scene, discuss it with Eisenstein, and rewrite it. Montagu's wife would type up the revised version and a secretary would then make copies.

Eisenstein read Bret Harte, Edgar Allen Poe, Jack London, and Ambrose Bierce. He studied photographs and met with people who had known Sutter personally. He used all of Cendrars' details, but introduced a new character, the circus artist Mary (a memory of Yanukova?), and a boxing scene with a mighty black man (*The Mexican?*). Eisenstein's usual violence was mixed with eroticism and erotic violence. In this bloody melodrama about an American Superman only the polyphonic use of sound and image revealed Eisenstein's love of experimentation. The screenplay included a well-developed musical arrangement of sounds, noise, melodies, and songs. Eisenstein wanted to treat the Gold Rush in a way different from Charlie Chaplin's interpretation. Un-like Stroheim's *Greed*, he did not aim for a dramatic or tragicomic effect. He wanted the film's sound to completely overwhelm and grip the viewer. In Cendrars' novel, Sutter dies in the Capitol Building in Washington because he has lost his court case. In Eisenstein's script, he dies when he hears that he has won his case. This was Eisenstein's compromise with the obligatory happy ending.

The script was written in the form of a narrative poem. Paramount did the math and came up with production costs of three million dollars. This was three times the average movie budget, and Paramount rejected the script on September 7 for financial reasons.

Eisenstein suspected that a feud between rival clans in the studio's leader-ship was behind the decision. Schulberg and Lasky were competitors. Any-thing one suggested would be blocked by the other. Lasky traveled to the East Coast to talk with Zukor, but had no luck persuading him to reverse the deci-sion. He returned with Dreiser's publisher Horace Liveright and a new idea: a film version of Dreiser's *An American Tragedy*. Paramount had purchased the rights to the novel in 1925. First Lubitsch was going to film the material, but Dreiser did not like that idea. Since Schulberg was against *Sutter*, Lasky sug-gested Dreiser as a compromise. Schulberg found it amusing that a Bolshevik would even think of filming a typically American story. Douglas Fairbanks supported the project wholeheartedly, since he hoped to reserve the lead for Mary Pickford's brother Jack. Montagu suspected that Lasky had never read Dreiser, otherwise he would never have taken such a risk. Eisenstein and his team were given twenty-four hours to consider the offer. They agreed to it. Eisenstein was thrilled by the material: 'The problem is not a simple one: make an Emile Zola from a Theodore Dreiser!' he wrote the Moussinacs.[154] They re-turned to the assembly line. By October 5 Eisenstein had finished the script and had sent it to Paramount to get feedback from the West Coast bosses (Schulberg), the East Coast bosses (Lasky), the Dreisers, and the Hays Office. The Hays Office had introduced the so-called Motion Picture Production Code, a set of self-censorship rules that Hollywood now followed. The novel was supposed to translate into a 2-hour long movie.

The hero Clyde Griffith has to choose between the working-class girl Roberta, who is pregnant with his child, and the rich Sondra who wants to marry him. An American career becomes a tragedy when Clyde tries to get rid of Roberta in a staged boating accident. In the end he hesitates, but the boat tips anyway, and Clyde is unable to save Roberta. He is caught, sentenced and executed in the electric chair.

Dreiser paints a broad social panorama that includes election campaigns, a judge's pathological obsession with fame, the hypocritical piety of a church congregation, and the desperate loneliness of the individual. Eisenstein did not turn the material into a 'boy meets girl' picture or into a whodunit about solving the murder, as Schulberg would have wanted. Eisenstein was concerned with the question of whether Clyde was a murderer or not. In Christian moral doctrine, the intention to murder equals the murder itself. For Eisenstein, Clyde was a replica of Dmitry Karamazov, but Eisenstein tried to solve the ambivalence of guilt and innocence (and of the individual and society) differently from Dostoevsky or Dreiser. Eisenstein made use of inner monologue. The novel was structured around a murderous inner conflict that pitted the dream of the establishment against love. Both failed. The conflict developed between an inner and outer voice. Eisenstein wanted to use the film medium to make the subjective objective and vice versa. He named E. T. A. Hoffmann, Novalis, Dujardin, Joyce, Gertrude Stein, and Dos Passos as his models. He did not envision inner monologue as a simple narrative voice-over. Instead he strove to imitate thought's rhythmic, asyntactic flow of words, sounds, and images. He interpreted visual and acoustic elements as an expression of the antagonistic conscious and unconscious. The visual and acoustic would change roles—both picture and sound could represent the conscious image at a given time. The other element would then remain symbolic or abstract. Eisenstein wanted this second element to be pure effect—like a black screen or an asemantic sound.

While they were working on the screenplay, Eisenstein met Erich von Stroheim, the director whose brutal imagination was kindred to Eisenstein. Stroheim was a controversial figure in Hollywood. Several movies had been taken away from his supervision, including the monumental opus *Greed*. Other directors would then finish his films, shorten and disfigure them. Not only large studios had fired the director. Even Gloria Swanson, an actress and the producer of his most recent work, *Queen Kelly*, finally dropped him. After 1933 Stroheim was given no more films to direct. Eisenstein and Stroheim met at a dinner thrown by Fox. After Eisenstein's toast, Stroheim supposedly jumped

up and screamed: 'Eisenstein, leave this place before it is too late. They're ex-
ploiting you spiritually and materially, but they'll never let you make a movie!'[155]
After the evening was officially over, Eisenstein was advised to avoid all contact with Stroheim in the interest of his good publicity. This report of the
event may have been shaped by the passing of time. Like Stroheim, Eisenstein
would soon be dropped by Hollywood, but at that point he was not yet ready
to recognize his fate.

Both Paramount bosses were enthusiastic about the Dreiser screenplay.
At least that is the impression they left with Eisenstein. But they gave the
script to David Selznick, an outside expert from MGM. Selznick was the
wunderkind among Hollywood producers and the son of a jewelry merchant
from Kiev. Selznick had advised MGM to purchase the rights to *Potemkin* and
thought that the film should be studied as intensely as Rubens or Raphael. On
October 8 Selznick wrote Schulberg: 'I have just finished reading the Eisenstein
adaptation of *An American Tragedy*. It was for me a memorable experience; the
most moving script I have ever read . . . . When I had finished it, I was so
depressed that I wanted to reach for the bourbon bottle. As entertainment, I
don't think it has one chance in a hundred . . . . If we want to make *An American
Tragedy* as a glorious experiment, and purely for the advancement of the art
(which I certainly do not think is the business of this organization), then let's
do it with a [John] Cromwell directing, and chop three or four hundred thousand dollars off the loss. If the cry of 'Courage!' be raised against this protest, I
should like to suggest that we have the courage not to make the picture, but to
take whatever rap is coming to us for not supporting Eisenstein the artist (as
he proves himself to be with this script), with a million or more of the stock-
holders' cash.'[156]

On that same day, October 8, the Fish Committee gathered in Los Angeles
to investigate Communist activities in California. They were particularly interested in Eisenstein's case and interviewed Fred W. Beetson on the subject.
Beetson was the treasurer and secretary of the Motion Picture Producers' Association on the West Coast. He was also the West Coast representative of
the Hays Office. The committee included Lieutenant-Colonel Leroy F. Smith,
who represented the Better America Federation, a group that was conducting
its own more subtle campaign against Eisenstein. The New York journal *The
New Republic* reported on the meeting on November 12, 1930 in an article entitled 'Redmongers Go West'. Hamilton Fish was allegedly very surprised when
he heard that Eisenstein planned to film *An American Tragedy*. He had never
heard of the novel and asked if it contained Communist propaganda. They
asked Beetson about the matter. Beetson assured the committee that Eisenstein
would never be allowed to make a propaganda film, and that Hollywood had

the necessary control mechanisms to prevent that.[157]

Eisenstein and his team learned nothing of Selznick's report, but they knew about Beetson's interview. Lasky took them to New York to see the locations for the forthcoming film. On the way there, Eisenstein wrote his mother: '13 October 1930. Arizona .... The scenario came out very well 'excellent', which seems to be everyone's opinion. But there are many questions in connection with the 'propaganda' theme, particularly now when even my name, as always, is being knocked about by the committee of Fish (in investigation of Communist Activities).'[158]

The campaign against Eisenstein and Paramount's internal battle were in full swing. The screenplay was used as an excuse to avoid the conflict. The studio directors doubted that Eisenstein could make a commercially successful movie. They discussed offering him the film *Broken Lullaby*. (Lubitsch made that film in 1932.) Mistrust towards Eisenstein, the press campaign (carrying with it potentially disastrous consequences for Paramount) and Selznick's evaluation of *An American Tragedy* finally led to the break with Eisenstein. The general economic depression and the crushed American Dream did not help the situation. The Paramount directorship thought that during this time of crisis a pessimistic film would flop with American viewers and be politically undesirable. Investors had not yet recovered from financial panic and prophesied another Black Friday. More than a film project was at stake; the issue concerned Paramount's reputation and the image of America itself. Eisenstein refused to make these connections in his enthusiasm for his new discoveries.

On October 22 Eisenstein and Henry Dana went to the Guild Theater in New York to watch the premiere of Tretyakov's *Roar, China!* The set reminded Eisenstein of *Potemkin*. He had not yet heard Paramount's decision and told Dana that there might be a press release tomorrow. The next day Lasky called Eisenstein into his office and announced that Paramount was terminating the contract. The official reason was that Eisenstein's script was too long. He asked Eisenstein to announce that a mutual agreement had preceded Paramount's decision.

They flattered Eisenstein and told him the script was simply too brilliant. They calmed him down and promised that Paramount would renew the contract once the political situation had stabilized and the campaign against him had come to an end. Eisenstein was anything but naïve, but he had underestimated the situation. He trusted Lasky and refrained from making aggressive statements to the press. Not until he learned that they had given the material to Sternberg and that Lasky had left Paramount in 1932, did he grasp the extent of the betrayal. Dreiser took legal action against Paramount—and lost.

The press tried to figure out what had gone on behind the scenes and looked for an explanation for the rupture. Eisenstein's later biographers would return to the question again and again. On November 14, 1930 Richard Watts wrote in *The Film Mercury* that Major Pease had probably persuaded Jesse L. Lasky and his colleague Mr. Zukor that Eisenstein posed a threat to Paramount's popularity. Marie Seton repeats Lasky's version of the story, which he allegedly shared at a cocktail party in New York. He is said to have told the columnist Ted Cook, Eisenstein's Hollywood landlord, that the studio had to protect itself from a deluge of protests and could not go ahead successfully in face of all opposition.[159] In 1934 Joe Freeman turned to Eisenstein for 'something authentic' about the conflict, since he wanted to write a book about the confrontation between a revolutionary artist and the supposedly non-propagandistic US film industry. Eisenstein offered an explanation based on the differences between Lasky (a romantic, sporting type) and Schulberg (the Wall Street 'clerk' type without fantasy or romantic risk). His screenplay had accentuated Dreiser's sociological tendencies against the wishes of the Paramount bosses who were already being blackmailed by Fish. But, according to Eisenstein, the capitalists had treated him in the most gentlemanly way and had considered their attempt to work with a Communist 'a noble experiment'.[160]

At Eisenstein's request, Paramount bought him a return ticket with a stopover in Japan. The press announced his upcoming departure. Eisenstein fell into a deep depression. In spite of all the flattery this affair was more than just a personal creative disaster. Hollywood had not merely crushed him (as it had Erich von Stroheim). Eisenstein felt that he had failed with his 'mission to the world', of which he had been convinced when he was in Europe. He knew how to make films that were as effective as Hollywood pictures, but he could not use Hollywood recipes and did not fit into their commercial calculations. Eisenstein had finally reached the heart of the world's film production, he had worked three whole years to get there, and now he had failed. During this period he met with D. W. Griffith in the Hotel Astor. Griffith was now a worn-out mythological figure in Hollywood. They discussed Griffith's new film *Struggle*, which had not yet been financed.

Eisenstein returned to Hollywood. His friends spread the news that he was now a free man. Samuel Goldwyn invited Eisenstein to his place, but MGM was no longer interested.

A Japanese entrepreneur suggested that Eisenstein make a film in Japan, but Eisenstein did not want to leave Hollywood. Montagu advised Eisenstein to go home; at least Paramount had arranged for the ticket. But Eisenstein did not want to go home defeated. When he was almost out of money, he mailed $100 to Dovzhenko in Berlin, remembering how strapped for cash he had been in Germany. A few days later Grisha won $3,000 gambling.

Eisenstein did not know what to do next. In this moment of total uncertainty, someone suggested launching a film project about Mexico. Eisenstein discussed his plans with Chaplin. Chaplin thought the idea sounded promising, but was not willing to finance the project. Eisenstein turned to Berthold Viertel, since Viertel was funding Murnau's independent project in the South Seas. Viertel could offer no money, but put Eisenstein in contact with Upton Sinclair. Eisenstein asked Montagu to work on the project, but Montagu declined and went back to England.

On November 4, 1930 Eisenstein wrote his mother about the break with Paramount: 'We parted as friends. It all occurred under the pressure of the anti-Soviet campaign. They want to rehire me in 9-12 months when the political pressure subsides.' He wrote that he would come home via Hawaii and Japan around December 10. He also mentioned that there was talk of a travel film about Mexico, but asked his mother to keep the information to herself. He had not yet discussed the matter with Sovkino.[161]

On November 18 Eisenstein was asked to leave the United States by the end of the month. His visa had expired. He spent that day in Santa Monica with Robert Flaherty, another director who had failed in Hollywood. Flaherty had some experience with independent film. His subjective presentation of people untouched by civilization (such as Eskimos or Polynesians), based on extensive camera observations of their lives, was an unexpected success and set a model for nonfictional filmmaking. He had just lived through the adventure of F. W. Murnau's film *Tabu*—the two filmmakers had started the project together, but Flaherty then abandoned it.

Sinclair was enthusiastic about supporting a radical Russian artist's film about Mexico. In America's left-leaning intellectual circles, Mexico was a fashionable theme, and Eisenstein a well-known name. He immediately became involved in extending Eisenstein's visa.

Eisenstein was 32 and Sinclair 52 when they joined forces. They had only met briefly once before, at Gillette's picnic. Sinclair came from a rich Virginia family that had gone bankrupt after the war. The father slid into alcoholism, and the son became ever more interested in Socialism. After his first marriage dissolved, Sinclair married Mary Craig Kimbrough, a faded Southern belle and daughter of a Mississippi judge who speculated in real estate. Her money allowed him to write. In the late twenties, Sinclair wrote a number of articles and several important novels, including *The Wet Parade* (1930). He was a safe bet for the Pulitzer Prize. His agent was even trying to promote him for the Nobel Prize. In the Soviet Union, Sinclair was the best known and most translated American author. Two million copies, or 195 titles of his work had already been published there. A complete 12-volume Russian edition of Sinclair's work came out between 1930 and 1932. His socialist leanings were well known. He corresponded with Stalin, was preparing for a trip to the Soviet Union, and had promised to write a novel about Americans who were helping to re-build the Soviet Union.

Sinclair and his wife knew several radical California millionaires who sup-ported Socialism and the Soviet experiment.

Mary Craig Sinclair made inquiries about the possibility of successfully producing a film. The information she gathered fueled her optimism. In order to finance the film the couple founded the 'Mexican Picture Trust'. They dragged Eisenstein to all the millionaires in the region. Salka Viertel was present at one of the dinners for lady millionaires. She said that not one of the ladies who had donated money had even heard of Eisenstein. Comrade S. Hillkowitz gave $15,000; Mary Sinclair herself put in $20,000—she had to take out a mortgage on her Pasadena home. Kate Crane Gartz donated $5,000. The banker Otto H. Kahn joined the group as an anonymous donor.

When Sinclair asked Eisenstein about production costs, Eisenstein men-tioned the sum of $25,000. Montagu said later that Sinclair should have asked someone else for an estimate. How was Eisenstein supposed to know? He had never produced a movie. Eisenstein allegedly got 'advice' from a bookstore owner in Hollywood, a man named Stade. In his youth, Stade had fought on the side of Pancho Villa. Eisenstein asked him how much it would cost to make a reasonably economical film in Mexico, mostly documentary, no pro-fessional actors. "Could it be done for—say—twenty-five thousand dollars?" The bookseller apparently replied: "Possibly." After this conversation, Eisenstein optimistically passed the information on to Sinclair.[162]

Mary's brother Hunter Kimbrough was named executive manager of the project. He worked as a broker, but had absolutely no experience in film. He was supposed to manage the money and organize the expedition. He would negotiate with the Mexican government, make travel arrangements, buy film stock, deal with the censorship committee, and organize translators, hotels, food, and vehicles.

Negotiations with Eisenstein's Moscow bosses went through Amkino, the film department of the Soviet foreign trade organization Amtorg. Lev Monosson, an intelligent and business-savvy man, was Amkino's boss. Monosson supported the venture, so Moscow permitted Eisenstein to spend more time abroad to make the first Mexican movie.

The contract that Eisenstein and Mary Craig Sinclair signed on November 24, 1930 stated that the filmed material (all positive and negative copies) would belong to Mary and that she could sell the material at any price. She was designated the sole owner of world rights to the film and had the option to copy-right the film in her name. Eisenstein was given full creative license on condi-tion that the picture would be 'non-political'.[163]

The contract guaranteed Eisenstein ten percent of the film's profits (or of the film's sale price), but only during the first 18 months after the film's pro-duction. "Hollywood must never know, of course, of the bargain price at which the great Eisenstein was secured by us," Mary wrote her friend Aline Barnsdall. Shooting was to be finished in four months—that was the deadline set in Moscow. Upton Sinclair thought that amount of time was completely reason-able. He knew that Eisenstein had needed only four months to film *Potemkin*. After Eisenstein consulted with Monosson about the contract, he got the par-ties to amend it slightly on December 1: the film would be distributed without a license on the territory of the USSR. This contract unleashed an adventure that has gone into film history as one of the greatest debacles ever. The scan-dal shook Sinclair's reputation as much as it upset Eisenstein's career.

The Mexican visas arrived on November 26. Just before he left, Eisenstein saw the edited, but still silent version of Chaplin's *City Lights*. He had had the opportunity to watch Chaplin at work on the set. The film started as an im-provisation in front of the camera. In takes and retakes, Chaplin corrected, developed, and perfected the scenes. In one case he used as many as seven hundred (!) takes for one shot.

This creative approach on the set would have been impossible in Soviet Russia where there was a chronic shortage of film stock, but it was unusual even for Hollywood. Eisenstein was deeply impressed by Chaplin's work method. In Mexico he would try to add his own twist to Chaplin's approach.

According to Marie Seton, Eisenstein later said that Alexandrov had been offered a film in Hollywood during this time. Eisenstein scolded him and was envious of his charm. He made Alexandrov turn down the offer.[164]

Salka Viertel took them to the train station, where Seymour Stern, Christel Gang and the Sinclairs were waiting. This was Eisenstein's last peaceful en-counter with his financiers. Two years later, Sinclair and Stern would also become involved in a bitter struggle over the film.

MEXICO
1931-1932

On December 5 the team crossed the Mexican border. Their arrival was dramatic: they were welcomed by Diego Rivera and a group of journalists but were immediately arrested by the police and were kept in custody until they managed to explain the grounds for their entry. Diplomatic relations between Mexico and the USSR had been severed in 1930, complicating the situation even more. Mary Craig Sinclair became incredibly active. A protest letter initiated by her telephone calls and telegrams signed by Einstein, Chaplin, and Shaw arrived in Mexico the next day. Twenty four hours after their arrest, Eisenstein, Alexandrov and Tisse were free to continue their travels. They reached Mexico City on December 8.

The investigation into their Communist activity was not abandoned until two US Senators intervened and wrote letters to the Mexican government on Sinclair's behalf. The Spanish ambassador to Mexico, Alvarez del Vayo (he had worked in Moscow and knew Eisenstein), also used his influence to make their lives easier. Eisenstein was declared an official guest of the government just before Christmas. Accusations that he was a Communist agent or a German spy were thus dismissed.

Shortly after their arrival Eisenstein discussed the formalities of making a film with the Interior Ministry. The chief of police agreed to support him; the Ministry of Education provided translators and advisors that doubled as chaperones: Dr. Adolfo Best-Maugard and Agustín Aragón Leiva. They were supposed to make sure that the film did not include material hostile to the government. The filmmakers had to pay for their 'services'. It was also decided that the Russians would send all filmed material to the government censorship office before they themselves had looked at it. Eisenstein agreed to these conditions: he had no other choice.

Both specialists assigned to Eisenstein were original personalities in their own right. Best-Maugard was a painter and had been Diego Rivera's associate in Paris, where he also met Nataliya Goncharova and Mikhail Larionov. After returning to Mexico, he published *An Approach to Creative Design* in 1925, in which he analyzed seven basic motifs (including the spiral, circle, zigzag, and straight line) and discussed dynamic symmetry and the golden section using Jungian psychology's notion of the archetype. In the late thirties he directed several remarkable movies. His ideas and way of thinking were kindred to Eisenstein and he introduced the Russian director to the history, customs, ethnography, music, and archaeology of his home country. But it was not Adolfo Best-

Mauguard, but Agustín Aragón Leiva, whom Eisenstein would later remember as his confidant. Best-Maugard was a homosexual aesthete, and Leiva was notoriously homophobic. During Eisenstein's stay in Mexico, Leiva was engaged in writing a pamphlet about homosexuals in the Mexican Government who had betrayed the Revolution. The list included Foreign Minister Genaro Estrada, whom Eisenstein would soon meet.

The painters Diego Rivera, Jean Charlot and Roberto Montenegro also gave Eisenstein tips and advice. (Montenegro later drew a picture of Eisenstein as a Spanish Conquistador on a fresco in the chapel of San Pedro and San Pablo.) Rivera invited Eisenstein over to dinner, where the director met Frida Kahlo. Eisenstein also visited David Alfaro Siqueiros. The conflict between Rivera and Siqueiros had not yet erupted publicly: Rivera admired Trotsky (who was to be exiled to Mexico in 1937) and Siqueiros took Stalin's side.

Hunter Kimbrough and Eisenstein were immediately welcomed by the US ambassador, who also promised to support the film. Similar conversations and meetings filled the first few weeks. In the evenings Eisenstein would usually visit the small theaters in Mexico City. He found their erotic atmosphere stimulating. He received permission to start filming on December 11. On December 14, he shot the first bullfights in Guadelupe. But for the moment that was it.

In order to get around more easily, Kimbrough bought a used Buick and Tisse paid $100 for a Cadillac that was almost new. The car was intended to transport film equipment, but Eisenstein liked to drive around in it too. He still had no idea what the film's topic was going to be or how he would structure it. He took inspiration from Rivera's stories, Anita Brenner's book *Idols behind Altars*, and Ambrose Bierce's reports about the Mexican Revolution. Eisenstein never mentioned John Reed's reports on the subject.

The camera team was made up of acquaintances, and Tisse found one more assistant of German heritage, Horst Scharf. Then Eisenstein met Arkady Boitler, a Russian film actor and Chaplin imitator who had emigrated to Mexico and offered his assistance. They planned to finish shooting the film in three or four months. However, they did little in the first three months and filmed almost nothing. Instead, they explored the country. Eisenstein went to Acapulco, where he met the Mexican President Ortiz Rubio. The meeting had been arranged by Alvarez del Vayo.

On January 16 there was an earthquake in Oaxaca. The group chartered an airplane and flew off to film the catastrophe. While they were shooting, the pilot made some extra money giving rich people air tours. Eisenstein quickly cut a short film, *El desastre en Oaxaca* (Earthquake in Oaxaca), which was immediately shown in the theaters. He also sent the film to Moscow, as proof of his activity.

Eisenstein soaked up this strange country, where modernity, the Middle

Ages and ancient Aztec culture lived side by side. He thought he could film a historical fresco without directing anything at all. He considered shooting a loosely connected series of episodes that would be united compositionally. The film would start with an orchestra playing. Then the musicians disperse and leave for different regions of Mexico, where self-contained stories occur. In the end, the musicians would return and start to play. In this way, Eisenstein could depict the shift of culture and eras that shaped the land and fascinated the director.

In late January, Eisenstein met Leopold Stokowski in Mexico City and asked him to compose the music for his film. Sinclair offered his help in writing the script and suggested that Eisenstein could use a Don Juan-like figure from Mexican folk songs as a compositional link. Sinclair shared a friend's idea with Eisenstein: the shift from story to story could be explained by the change of religions in Mexico. But Eisenstein refused to be pinned down. He began to film what attracted him: bullfights, fiestas, funeral rites, landscapes, pyramids, religious ceremonies.

On January 24 Sinclair showed the first Mexican shots to a group of friends who included Einstein, Seymour Stern, Berthold and Salka Viertel. They were all thrilled. Mary Craig Sinclair immediately decided to double her investment in the movie. After these first impressive images her friends promised a sure profit. However, Eisenstein asked Sinclair never again to show excerpts to anybody before he had viewed and edited the material.[165]

On January 30 the group left to film in Tehuantepec, a tropical region in the southeast near the Gulf. They traveled on horseback to reach their location. After vaccinations against cholera and typhus, the Russians all developed fever of 104° F; they all suffered. Alexandrov and Eisenstein were confined to their beds; to make things worse, Eisenstein also got the flu. The unusual food and bad water gave all of them diarrhea. February was marked by physical weakness and various illnesses. But the Tehuantepec footage still depicts a natural paradise and shows Gauguinesque episodes of sensuous girls languishing in hammocks. Three old women made sure the foreigners with the cameras did not harm the girls.

The difficulties soon overwhelmed them. There was no infrastructure and absolutely no technical support for the film project. They had to send the material to Hollywood to be developed. On its way back to the Mexican team, the footage had to pass censorship twice: once at the Mexican embassy in California, then in Mexico City. Tisse worried that the tins of undeveloped film would be opened by careless officials at the border—this did happen occasionally. Kimbrough was in charge of keeping track of the film that was sent back and forth, sometimes lost, sometimes exposed. Sluggish Mexican officials and ubiquitous corruption at all levels of bureaucracy did not make his task any easier

In spite of illness and chaotic production methods, they worked 16 hours a day non-stop. In March, the team took a plane to Yucatán, where they wanted to film the ancient pyramids. However, the weather was often so bad that they were forced to sit around idly. They therefore made extremely slow progress, and their expenses continued accumulating. Sinclair postponed his trip to the Soviet Union in late March and instructed Kimbrough to limit the Mexican expenditures to $36,000 so there would be enough left for postproduction. Kimbrough was to start arranging for the Russians' return visa to the United States.

Eisenstein's passport expired once again. He also knew that he would need at least another six months to finish the film, so he asked Soyuzkino (Sovkino's successor) to extend his contract three more months.

The letters from Moscow began to worry him. On March 1 Pera wrote: 'There's an upheaval coming. It's in the air. The official attitude towards you is changing. I'm not sure how your American work is going to influence all of this. Don't get mad at me, but America is the wrong approach now. Six months won't be enough anyway, so it would add up to another year or so.'[166] Pera reported that all artistic groups had been dissolved; institutions had either shrunk or had started over from scratch; Shklovsky had publicly denounced the Formalists. She reproached Eisenstein for never having written his boss Konstantin Shvedchikov, the head of Sovkino. She summarized the film functionaries' general opinion about Eisenstein: Eisenstein had received permission for a three-month business trip and had stayed away a year; in other words, the best director had been unavailable for a whole year, and he had not even made any movies. Eisenstein did not respond to Pera's reproaches. Instead, he asked her to come to Mexico and work as his assistant. She, however, was not allowed to leave the country.

At this point, the camera team was still in a good mood. Sinclair had seen eight thousand meters of film and was excited by the footage. Eisenstein sent him first press photos to launch the publicity campaign. Eisenstein's creative plans were slowly taking shape. The film was going to consist of six short stories. The first took place among young girls in the tropics during some mythic era; the second would deal with the era of colonization. Eisenstein wanted to shift from showing matriarchal forms of society to the patriarchal story of the 'right to the first night'. He would move from the girls' daydreams and feminine harmony to male urges. The third episode, 'Maguey', was structured around a story of violence and counter-violence. The fourth story, 'Fiesta', took place just before the 1910 Revolution. It would be baroque and show bullfights, jealousy, *spanité*, Catholic Mexico's Golgotha plays and cathedrals built on top of Aztec and Mayan pyramids. The next story would depict the

Civil War and would focus on the figure of Soldadera. The Soldadera follows armies and takes care of the soldiers; she bears a child and does not hesitate to pick up a dead man's gun when necessary. Finally, the epilogue would connect modern Mexico with primeval cyclical time in the carnivalesque festival of the Day of the Dead.

After the historical dialectics of his Russian films and the socio-psychological dramas of his Hollywood scripts, Eisenstein was now confronted with mythological ways of thinking. He experienced the mythic mindset in everyday life. This way of thinking overwhelmed him—it seemed not to distinguish between life and death, body and spirit, object and subject, male and female. Sensuality and sexuality acquired completely new meanings. In Mexico Eisenstein discovered his own sexuality and lost his virginity. The experience was apparently so moving that he felt he had to tell Pera about it: 'You know that I have never gone all the way with the objects of my infatuation. I would interrupt things half way there and would justify my behavior with pity, love of humanity, or outside circumstances. I have often complained to you about this block. I have long considered this to be a sublimation of the sexual sphere, my super-asceticism has developed repressive mechanisms so that my lust is suppressed as soon as it comes to the surface. Just now I was madly in love for ten days and got everything that I desired. You can't imagine what it means to suddenly get 100%, after you've spent 10 years going 99% of the way, but then always breaking things off because of some hesitation. I never would have guessed. This will probably have huge psychological consequences.'[167] Eisenstein signed the letter 'little school boy'. His encounter had not been with a woman, but with a man from Guadalajara, Jorge Palomino y Cañedo. Cañedo was a historian of religion and came from a wealthy aristocratic family. Eisenstein had met him in September 1931 in Mexico City.

In Eisenstein's eyes, the Mexicans were a 'a race of young people, where the men have not yet lost their early femininity, nor the women abandoned their puerile pranks.'[168]

He interpreted Mexican architecture as the materialized unconscious that had been liberated by drugs and projected onto the outside world. After a long hiatus he again began to draw. (He had sketched his last theater designs in 1923.) He drew bullfights and ritual dances, Golgotha, Christ and other martyred, but beautiful bodies: Torero, the Bull, Sebastian, King Duncan, Werther—a series of agonizing deaths. The sketches were a kind of *écriture automatique*, a flood of the unconscious.

After Murnau and Flaherty had finished their Polynesian project *Tabu*, Eisenstein began his adventure of a European among 'primitive' people. His sentimentality came to the surface and evoked a sensual euphoria. He experimented with drugs; he tried to 'think mythologically' and apply this way of thinking to film. He wanted to know which came first: did death follow life or did life come after death?

The 'Maguey' episode was built around the tortured body. First a girl is raped. After her groom, a peasant, takes bloody revenge, he is executed.

Should he place the violence and death of 'Maguey' after the tropical scene with the young girls? That way he could turn everything on its head and celebrate death as resurrection. Eisenstein projected the revolt of poor peasants and dishonored men onto biblical matrixes. The young martyred groom's name was Sebastian; his death would be depicted in a montage with Corpus Christi, the celebration of Christ's body that Eisenstein had filmed in Yucatán. The way the peasants were buried—standing up in their own graves—offered another compositional parallel with the Golgotha-theme. However, the raw brutality of the execution—the heads of the buried men would be crushed like nuts by horses' hooves—prevented the cutters who later edited the scene from following Eisenstein's design.

The film was supposed to move abruptly from mythical and colonial eras to a historic era—to Civil War and Revolution. Eisenstein could imagine no other frame for the film.

The team spent the month of April in Izamal on the Yucatán Peninsula at the ancient Mayan pyramids. In Merida, also in Yucatán, they experienced a mixture of Catholic Spain and old Mexico. Here Eisenstein filmed two men carrying cacti in the shape of crosses, an ancient form of religious penance. They also wanted to capture religious festivals on film, but the believers would not let them and knocked over the camera. Eisenstein was forced to recreate the ceremony in Izamal, where those particular rites were unknown.

At this time a notice reached Eisenstein from New York that Paramount wanted to offer him a project to be filmed in India based on texts by Rudyard Kipling. Tisse received an offer from Praesens-Film. These offers proved that they had not yet been forgotten. Eisenstein sent pictures from his Mexican film to Paris, London, and Berlin and assured Sinclair that he maintained wonderful links to the most important European film journals. He advised Sinclair on how to deal with Louella Parsons, the mightiest columnist in Hearst's press empire, since she knew how to organize the best whisper campaign in Hollywood. Whenever Sinclair expressed his doubts, Eisenstein pacified him and said that he had filmed *Potemkin* in the same way.

On May 4 the group arrived at the Tetlapayac hacienda to shoot the 'Maguey' episode. The owners and the peasants played themselves. The ranch belonged to the 80-year-old Don Alejandro Saldívar. He refused to take money from the team; the filmmakers only had to pay for their own food and for the peasants' lost work time. The ranch was surrounded by geometrical, gray-green Maguey cacti. The locals made *pulque*, a light milky drug, out of the plants. Unfortunately, the rainy season soon started and they were only able to film a few hours a week.

Eisenstein filled dozens of thick notebooks with his notes, and asked Sinclair to send him books for his research, including Isaac Don Levine's just published volume *Stalin*, a fictionalized biography that made use of revelatory memoirs by the 'renegades' Trotsky, Georgy Besedovsky, and Boris Bazhanov (Stalin's defected secretary). Levine's book centered on the disclosure of Lenin's secret testament, which deprived Stalin of the right to power. Eisenstein intended to use the forced interruption to finish his book on film theory. His advisor Leiva said that Eisenstein looked like a 60-year-old man, even though he had just turned thirty-four. While everybody else was out partying, Eisenstein sat in his cell and read. He allegedly told Leiva that his life's work was to study. Eisenstein kept up a lively correspondence during this time. He wrote to Magnus Hirschfeld and received a letter from Alexander Luria with an invitation to Central Asia. Luria was organizing an expedition with Wolfgang Köhler, Jean Piaget and Kurt Lewin to study the historical laws of perception. Eisenstein was dwelling on those laws in Mexico on his own: he had read Lucien Lévy-Bruhl's *Primitive Mentality* and twelve volumes of James Frazer's *The Golden Bough*, which he had purchased in Paris and California.

He was all alone—miles from the defunct Association of Revolutionary Cinematography (ARK), the infighting at home, and the intrigues in Hollywood. He was living outside socialism and capitalism: he was using a modest sum donated by California millionaires to make a Mexican movie. Sinclair, the Soviets and time were on his back. He did not yet sense just how shaky his position really was. He thought he would be able to overcome his momentary difficulties. Eisenstein had always been an individualist and trusted only himself. However, he had no experience in independent film. Up to this point his projects had been generously financed and had known few limitations. Now both money and know-how were in short supply. Sinclair kept writing Eisenstein about his efforts to find new investors. He complained that he spent all his time writing petitions and no longer had any time for his novels. Even if the team lived simply, Sinclair knew that the expenses would double. Twenty-nine thousand dollars had already been spent; the rest was intended for the editing phase. However, not even a third of the film had been shot. Eisenstein, Tisse, Alexandrov and Kimbrough were not even being paid an income beyond their expenses.

Sinclair watched Murnau and Flaherty's *Tabu*. He compared Eisenstein's footage with that film and his own expenses with those of the 'Polynesians'. According to Sinclair, Murnau had worked with a budget of $75,000; *Taboo* brought in a $135,000 profit during its first week in the theaters. Sinclair used this example to ask for another loan from the Amalgamated Bank in New York. His argument did not fly. He then tried to sell the production to Otto H. Kahn and wrote that the film promised to be the greatest sensation the art world had ever known.[169] For the time being none of his attempts to find money met with any success. In June Kimbrough reported that the team was down to $2,000 and would need about $15,000 more; they were having problems with lighting and Eisenstein worked too slowly and too carefully. In the meantime Amkino director Lev Monosson reported on changes in Moscow. The new film chief Boris Shumyatsky was of the opinion that Eisenstein had spent enough time abroad. The little film about the Mexican earthquake did not justify his absence. Soyuzkino was still paying the employees' families: the sum was substantial and it was time for them to come home. Eisenstein was expected to make another movie for the anniversary of the Revolution (this time it was the fifteenth). Monosson said that Moscow had not responded to his request for an extension of their travel permit. Only Eisenstein himself finally met with success in that area: he received an extension until November. In order to improve Soyuzkino's mood, Eisenstein and Alexandrov promised to write a screenplay immediately. They would contrast socialist industrialization with the depression in the capitalist economy.

Eisenstein demanded that Sinclair put the film's entire budget, $50,000, into the Mexican half of the project. Once the footage was complete, Eisenstein said, they would find money to edit it in Hollywood. But first the film needed to be shot. The weather was ruining all their plans. They had planned to spend three weeks at the hacienda; now they had been there six weeks and there was still no end in sight.

Sinclair was desperate and came up with the following idea. The Gosizdat publishing house owed him a large sum of money for the Russian editions of his work. On June 20 he wrote the publisher Artashes Khalatov and requested that his royalties be transferred to the United States. This was a highly unusual practice for Gosizdat. The publisher would always pay part of the sum in hard currency, but the rest was supposed to be handed out in the Soviet Union in rubles. Sinclair justified his request by stating that he would not spend the money on himself, but would invest the entire sum, $25,000, in the film. He asked Monosson for advice and sought support from influential people in the Soviet Union. He wrote beseeching letters to Lunacharsky, Radek, Gorky, and Boris Pilnyak, who had spent 1930 in California. Sinclair was ready to travel to Moscow to take care of the details, but his wife fell ill. His son David went to Moscow instead to negotiate the deal. After several conversations Gosizdat agreed to transfer $5,000.

In the meantime, relations were souring on the set. Kimbrough thought that Eisenstein and his demands were greatly exaggerated. Since he had seen the film's script—Eisenstein had had to write it down for the Mexican authorities—he had begun to economize the little money that was left. He put more and more pressure on Eisenstein; Eisenstein became more and more irritated. In letters to Moscow, Eisenstein complained about chaos, heat, fever, and Kimbrough's incompetence. July was an unlucky month. One actor was bitten by a snake; another suffered a serious head injury while shooting the execution; another, Félix Balderas, killed his sister with Tisse's pistol and was arrested. Work on the movie ground to a halt. The actor was finally allowed to work on the set under police supervision, but this situation made work difficult and spoiled the mood at the hacienda. Katherine Anne Porter, who visited the team in Mexico, described the incident in her novel *Hacienda*. Eisenstein fell ill.

In his letters to his brother-in-law, Kimbrough started a massive attack, even intrigue, against the capricious director. He wrote that Eisenstein was arrogant, sexually perverted, and a liar. He was absolutely crazy about bullfights, fiestas, and funerals; filmed only that material, and wasted time and money.[170] Eisenstein aggravated Kimbrough's mood with a silly joke. When it was time to meet Kimbrough at the train station, Eisenstein inspired the people at the hacienda to stage the event like a scene from a western. They put on masks, dressed up like train robbers and 'kidnapped' Kimbrough from the train. The joke went too far for Kimbrough. He complained to Sinclair that Eisenstein had hired Mexicans to kill him.

Around this time, Sinclair found new hope on the financial front. In August, MGM purchased the rights to film his novel *The Wet Parade*. He spoke to MGM's production chief Irving Thalberg about his difficulties with the Mexican film. Thalberg hinted that he might be able to finance the postproduction. Sinclair immediately wrote Eisenstein and suggested turning the hacienda story into a separate movie. That episode was made for Hollywood: it was a Mexican picture with a story, a dramatic plot, characters, and exotic landscapes. Eisenstein could cut that story first; they would release the film, and use the profit to finish making the longer film.[171]

Eisenstein knew that he would never get permission to make a second movie, so his reply to Sinclair was the independent filmmaker's classic response to financial pressure and compromise: he rejected the suggestion. He said making the short film would be the same as taking the scene of Polonius' death out of *Hamlet* and turning that into a new drama.[172] Eisenstein tried to make Sinclair feel better about the huge amounts of 'wasted' film stock and compared this film to *October*. In that movie he had cut around 80,000 meters of footage to

2,100 meters; he would have to do the same thing here. Sinclair had trouble following Eisenstein's train of thought. Eisenstein had to enlighten Sinclair about the basics and nuances of a film production.

In a letter to Monosson, Eisenstein reacted even more sharply to Sinclair's offer: 'Sinclair's last 'brilliant' idea: to make an independent movie out of the middle episode..! True, it is hard to find a worse novel (from a compositional point of view) than the ones that Sinclair puts together. Why should my film have to follow those same principles?'[173]

On August 31 Eisenstein began filming the Day of the Dead in Mexico City. His serious disagreements with Kimbrough led to tensions in the team. Sinclair's suggestion of including MGM did not appeal to Eisenstein at all. He would have preferred Paramount or Laemmle's Universal Studios. One of Universal's agents in Mexico promised support, but Sinclair had to curb Eisenstein's enthusiasm. He had already shown Carl Laemmle excerpts. Laemmle was only interested in the finished product. Monosson brought a ray of hope into this desperate situation. Amkino was willing to invest $25,000, but the money could be used *only* for the postproduction. Monosson wrote Sinclair that he did not think releasing a part of the film separately was a good idea.

This financial support encouraged Sinclair and he agreed to allow Eisenstein to develop his artistic ideas and to finish the film the way he envisioned it. But the team still was not making any progress. Alexandrov fell seriously ill and spent a month lying in bed. He moved in with an acquaintance in Mexico City, a Russian doctor who took care of him. Kimbrough said Eisenstein would never finish the film.[174] Mary Craig Sinclair was in despair and demanded that her husband take decisive measures to tame Eisenstein's 'disobedience and extravaganza'. On September 12 Sinclair collapsed under the pressure and had to spend two weeks in the hospital. After his release he threatened to stop all funds if he didn't receive a production plan that would allow him to estimate deadlines and expenditures. Forty-three thousand dollars had already been spent. On October 23 Sinclair even set an ultimatum, whereupon Eisenstein and Alexandrov sent him a schedule. According to that plan, they would still need 120 days on site and $35,000. Kimbrough had now written Sinclair, 'He's like a negro. Kind words and consideration are not enough.'[175]

In late October, while Eisenstein was filming several scenes in a tropical region near the Pacific Ocean, the Mexican government asked Eisenstein to make an official film starring General Calles, the second most powerful man in government. The government would cover all costs, including salaries. The perk that interested Eisenstein most, however, was the support of the army. He needed soldiers for the episode about the Civil War. General Calles promised to provide 500 soldiers, 10,000 guns, and 50 canons for free. Eisenstein could also count on the support of the railroad. Of course, Kimbrough would have to give away little 'presents' here and there. Eisenstein enthusiastically agreed to the Mexican government's offer.

MGM sent a camera team to Mexico in October. They even filmed at the same hacienda! Eisenstein was very upset and said that Sinclair had told Irving Thalberg way too much about his movie. Sinclair defended himself and said Eisenstein should hurry up and beat the competition. Otherwise his film would be seen as an imitation of *Viva Villa!*

The prospect of working with the government gave Eisenstein confidence. He broke his silence and began denouncing Kimbrough in letters to Sinclair (in much the same way as Kimbrough had already written about him). While Kimbrough called Eisenstein a blackmailer who constantly threatened to stop filming if his demands weren't met, Eisenstein wrote Sinclair that Kimbrough wasted money, gambled, was perpetually drunk, staged orgies in bordellos, wreaked havoc during production, and made anti-Semitic remarks.[176] When Tisse was questioned about the matter, he said that Kimbrough had only drunk with the officers to speed up production.

Sinclair was now confronted with two opposing statements and was at a complete loss. He talked to Monosson, who did not believe that the Russian 'boys' would purposefully waste time in malaria-infested Mexico in uncomfortable surroundings. He advised Sinclair to go to Mexico himself, so he could get a first-hand picture of the situation, but Sinclair's health did not permit the journey.

On October 27 Sinclair signed a contract with MGM that guaranteed him $18,000 for a film version of his novel (the film came out even before Eisenstein left Mexico). The contract allowed him to transfer his wife's share of the project into his own name and to carry the entire responsibility. Now Sinclair was firmly counting on Amkino's promised investment. But the situation changed in November. Monosson was called back to Moscow. Viktor Smirnov took his place; though he wrote polite letters to Sinclair, he knew nothing of the agreement and took no initiative in the matter.

Eisenstein was meanwhile filming the 'government film' with the Mexican president, politicians, generals, and other official figures. He wanted to use some of the shots for his own film (as satire), but they were as stiff as a court chronicle. This footage was not used in any of the later versions of Eisenstein's film. Furthermore, his compromise was strongly condemned. There was nothing satirical in the material, according to one critic; in fact it was even fascistic in tone since it supported the reactionary Mexican government.[177] Leiva wrote Seymour Stern: 'Eisy has got in acquaintance with the racketeer

in chief [General] Calles; he is in the film, altogether with the imbecile President we have. I see this as dangerous stuff for the standing of Eisy among the
advanced people, as it is no more a secret that Calles is the wealthiest Mexican, a fascist of the worst kind . . . . I cannot imagine [him] in the film otherwise than in a sarcastic mood. We must refrain of doing any comment until
we'll see the film complete.'[178]

While Eisenstein was working on the commission, he also filmed the Day
of the Dead for his own film. To do this, he had to trick his 'advising observers'. He borrowed skeletons from a medical institute, dressed them up as a
banker, a general, and an archbishop. He filmed these dead dolls on the roof of
his hotel. The use of the skeletons in parallel montage to the stiff, official pictures was to have a sarcastic effect.

By November only $6,000 remained. Sinclair suggested that they give up
on the 'Soldadera' episode completely and try to finish the stories that had
already been started. At this point, not a single episode had been filmed in its
entirety. Sinclair was becoming suspicious and thought this lack of completion was one of the director's mean tricks. Eisenstein complained about
Kimbrough; the two men were only able to communicate via Alexandrov.
Eisenstein was also outraged that Sinclair had started showing material to
the press. He was shocked by Edmund Wilson's article in *The New Republic* on
November 4. The influential critic had written that in Mexico Eisenstein enjoyed total creative freedom for the first time in his life. This would be his first
truly free film. Because of his marred reputation at home, Eisenstein could not
possibly let Wilson's statement stand. He sent a response to the journal on
November 9, mailed a copy to Amkino, and discussed the matter with Sinclair.
Sinclair argued that the order to remove Trotsky from *October* had convinced
the entire Western press that Wilson was right, but Eisenstein was not persuaded. Eisenstein's correction to Wilson's article was not published until
December 9. To strengthen Eisenstein's position, Sinclair wrote an article for
Pravda on November 7: 'I am collecting money for a film that Eisenstein is making in Mexico; this is a brilliant victory for Soviet film technology. I hope to
visit Russia next summer and to gather material for a novel about American
participation in the socialist restructuring of agriculture. I plan to write a screenplay for Eisenstein on the same theme.' This was of little help to Eisenstein.

Right around this time another dramatic story with unexpected consequences came to an end. The father of Fred Danashev, a technician who supervised the development of the Mexican film stock in Hollywood, was a Russian émigré. In the mid-twenties he had returned to the Soviet Union to help
build the film industry. Now a political trial had started against the
'Promparty'—against a fictitious conspiracy of engineers. The engineers were

blamed for all the mishaps and the slowed tempo of industrialization. Fred's father was sucked into the current and accused of sabotage. Fred asked Sinclair to write to Stalin. On November 21, one month after Sinclair's petition, a telegram arrived with the answer. After a few sentences about Anatoly Danashev's fate (Stalin promised to arrange an amnesty if Sinclair insisted; the GPU had clear proof of his guilt), the letter added: 'Eisenstein loose [sic!] his comrades confidence in Soviet Union. He is thought to be deserter who broke off with his own country. Am afraid the people here would have no interest in him soon. Am very sorry but all assert it is the fact.'[179] Sinclair immediately wrote back in Eisenstein's defense: Eisenstein had long ago had the opportunity to sever ties with Moscow, when he had been so sharply attacked in the United States. Instead, he had always remained loyal. He was not to blame for his long stay in Mexico and would return to the Soviet Union as soon as the film was finished.

At first Sinclair did not want to tell Eisenstein about the telegram, so as not to worry him,[180] but Eisenstein heard about the aggravated situation at home from other sources. Since the summer he had been bombarded with letters demanding his return. Shumyatsky had already sent him an ultimatum on July 27: 'We expect your return without regard to the Mexican film. That is only one episode in your artistic career. There is a huge field of work here that is waiting for its masters. That is why we are so impatient. Your great distance from Soviet cinematography is unacceptable. Of course Hollywood and a theoretical experiment there are not bad things, but the work waiting for you in the USSR is one hundred times more important. Good bye and may we see each other soon in Moscow'[181]

On September 9 Esfir Shub beseeched Eisenstein, 'You should return as quickly as possible. Whatever you've shot, there must be enough for your movie.'[182] In November, his mother sent him a disquieting telegram. He answered that the rumors about his defection were a fantasy of the White press: 'Ma loyalité inébranlable [My loyalty is unshakeable].'[183] But on November 27 a dramatic telegram arrived from Pera. Stalin's opinion that Eisenstein was a deserter must have become known in Moscow as well. 'Pray you urgently believe. Your situation unbearable most most serious. Impossible stay Mexico longer week more. Understand. Impossible give details. Wire immediately. Shutko list exact data arrival if necessary. Grisha must finish film alone. No Kindergarten this time. Pearl.'

Eisenstein must have sent a telegram to Kirill Shutko immediately (unfortunately the letter was lost—Shutko was arrested in 1937 and his archive disappeared); Pera sent another telegram that same day: 'Your answer Shutko absolutely silly. Misunderstand absolutely situation. Last word come immediately if not late. Pearl.'[184]

Eisenstein could not have known that Stalin's mistrust was founded in a real precedent. In 1929 and 1930 a wave of Soviet citizens never returned home. Many of them left diplomatic posts. However, it had not escaped Eisenstein that Malevich had been arrested the previous year, after his return from Germany, and was released only thanks to Shutko's intervention. Eisenstein thought that he, the director of the most revolutionary Soviet film, did not need to worry about such things.

That Stalin declared Eisenstein a deserter had other consequences as well. One of the film's financial backers, Comrade Hillkowitz, threatened to take his money out of the project because he did not want to support an 'anti-Soviet' person. Amkino hesitated to pay out the promised $25,000 and gave Eisenstein's unreliable position as the reason. Soyuzkino would occasionally interrupt its payments to the families. Eisenstein asked Sinclair to intervene and to give the family members $250 a month. Sinclair paid out of his own pocket.

In order to save his hide, Eisenstein made the pro forma suggestion to Amkino to edit the film in Moscow. When Sinclair heard about the offer, he was unpleasantly surprised. This had not been part of their agreement! Eisenstein did not actually want to cut the film in Moscow either, and hoped that Sinclair would make some other arrangements for him so he could finish the film in Hollywood. Eisenstein's two-facedness quickly became his undoing.

While Eisenstein was finishing the hacienda episode and preparing 'Soldadera', Sinclair mailed a report to Stalin on December 3. He included an article on the film that the *New York Times* had published on November 29. However, Sinclair did not know that December 9 Stalin was given a whole press folder full of recent articles on Eisenstein. A letter by Shumyatsky accompanied that report. One of the newspaper clippings in the folder announced that King Vidor would make a film about Stalin with Eisenstein as assistant and advisor. 'A second *Ben Hur* will be made.'[185] The script would be based on the book by the *Trotskyite* Isaac Don Levine. Shumyatsky's letter concluded: 'The revived interest in Eisenstein proves that American and German film place some hope in him.'[186] One can only guess what effect this material may have had on Stalin, but Amkino was ordered to sever contact with the renegades immediately and to cancel the payment to Sinclair. On December 25, 1931 Eisenstein received official notice that he and his two coworkers were considered to be 'deserters'.

Sinclair was shocked by Amkino's breach of contract. He demanded that Kimbrough return to Pasadena immediately and report on the filming.

Eisenstein spent Christmas 1931 at the hacienda; his camera team went to Mexico City. He wrote Seymour Stern: 'in the *best company I can imagine*—and that is completely *alone* on the hacienda . . . . I, myself, am like the wandering Jew, or Dante, touring through hell—getting out of one trouble only to get in another—and usually worse one!—out of one mess in another. 'Mass move-ment'—the glorious title accompanying my career should be really written 'mess movement' . . . . But I am really getting desperate of . . . not getting des-perate and continuing to have the most stupid optimism in the world!'[187]

Work progressed much more quickly without Kimbrough, and Eisenstein asked Sinclair to give him full financial authority; Kimbrough was just embez-zling and gambling away the funds anyway. But after his conversation with Kimbrough, Sinclair made a different decision. He granted Kimbrough com-plete authority.

In response, Eisenstein gave Sinclair an ultimatum on January 29. He would not shoot a single meter of film if Kimbrough stayed. Sinclair reacted coolly to Eisenstein's threat (he may have been prepared): the threat amounted to a breach of contract, and the trust would now have to take measures to protect its property. In the meantime, Sinclair had received a report from Amkino on Eisenstein's method of filming *October*. When the budget had been reached, Eisenstein had simply asked for more—and he got it. On January 12 Sinclair responded to Eisenstein's ultimatum with one of his own: the director would have to accept Kimbrough, compile a compulsory time line for the end of shoot-ing, and cancel the 'Soldadera' episode. Otherwise Sinclair would stop the film immediately. After this threat, Sinclair received a plan from Eisenstein and called it absurd.[188] His reaction was understandable: Eisenstein promised to shoot more in 30 days—just before the rainy season—than he had filmed in the past year.

Eisenstein was completely worn out; he lost his hair; his teeth had been aching for a month. On January 20 the dentist pulled seven teeth and Eisenstein went to see a neurologist. Eisenstein pleaded with Sinclair to ask his lawyer in Mexico about Kimbrough, if his own word was not enough. But Sinclair remained firm. He again tried to sell the film, this time for $145,000 and fifty percent of the profits. When his efforts failed, Mary and Upton Sinclair sent Kimbrough a telegram on January 24: 'Permit no further shooting. Come home immediately. Bring party.'[189] In response, Eisenstein withdrew all complaints against Kimbrough on January 25 and apologized in a letter attested by a no-tary. He accepted Upton Sinclair's brother-in-law Kimbrough as production director and agreed to all the points demanded by Sinclair. Alexandrov apolo-gized for the latest delays and blamed them on Eisenstein's illness.

However, two days later Eisenstein wrote to Moscow that he had been forced to make concessions.

In late January, Sinclair allowed ten more days of shooting with a budget of $1,000. Eisenstein would have to renounce the 'Soldadera' episode in writ-ing.[190] Eisenstein made one last effort to save the scene and asked Salka Viertel to mediate: 'I have exhausted my powers of persuasion. I shall do everything he wants . . . . I accept Kimbrough, everything, anything . . . . if only they let me finish this film. I have worked under most incredible harassment, no, not worked—fought . . . . Use your Medea flame and convince him (but especially *her*) to let us finish our film.'[191] Eisenstein, who had just agreed in writing to strike the 'Soldadera' episode, elaborated in the letter that 'Soldadera' was the most important part of the whole film. Without 'Soldadera', the work had no meaning. Salka showed Sinclair the letter, which naturally described Eisenstein's problems with Kimbrough, and the situation escalated even more as Salka Viertel put more facts on the table: 'Selznick authorized me to tell Upton Sinclair that he would like to see all the film Eisenstein had shot as he intended to buy out the Pasadena group and finance the picture himself . . . . That evening Eisenstein telephoned from Mexico and I told him of Selznick's offer. Afterward I called Upton, repeated what Selznick had said, and added that I had to talk to Sergei. But Mrs. Sinclair was adamant. She was deter-mined to call an end to the Mexican venture, and that was that. 'Mr. Eisenstein was notified days ago that the production would be stopped. The film belongs to the Pasadena group and can neither be sold nor financed by anybody.'[192]

Sinclair said that Eisenstein had played him false and terminated their cor-respondence. On February 5 Sinclair ordered Kimbrough to break off filming and to leave Mexico with Eisenstein within two days. This decision was has-tened by a telegram from Amkino that informed Sinclair that Eisenstein's resi-dence permit had expired and demanded his return. The affair was over. On February 12 Kimbrough reported that they were on their way back to the US.

Several months later Sinclair wrote of these events in his autobiography *American Outpost* (1932). He described the order to end the filming as a short circuit. He himself had stood between two fires: Eisenstein and his wife. After hearing the accusations against her brother, Mary Sinclair had had a hysteri-cal attack and had screamed that Sinclair needed to put an end to all of it.

Instead of spending four months in Mexico as planned, Eisenstein stayed fourteen months and shot about eighty thousand meters of film—three times the agreed amount. Sinclair had already spent twice the original budget and significant expenses were still ahead. Mary gathered relatives and lawyers for a final consultation that sealed the film's fate. She is usually given the blame for the film's end, but Sinclair used her as a shield: female hysteria, family honor, and fear of losing money were very understandable reasons for bowing out. However, the Mexican adventure was really the story of two men, Sinclair and Eisenstein. Sinclair had lost faith in Eisenstein and in Eisenstein's integrity. On a personal level, he was deeply disappointed. Without thinking, both men had shown outsiders their letters and had read other people's letters without considering the possible consequences. Eisenstein had lost his diplomatic touch and denounced a close relative of the family—Mary's brother and good friend—as an unemployed lecher for whom the Sinclairs had found a job doing the film. Sinclair showed Eisenstein Kimbrough's letters. Kimbrough's unconscious anti-Semitism hurt more than Major Pease's attacks. The dishonest game involving Eisenstein, his Moscow bosses, Amkino, and Sinclair convinced the latter that Eisenstein was cheating him and playing a cunning game. Sinclair believed that Eisenstein had refused to bring a single episode to completion so that he could later turn the footage into four or six separate movies; Eisenstein promised to accept Kimbrough, but then he immediately denied his own words and told everyone he had been pressured. He had agreed to forfeit the 'Soldadera' episode, but the letter to Salka Viertel proves he was still preparing to shoot it. Sinclair understood that Eisenstein was unpredictable and more than he could handle. When Shumyatsky came to Pasadena in 1935, Sinclair told him about the affair and was pleased when Shumyatsky confirmed his suspicions: "Well, he outsmarted you, that's all.' And we had thought we were dealing with idealists and comrades!'[193] Sinclair later noted.

Of course the problem was not that simple. Sinclair was inexperienced in filmmaking and could not deal with the weather problems, the chaos, the shortage of money, and a stubborn director. He obviously did not want to admit his own failure even to himself. His frustration turned into a flood of denunciations against Eisenstein in his letters to Eisenstein's friends and superiors. Eisenstein had stayed in Mexico at Sinclair's expense instead of returning to Russia. His Mexican friends were all Trotskyites and homosexuals! In a letter to Marie Seton, Sinclair even explained the conflict between Eisenstein and his brother-in-law Kimbrough in terms of a well-bred (i.e. conservative and heterosexual) aristocrat's shock over the manners of a (leftist and homosexual) artist and Jew.[194]

Claims that Eisenstein was a pervert were based mainly on Eisenstein's sketches, which both Kimbrough and Sinclair considered to be pornographic. When customs officers opened the camera team's suitcases full of stills and equipment in Kimbrough and Sinclair's presence, they also discovered Eisenstein's drawings. The policemen, according to Sinclair, said that was 'the vilest stuff' they had ever seen; Sinclair himself was horrified by pictures of copulating animals and people in obscene positions. He was particularly shocked by a drawing of Golgotha: Christ's erect penis was so huge that one of the crucified robbers was able to take it in his mouth. The sketches had been drawn very carefully, in two different colors, which appalled Sinclair even more. Only a short time later, the New York gallery owner John Becker purchased the sketches and exhibited them—as art objects—for the first time.

Rumors of Eisenstein's 'perversion' spread quickly. Sinclair wrote to Eisenstein's friend Professor Dana, 'Suppose also I should tell you that the great artist is a sexual pervert, and that he shipped into the United States an enormous mass of unthinkably filthy drawings and photographs . . . . made with our money? He shipped this in the baggage belonging to us and including all the priceless stills of the expedition. The whole thing was seized by the United States Customs Authorities, and we very nearly had all our property confiscated and a frightful scandal in the newspapers.'[195]

On November 15, 1932 Leiva wrote a letter to Stern: 'Concerning the perversions, I think that the charge is childish. Eisenstein is not a saint, yet he never drinks or smokes or goes to wild parties. He is suspected to be a homosexual, but you know that thousands of innocents live under that suspicion. He made here heaps of . . . . drawings. But he never intended to publish them or to exhibit.'[196]

After the group's departure, Leiva did not believe that they would leave for good. He still thought they could work things out. At the US border in Laredo, Eisenstein's entry visa was rejected. They spent the best part of a month, until March 12, without money in a dirty little hotel waiting for a transit visa. Sinclair did not send them a cent. They had to borrow money or earn it. They filmed shorts about the Mexican dancer María Tereza Montoya and sold them for $1,500 a piece. Kimbrough left on February 24. Seymour Stern, Sinclair and Amkino began the battle to get the Russians a transit visa. Stern wanted to organize a protest, but Pickford, Disney, Chaplin, Lubitsch, DeMille and Vidor did not wish to sign another petition for Eisenstein. Only Schulberg and Sternberg would still agree to do something about the matter.

Eisenstein had a month to process his trauma. He had spent more than a year in Mexico and had still not finished his film. In Moscow, his reputation was shot; his relationship with his loyal assistant Grisha was in shambles. He had written off Sinclair and discovered traits of his own tyrannical father in the American writer. In many ways, the history of this film's creation had been much like his other films. There was an approximate screenplay that could never be realized completely; he repeatedly had to limit himself or select only a few episodes. But until now he had always worked under huge time pressure and under political pressure from above. He had had to finish his earlier films in a short time period, because the date of the premiere was always set at the beginning of production. There could be no extensions, since the date had nothing to do with the film and everything to do with the anniversary of the Revolution. The pressure to finish a state commission on time was increased by the substantial means—not only financial—that stood at his disposal. The army and naval fleet with their organization, logistics, technology, thousands of extras could fill huge spaces—for free! The costs hardly even mattered. As soon as these pressures were gone, Eisenstein let the filming go on fourteen instead of two months and became 'completely absorbed' in his material.

For Sinclair, who had as little knowledge of film production as his brother-in-law Kimbrough, the project was hopeless from the start. Mexico was a cheap country, but $50,000 was a laughable sum for the film that Eisenstein was planning. MGM spent ten times as much for smaller productions. Eisenstein knew that in Hollywood his salary alone would have exceeded Sinclair's entire budget. Had he really been wasting time? Did he really spend a whole year waiting for Paramount to renew its offer, as Sinclair suspected?

In his lust for people, exoticism, and sensuality, Eisenstein became addicted to Mexico. Even though he had been pushed off to the margins, he was filled with the idea, the mission even, of making a movie for the whole world. In Mexico, he discovered what was lacking in European, American, and Soviet film. His fiasco was painful, but he did not believe that all was lost. He thought that he could still save the project in the editing room.

After seven senators became involved (Sinclair had asked them for help), the Russians finally received a transit visa. However, they were not allowed to travel to California, and were only permitted to pass through New York on their way to Europe. The visa was valid for a month. The threesome crossed the border March 14, where Eisenstein was immediately interviewed by a correspondent of the *New York Herald Tribune*.

Sinclair wrote Eisenstein a telegram: 'Trustees approve proposition you made to Amkino to cut picture in Moscow . . . . Will ship film via Bogdanov. Also your trunks and boxes. Your statements that picture incomplete are damaging. Insist you do not make such statements again.'[197] They rented a car and drove to New York.

Eisenstein now got to know the colonial south. In order to make some money, he once again gave lectures, including one in New Orleans, in an African Baptist church. These delays annoyed Sinclair. He promised to send the positive to Moscow by April 1, and simultaneously threatened to sell the negative if Eisenstein did not leave the country within two weeks.

Eisenstein arrived in New York on April 1. First he stayed at the Hermitage Hotel on Times Square, then moved to the Barbizon Plaza. Once the Mexican footage found its way to New York, Eisenstein immediately showed it to all his friends. Sinclair ordered his lawyer to stop the showings and to send the copy back to him. Amkino asked Sinclair if he would pay for the team's tickets home. Sinclair was outraged by the new request for money (Paramount would have paid!), by the delayed departure, by the things Eisenstein was saying in interviews. Sinclair was worried about his reputation.

So Sinclair threatened to destroy Eisenstein's reputation if the director in any way attacked him or his family in public. In November 1931 Sinclair had still defended Eisenstein to Stalin, but in March 1932 he dangerously blackened Eisenstein's name to Soviet officials. On March 19 he even painted a picture of a deliberate deserter in a letter to Amkino representative Smirnov. Eisenstein had tarried in Mexico because he wanted to make use of every opportunity to stay in the US. His Hollywood agent had been trying to arrange a contract and had finally offered him the three-million-dollar Paramount production in India. To top things off, Eisenstein had arranged for a Spanish entry visa through his friend Ambassador del Vayo. He, Sinclair, had been a slave to this traitor for 16 months! He also described the incident with the drawings in detail. Sinclair ended the letter and pathetically declared that he had fulfilled his duty and had returned Eisenstein to the Soviet Union.[198]

Of course, this version served his own purposes: he wanted to present his decision to end the shooting as a political measure, not as a private or financial disaster.

On April 5 Sinclair ordered that the film be placed exclusively at his disposal (however, Amkino only followed the order after Eisenstein's departure) and denied Eisenstein any access to the material. He promised to send the film off on the next boat, but he was worried that Moscow would make a duplicate of the negative, i.e. illegally copy the material. For that reason, he wanted someone to go to Moscow and keep watch over the film. Sinclair also knew that he would have to pay $15,000 in customs for importing the edited film. He weighed all these factors before he decided—after Eisenstein's departure—that he would keep the copy in the United States and have someone else finish it.

Many of Eisenstein's American friends had doubted that Sinclair would keep his promise and send the film to Moscow. They tried to extend Eisenstein's visa so he would be able to finish the film in New York. The lawyer Enos S. Booth started negotiations with Sinclair. Lincoln Kirstein, the publisher of Hound and Horn, wrote on April 30, 1931 in Arts Weekly that this was the most opulent material he had ever seen. It reminded him of Caesar's burntdown library in Alexandria, and Rubens' copy of Leonardo da Vinci's Battle of Anghiari. However, the loss of these works, said Kirstein, was less upsetting than the possible loss of this film. This was clearly an attack against Sinclair, who had barred Eisenstein from his own material and was acting like a banker rather than an artist.

Sinclair responded to this pro-Eisenstein campaign by announcing that he was writing an autobiography that would uncover the background to the Mexico film and explain his own role in its creation. He, Sinclair, had produced the film in order to support a revolution in film art and had never intended to make a profit. The money was to go to the newly founded Sinclair Foundation, which would donate his books to libraries all around the world. Sinclair's position was reinforced by a campaign to nominate him for the Nobel Prize. That movement was supported by 405 European and American intellectuals who included Einstein, Bertrand Russell, and John Dewey. But this was just a taste of the scandal that would rage in the press for two more years.

Amkino meanwhile convinced Eisenstein to go home. He had no one to talk to. He posed for the Russian Futurist David Burlyuk, who had moved to New York in 1922, and for the Mexican Jean Charlot, whom he told that he was afraid of being reprimanded in Moscow for his long absence. He told the dancer Sarah Mildred Strauss, who showed him around New York, that he was returning to Moscow for his mother's sake. On April 19 there was a farewell dinner for Eisenstein and Tisse, arranged by Dreiser. Friends and journalists saw them off at the harbor. Alexandrov stayed in America.

While their ship was crossing the Atlantic, Eisenstein wrote Moussinac that he would have liked to see Paris one more time, but that was impossible. He could also have stopped over in England, but decided that Bremen would be the goal of his journey. Nine days later he reached Berlin and stayed at the Hotel Savoy in the Fasanenstraße. He later reported that Hitler had lived above him.

In Berlin, Eisenstein met Hans Feld and Martha Feuchtwanger. He also saw Valeska Gert again. Lotte Eisner, a critic for *Film-Kurier* and one of the most original interpreters of German Expressionism, interviewed Eisenstein about the montage of the Mexico film. His Berlin friends, who had last seen him a year and a half earlier, thought he had aged by a decade. He had gone almost completely bald.

In several interviews, Eisenstein said that he would soon make a film travelogue of the Soviet Union and *The Twilight of the Gods*, a movie about his experiences with capitalism.

On May 6 Sinclair arranged for all the positives to be sent to Los Angeles, but did not tell Eisenstein. On May 8 Eisenstein traveled to Moscow with Brecht, who had been invited to the premiere of his film *Kuhle Wampe*.

The two artists met for the first time and did not get along. Their 'nonmeeting' was hardly a coincidence. Brecht admitted that it had not been *Potemkin* that made him a Marxist. He found questionable the strong emotional shock that Eisenstein forced his audiences to experience. He thought Eisenstein deprived the audience of the necessary distance and analytical ability to understand what was being presented. Eisenstein's films totally monopolized the viewer and made him easy to manipulate, susceptible to any given ideology. For Brecht, fascism's success only confirmed the danger of the anesthetizing effect of art. For Eisenstein, Brecht was the German version of Tretyakov. He found his didactic plays to be rhetorical, scholastic, hence ineffective and—boring.

Shortly before his departure, Eisenstein mailed a $15 check to Lester Cowan, the secretary of the Academy of Motion Pictures in Hollywood. The sum covered the annual membership fee of the director's guild. That straw was meant to keep him in touch with the world he had left behind.

On May 9 Eisenstein arrived in Moscow. Almost three years had passed since his departure. He would never cross the border again.

THE RETURN
1932-1934

Eisenstein was met at the Belorussian train station by his mother, the film chief Shumyatsky, his friends (Strauch, Glizer, Atasheva) and photographers. His luggage consisted of thirty-two huge suitcases full of books. He was driven to his apartment in an open car. Only slowly did he begin to grasp the changes that had taken place at home.

In 1930 film production in Moscow gradually began to move to the new Soyuzkino studio on the edge of the city near the Potylikha settlement on the Sparrow Hills. By 1935 the studio would be the largest in the country and be renamed Mosfilm. Boris Shumyatsky started large-scale activities designed to turn Soviet cinematography into a self-sufficient industry. The expansion of cinema formed one part of the gigantic upheaval of the first Five-Year Plan, since the Party needed an effective medium for creating the new Soviet identity. As of 1930 much more money was being invested in film than before: in 1927 the state put four million rubles into the industry; in 1937 the subsidies had grown to 225 million rubles a year. The new funds allowed for previously unimaginable expansion, but growth was hampered by technological, economic, and ideological constraints. After 1927 the film industry received no hard currency from the state, which meant that factories had to be built to provide film stock and technology that had previously been imported from Germany. The import of foreign films was gradually frozen. Between 1930 and 1946 only few foreign films (a potentially confusing source of competition) entered regular film distribution. At first, Soviet film production decreased considerably. In 1928 the USSR still produced 124 films; in 1930 only eleven were completed. This drop was connected with the transition from silent to sound film and the switch to domestic resources. In the meantime the number of cinemas exploded. The few films made were copied endlessly onto domestically manufactured positive stock and distributed across the country. The viewing public was thus much more intensely confronted with the 'most important of the arts'. Distribution policies also changed. In the 1920's the playbill had still been renewed every other week, but in the 1930's movies were replaced only once a month. Since cinema remained the only accessible means of entertainment, audiences were at the films' mercy and had to consume ideology as entertainment. Cinema was now controlled by a central organ that could become involved at any level of production and distribution: it reviewed screenplays, finished films, arranged test showings and made personnel decisions about directors, casts, costumes, and music. Stalin viewed cinema, which gradually came under his personal supervision, as a collective creation of film-makers and himself. 'The leader of our Party and our country, the leader of the World Revolution, Comrade Stalin, devotes a great deal of attention to art and finds the time to watch our best films, to correct their errors, to talk to our masters and indicate the direction that each of them should take.'[199] This assessment by Shumyatsky in 1935 is not merely an obligatory rhetorical flourish of the times; his statement is also completely truthful.

Film was only a small part of the larger upheaval. The first public trials took place in 1931, first against the 'Promparty', then against Mensheviks. A wave of 'sabotage' hysteria preceded the actual trials. In public meetings voices would demand the death penalty for saboteurs. Pilnyak wrote, 'it smells of blood here.'[200] After the trial, the death sentences were revoked and the engineers continued their research in prison, but the trials were formative for the behavior of the intelligentsia. Its silence was not tolerated by State and Party apparatuses; instead silence was prosecuted as a crime. The artistic psyche was supposed to change. People took drastic measures: Mayakovsky committed suicide in 1930; the Association of Proletarian Writers (RAPP) led aggressive campaigns against disloyal writers, such as Zamyatin, or against those like Pasternak, who were 'simply poets.' On April 23, 1932 the Party decided to dissolve all artistic organizations. Artists at first interpreted this resolution as liberalization, since the decree also affected RAPP, the one literary group that embodied the direct interference of the Party apparatus in literary life.

During this time, while Eisenstein was still far away and RAPP was stirring up public opinion against the art world's bourgeois fellow travelers, the *Potemkin*-director Eisenstein was classified as a member of the petty bourgeois intelligentsia who had been tagging along with the proletariat. His origins and mental orientation had blocked his understanding of key stages of the Socialist Revolution. Instead, he had led himself down the dead-end path of montage theory, as proven by *October* and *The Old and the New*.

Eisenstein had trouble understanding such ideological nuances and following the new rules. At first, he was shocked at how ugly everything was around him: the new houses, his old apartment. There were gaping holes in downtown Moscow because many buildings, and especially churches, had been razed to free space for the reconstruction of the city.

After a three-year interruption, after numerous letters calling him home to help establish Soviet cinematography, what great task was he supposed to accomplish? Shumyatsky offered Eisenstein a musical! Eisenstein declined and felt mocked. Was he supposed to imitate Hollywood? Unlike the average Hollywood director, Eisenstein could never have enthusiastically embraced the idea of making commercial entertainment.

Eisenstein was still waiting for the footage from his Mexican film. On June 4, 1932 Sinclair announced that the film would not be cut by Eisenstein in Moscow, but by another Hollywood director. In July, Sinclair offered to sell the complete negative to Amkino—for $75,000. The price was justified, he said, because there was enough material for three films.[201] When Amkino agreed to buy the negative at that price, Sinclair increased the price to $100,000 and wrote a letter to Stalin explaining himself.[202] Then he gave the material to MGM. Sol Lesser cut *Thunder Over Mexico*; the rest of the material was to be auctioned later at the price of one dollar per meter.

Eisenstein knew nothing about the negotiations with Sinclair. He twice wrote Alexander Stetsky, the new Propaganda Chief of the Central Committee, who had replaced his good friend Krinitsky, to try to find out what was going on. He never received an answer. When he found out the truth in August from newspaper clippings sent to him by Seymour Stern, he locked himself in his apartment and considered committing suicide.

During this time Eisenstein met the Englishwoman Marie Seton, who witnessed his trauma. Seton was astonished by how poorly Eisenstein lived in comparison with other Soviet artists. Paint was peeling everywhere in the old building; the doorbell hardly worked; the hallway was narrow and dark; a moody peasant woman ran Eisenstein's household.

These circumstances stood out, because in the thirties the first signs of comfort were appearing in the lives of Soviet citizens. There were new service complexes, affectionately called 'Americans', opening in Moscow; the first Soviet perfumes appeared on the market with metaphoric names such as 'Red Moscow' or 'Dawn of Freedom'. However, the wives of the artistic elite continued to use French brands and kept their own household help. Peasant women, who lived in Moscow semilegally and had fled hunger in the collective farms or imprisonment in Siberia, were a source of cheap labor.

Eisenstein was obviously not bothered by his simple lifestyle.

At first he gave lectures on his impressions abroad, Mexican theater, and the US film industry. On October 1 he was appointed Chair of the Direction Department at the film school GIK. He was offered a film project in Persia. He thought that the tragic fate of the writer and diplomat Alexander Griboedov, told in the vein of Tynyanov's novel *The Death of Vazir Mukhtar*, would fit his current mood. But after such a long, ambivalent absence, it was impossible for him to leave the country. Two cameramen were sent to Persia instead, and Eisenstein's project remained on the drawing table. Eisenstein knew a lot about high-level intrigue; he understood that he would have to approach the leader himself. When Eisenstein was still in Mexico he gave his friend Strauch written advice on how a film director should behave: 'pressure them, be diplomatic, grovel, be sly, and then pressure them again.'[203] Why wasn't he having any success? His friends in high places had changed jobs. Stalin kept shifting them from one post to the next, opening up the hierarchy for newcomers, and moving the old ones around on the official carousel. Krinitsky was gone; Raskolnikov was serving abroad; Shutko had lost his influence. Martemyan Ryutin headed the commission for film innovations.

Stalin also placed his bets on literature. He visited Gorky frequently and met with writers, whom he addressed in a light and ironic manner. Writers were enthusiastic about him. On October 26, 1932 a fateful meeting took place in Gorky's apartment. Stalin formulated his demand for a new artistic method; after the meeting, Alexander Fadeev summarized these ideas in an essay. Two years later this method was officially adopted as 'Socialist Realism'. This rapprochement between the leaders of the Party and literary circles was interpreted as a sign of liberalization. At the same time, however, there were more arrests. The Ryutin group was declared counterrevolutionary because Martemyan Ryutin had demanded an end to collectivization and to Stalin's rule. Famine in the countryside reached catastrophic proportions; the death toll surpassed eight million. On November 9, 1932, Stalin's wife, Nadezhda Alliluyeva, unexpectedly committed suicide. Moscow rumors had it that she might even have been killed.

Eisenstein seemed far removed from these events; he was off suffering his own Mexican trauma. As another director was cutting his film in America, a harsh discussion in Moscow dismissed montage as a mere formalistic device. In order to disprove that absurd thesis, Eisenstein wrote the essay "Eh!' On the Purity of Film Language' in which he analyzed fourteen shots from *Potemkin* that had become classics—because of clever montage. He was influenced in his analysis by conversations with the Gestalt psychologist Kurt Koffka, whom he had met at Luria's home.

In late October Eisenstein traveled to Armenia and Georgia in order—according to the official version—to prepare a screenplay. He stayed until December, licking his wounds. At this time the Caucasus was a place of refuge for over-stressed Moscow intellectuals, including Andrei Bely, Boris Pasternak, and Osip Mandelstam.

The new chief of cinematography and Eisenstein had nothing in common. Shumyatsky was developing a pragmatic program for a new Soviet movie industry that would reach millions of viewers. He wanted simple, intelligible stories, pretty stars, clear messages, light music, no formal experimentation— the opposite of the standard for revolutionary film that Eisenstein had set in the twenties. Shumyatsky thought that Eisenstein's generation was passé and placed his bets on the younger filmmakers. The Mexican trio had dissolved:

Tisse was racing cars in the desert and Alexandrov had taken over the assignment that Eisenstein had turned down. Grisha filmed the comedy *The Happy
Guys* using all of Hollywood's tricks. After the inevitable quid pro quo, the
shepherd and maid become stars of the music hall. The movie's musical numbers distracted the audience from all thoughts and worries. In one episode,
the rehearsal of a jazz orchestra degenerates into a hilarious fight scene.
Eisenstein helped Grisha with the film's montage, but felt that he had been
betrayed. He had lost Grisha to a new understanding of cinema and to a woman.
During the work on *The Happy Guys*, Grisha fell in love with his lead actress,
the blonde soprano Lyubov Orlova.

Eisenstein tried to counter this state-ordered kitsch with his own idea of a
comedy. He used the film project *MMM* to process his impressions of the
changes in Soviet life. He himself had returned home as a quasi-foreigner. In
MMM he described everyday absurdities from the perspective of foreign visitors. Eisenstein's visitors were time travelers from the 16th century who suddenly show up in Moscow in the 1930's. Eisenstein played freely with anachronisms. Warriors from Russian fairy tales conquered *byt* (everyday life), rode
on packed streetcars, and held their ground against the police. Boyars from
the time of Ivan the Terrible acted like rich repatriated citizens.

He wrote the screenplay in free verse: this was the only literary form that
resembled montage and could express his concept of inner monologue, which
lay at the core of the comedy. He envisioned Strauch and Glizer in the lead
roles. This was the first film sketch that showed off his notoriously wicked
sense of humor. Eisenstein depicts a bourgeois version of life, or rather a petty-
bourgeois imitation of bourgeois life. He describes the life of a Soviet conformist, Maxim Maximovich Maxim (hence the title *MMM*), who runs the Intourist-
office and resembles heroes from Mayakovsky and Erdman's satirical comedies. Much like the American absurd burlesque, Eisenstein's comedy exposes
the technique of laughter and relies on constant defamiliarization. The director and the scriptwriter—both star in the film—develop the plot as a game of
chess by moving the film's characters: the actors regularly step out of their
roles, but are still confused with their dramatis personae. Even film technology
itself is part of the game: in order to objectify the inner monologue, the hero swal-
lows a microphone as everyone else waits to hear his 'innermost' secrets.

Eisenstein was generously remunerated for his work on the script—he
received 18,000 rubles in three payments. *MMM* was released for production
in March 1933. Eisenstein had already finished casting when the production
was suddenly stopped. This happened to a number of comedies of the time.
Nikolai Erdman (who wrote Alexandrov's script) was working on the set when
the GPU came to take him away.

In May Eisenstein planned to devote himself fully to the textbook *Direction* and simultaneously came up with a grandiose plan for a book on the psychology of art: art's *Grundproblem* ('Fundamental Problem'). Eisenstein attended lectures by the linguist Nikolai Marr and studied the results of his friends' (Luria and Vygotsky) psychological research. Not until June 29, 1933, one year after his return, was he confirmed as a film director at Soyuzkino's Moscow studio. The confirmation didn't come out of the blue—Eisenstein was assigned a film about Moscow.

Eisenstein made notes for this historical film during the first ten days of June. During this time Moscow was supposed to host an international congress on city planning, but the Soviets unexpectedly canceled the meeting at the last minute. A dramatic story had preceded the congress. Many internationally acclaimed architects, such as Gropius, Le Corbusier, and Hans Poelzig had participated in a competition to design the new Palace of the Soviets that was to replace the demolished Church of Christ the Savior. All of their proposals had been rejected. Sigfried Giedion, Secretary of the Association of International Architects (CIAM), wrote a letter to Stalin in their name. He expressed their bewilderment over Soviet Classicism, Moscow's new line of architecture. This letter probably led to the cancellation of the congress. The international architecture elite was indignant about the plans for reconstructing the Soviet capital, which had been presented by Lazar Kaganovich in a 1931 speech. Ten Soviet architecture offices would continue to work on the project for four more years.

Eisenstein presumably knew of the dramatic events surrounding the architecture congress, since he had participated in a discussion of proposals for the Palace of the Soviets in the spring of 1933. That he sketched his first ideas for the film during the planned congress is hardly a coincidence. He certainly knew of the reconstruction projects, since his film was to illustrate Moscow's new understanding of history through its architecture. The city was being rebuilt according to Stalin's general plan, presented by Kaganovich, much as peasant Russia had been rebuilt according to Stalin's General Line.

In spite of the distrust expressed by Stalin during Eisenstein's absence, the director once again received an important state commission. *October* had cemented the image of Petrograd as the city of revolution and as Lenin's city; now he was supposed to capture the birth of Stalin's Moscow in effective film images.

Eisenstein intended to transfer the main principle of his Mexican film to the Moscow project. The first draft of his screenplay included three main trajectories: history of the Russian and Soviet states, transformation of nature, and creation of a new city architecture according to the plan for general reconstruction. *Moscow* interpreted the state's idea as a new vision of a *Gesamtkunstwerk*, as the unity of history, nature, and art.

Stalin's general plan rested on the ideology of an absolute center—a city that materialized the utopian dream of a unique country. Grandiose architectural plans for building a subway, canals, and skyscrapers tested the limits of depth, height, length, and breadth. Moscow, a northern city without access to the sea, was declared the capital of five seas and built like a southern Mediterranean metropolis. New buildings had open terraces and broad balconies. This water cult revived the old imperial dream: an empire becomes a world power by conquering waterways and controlling access to the sea in order to dominate trade. Russia had long been cut off from the water. Stalin's gigantic plan envisioned changing the landscape by connecting all the seas through canals. Then Moscow really would have access to all the waterways. This dream had its origin centuries earlier, when Ivan the Terrible fought wars over the Baltic Sea and Empress Catherine battled for the Black Sea. In this new project Eisenstein planned to shape this anachronism in a dramatic way, rather than taking the funny approach of MMM.

Moscow in the 1930s was still far removed from this grand vision—its streets were narrow and curved; its houses were chaotically scattered about. Monasteries and warehouses blocked the view of every big square. The city was cut up by little alleys and dead ends. Stalin had the streets broadened: houses were moved over several yards; all the trees were chopped down on the garden ring. Historic buildings and old churches, especially those that blocked the view and obstructed the squares, were torn down mercilessly. A battle raged about the future of St. Basil's Cathedral on Red Square; it was finally allowed to stay. The center was purged. The new open spaces would be filled with colossal buildings; the new, broad, straight lines completely restructured Moscow. While the utopian architecture of the 1920s was dominated by glass expressing the transparency of relationships, the buildings of the 1930s were dressed in thick coats of stone and plaster. Wood was replaced by marble and granite.

All this construction lasted several years and filled everyday life of Muscovites with chaos, noise, and dust. The city was slowly transformed into an encrypted book whose writing was not accessible to everybody. The foundation of the Theater of the Soviet Army was built in the shape of a star, but that was only visible from an airplane.

Eisenstein, who could manipulate architecture like no other Soviet director, was supposed to teach the ignorant audience how to read the new symbols and to create a correspondence between the film and the state's utopian architecture. The Komsomol was put in charge of the film that was supposed to cover everything: industrialization (from Peter I through the 19th century), battles of liberation against the Tatars and Napoleon, three revolutions.

Eisenstein was fascinated by the scope of the new utopia, but he did not know what to do with its actual existence, so his sketches remained very abstract.

He planned to use city architecture to structure history with the help of a model from Elizabethan theater. Four elements—water, air, fire, and earth—determined the plot as a geometrical figure. He interpreted historical dialectics as the dialectics of nature, but transferred them into alchemical concepts. Eisenstein wanted to create a system of huge correspondences—one event would be reflected in another, a small story would be mirrored in a larger one. The story (*syuzhet*) was based on the principle of metaphorical transference. The history of a class was reflected in the history of a family; the history of the family in the history of an individual; the individual's history in the history of the city; city history in the history of the state. The state's history was represented by the four natural elements. However, Eisenstein did not have any ideas for the plot (*fabula*). He thought that it might be possible to realize the transformation from the material to the immaterial: Moscow's architecture would complete this process over the course of the film's development. In *Glass House*, Eisenstein had to transfer metaphors into real, literal and material objects. Now, in *Moscow*, he had to transform material, literal objects into metaphorical concepts. Thus the four material elements turn into tropes, for example 'the air of freedom' or 'the fire of the Revolution'. They transmogrify into heraldic emblems that manifest history. *Moscow* had to make do without the actual architecture of the city (the old architecture had been destroyed, the new plans weren't finished yet) and work with cardboard models. This was in effect a film about a history that had been placed into the world of the film studio and had mutated into a play of *theatrical elements* that superseded historical processes. Eisenstein's method of equivalence (liberation from the Tatars equals war against Napoleon) eventually made time stand still, or rather, eliminated time altogether. History turned into an eternal play without progress in a metaphysical theater set, into a *perpetuum mobile* (yet another reference to alchemy).

The two projects—MMM and *Moscow*—had one thing in common: they were structured around an inner monologue. Eisenstein even played with the idea of giving this inner voice to Lenin.

He looked for an author who would write the script to *Moscow*, but could not find anybody. In 1933 an editor introduced Eisenstein to Andrei Bely. Eisenstein went to a private reading of Bely's book *The Art of Gogol* and was thrilled by the author's discussion of the changes in Gogol's color palette. He immediately led a discussion of the book at an evening for the poet in the Polytechnic Museum on February 27. Bely had just finished his novel *Moscow*; the final chapters were published in 1932. Meyerhold wanted to stage the book in his theater, but Bely's vision of the chaotic city as a maze and spider web had little in common with current State policy.

Eisenstein asked Alexander Fadeev, a writer close to Stalin, to collaborate on the screenplay. Fadeev answered in a letter on August 22 that he could not accept the offer because he and Eisenstein, whom he deeply respected, were walking different paths. Fadeev was also planning to spend several months in the Far East, so he suggested that Eisenstein turn to his colleague Pyotr Pavlenko.[204] Pavlenko was an adventurer. He had worked in China for a long time; now he was close to the GPU and suggested that his writer colleagues hide in the closets of interrogation rooms to experience interrogations and torture. Eisenstein did not take Fadeev's advice. When the newspaper *Kino* announced that Eisenstein and Fadeev had signed a contract to write the script to *Moscow* and that the film would be ready by October 1, 1934, Fadeev had already turned down the offer. The date was also unrealistic for the studio. Since a film of this scope could never be finished that quickly, the project was scrapped altogether.

While Eisenstein was preparing *Moscow*, he also resurrected an old American idea and tried to sell it to the studio. He even met with success. On July 23, 1933 Eisenstein signed a contract with Soyuzkino to write the screenplay to *The Black Consul*. The story was about an 18th-century slave rebellion in Haiti that had been supported by monastery authorities, but was betrayed by Napoleon. It also dealt with the mutation of a revolutionary into a dictator. The revolutionary protagonist Henri Christophe was crowned Emperor of Haiti. Another point of controversy was the figure of General Toussaint-L'Ouverture, a 'black Robespierre' or 'black Napoleon'. He began as Haiti's revolutionary leader, then became the dictatorial governor, and was finally arrested in 1802 on Napoleon's order and deported to France, where he died in the dungeons. This story had already inspired a number of writers. Eisenstein referred to John W. Vandercook's *Black Majesty* (1928), Percy Waxman's *The Black Napoleon* (1931), and Karl Otten's *Der schwarze Napoleon* (1931). When Otten heard about Eisenstein's interest from his Comintern friends in September 1932, he suggested that Eisenstein film his novel. But Eisenstein decided to ask the Soviet literary scholar Anatoly Vinogradov to collaborate instead. Vinogradov had also worked with the story and published his own novel *The Black Consul* in 1933. Eisenstein envisioned Paul Robeson in the leading role. The project began to stall, even though Eisenstein followed orders and turned his attention away from the central figure of the tyrant to one of Toussaint-L'Ouverture's adjutants, Jean-Jacques Dessalines. Dessalines had remained true to the idea of freedom and led the slave's war of liberation to the end. However, he also had the people crown him Emperor in 1804.

The Mexican trauma welled up again in the summer of 1933. The press screening of *Thunder over Mexico* took place in Los Angeles on May 10, 1933. The film was attributed to Eisenstein. The story 'Maguey', which Eisenstein intended to be two reels long, was stretched out over six reels. Sinclair had succeeded in turning one episode into a full-length film. The press published euphoric reviews by Chaplin and Fairbanks. Sinclair announced that Sol Lesser had cut the film according to Eisenstein's original plan. However, the *Los Angeles Times* wrote on May 14, 1933, that without Eisenstein's montage the film had turned into a 'series of exquisite still pictures in a reasonable (but conventional) dramatic sequence.' Lesser's version reminded the journalist of a Beethoven symphony scored for a string quartet, or the theory of relativity explained in a newspaper column.

The screening triggered a wave of open letters, accusations, denunciations, and explanations. In June 1933, Seymour Stern and Agustín Aragón Leiva founded the International Defense Committee for a Mexican Film. They tried to ban the premiere of *Thunder over Mexico* and have the film reedited. Their actions unleashed protests all over Latin America, from Peru to Brazil and Argentina. Even a Rumanian prison in Transylvania joined their efforts. Several letters denouncing Sinclair were sent to the Nobel Prize Committee in Stockholm—Sinclair's name was being considered for the Nobel Prize. Sinclair was accused of destroying the work of a genius in a barbaric manner. He defended his decision with the argument that not a single Eisenstein film had been cut by Eisenstein himself. Sinclair wrote to Eisenstein's friends and defenders and threatened to spread truths about Eisenstein that he had so far kept quiet. He reiterated that Eisenstein had used the delays in shooting to stay in the United States and threatened to publish Stalin's telegram as proof. Sinclair said that he had only interrupted the work to force Eisenstein to return to the Soviet Union. He had kept Eisenstein from becoming a second Sergei Rachmaninoff or Feodor Chaliapin. Russian and American Communists should be thankful to him. In Sinclair's statements, the sum he had spent on Eisenstein grew from $53,000 to $120,000![205]

Eisenstein sent a 30-page letter telling his side of the story to the journalist Joe Freeman; he wanted Freeman to publish his statement. Freeman declined and forwarded the letter to Amkino, since Sinclair supported his orthodox Communist newspaper *New Masses*. Freeman only responded to Eisenstein after Sinclair ran for California governor as a Democrat in 1934 and became a target of leftist radicals. The Moscow press ignored the Mexican story, since Sinclair was still a 'friend of the Soviet Union'.

Since Freeman had not responded to his letter, Eisenstein feared that Shumyatsky had interrupted his channels of communication. He then turned to Louis Fischer, the Moscow correspondent of the liberal paper *The Nation*, and asked him to negotiate with Sinclair. Fischer wired Pasadena that Eisenstein was willing to cut the film within four months and asked where Eisenstein's part of the profit was. Sinclair responded that Eisenstein had broken the contract. Even if he, Sinclair, were personally willing to pay Eisenstein, he could not legally give him a share of the profit.[206] At this time, the film had made about $30,000. Eisenstein suggested that Sinclair send him a duplicate of the negative in lieu of his share of the profit, so he could cut his own version. Sinclair refused this suggestion, since it would endanger 'his' film. On July 25 Fischer pleaded with Sinclair in a telegram. If Sinclair did not accept Eisenstein's offer, that could only mean that he, an artist himself, was depriving another artist of his work. Fischer described Eisenstein's extreme depression and hinted to Sinclair that Eisenstein might do something rash.[207] A week passed before Sinclair responded. He said that his offer to Soyuzkino to sell the material still stood. He did not have the money to make a duplicate of the negative; maybe the profit would later cover the cost of a second negative for Eisenstein. On August 4 Fischer reminded Sinclair of the negative; Sinclair did not respond. Pera Atasheva gave copies of Sinclair's and Eisenstein's Mexican correspondence to Fischer in the hope that he might publish them and use them to pressure Sinclair. Fischer adamantly refused to publish the letters. Eisenstein had a nervous breakdown and was sent to the Caucasus, to a sanatorium in Kislovodsk.

Sinclair had meanwhile written Eisenstein's friend Professor Dana several times enlightening the professor about the 'sexual pervert' and potential émigré. Dana sent copies of these letters to Moscow. Pera Atasheva wrote Dana on August 18 that Eisenstein was doing very poorly and to please stop forwarding Sinclair's letters. As Eisenstein's assistant, she tried to defend him and wrote that the director was only interested in finishing his work of art, as proven by his letters to Sinclair, but that Sinclair refused even to respond. Now that Eisenstein had returned to the Soviet Union, he was not in a position to prevent or harm the film's distribution, and Sinclair's worries were therefore unfounded.

The International Defense Committee for a Mexican Film demanded that Sinclair stop destroying Eisenstein's political position in the Soviet Union with claims of sexual perversion and disloyalty. In 1933 the New York premiere of Sinclair's film went off without incident, in spite of protests and a large police force outside the theater. Meanwhile, Sinclair had Sol Lesser cut a second film, *The Death Day*. He published the announcement on his campaign stationery.

In September Eisenstein left Kislovodsk for Kabardino-Balkariya's capital Nalchik, a former Russian fortress in the foothills of the Caucasus. Betal Kalmykov, First Secretary of the region and a friend of Isaak Babel, housed Eisenstein in a Party sanatorium and asked if he would like to take part in an auto-rally. The republic had just announced a competition to design the capital city. Eisenstein looked through the projects, made fun of them, and designed a few himself. His drawings took the mountainous landscape into account and imitated the shape of the national headgear. This amateur occupation with architecture seemed to be a sublimation of the interrupted film *Moscow*.

After his return from the Caucasus, Eisenstein resumed teaching at the film school GIK. He lectured on composition in film and literature. He chose scenes from Dostoevsky's *Crime and Punishment* and Leskov's *Lady Macbeth of Mtsensk* in which domestic violence plays itself out in cramped rooms. He planned to lead an English-language seminar at GIK in December. Applicants included the American Jay Leyda, the Englishman Herbert Marshall, and in 1936 an Irishman named Samuel Beckett.

Eisenstein's Russian students were given English lessons by Ivy Litvinova, wife of People's Commissar for Foreign Affairs Maxim Litvinov. Eisenstein frequently met with her at her house or at the dacha.

Rumor had it that Eisenstein had stopped working and had no more plans. His income was now modest in comparison with his colleagues. His salary at the film school (792 rubles) was three times an engineer's income, but only a tenth of Meyerhold's monthly earnings. Once the center of attention, Eisenstein had now been written off. During this time, Boris Pasternak told him that he was like a 'church that had not yet been destroyed'.[208] Mean-spirited intrigues against Eisenstein were making their way through the highest echelons, led by Boris Shumyatsky, whom Eisenstein obviously irritated with his arrogance and careless jokes. In the eyes of the mighty, the Revolutionary artist had turned into a 'bourgeois reactionary'.

A reminder of Eisenstein's former image unexpectedly came from Germany. In February 1934 Goebbels demanded of his artists a National Socialist *Potemkin* during a speech at the Berlin Kroll Opera House. Two years later his wish was fulfilled. Carl Anton filmed *Weiße Sklaven* ('White Slaves'), which described the 1905 mutiny of Russian sailors from the point of view of the officers. On March 9, 1934 Eisenstein responded to Goebbels' speech in an open letter to *Literaturnaya gazeta* that was translated and reprinted in *Film Art* and the German émigré newspaper *Pariser Tageblatt*. Eisenstein essentially denied National Socialist art the existential right to call itself art. 'Truth and National Socialism are incompatible,' since that regime was based on lies (such as the Dimitroff trial), contempt for humanity, and mass terror. However, 'the higher the work of art, the more fully the artist has succeeded in comprehending, feeling and communicating this creative burst of the masses themselves.'[209] At this time, Eisenstein—like Meyerhold—believed that fascism would soon self-destruct and that the German proletariat would show who was 'the subject of history'. His arguments against art in the service of the Nazi Party bureaucracy—and his defense of Soviet art—was put into a macabre light by the events of 1934. Only two months later Osip Mandelstam was arrested; he later attempted suicide in prison.

Shortly thereafter the American critic and Trotsky's translator Max Eastman published *Artists in Uniform: A Study of Literature and Bureaucratism.*[210] The book was a sensation in the West and a scandal in Moscow. The author sharply criticized the Soviet apparatus' crushing of Russian writers, writing as a knowledgeable insider of the literary scene. All over the world discussions of the book equated the ways in which the National Socialists and the Russian Communists used their artists. On July 18, 1934 Karl Radek finally had to respond in *Izvestiya*. He dismissed Eastman's accusations by pointing to concentration camps and book burnings in Germany. In that country poets were physically destroyed. In the Soviet Union they were merely forced actively to apply their art to the construction of Socialism. In this polemic Radek basically invalidated Eisenstein's argument against Goebbels, according to which art could not be created under pressure from the Party. However, nobody seemed to make that connection. Even Eisenstein himself did not openly acknowledge the dissonance; after all he had made all of his films in the 1920's on order from the Party.

While people in the West still listened to Eisenstein, he was increasingly ignored at home. On November 18, 1934, shortly after the premiere of *Chapaev*, directed by Eisenstein's students Sergei and Georgy Vasiliev, Shumyatsky published an article in *Literaturnaya gazeta* called 'The Best Soviet Film'. He sharply attacked Eisenstein, who had frequently complained that the bureaucratic apparatus and outdated theater aesthetics had aborted the development of Soviet cinema. Eisenstein responded in an open letter to the editor, which was never published: 'My behavior is presented as that of a costumed bandit, a Mafia-member, an Al Capone. You might think I wanted to blow up Potylikha [the location of the new studio] or the film headquarters.'[211]

Alexandrov's film *The Happy Guys* was finished in the summer of 1934. Critics panned the movie for its saccharine kitsch, but Stalin praised the film highly. Alexandrov advanced to the status of most-favored director. Eisenstein's former assistant had usurped his place. Foreign journalists who had once come to interview Eisenstein now talked to Alexandrov. This only confirmed the general belief that Eisenstein was burned out.

In 1933-34 a house was constructed for film workers between Malaya Nikitskaya and Povarskaya streets, just behind Dom Kino, the House of Cinema. Alexandrov took over the cooperative's leadership. The apartments were very comfortable and had generous layouts. Eisenstein intended to occupy two apartments in the house—three rooms for himself and a studio for his mother.

His mother was becoming pushier. She no longer wanted and was no longer able to live alone in Leningrad. Her place was also searched in 1934; all remaining gold and silver items were confiscated. Eisenstein supported her and paid her 300-500 rubles monthly; the exact sum depended on his own income. He asked his mother to go to Shumyatsky and ask for the apartments. He advised her to describe his depression, since Shumyatsky would be the one to finally decide if Eisenstein would receive an apartment. He did not get one.

He had lost his leading role. He had not made a single film since 1929; his social presence had shrunk to zero; he was merely a teacher at the film school.

In 1934 Eisenstein's old friend Axyonov wrote a monograph on Eisenstein in an attempt to put the director back into the spotlight. Eisenstein corrected several versions of the manuscript and turned his life into a legend, but the book was never published in his lifetime.[212]

It is amazing that Eisenstein, the most politically exposed director of the twenties, was allowed to live such an apolitical life after his return home. This was only possible because 1932 and 1933 had brought a short liberal pause. The wave of arrests came to an end in 1933 and many people were released from prison. Even the banned opposition leaders Lev Kamenev and Grigory Zinoviev were allowed to return to the capital. Bukharin was demoted to the post of editor at *Izvestiya* in 1934; this amounted to his resignation from politics. He tried to turn art into a refuge for the individual personality: against the backdrop of the easy victory of fascism in Germany this says much about Bukharin's utopian despair.

After his return, Eisenstein had difficulty adapting to the new rules of behavior. Even his clothes seemed extravagant. Muscovites now dressed very formally—dark suits and ties were obligatory. Eisenstein's shaggy, yellow tweed jacket from America stood out. People experienced Eisenstein as arrogant, reserved, cynical, and unfriendly.

The image of the new Soviet artist—an open person without doubts— had been formed during his absence. Leading directors like Pudovkin and Dovzhenko traveled around the country visiting collective farm and factories in order to meet with the workers. Meyerhold gave a speech at the inauguration of the Dnieper hydroelectric plant. When Pasternak returned from such a tour of collective farms in 1932, it took a long time for him to process the suffering that he had seen. In Moscow, artists were pampered and received special rations—Spanish oranges, rare Russian fish, dachas, apartments, cars. The peasants, however, were starving. The most basic needs of the exploited workers on construction sites were ignored. In August 1933 one hundred twenty writers were sent out to document the building of the White Sea Canal. They were to turn the life stories of forced laborers—criminals and enemies of the people—into novels, plays, and poems. Eisenstein was spared these appearances *in front of* and encounters *with* the builders of socialism. He was unable to give fiery speeches, since he did not have a film to accompany them. Instead he had only 'flawed opinions on film art'. His depression and heart attacks secured him recovery time in the spa while his artist colleagues made excursions 'into life'. He tried to avoid all social engagements, even among small circles of friends. Louis Fischer's wife Markoosha was hurt that Eisenstein shunned her invitations. Rumors spread that Eisenstein was interested only in himself, his theory, and montage.

His colleagues were completely indifferent to his theories. Two 'classmates', the directors Mikhail Kalatozov and Sergei Bartenev, published an article in which they sharply attacked the practice of montage.[213] In order to reconcile *Potemkin* with the flawed theories of montage, the critics reinterpreted the reasons for the movie's success. *Potemkin* had been made not by Eisenstein's montage, but by the well thought-out scenario. That scenario, in turn, had strictly followed the logic of real events, which meant that the film's human author was irrelevant. *Potemkin* had been created by history itself. In other words, the little that was left Eisenstein—his most famous film—had been taken away.

Eisenstein accused Soviet cinematography of having entirely succumbed to theater. Meyerhold advised Eisenstein to direct a theater production, preferably opera. On August 20, 1934 Eisenstein announced demonstratively that he was going to the Theater of the Revolution to direct the play *Moscow 2* by Nathan Zarkhi, a writer best known for his film scripts. A Leningrad paper even published an interview entitled 'Why I Left the Cinema'.[214]

The situation was somewhat paradoxical. He was not allowed to make the film *Moscow*, and he criticized cinema for being too much like theater. Therefore he decided to work in the theater and direct a Moscow project written by one of Pudovkin's screenplay writers! The premiere was scheduled for January 1935. His connection to the Theater of the Revolution hinged on one detail: this was the workplace of his friends and neighbors Maxim Strauch and Judith Glizer.

There were six characters in the play: five people and a stone guest. The subject was the hero's confrontation with his monument, a situation that Eisenstein found to be somewhat autobiographical. The hero was a worker-activist for whom a monument was erected on Pushkin Square right next to Alexander Pushkin (who wrote his own play about Don Juan and the stone commander). After the statue's completion, the worker's life reeled out of control. Everybody—his wife, his colleagues, he himself—compared the real person to his monument. If he wanted to have a drink, he now had to ask himself if his monument would approve. The man lived in permanent conflict with his super-ego and was barely able to process the confrontation between social and individual behavior.

During a lecture at the film school Eisenstein said that when he heard of the subject —a man and his monument—he knew that the play was right for him. He simultaneously began rehearsing Shakespeare's *Julius Caesar*, a drama in which a person's value is determined by his or her success as a conscious player in the historical arena. In *Moscow 2* this same subject was to be worked out comically. The play would lead the way to new standards of behavior in the tradition of Tretyakov's *I Want a Baby!* But Eisenstein only had luck with apocalyptic tragedies about the destruction of the old world. His attempts at comedies about building a new world met with a different fate.

Eisenstein and Zarkhi worked together on the plot. The dialogue had not yet been finished when Zarkhi died in a car accident in 1935. Pudovkin, who had been at the wheel, survived, and the incomplete play was canceled by the theater's general director Alexei Popov.

Eisenstein found himself back at his desk. He studied *Alice in Wonderland* by Lewis Carroll and asked his friends in the West to send him all the secondary literature they could find. He had been working on the textbook *Direction*, a work about the art of mise-en-scène, since June. He developed a simple situation—a soldier returns from the front—in different genres—expressionist drama, everyday comedy, high tragedy. Using a long, rational approach to the creative process, he would find the only possible artistic solution for every single little gesture and detail. His textbook and his course on direction used the classical Socratic method.

In the days leading up to the Writers' Congress Eisenstein visited Gorky. Gorky suggested a film topic—the fate of homeless children—and offered to write the script himself. Gorky had already suggested that material to almost every filmmaker he had met. Eisenstein declined. He had little sympathy for sentimentality, and was uninterested in the material and Gorky's views on the education of the new man. Eisenstein took part in the Writers' Congress from August 17 to September 1, 1934.

At the congress, Karl Radek gave a speech—all details of which were approved by Stalin in advance—that condemned all of western modernity, including the inner monologue. Joyce was dismissed as decadent; the ongoing translation of *In Search of Lost Time* was stopped one year later.

The congress was not only significant for writers. This is where the course was set for a new understanding of art and artists, including film and filmmakers. During his speech at the congress, André Malraux expressed bewilderment that Soviet functionaries placed greater trust in criminals than they did in artists. Art had nothing to do with following directives; art was about free imagination and experimentation. The congress unexpectedly brought Eisenstein a job offer from Malraux that saved him from immediate worries: Eisenstein's dry spell was not only creative, but also financial. Pera had already been forced to sell his silver and copper things. The contract with the Mezhrabprom studio to work as an expert advisor for the film version of Malraux's *La Condition humaine* ('Man's Fate') came at just the right time. Albert Gendelstein was supposed to direct the film. After the congress, Eisenstein traveled to the Crimea with Malraux and Babel to work on the script. Six months later, in March 1935, Malraux was back in Moscow. Now Meyerhold was supposed to direct the stage version of his novel. Ehrenburg had already translated the book, but the project was never realized. The film was also left on the drawing board.

Eisenstein signed additional lucrative contracts to work as a screenplay advisor for various Ukrainian studios. Those contracts secured him 1,000 rubles a month plus expenses and transportation. He spent all of September in the Crimea and also visited Odessa. Marie Seton came to meet him; they spent their vacation together in Yalta, something Eisenstein had not done in 17 years. They shared a room in the holiday complex of the Yalta film studio, but their relations remained platonic.

One evening Pudovkin knocked on their door and asked to spend the night in their room; his room was full of bedbugs. Eisenstein became very nervous, but since Marie Seton didn't mind, he let him sleep on the couch. Pudovkin observed the situation; in the morning he advised Seton to forget about Eisenstein. Eisenstein, on the other hand, thought he owed Seton an explanation of his sexuality.

Seton later included Eisenstein's analysis of his sex life in her biography. He told her of the love-hate relationship with his mother, his romantic-bourgeois relationship with an actress who was later seduced by Alexandrov, his encounter with a prostitute whom his friends had sent him as a joke, and his fear and revulsion of sex. He told her of his long-standing intellectual preoccupation with homosexuality and how he had solved his conflicts through sublimation—the relief he had found in Freud's vision of Leonardo.[215] 'My observations led me to the conclusion that homosexuality is in all ways a retrogression—a going back to the state where procreation came with the dividing of the cells. It's a dead-end. A lot of people say I'm a homosexual. I never have been, and I'd tell you if it were true. I've never felt any such desire, not even towards Grisha, though I think I must in some way have a bi-sexual tendency— like Zola and Balzac—in an intellectual way.'[216] There is a remarkable slip of the tongue here. In later diaries from 1943, the amorous rivalry with Grisha still plays a role, but the woman becomes interchangeable. At one point, Eisenstein mentions Vera Yanukova,[217] a bit later it is Irina Meyerhold;[218] in both cases, the real issue at stake is Grisha's betrayal of Eisenstein. Eisenstein even thought that the invented love affair between Prince Kurbsky and Ivan's wife Anastasia in his film *Ivan the Terrible* reproduced the traumatic situation between himself (Ivan), Irina (Anastasia), and Grisha (the false friend).[219]

Marie Seton believed Eisenstein and accepted his stories of inhibited erotic adventures, all of which had a tinge of trashy romance novels. She also reported a number of concrete observations from Eisenstein's everyday life. She noticed that he never drank tea (unlike most Russians) and never kept wine or sweets at home. His excursions to the Crimea were the only luxury in his life. He slept in nightshirts and wore silk pyjamas during the day—Seton gave him a red and a blue pair. Montagu sent him socks and shirts from London. Eisenstein thought that his own taste in clothes was much too vulgar and that his fat body looked silly.

At this point in time marriages to foreign women—usually English or American—were not as rare as people think today. Pudkovin was having an affair with an English dancer who had followed him to Moscow, but he did not want to divorce his wife. The playwright Alexander Afinogenov had an American wife; even the People's Commissar for Foreign Affairs Litvinov was married to an Englishwoman. Eisenstein started a 'platonic love-affair' with Marie Seton. She listened to him attentively and wanted to help him with the Mexican film, which she did in 1939 by editing another version called *Time in the Sun*. In 1952 she wrote the first biography to be published after Eisenstein's death.

Eisenstein needed Seton—a devoted foreigner who sent him books. His wish lists were long and he put a lot of thought into them. He was interested in new books on psychology and art history that he could not get in the Soviet Union. He used to be able to buy books because he published articles abroad. By now his main publishers, *Experimental Cinema* and *Close Up*, had gone under. His relationship with Marie Seton was a pragmatic affair—she was a small window to the world outside his prison at home.

In October, Eisenstein returned to Moscow and continued working at the film school. He prepared a new series of lectures and was presented with new students, who included Jay Leyda and Herbert Marshall. However, most of his students were children of workers and peasants. They were minimally educated, knew little about the history of art, and had a poorly developed sense of composition. Their knowledge of literature and theater remained sketchy.

Eisenstein believed that he first had to work to develop their personalities, their body and spirit, and train them to perceive things. For two years, he conducted a program intended to train directors that looked like a plan to shape a Renaissance individual. Eisenstein turned class time into an exciting process. He did not lower the level of instruction to accommodate his audience's lack of education. Instead, he used his students to test his own ideas and theories.

Every lecture and every seminar turned into a grandiose dramatic presentation, a theatrical act, a dispute in the form of a Socratic dialogue that led to a climax—the solution to staging a scene. Eisenstein provoked and poked fun at his students. He placed great demands on them, since his models of thought were very unusual.

He had lost his entourage of devoted assistants who looked up to him and were willing to do anything for him. They were replaced by his students. With them he could still discuss dramatic material that had almost disappeared from the present. They covered Dostoevsky (who was slowly becoming taboo), the history of the Haitian revolutionary who ends up a dictator (not suited for the Soviet Union in the thirties!), *Lady Macbeth of Mtsensk*, Nikolai Leskov's story of erotic passion and crime. He could never have used this material to make films, since suffering, death, misfortune and eroticism had been banned from art. Society on the 'outside' was grooming people who knew no scruples and had easy answers for all of life's complicated questions—there was no room for Hamlet or Faust. In the auditorium at the GIK (renamed VGIK in 1934) refuge, Eisenstein preserved old ideas about personality and the contradictory nature of art.

Pera Atasheva took over the huge job of being Eisenstein's lecturer and assistant. She collected information about all the subjects that interested him. She lugged home books from the library, took care of his correspondence, and negotiated with publishers. She typed his articles and put page after page of dictation on paper. She also worked as his assistant at the film school and gathered his shorthand lectures into a typed book manuscript, which Eisenstein then edited. Without her help Eisenstein never would have finished his book on directing.

On October 27, 1934 Eisenstein married Pera Atasheva. They kept the marriage a secret from his mother. They continued to live apart and their relationship remained platonic: they even used the formal pronoun *vy* to address each other. The marriage came about after even the vaguest hint of tender friendship had passed. They had become emotionally distant even before Eisenstein spent his vacation on the Crimea with Marie Seton—jealousy was probably not an issue. But Pera still took care of all practical problems for the overgrown child Sergei. She remained the honest manager of Eisenstein's household, his surrogate mother, sister, nanny—a sexual relationship would have amounted to incest, so it did not exist.

On Pera's birthday, November 19, 1934, Eisenstein gave Pera, who had accepted the strange role of his companion, his portrait with the dedication: 'On this day I will always be thankful to your parents.'

At the time (and later), there were a number of speculations about the reasons for this sudden marriage of convenience. One explanation might be the law passed on March 1, 1934 that made homosexuality a crime. Previously, only rape and illicit relations with minors were illegal. Now homosexuality per se had become a punishable offense that could earn one a prison or camp sentence of up to eight years. In January there had been mass arrests of homosexuals in Moscow, Leningrad, Odessa, and Kharkov—most of the people arrested were artists. The master of ceremonies Alexander Alexeev received a two-year sentence—rumors about his sentence ran through the art world. On May 23, 1934 Maxim Gorky published an article in *Pravda* that condemned homosexuality as a 'phenomenon harmful to society' that ruined proletarian youth and was conceivable only in bourgeois countries: 'If we stamp out homosexuality, Fascism will disappear all by itself.' The People's Commissar for Justice, Nikolai Krylenko, did not merely equate homosexuality with degeneration; he considered it counterrevolutionary. Homosexuality became a political crime under the jurisdiction of the state security organs.

One year later, on October 17, 1935, a decree was passed that made the ownership of pornographic material illegal and punishable with up to five years of prison. Eisenstein's drawings might fall into this category. He recalled how his heart had stopped at the border once before. A customs officer had flipped through Eisenstein's volume of de Sade. Luckily Eisenstein had not yet read the volume and the illustrations still stuck together. Eisenstein avoided a scandal only because the customs officer had never heard of that author. The Soviet people's erotic innocence and the newly discovered classical ideal of the family were now guarded as carefully as the people's ideological purity.

Even if Eisenstein was only latently homosexual, rumors of his 'abnormality' traveled not only in American and Mexican circles. As a married man he would be harder to blackmail.

During this time Eisenstein again became intensely interested in ecstasy. He did not try to access the unconscious through dreams, as the Surrealists had. Instead he sought out changed states of consciousness, triggered by drugs, orgasm, or—art. In the last case, rhythm, color, and image acted as a form of narcotic that dulled the conscious mind. The experience of masses in movement, intensified by film, also had a strong erotic effect. Since Freud had not dealt with these parapsychic states in classic psychoanalysis, Eisenstein turned to one of Freud's 'disloyal' students. In July 1934 he wrote a letter to the Marxist Freudian Wilhelm Reich asking for a copy of his book on orgasm.[220] Reich, who was already living in exile in Copenhagen, answered immediately: 'I was particularly pleased to hear from a leading comrade in the artistic field that art has a great deal to do with the central problem of the living substance, with orgasm.'[221] The German composer Hanns Eisler, with whom Reich had discussed this issue, had denied any correspondence between music and sexu-

ality. Eisenstein's interest in orgasm was connected to his study of the ecstatic state. However, for Eisenstein sex was only a 'stopping-place'. Sex was
merely a short-lived, if the 'most common', transition to ecstasy (something
for everyday use)—art, on the other hand, offered a much more intense ecstatic experience. Art de-sexualized and socialized ecstasy, though it also
largely suppressed the mind's logical capacities.

In November 1934 Eisenstein was finally assigned a four-room apartment
in the House of Film Workers next to the Potylikha studios. The studios were
at the very edge of the city. (The building had already been torn down by the
late 1950s, when Moscow grew to the southwest and the street was extended.)

He asked Marie Seton to move in with him and promised to keep her room
available. She agreed.

In mid-December 1934 Paul Robeson came to Moscow with his wife. Marie
Seton had arranged the meeting. Eisenstein and Robeson got along splendidly
right from the start: they shared a philological interest in mythological forms
of thinking. When Robeson heard of Eisenstein's research, he recommended
the French sinologist Marcel Granet's recently published book *La Pensée chinoise*
('Chinese Thought'). On December 26, the Second Day of European Christmas, they ate turkey together. On New Year's Eve Eisenstein threw a party in
Robeson's honor at the House of Film on Povarskaya Street. The guest performed two songs by Modest Mussorgsky.

Towards the end of the year the situation suddenly became more sinister.
On December 1, 1934 Sergei Kirov, a high-ranking Party official and First Secretary of the Leningrad Regional Party, was murdered. As if arranged in advance, special courts were legalized that same day. The courts had the right to
try 'terrorists' over a ten-day period without a conventional trial, an appeals
process, or the possibility of amnesty, and to sentence the accused to death.
This maximum sentence was to be executed immediately. The 'Kirov assassin'
and thirteen other people were immediately sentenced and put to death.
Whether the GPU (renamed NKVD in 1934) was guilty of this political murder remains unclear to this day. The assassination provided a welcome excuse
for a broad wave of terror. The official explanation for the act of terrorism was
a conspiracy by the opposition, led by the former Party leaders Gigory Zinoviev
and Lev Kamenev. On December 6 newspapers published notices of summary
executions of members of 'counter-Revolutionary terrorist organizations' in
Moscow and Leningrad. Tens of thousands of innocent people were arrested
and deported. Kamenev and Zinoviev were arrested on December 16 (the press
report came out on December 22) and sentenced on January 18. At the same
time, the Bolshoi Theater hosted the All-Union Creative Conference of Soviet Film
Workers, where all the 'distinguished film workers of the country' gathered.

INSIDE THE IVORY TOWER
1935

The conference met on January 8-11 in the Great Hall of the Bolshoi Theater. Its significance and orientation can be compared to the Writers' Congress that had met six months earlier. The Writer's Congress united all Soviet literary workers in one union with a single platform. The Party did not need to create a union to control film workers. The rigid and highly centralized structure of film production meant that the industry could already be controlled from above. On January 11 the first pages of *Pravda* and *Izvestiya* were covered with telegrams greeting Stalin, and the leader's own welcoming words. The second page was filled with snapshots of Soviet film artists. The photographs of Pudovkin, Kozintsev, Trauberg, and the Vasiliev brothers were accompanied by the caption 'Director'. Eisenstein's caption read 'Extraordinary World-Class Director'.

Sergei Dinamov, the Party authority on culture and a Shakespeare scholar by profession, gave the opening speech. He talked for almost four hours and stated that Eisenstein had directed only one great film in his life: *Potemkin*. Since then, Eisenstein had only made bad movies and had wasted his time on a confused, Formalist montage theory, the throws of which Soviet cinema was only beginning to shake off. For the last five years Eisenstein had remained *silent* about *all* the great achievements of Soviet life and Soviet cinema. Eisenstein was the second speaker. He did not explain why he had not made a movie for six years, nor did he say a word about Mexico. He tried to defend his assessment of the development of Soviet cinema and to present the results of his research, which he considered more important than filmmaking. He was deeply convinced of the significance of his theoretical work and its practical utility. The ultimate goal of his research was to determine the exact formula for the creation of an absolutely effective and brilliant work of art. Marie Seton, who was still living with the Afinogenovs in Moscow, said that theory now seemed more important to Eisenstein than any film he might make. He intended to write several books simultaneously.[222]

Even before his travels to the West, Eisenstein had discussed this research project with Alexander Luria, Lev Vygotsky, and Nikolai Marr. He wanted to use the scientific method of experimentation to examine art (especially film) as an imprint of patterns of thought and to explain aesthetics from the perspective of psychology and cultural anthropology. Eisenstein had thus far conducted the actual work on the project by himself. He had merely discussed several issues with Vygotsky, but Vygotsky's premature death in 1934 cut short these consultations. Eisenstein's thoughts on the effect of art made him conclude that, in the culminating moment of ecstasy, art provoked an affect that took the recipient back into early forms of thinking (which Eisenstein called 'sensual thinking'). He believed that this affect lamed brain cells' ability to differentiate. Art, then, had an effect similar to that of alcohol, drugs, or schizophrenia and could plunge the recipient into the deepest hell of collective barbarism—into cultural regression. The regression of Europe's two most progressive and most revolutionary states, the outbreak of mass psychosis and hysteria in Germany and the Soviet Union, influenced Eisenstein's hypothesis. His Mexican experience also contributed to his theory. The crisis that followed Eisenstein's revelation was so severe that in 1933 and 1934 he was ready to abandon art. He did not want to contribute to cultural regression. He discussed his dilemma with Vygotsky, who advised him to continue working as an artist.

Eisenstein dedicated much time to religious mysticism, symbolic forms and rituals, and Jacob Böhme's spiritual experience. He read detective novels as a modern form of the mystery play: the detective's flash of inspiration leads him to make causal connections between a string of apparently unrelated events.

Eisenstein presented the core of his thoughts in his long conference speech.[223] He used several distinct examples to illustrate his hypothesis:

1. The director wants to tell the viewer that the ship's doctor has died. Instead of showing the body washed up on shore, he focuses on the doctor's pince-nez for the maximum intensity of effect—see *The Battleship Potemkin*.

2. King Lear goes insane. His lament unites with the storm raging about him—maximum intensity of effect.

3. Capitalism has ruined a farmer. In his monologue the hero of John Steinbeck's *Grapes of Wrath* equates real horses sold at market with the abstract values of work, pain, and bitterness—maximum intensity of effect.

4. Gogol changed the first version: 'Taras Bulba shrugged his shoulders and rode off to his camp' to: 'Shrugging his shoulders, Taras Bulba rode off to camp'. Why did Gogol do this?

5. Tolstoy condemned ownership. To illustrate his point, he invented a horse—a strider—and gave that horse language.

What do Tolstoy, Gogol, Steinbeck, Shakespeare and Eisenstein all have in common? In order to create an effect that is not merely informative, but strong and emotionally compelling, these artists have (1) equated a part with a whole, (2) attributed a human state to nature, (3) equated a thing with a concept, (4) elevated the act of movement over the object in movement, and (5) led the recipient back to totemism.

The common denominator in all of these operations of transformation lay for Eisenstein in the return to the specifics of a way of thinking that encompassed totemism, animism, isomorphism of macro and microscopic worlds, identity of part and whole, of subject and object—in short a return to earlier forms of thinking. He studied so-called primitive forms of thought in Frazer's *The Golden Bough* (1907-1915), Lévy-Bruhl's *La Mentalité primitive* (1922—the Russian translation was published in 1930 with a preface by Marr), Granet's *La Pensée chinoise* (1934), Wilhelm Wundt's *Elemente der Völkerpsychologie* ('Ethnic Psychology', 1912), and Heinz Werner's *Einführung in die Entwicklungspsychologie* ('Introduction to Developmental Psychology', 1926). Eisenstein had had his own encounters with 'mythological' thinking in Mexico.

The Freud circle's study of the unconscious, Jung's exploration of the symbolic, Lévy-Bruhl's work on early forms of thinking, Vygotsky's research on child psychology, and Marr's theories on the development of language were all based on extensive empirical and experimental material. By dynamically linking psychology, ethnography, etymology, anthropology, aesthetics and art, Eisenstein sought to locate the moments when sensual thinking erupted in everyday life, in the creative process, in a work of art and its reception. Since logical, rational thinking exhibited regular patterns, Eisenstein believed that sensual thinking must also be governed by patterns and distinctive structural features. His own analysis of effective artistic techniques and works of art had convinced him that the patterns of early thinking formed the foundation of all elements of form. Eisenstein was not the first to attempt to describe these patterns. His innovation lay in his approach: the recognition of the structure of these forms of thinking should be utilized in the practice of art and in the training of artists. At the same time analytical thinking should not be disregarded— in order to protect one from emotional chaos and mythological barbarism.

Eisenstein made a dialectical correction to psychoanalysis, since he viewed the antagonist model of coexistent conscious and unconscious psychological processes as a unity of opposites. He introduced the notion of the 'dyad' in order to describe the effect of a work of art (and the work of art itself) as such a dynamic unity: 'the dialectic of a work of art is constructed upon a most interesting 'dyad'. The effect of a work of art is built upon the fact that two processes are taking place within it simultaneously. There is a determined progressive ascent towards ideas as the highest peaks of consciousness and at the same time there is a penetration through the structure of form into the deepest layers of sensual thinking. The polarity between these two tendencies creates the remarkable tension of the unity of form and content that distinguishes genuine works.'[224]

Eisenstein's speech was met with a strange reception by the conference participants. None of the subsequent speakers seriously addressed Eisenstein's questions. Leonid Trauberg called them 'a museum of fantastic illusions' and said Eisenstein himself was a doll in a wax museum. Eisenstein's path—like those of Kuleshov and Vertov—led to the twilight of the gods.[225] On the second day, Dovzhenko spoke. He said that Eisenstein had better watch socialist women in labor instead of delving into Polynesian birthing rites and mythology. Eisenstein's erudition was destroying and disorganizing him. A new film was needed, not new theory that was a dangerous, mysterious mixture of 'that whole Freud complex' and comprehensible to no one.[226]

Eisenstein's erstwhile friend Yutkevich found a formula on which they could all agree: Eisenstein was sitting in an ivory tower destroying himself with theory. He was doing nothing, or at least not what Soviet society expected of him. Pudovkin was criticized as much as Eisenstein, which made that director insecure—after all, his film *Mother* was a harbinger of Socialist Realism! Pudovkin had also spent a long time in Germany at the beginning of the 1930's, but he had not stayed away as long as Eisenstein and had even brought back a half-finished film, *The Deserter*, about the battle of the German proletariat. As an actor, Pudovkin was able to gauge the atmosphere in the room better than Eisenstein. He noticed that everybody was sick of speeches and theories and tried to lighten the mood. He alone said that Eisenstein was a philosopher, galaxies away from the rest of us. However, the audience laughed (according to the conference transcript), and Pudovkin's support turned into an ironic blow when Pudovkin added that galaxies were something very distant, murky, and unclear.[227]

Eisenstein's friends did not say a word. The Georgian Nikolai Shengelaya apologized that he had come too late to hear Eisenstein's lecture. Esfir Shub kept silent. His former student, Sergei Vasiliev, now the celebrated director of *Chapaev*, advised him to take off the Chinese cloak of a wise man and to step down into Soviet reality.[228] Why was Eisenstein teaching instead of making movies, someone called out from the audience.

Only one critic, Nikolai Lebedev, referred to Eisenstein as a great researcher, who should really receive two million rubles and a studio for experiments; if people waited calmly, he would find the topic for his next film.[229]

Lev Kuleshov, who was himself scolded for being a bourgeois director and a Formalist, finally said on the third day of the conference: 'A word about Sergei Mikhailovich [Eisenstein], whom people have been burying prematurely. Very many comrades have talked about Sergei Mikhailovich as if he were dead . . . . Yutkevich said that knowledge exhausts people and that he is afraid that this is happening to you. Dear Sergei Mikhailovich, it is not knowledge that exhausts people, but envy.'[230] Naturally, envy formed part of the attack: people were jealous of his early international fame, his idiosyncrasies, his sharp tongue, and his strangeness.

News about a trick that Eisenstein had once played on Shumyatsky spread quickly. In response to Shumyatsky's question about what he wanted to film next, Eisenstein suggested Ivan Barkov—a writer who had been suppressed and forbidden under the Tsar. The poorly educated professional communist Shumyatsky sent his assistant to the Lenin Library to get Barkov's 'illegal revolutionary works'. The assistant did not know how to gently tell his boss that Barkov had been banned as pornography. Shumyatsky did not speak at the conference. Instead he published a book in 1935 with his program, 'A Cinema for the Millions'. An excerpt from the book was published in *Pravda* on January 11 in connection with the conference.

According to Marie Seton, Eisenstein remained as enigmatic as a sphinx during the debate; he did not show his nervousness and dismay. She later asked him why none of his colleagues had responded to his theories. He blamed himself, thought that he had presented his ideas poorly, and felt even more miserable. In spite of this defeat, he did not give up his research project and spent the next twenty years returning to the expansive book that he first called *Grundproblem* ('Fundamental Problem') and then *Method*. However, he never again spoke of the project in public.

After the third day of the conference, Eisenstein asked Marie for a few pounds—as consolation—so he could go to Torgsin, a hard currency store, and buy a book about Leonardo da Vinci that he had been eyeing for a long time. The monograph included Leonardo's studies of the body's proportions. Seton left for England that same evening, but promised to return as soon as he had moved into his new apartment.

The reservations about Eisenstein were openly demonstrated on January 11. For the first time ever, film workers were awarded state honors. Alexandrov and Vertov received the Order of the Red Star, a military decoration. Mikhail Kalinin joked that Alexandrov had been recognized for courage and bravery in coping with film comedy. Pudovkin, Dovzhenko, Ermler, Trauberg and Kozintsev were awarded the Order of Lenin. Eisenstein—like Kuleshov and Tisse—was given only the title 'Honored Artist', a third-rate award in the lineup. This humiliation affected him deeply. The awards affirmed only the newly established pantheon of Soviet film, where there was temporarily no room for Eisenstein. In 1935 Stalin made yet another director his personal favorite: Alexander Dovzhenko, who was collaborating closely with his friend and mentor Joseph Stalin on the film *Aerograd*.

For someone less obsessed with power and dominance, the public spectacle of humiliation that took place in the same building where Eisenstein had celebrated the triumph of *Potemkin* as a 27-year-old might not have been as effective. But this show was perfect. The organizers hit Eisenstein where he was most vulnerable—they attacked his ambition. During the three-day campaign of destruction, Eisenstein was lectured, scorned, insulted, reprimanded, and ridiculed like a little boy by the Soviet cinema public, his colleagues, former friends, admirers, and students. The possible consequences of this exercise—ranging from loss of the right to work to incarceration—had already been demonstrated by the fate of other artists. Might fear have crept into the wounded vanity? Now Eisenstein knew what was expected of him.

Having turned thirty-seven in January, he had his hair cut short and tossed out his extravagant foreign clothes. He donned strict dark suits that made him look more like a scientist than an artist. The conference's derisive reprimand, implicit threats and degrading accolade were forms of extortion that forced him back to work. Two weeks after the conference and the awards ceremony he announced his plan to direct a film based on the script *Bezhin Meadow*.

The combination of this third-rate award and an unsatisfactory standard of living tempted Eisenstein to join his colleagues in their corruption. Meyerhold now made 6,000 rubles and had moved into a beautiful apartment on Bryusov Alley in a building designed by Ivan Rerberg. Pudovkin and Alexandrov had received nice apartments in the center of town. Moscow artists were accumulating mahogany furniture and building luxurious summerhouses. They collected art and drove cars. They could even spend their summer vacations abroad and traveled to the French Riviera and Karlovy Vary. Eisenstein was still living in one room of a communal apartment with five other tenants, and his new home lay in the outskirts of the city. He received the fairly modest income of a teacher at the film school. He still had the specialist contracts—as of January 1, 1935, nine thousand rubles plus expenses in Tajikistan, as of January 3, 1936 the same deal with Azerfilm in Baku—but this income was not comparable to the earnings of his former student Grisha Alexandrov. Besides, if Eisenstein had not expressed his intention to make a topical film, these contracts might have been terminated immediately. The conference had not merely slighted his vanity, but had also shown Eisenstein what might await an 'exceptional world-class director': the life and income of an average Soviet citizen. Eisenstein opted for something different.

Eisenstein's mother was also pressuring him to change his lifestyle. She wanted to move to Moscow and to arrange the life of her famous son accordingly. In September 1935 Eisenstein moved into the spacious four-room apartment that he had furnished in May. He wrote to Marie Seton that he had decided to spend the larger part of his income on furniture. He asked her for a Victorian mirror and for decorative bouquets of wax flowers. In the spring of 1936 he helped his mother settle into his room on Chistye Prudy Boulevard. He sent her a list of the items that she absolutely had to bring him: grand piano, wardrobe, the round table, bed, dishes, her Kuznetsov porcelain tea set, the samovar (he wanted petty-bourgeois comfort), tablecloths (he owned none), and silverware. As of July 1936 it was possible to build private houses (declared as dachas) in the suburbs of Moscow, Leningrad and Kiev. Eisenstein requested such a dacha and his mother put all her energy into the construction of a spacious summerhouse with seven rooms. She would reside on the ground floor and Eisenstein on the floor above.

Eisenstein now lived in luxury by Moscow standards: he and his mother could inhabit twelve rooms in a city where many generations often shared one room in a communal apartment. But unlike the homes of many Moscow artists, Eisenstein's new living space left anything but a bourgeois impression. The furnishings struck visitors with their extravagance. A wooden angel from a church stood in as a tie and suspender rack in his city apartment. Sometimes a Menorah took over that function. Right next to it hung a boxing glove with Harpo Marx's autograph. Everyday things appeared as carnival props. The furniture seemed to be fragments of theater sets or might have come out of film storage: a brocade chair stood next to a Bauhaus piece; the chandelier was made out of the remnants of four old cameras. Autographed portraits of Einstein, Asta Nielsen, and Meyerhold hung next to Corrida-postcards. The enormous bed was covered by a bright Mexican rug. But most of the space was taken up by books. The library grew relentlessly and was organized idiosyncratically: Stanislavsky stood next to the Bible; Hegel was up-side-down, since that was how Lenin thought Marx had dealt with Hegel's dialectic; a Repin album served as a costume history. Eisenstein's surly Russian housekeeper Aunt Pasha cooked according to American recipes.

After the apartment and the summerhouse were furnished, his mother decided that the only thing missing was a suitable wife. She should naturally be of good stock, suited to the famous son and his mother. When his mother found out that the only woman in Eisenstein's life was Pera and that the housekeeping money already went straight to her, she was outraged. She had a more appropriate partner in mind: Elizaveta Telesheva, a director at the Art Theater, pretty, plump, like a picture by Kustodiev.

Eisenstein had met Telesheva during the preparations for *Bezhin Meadow*. She was supposed to play a leading part, the Chair of the Kolkhoz. Like Yulia Ivanovna, she came from a rich merchant family, was widowed and had an almost grown-up daughter with whom she shared a large apartment full of antiques on the Tverskoy Boulevard in the center of town.

Telesheva was a true society lady and got along splendidly with Yulia Ivanovna. She knew Moscow's theater elite well and often had soirées at her home. She was deeply impressed by Eisenstein. In order to conquer Eisenstein, the two women devised a tactic that exploited one of his weaknesses: he was a gourmet. Telesheva knew a thing or two about fine dining. Her feasts were exquisite and opulent: pickled delicacies, caviar, mushrooms, salmon, sturgeon, suckling pig with horseradish, large piroshki, small piroshki, kulebyaka … All this was just an overture; entrées followed. Eisenstein ate like Gargantua, Glizer recalls, like Brecht's Galileo in the last act, as if the whole point of life lay in eating. He ate and ate and demanded to be entertained with gossip from the Art Theater. And the theater's rumor mill was known to cook up unbelievable intrigue! Bulgakov, whom Eisenstein had met at Telesheva's, had just immortalized the theater's gossip in his *Theater Novel*.

Soon he became impossibly fat. His heart could no longer keep his corpulent body running. In October 1935 the doctor put him on a diet: little meat, lots of vegetables, nothing sweet and no alcohol. Eisenstein was a teetotaler anyway.

Telesheva often visited Yulia Ivanovna at her dacha and spent whole days there helping Yulia Ivanovna arrange things around the house. Pera was pushed into the background, but the wedding with Telesheva never happened. At the most they had an intermittent affair. Eisenstein never divorced Pera, but when Elizaveta started playing the role of 'official wife' for the outside world, Pera took offense and resigned from her position as assistant and manager of his household. Telesheva took over: she gave his money to the housekeeper and later to the chauffeur, she took care of finding gas rations, paid laundry bills, and wrote long letters to Eisenstein complaining that he didn't have time for her and didn't want to live with her. But she was forced to accept his problems with women—the difficulties had evidently remained.

His chaste relationships with women stood in marked contrast to the incredibly daring erotic fantasies that Eisenstein unloaded in his jokes and especially his drawings that shocked his prude contemporaries. A whole set of vulgar pin-ups hung over his bed in his summerhouse, just like in a sailor's cabin. One visitor remarked on the contrast between the pictures and Eisenstein's outer professorial appearance. Another considered Eisenstein to be a cynical satyr.

The state's naïve campaign in support of consumption and the newspapers' pictures of workers out shopping had nothing to do with the new bourgeois way of life among the intellectual and artistic elite. Their privileges were carefully promoted and protected. While it was hard even to find bread in the twenties, in the thirties French wine and Russian caviar returned to the table. Old servants appeared in the artists' households. The poverty of the general population was no longer a transitional phase, but simple reality.

The Stakhanovite movement (on July 31, 1935 the miner Alexei Stakhanov fulfilled 14 daily work quotas in a single shift) returned the cult of the select few to the society of 'declared equality'. The cult reached its apogee in the worship of Stalin and in the staged hysteric surges of the people's love for their leader at the Stakhanov Workers' Conference in November 1935.

While 1934—especially the last few months—seemed to be an overture to a new wave of terror, the following year was more relaxed. There was a people's carnival in Moscow in July. Stalin called on everyone to be happy and coined the new slogan: 'Life has become happier and more joyful.' Before the new constitution was introduced in 1936, there were rumors about an upcoming democratization, the legalization of the opposition, and the introduction of parliamentary democracy! People even spoke of a party of intellectuals led by Gorky. The churches were allowed to ring their bells and people were allowed to celebrate the New Year. Even Christmas trees, banned in 1929 as a capitalist remnant, were permitted. However, the superficial reanimation of public life only covered up the secret arrests. The son and husband of the poet Anna Akhmatova were arrested. Gorky fell into disfavor and was denied an exit visa to Italy. After military rank was re-introduced in the Red Army in September 1935, it seemed time to divide the writers and directors into a first and second class as well. On November 24, 1935 Lili Brik wrote Stalin that Mayakovsky was being forgotten. Thereupon Stalin declared him the country's best state poet. Meyerhold immediately decided to stage *The Bedbug* again and to dedicate the performance to Stalin.

Eisenstein left his ivory tower in 1935. He stepped into life and accepted the role of the privileged Soviet artist. The next two years were marked by a number of changes—a new apartment, a comfortable summer home, a new partner—these were all consequences of his decision to make a new movie, a long overdue sign of his loyalty. The temptation to film again was also too real. Since his return, Eisenstein had been unable even to start filming the projects he favored. The materials he had been offered—a musical comedy, or a monumental historical film about Stenka Razin—were perceived as a form of mockery. His experiences in Hollywood and with independent film had been crushing, so all that was left was production at home—if he was ever going to return to cinema at all. He was not allowed to stay on the sidelines: external pressure was reinforced by pressure from inside. His personality and his form of creativity could not cope with eternal isolation. Once again Eisenstein looked into the mirror and saw Freud's portrait of Leonardo da Vinci. He was no longer interested in his emotional apprehension or the sublimation of homosexuality. His attention had turned to the traits of an amoral scholar who created machines of destruction on order from his patron and who was pathologically unable to finish his work. This would also be Eisenstein's fate.

Eisenstein underwent a huge transformation. The eccentric youth with a head of curls turned into fat, solid, bald man. Even his handwriting changed as if it had been folded over in the mirror—the slant moved from left to right.

BEZHIN MEADOW:
FATHER AND SON
1935-1937

Eisenstein's decision to film *Bezhin Meadow* may have been over-hasty. Mosfilm had purchased the script a year earlier. Since then no director had wanted to shoot the material, and the studio itself was hesitant to jump into the project, which was sensitive from a number of viewpoints. Both the theme and its dramatic interpretation shocked the artists and the people in charge. The screenplay was based on an event that the media had beaten to death over the last three years. The 14-year-old boy Pavel Morozov from the village of Gerasimovka beyond the Urals had exposed his father to be an 'enemy of the people'. The father was sentenced to ten years' imprisonment (a euphemism for summary execution). After the event, Pavel and his little brother Fedya were murdered by their grandfather and the grandfather's cousins. The murderers and their accomplice, Pavel's grandmother, were convicted and executed.

The screenplay had been written by Alexander Rzheshevsky for the Children's Commission of the Central Committee of the Komsomol. The first page read: 'Narrative manuscript for a sound production'.

The author, who had begun his career as an actor, had been noticed at the end of the twenties for his 'emotional screenplay'. The phrase referred to his style—his scripts were written in blank verse, in short, clipped sentences and richly adorned with hyperbolic epithets. Pudovkin and Nikolai Shengelaya had made films using Rzheshevsky's material, *A Simple Case* and *Twenty-Six Commissars*—both films were considered to be among their directors' less successful works. After these flops, the author had been written off as unlucky. Rzheshevsky's prose was not convincing from a literary point of view, his characters were two-dimensional, his plots unmotivated. The new script was full of folksy-naïve and macabre jokes: 'Give us machines, otherwise the harvest will spoil,' [said the farmers]—'Then we'll lock you up,' the Commissar answered with a calm smile. And the farmers joyfully cried, 'Let's go to Ivan Ivanovich! Off we go to the GPU! With the greatest pleasure!'

Rzheshevsky's child hero was dramatically uninteresting. He was an imperturbable little angel in a pioneer scarf at the side of his eternally drunken father. The screenplay attributed the son's murder to the father in order to make the conflict more dramatic. What did Eisenstein think he would find for himself in this strange, grotesque 'narrative manuscript'? Neither the son nor the father was allowed to have any doubts, otherwise the ideological superstructure would collapse. With which of these two could the director sympathize in a merciless time that was becoming more and more bloody as the production of the film progressed? For the studio, which was uncertain about which director to assign to the project, Eisenstein's name still guaranteed success.

The screenplay combined two temporal layers—memories of Turgenev's times and the contemporary reality. Eisenstein cut the Turgenevan reminiscences from the script—only the title of one of Turgenev's *Sportsman's Sketches* remained. Eisenstein placed all his bets on the effect of the image. He told his American student Jay Leyda that he would unite the whole of visual culture in this film. The film would discover the Russian landscape through impressionism, Japanese prints, Spanish and Dutch art. This layer of culture would help to tear the story out of current politics and project it onto a mythological plane. However, this time Eisenstein would not focus on the oedipal revolt of the son, but on the drama of the father who wants to save his own flesh and blood from the state but has to take revenge on his boys. This inversion was not only politically completely unacceptable, it was also beyond Eisenstein's auto-biographical experiences with his own father.

Eisenstein found several pleasant distractions from the screenplay, which he tried to enrich with facts from the real court proceedings. He was a member of the jury of Moscow's first International Film Festival (two years after Venice hosted the first film festival ever). The event lasted from February 21 to March 1. The competition included movies by King Vidor, Cecil B. DeMille, René Clair, Walt Disney, Julien Duvivier, Jacques Feyder, Marcel L'Herbier, Alexander Korda, Alessandro Blasetti, Gustav Machaty, Henry Koster (Hermann Kosterlitz), and MGM's Mexican production *Viva Villa!* by Jack Conway. In an interview Eisenstein said that Disney's *The Three Little Pigs* was the best entry. However, three works of Socialist Realism shared the first prize: *Chapaev*, *The Youth of Maxim* and *Peasants*. Boris Shumyatsky chaired the jury, which also included Eisenstein, Pudovkin, and Alexander Aroseev, the chief of VOKS. Eisenstein at least managed to get Disney a third prize behind René Clair's *The Last Billionaire* for 'visual culture and clever musicality'.

The Peking Opera was also playing in Moscow at the time, starring the famous Mei Lanfang. The Chinese star was celebrated and honored by everyone. Eisenstein met with him on March 12 and suggested filming *Rainbow Crossing*, a performance in the opera's repertoire. By March 29 they had already started recording the soundtrack at the Mosfilm studio. They would shoot at night after the performance: the actors were completely exhausted and unaccustomed to repeating the technically complex and physically demanding scenes so many times in a row. Eisenstein insisted on finishing the work. Mei Lanfang took the film back to China; Eisenstein was afraid that in the Soviet Union it might be confiscated and disappear.

The central administration returned the script for *Bezhin Meadow* on March 20 and demanded one more revision. The screenplay did not pass censorship until May 17, when Eisenstein finally received permission to proceed with shooting. Tisse had just returned from the Far East, where he had filmed *Aerograd*. Eisenstein was assisted by Mikhail Gomorov, who had already worked on all of Eisenstein's previous films, Pera Atasheva, and his students (including Jay Leyda). The young composer Gavriil Popov, who had been in charge of the soundtrack to *Chapaev*, wrote the music. The sound engineers were Leonid Obolensky and Boris Volsky.

The father was played by Vakhtangov's student Boris Zakhava, the head of the collective farm by Elizaveta Telesheva. She also advised Eisenstein on matters concerning the actors. Two days a week Eisenstein would devote four hours to casting the people his assistants were considering for roles as village dwellers. He would look them over in groups of five; those who passed inspection were photographed and registered. He was just as thorough picking extras for the mass scenes. The assistants had narrowed down a group of 2,000 children to 600; Eisenstein took 200 of these into serious consideration, but he still had not found a boy to play the lead role.

In the penultimate group of boys Eisenstein suddenly noticed Vitya Kartashov, the son of a truck driver. Everybody else was against him. His hair grew every which way, his pigmentation was uneven (he had big white spots on his face and neck), and his voice was stiff. But Eisenstein was convinced that this boy was his one and only Stepok.

On the morning of May 15 Eisenstein flew to Arvamir, a city in the Krasnodar region along the Kuban river; from there he departed for the Soviet collective farm 'Stalin' (formerly 'Gigant'), where the mass scenes were being filmed without sound. Eisenstein had already filmed at this location—this is where he shot the changes to *The Old and the New* that had been demanded by Stalin. He filmed with several cameras at once and explained to Jay Leyda that he would use the images like a fugue and would bring the voices together on the editing table. First he would work on one voice—close-ups of the character. Then he would shoot the rear projection shots, then film the actors in front of a translucent screen. Music and sound came last.

The two women on the set—Telesheva and Pera—did not get along. But they both took care of Eisenstein, so he was content. Occasionally he would return to the capital to remodel and furnish his apartment.

In early July they began shooting in Kharkov, this time with sound. Eisenstein was ill with food poisoning when he arrived from Moscow. At his request, two square kilometers of the landscape were cleared of telephone poles and electric lines because they disturbed the composition of the picture. They shot a harvest using 150 tractors that had been taken from various collective farms just for the film. When the rainy season set in, they traveled south to the Kuban Steppe. That summer the press reported on the film frequently. In July *Komsomolskaya pravda* published four long articles by Mikhail Rosenfeld about the work on the set.

In late August 1935 the team returned to Moscow and started filming on the sound stage. 'The image behind the camera was just as strange as the one in front of it,' Jay Leyda wrote in his production diary. 'A group of family and friends stood in a half-circle behind the camera team: relatives, studio directors from all over, other directors, students . . . . French writers, English aesthetes, German émigrés, American tourists. As soon as Tisse picked up the camera and Eisenstein lifted his candy-colored baton to move to the other side of the enchanted forest, everybody got up, grabbed their wicker chairs and old boxes, and rearranged themselves among the holes in the ground and the dirty puddle to watch Eisenstein with total absorption.'[231]

On the set preparations were in progress to film the destruction of a church. It would be a reenactment; the campaign to tear down and change the function of many churches had raged several years earlier. On December 5, 1931 the Church of Christ the Savior had been razed in Moscow. At this point the leadership was still planning to build the Palace of the Soviets in its place, but the construction was being held up because the Moskva River kept flooding the foundations. In the center of Moscow there remained only emptiness—a gigantic hole. The faithful saw this as an act of God, who seemed to be taking revenge even for small things: When Eisenstein went to view original props and vestments for his film orgy of destruction in the church in October, he caught what he thought was smallpox. Superstitious as he was, he decided that the infection was a bad omen. He was put into quarantine for three weeks, but it turned out to be only a serious case of the chicken pox. All seven thousand employees of the studio were vaccinated prophylactically. Eisenstein joked that they had missed a huge promotional opportunity—imagine if all the employees had been marked with his initials—SM (Sergei Mikhailovich). Only Pera Atasheva was allowed to visit and take care of him during his illness—his food was handed to him through a slit in the door. After his hospital stay Eisenstein had to go to Kislovodsk to recover: his heart had barely survived the high fever. He wrote Marie Seton that his beauty had suffered somewhat from his illness—a few large scars would remain. While Eisenstein was in the hospital and recovering in the Caucasus, the filmed material was shown to friends and acquaintances in Moscow. His mother wrote that Ehrenburg was thrilled, but that he did not like the dialogue. Shumyatsky and his representatives also viewed the material; in spite of some critical comments, their evaluation was largely positive.

He was able to return to work in December. However, the team had to stop filming again for three weeks in January. Eisenstein had caught the flu even though the winter of 1936 was very mild. On January 28, 1936, as Eisenstein was lying in bed, *Pravda* published the article 'Chaos instead of Music', a harsh attack on Dmitry Shostakovich's opera *Lady Macbeth of Mtsenk*. In the recent past, that opera had been a showpiece. All important foreign guests had been dragged to see the perpetually sold-out performance. Stalin went to the opera on January 26. Shostakovich suspected that Stalin himself had authored the anonymous critique that had then been formulated by the editors. Stalin was gearing up for a new campaign of destruction, and Shostakovich was only one of many victims. The Committee for Artistic Affairs, founded only a week earlier to centralize all aspects of artistic life under the leadership of Platon Kerzhentsev, was assigned the task of heading the campaign 'against Formalism'. The term 'Formalism' had been used since 1933 in contrast to Socialist Realism. Now it was given new nuances. In the past, artists had been criticized for their 'reactionary ideological positions'. Now aesthetic criteria alone sufficed to make an artist 'counterrevolutionary'. In the lead article against Shostakovich, Formalism received a new synonym: 'Meyerholdism'. The field of attack quickly broadened. On February 13 *Pravda* published another article, this time about Formalism in film: 'A Rough Outline instead of Historical Truth'. The article's main topic was the Ukrainian film *Prometheus* by Ivan Kavaleridze. In the same issue, the paper demanded that the discussion be expanded to include all forms of art, since 'the *leftist deviation* has taken root in all areas'—in literature, painting, architecture. Other press organs were called upon to join the discussion. On February 14 *Komsomolskaya pravda* published the article 'Against Formalism and the Leftist Deviation in Art'. Here, James Joyce (especially *Ulysses*) and the school of the painter Pavel Filonov were included in the list of deviationists. The Constructivist architect Konstantin Melnikov was the next victim; he was followed by the dramatist Mikhail Bulgakov.

After these massive attacks Shumyatsky reviewed Eisenstein's footage on February 25 and criticized his depiction of the class struggle in the village. The real event had begun to look like the Biblical drama of Abraham's sacrifice. He reproached Eisenstein for his mysticism and aestheticism. In February, there was a meeting on Formalism in the House of Film. Eisenstein was absent. However, he wrote a letter that was published on March 11 in the paper *Kino*. In the letter he expressed hope that the Party line set by *Pravda* would save art from Formalism and naturalism. 'I have spoken of my personal mistakes in the past. Now I will prove in seventeen days that I have understood everything and will rework my film accordingly.'[232] To strengthen his position, he promised in another article: 'This will be a film about a heroic childhood!'[233] Press photos showed tractors decorated with flowers with the caption, 'They're going to work on the movie *Bezhin Meadow*!'

The joyful mood was merely a façade. Ten days later, on March 27, Eisenstein wrote in his diary: 'Can a vocation involve this much disgust and apathy? If there's no joy in it, only difficulties, why the hell am I making this movie? I've begun the montage—no curiosity, no interest at all. What do I want anyway? I only want to write the book. Only the book. Why did I start making this film? Is it my lack of principles? I should have gone into exile like Dante, if only to write this book. The book is my mission. Could I possibly be deaf to the voice of creative failure that started after *Potemkin*? It all became obvious in the night after the tragedy of *October*. But I'm like a whore. I can't withstand the temptation to flirt with my own creativity. I say no, but then I do it anyway. No principles at all. Nothing—not even last January—should have forced me to make this movie. These failures don't come from nowhere. This will be my last attempt. After this an attic room, hunger, whatever, but I'll be principled. I'm not a director. I'm not a cinematographer. I have to write my book.'[234]

By the 'night after *October*', Eisenstein probably meant the forced last-minute cuts to that film; 'last January' certainly referred to the conference with its scorn and awards that Eisenstein experienced as a deep humiliation. 'The book' was his ongoing project *Grundproblem*; its basic ideas had been mocked at the conference. On March 31 Eisenstein wrote a nighttime entry: 'I saw *We From Kronstadt*. But somebody has got to preserve cinema culture. What I saw isn't even another level, it's like heaven and earth.'[235] *We From Kronstadt* had been directed by Efim Dzigan and was based on a script by Eisenstein's new friend Vsevolod Vishnevsky. Vishnevsky was the son of the first Russian film historian and a celebrated author of revolutionary plays; his *Optimistic Tragedy* presented the Kronstadt anarchists from the point of view of the Bolsheviks, the real victors of history. Though praised as a great achievement of Socialist Realism, Dzigan's heavy-handed epic film about the revolt of revolutionary sailors did not have an ounce of *Potemkin's* force. In a review that had been ordered from above, but remained unpublished, Eisenstein naturally praised the film as a 'successor in the *Potemkin* line', and thanked the author 'for this exceptional work of film art from the bottom of his heart.'[236] But the same March 31 diary entry ends: 'Emptiness. Loneliness. Where is art? Where has it left to go?'[237]

Eisenstein did not have the option of exile or the attic room. He could not possibly interrupt *Bezhin Meadow*, a state assignment. Within two weeks he needed to quickly rewrite the script. He had the help of Isaak Babel, who was working as a script editor at Mosfilm at the time.

Eisenstein placed great hopes in Babel, or rather in Gorky, to whom Babel had a direct line. He also hoped that Babel could get something more out of the material. In 1928 Eisenstein had been so deeply impressed by Babel's father-son tragedy 'Sunset' that he had even wanted to film it. Babel had not published anything recently; he was writing a novel about collectivization and living fairly well off of his Mosfilm job. He did not want to risk anything with this film—he had a wife and small child. Erwin Sinko, who shared an apartment with Babel in Moscow for a time, wrote in *Roman eines Romans* how he had met Eisenstein on May 23, 1936. It was very hot, and Babel had opened all the windows and doors: 'A man in shirtsleeves was crouching next to him, all bent over, his head buried in his hands. His shirt had slipped out of his pants in the back, his shoulders and his broad back were shaking as if he had the chills.'[238] Eisenstein had come to Babel looking for help. The government commission, which included Vyacheslav Molotov and Anastas Mikoyan, had seen the half-finished film and decided to destroy it, since it followed the line of a recently criticized article by Bukharin, in which the chief editor of *Izvestiya* had completely misunderstood Russian history and had painted the Russian peasants in bleak colors. Eisenstein, like Bukharin, had succumbed to mysticism in a barbaric fashion. He had soaked his film in mysticism, naturalism, and Formalism. Eisenstein hoped that Babel could appeal to Gorky to save the film. After Eisenstein left, Babel told Sinko that the authorities had hinted to Eisenstein that they might use his well-known abnormal sexual inclinations against him.[239]

Gorky died on June 18, and Babel did not have the power to change the order to remake an almost completed film. He himself had to write the new dialogue, and Eisenstein had to replace all the actors. Instead of Boris Zakhava, who looked like Mikhail Vrubel's painting of Pan, he cast Nikolai Khmelyov—on Telesheva's recommendation. Khmelyov was a very tough actor from the Art Theater: Bulgakov envisioned him in the role of the sadistic General Khludov in his own play *Flight*. Pyotr Arzhanov from the Tairov Theater would now play the GPU-chief. He had been trained to act dramatic, heroic parts. He replaced the friendly storyteller Vasily Orlov.

This blackmailing of Eisenstein took place at a time when people were expecting a democratic constitution that promised new freedoms (the equality of all citizens regardless of their social origin, freedom of expression, the press, and religion) and political amnesty. Eisenstein's case proves that for Soviet citizens the last remaining form of freedom—private life—no longer existed. Life was 'organized' around innumerable institutions, organizations, and gatherings; even erotic dreams were supposed to be transparent. The utopian vision of a glass house now revealed its sinister side to Eisenstein.

In July, Eisenstein lost his devoted student Jay Leyda. Leyda went to New York to take the position of assistant-curator at the newly founded film department of the Museum of Modern Art. He had been offered the job on his teacher's recommendation. Eisenstein gave him a complete copy of *Potemkin* and several of his writings, including the screenplays to *An American Tragedy* and *Sutter's Gold*. In consolation, Eisenstein received the support of his former teacher. Meyerhold, who was hounded by persistent accusations of Formalism, gave a lecture on June 13, 1936 in the Leningrad House of Film on 'Chaplin and Chaplinism'. He spoke more about Eisenstein than about Chaplin. After the master returned to Moscow, Eisenstein paid him a visit and thanked him. Meyerhold gave him a portrait of himself with the inscription, 'I am proud of the student who has already become a master. I love the master who has founded his own school. To this student, this master—Sergei Eisenstein—my admiration.'

Around this time, several writers went to Paris to take part in the International Congress in Defense of Culture. Vishnevsky saw *Thunder over Mexico* on that occasion. The film was announced as Eisenstein's masterpiece, and promoted with a quotation by Chaplin: 'The best film I have ever seen'. The film was successful and received good reviews. Vishnevsky wrote from Paris that the movie had thrilled him. His congratulations only irritated Eisenstein. His mood was dark; his relations with the script editors and supervisors were becoming more and more complicated. Rzheshevsky was scheming against Eisenstein because the script had been rewritten. The material was supposed to be adapted for a children's movie. Rzheshevsky declined the assignment, so Eisenstein's assistant Zaitsev took over the job.

After the June festivities celebrating the new constitution, the complete change of course which the show trials represented was jolting. On July 15, 1936 a public trial against Kamenev and Zinoviev was announced. The two had allegedly collaborated with the Gestapo. The papers were filled with exalted slogans: 'No mercy for the enemies of the people! Shoot the murderers!' This campaign of rhetorical destruction against political opponents followed the same patterns as the anti-Formalist campaign, which had attacked aesthetic opponents. On July 21, 1936 an open letter from Soviet writers appeared in *Pravda* under the headline: 'May They Disappear from the Face of the Earth!' The letter's sixteen signatures included Vishnevsky, Pasternak, Leonov, and Afinogenov. They demanded the death of the traitors. The same issue branded Bukharin, Tomsky, Rykov, Radek, and Pyatakov as members of a terrorist organization. Tomsky thereupon committed suicide.

During the trials Babel and Sinko were spending time together in Odessa. Babel joked around and said that the trials would end just like the Promparty in 1930. But on August 25, ten days after the beginning of the trials, the executions were announced—the report came as a huge shock. All hopes for liberalization were shattered. A three-year period of terror followed, involving mass arrests and more show trials, during the course of which about nine million people were deported to prison camps and around three million people were executed. The victims included politicians, military men, economists, diplomats, scientists, and artists.

On July 14, one day before the trials were announced, Eisenstein wrote in his diary: 'The dacha is being built in Kratovo. To do that, I had to sign a contract for the textbook *Direction*. The dacha will be there, but what about life... I haven't moved a finger since last Sunday. I've been sitting around like a bump on a log. Can I lead such a brainless life? I've got to end it. Do I have to? Why? What for? Shakespeare, I shake your hand. And yours, Michelangelo. Everything is empty. The day before yesterday, after a walk in the forest, I bawled for an hour and chewed on my pillow. I can't, don't want to, won't do anything. I don't understand anything. What is the matter? Babel hasn't called. I can't even work. I can only numb myself the way you numb fish with dynamite. Why am I keeping silent? I need to change my name. *Why not?* My name has nothing to do with what it used to stand for. How about Ivanov, Petrov...'[240]

In spite of his deep depression, which he again tried to treat with the help of Kannabikh's hypnosis (just like Meyerhold's wife Zinaida Raikh, who suffered from serious anxiety neuroses), Eisenstein returned to work on July 22. He filmed in Yalta and Odessa, using a new script and new actors. On August 21 he obediently signed a letter demanding the death of the murderers.

He spoke to nobody of his fears, but at exactly this time he wrote a highly revealing letter to the German actor Werner Krauss, whom he had greatly admired in *The Cabinet of Dr. Caligari*, *Secrets of the Soul*, *The Trousers*, and *Looping the Loop*: 'I never would have expected to meet you among the lackeys in *Dr. Goebbels's Cabinet*. I never would have expected such meanness, even in the very depths of your soul. But perhaps you managed to slither into the position of man and artist in *Looping*, when you wet your ... *Trousers*?'[241] He never mailed the letter; he had probably written it on order. Eisenstein repressed his new assignment and the possible autobiographic undertones of the Krauss potrait with word games and stylistic exercises. On November 11 he returned to Moscow, where he shot several scenes in a studio. Babel was editing his translation of André Gide, which was supposed to appear in the magazine *Znamya*. Gide was in the Soviet Union during the show trial, but he was not allowed to attend the meetings of the court or meet with Stalin. On December 3 Soviet citizens learned of Gide's 'betrayal'—the book *Return from the U.S.S.R.*—in a *Pravda* article. The accusation read: 'Gide has accused all Soviet writers of cowardice, of having no personal opinions and no talent. According to Gide, a truly talented writer should stand in opposition to the government and its leaders, and call to battle against the government.' The Soviet campaign against Gide called upon international authorities like Romain Rolland and Lion Feuchtwanger, who was visiting Moscow at the time. Shortly thereafter a pun coined by Eisenstein ran through Soviet circles. The play on the words Gide-Yid pointed out how 'friends of the Soviet Union' could spontaneously turn into enemies

and poked fun at the stiff seriousness of the campaign that involved many prominent artists, including Eisenstein himself.

Eisenstein showed Feuchtwanger the raw cut of *Bezhin Meadow*, which lasted
about five hours. He was sorry that he would still have to cut the film much
more; he was proud of the night scenes that he had filmed in daylight.

In December Paul Robeson came to Moscow and promised Eisenstein that
he would be available for film work the following year—from July to October.
The friendship between the two men led to absurd rumors.

In early January 1937 Eisenstein once again fell ill with the flu, but he wrote
Leyda that he would be done filming in three to four weeks. On February 1 he
again wrote that he was almost done with the film and was itching to get back
to his book. He was worried that he would not have time to write, since two
more projects were waiting for him: a film about the Spanish Civil War and
the project with Paul Robeson. Eisenstein asked Leyda to send him book cata-
logues and to keep him up to date on new publications in the areas in which he
was most interested, namely psychology and art history. On January 17 he was
named professor at VGIK. Five days later, on January 23, a new trial started;
seventeen high party officials were accused of diversion, espionage, and murder conspiracies. Karl Radek, Leonid Serebryakov, Yury Pyatakov and Georgy
Sokolnikov were the principal defendants. All but four of the seventeen were
condemned to death; Radek was one of the exceptions. Feuchtwanger attended
the trial and wrote about it on January 27 in *Pravda*. Only writers, Feuchtwanger
argued, could explain the acts of the criminals, which were beyond rational
thought. Isaak Babel, Andrei Platonov, Yury Olesha, as well as Konstantin Fedin,
Yury Tynyanov, Nikolai Tikhonov, Alexander Fadeev, Alexei Tolstoy and Pyotr
Pavlenko had to publish individual statements on the trial and demand merciless sentences. Several writers hid out at home in order to avoid signing the
collective letters demanding the officials' executions. This withdrawal was
useless: in 1936 Pasternak had courageously refused to sign an open letter but
his signature was published in the paper anyway.

On January 17, 1937 Bukharin, the chief editor of *Izvestiya*, disappeared from
the pages of the paper; on January 24 Radek mentioned Bukharin's name in the
course of the trial. The announcement of a new trial followed immediately:
Bukharin and Rykov were arrested on February 27. Their trial took place in
March 1938. A broad ideological campaign was launched beforehand that aimed
to 'root out' Bukharin's influence and claimed the lives of several artists. Nikolai
Ezhov was appointed the new chief of the NKVD, so this bloody period was
named after him: 'Ezhovshchina' or 'The Great Purge'. In April Ezhov's predecessor Genrich Yagoda was arrested as a Gestapo spy. The arrest of his relative
Leopold Averbakh, literary critic and influential leader of RAPP, followed suit.

People disappeared overnight. On February 8 Eisenstein publicly denied reports of his arrest in *Izvestiya* because the Paris *Cinémonde* had published the note: 'Eisenstein est-il en prison?' on December 17, 1936.

In the meantime the NKVD continued collecting information against Eisenstein. Edmund Stevens, an American journalist, wrote a fitting denunciation and sent it to the judge David Raizman. The letter accused Eisenstein of maintaining relations with Trotskyites. In Mexico Eisenstein had spent time with Trotsky's friend Rivera; in New York he had met with Anita Brenner, Rivera's friend. He was also acquainted with Bertram Wolf, Elliot Cohen, and Herbert Solo, all Trotsky followers from the American branch of International Workers' Aid. In his conversations with Anita Brenner, according to Stevens, Eisenstein had repeatedly expressed his sympathy for Trotsky and had said that he considered Trotsky's deportation a great loss for world revolution.[242] Eisenstein never learned of this denunciation.

On March 4, after his recovery, Eisenstein returned to work on the film, but only three days later the project was stopped for good on order from the main film administration. In an attempt to protect himself in the anti-Formalism campaign, Shumyatsky had ordered that the unedited footage of the second version be taken to the Kremlin and shown to Stalin. The 'First Viewer's' complete inability to comprehend why white doves repeatedly flew out of burning houses—Eisenstein had been testing the possibilities for contrasting fire and night, white and black—apparently ended in a tantrum. After such a response the solution became obvious. Shumyatsky suddenly began to accuse Eisenstein of wasting resources: three million rubles had already been spent on the film. By this time artists had become very familiar with these tactics. When authorities had demanded the discontinuation of the Art Theater's most popular play, *The Days of the Turbins*, they held the play's high production costs against the author Bulgakov. On March 5, 1937 the Central Committee passed a resolution that demanded the immediate cancellation of Eisenstein's 'politically misled, anti-artistic production'. The guilty parties were to be held responsible.[243] Shumyatsky tried to deflect the accusations from himself and pass them on to Eisenstein. He condemned the film *Bezhin Meadow* and its director. The film suffered from subjectivism, mythologism, a Biblical orientation, showed traits of Formalist degeneration and depraved ideological content. The paper *Kino* reported on the matter on March 24 and demanded that film *leadership* be strengthened, so that such grave mistakes would not be repeated. The paper's formulation let the inner circle understand what kind of intrigue was going on behind the scene and who might be blamed for the film.

There was a three-day conference in Moscow March 19-21 that condemned *Bezhin Meadow*. Eisenstein was called upon to do public penance. He did this by

publishing the article *The Mistakes of Bezhin Meadow*, but that was only the beginning.[244] The film was condemned in discussions that took place everywhere—in the studio, the film school, the Writers' Union, and the Committee
for Artistic Affairs. Eisenstein had to attend all these meetings personally and
give talks. He did it all and was as obedient as a polite little boy.

On May 28, 1937 a book was published devoted exclusively to the 'mistakes of *Bezhin Meadow*'. It included essays by Shumyatsky, Evgeny Veitsman,
Ilya Vaisfeld, and Eisenstein himself. The director was reprimanded for not
being able to make an up-beat movie after three Hollywood scripts about the
downfall of individuals. Once again, the director had produced a film about
disaster.[245] His collective farm workers acted like barbarians, the decoration of
a clubhouse was shown as the destruction of a church, his Soviet Pioneer appeared as a silent angel, and the boy's father—an obvious class enemy—looked
like Pan in a painting by the Symbolist Vrubel. Eisenstein had proven that he
knew nothing at all of reality, and had thus ignored the foundation for the
development of Soviet art: the unlimited, omnipresent power of the Party. The
Central Committee finally had to step in and stop this pathological production. The critics Vaisfeld and Veitsman needed to support their accusations
theoretically, so they discovered the roots of Eisenstein's mistakes in his theory,
in his enthusiasm for inner monologue and his dubious fascination with myths.
This propensity had led him to anthropomorphize nature and to present a clear
case of class warfare as a Hellenistic tragedy in a Nietzschean spirit, as a mystery play with choruses and mythological figures who succumb to their irrational fates: 'Nietzsche, Lévy-Bruhl and Joyce are no help for a Soviet artist'.[246]
Eisenstein admitted that he had relied too much on his spontaneity and creativity (!). Since his creativity was undisciplined, subjective, and anarchical, it
had led him to false generalizations. He condemned his individualism as pathological and identified as degenerate his experiments with unusual composition, lighting, camera angles, still shots and masks in place of realistic characters. His personal aesthetic had led to this political failure.

This conclusion matched the tone of the anti-Formalism campaign;
Eisenstein's film, like Shostakovich's opera, became a precedent. Eisenstein
also had to condemn his own life as a 'political mistake'. He had been isolated
from the vigor of the masses—in his research laboratory, the film school auditorium, his own eggshell. The studio collective would now help him to rot out
this pernicious individualism.[247] Eisenstein did not put a lot of effort into the
words he used; instead he followed the prescribed rhetoric of the time. His
film was banned along with Abram Room's *A Severe Young Man* (based on a script
by Yury Olesha), Kavaleridze's *Prometheus*, the comedies *Once in Summer* and
Lenochka and Grapes. In July the journal *International Literature* published an En-

glish translation of Eisenstein's essay 'The Mistakes of *Bezhin Meadow*'. News about the case spread through the foreign press, accompanied by dramatic details about the destruction of the negative and of the only positive copy. After all the humiliating meetings, Eisenstein was given the opportunity to voluntarily leave his job at the film school.

He took the final blow lightly. His diary reads merely, 'Today production of *Bezhin Meadow* was stopped.' No further comment. He took notes on the German book *Die Urgeschichte der Bildenden Kunst* ('The Prehistory of the Visual Arts'), Vienna 1925, and on the biography of François Delsarte, a theoretician of expressive movement, published in 1874.[248] The Great Terror made him fear for his life, but the end of the film did not mean much to him. He had known the risks when he decided to film that material. He had shown the Party his willingness, and thought that art would save him from ideological banalities, but the simultaneous flirt with power and with his own creativity had lead to a catastrophe.

Now he had been catapulted into the freedom he had longed for a year earlier: 'I have time to time. I have a time to look my own hand writing.'[249] Naturally, he still had to show his loyalty; on April 16 he wrote an obligatory letter to Andrei Zhdanov asking for permission to correct *Bezhin Meadow*. He wrote letters explaining the situation to Stalin and to the government. He asked them for trust and the permission to continue working. He mentioned a 'safe' source, Vishnevsky's *We the Russian People*, about the origins of the Red Army.

Three days later, on April 19, Shumyatsky passed the letter on to Stalin and added his own two cents. He did everything he could to protect himself and to place all the blame on Eisenstein. He reported to his supreme supervisor that several comrades were energetically trying to find Eisenstein work, but that he himself was against it. Of course, the final decision lay in the hands of the Central Committee. Eisenstein had mentioned many times, Shumyatsky wrote, that he would take his own life. In spite of that 'blackmail', Shumyatsky suggested that Eisenstein be denied the right to practice his profession. He also expressed the desire that more newspapers publish the Central Committee resolution banning *Bezhin Meadow* and discuss the pernicious elements of Eisenstein's artistic principles on an even larger scale.[250]

The Central Committee rejected Shumyatsky's overeager approach: Molotov drafted an alternative proposal that gained the support of Zhdanov and Voroshilov: 'The suggestion has been made to Comrade Shumyatsky that Comrade Eisenstein be used and be given a new assignment (a subject). The script, text, etc. need to be confirmed in advance.'[251] Stalin preferred this approach to the one drawn up by Shumyatsky and Kaganovich, so the film chief was forced to comply. Eisenstein's fate was thus sealed on May 9. So far no documents have revealed whether Eisenstein knew of the protection of his high-ranking patrons.

In May 1937 he went to take a cure: his heart and his nerves could not handle the pressure. After his treatment he had to start working on a 'suitable' screenplay. 'I feel like I'm in a glass coffin,' he wrote Pera, 'could that be why I dreamed of the Glass House?'[252] The studio leadership, however, could not allow a director as dubious as Eisenstein to work on the script of a writer as famous as Vishnevsky. This decision was upheld even after Eisenstein's friends and colleagues Boris Barnet, Mikhail Romm and Alexander Medvedkin signed a petition in his favor. Eisenstein was also forbidden to film Feuchtwanger's novel *The Pretender*. While Eisenstein recovered in Kislovodsk, Vishnevsky wrote him long letters almost every day. On May 18 Elena Sokolovskaya, the Mosfilm director, said that she would try to get him the script *Rus* ('Russia') about Alexander Nevsky.

Eisenstein's plans to make a film about Spain were also shot down. His offer to film *The Lay of Igor's Campaign* was ignored. Shumyatsky rejected everything that had anything to do with Eisenstein. On June 5 the director wrote Elena Sokolovskaya from Kislovodsk: 'I am trying to avoid all intellectual activity. I am trying to gather the necessary strength. But two hypothetical themes still came into my head. One—the fight against espionage and diversion. The theme is topical, but it seems that for me it's taboo. The second theme that interests me is race. Robeson is determined to work with me. There is some unexpected historical material: Pushkin's fragment about the Moor of Peter I. That could free me. I'm also interested in Persia, but you could hardly do that without a trip to the site. At least a little excursion. I already wanted to go there in 1933, but they sent [Vladimir] Erofeev and [Anatoly] Golovnya instead and they botched it.'[253]

After the nation-wide celebration of the Pushkin anniversary in June of 1937, the Pushkin idea showed good timing; the other suggestions were appropriate as well. But none of them were even considered. Instead, Eisenstein began to work on the study 'Pushkin and Cinema' but never finished it. He picked up the idea in his broader project 'Soviet Film and Russian Culture', which was also supposed to include the essay 'Gogol and Cinema Language' that he had started in 1933. He would not complete any of these texts.

Eisenstein's financial situation was dismal. He no longer received a salary either from the studio or the film school. His mother had to cash her securities and sell some old books from Eisenstein's library. Elizaveta Telesheva approached Vladimir Nemirovich-Danchenko and asked him to arrange for Eisenstein to direct something at the Art Theater. Nemirovich-Danchenko naïvely wrote Shumyatsky, who told him to avoid Eisenstein. He suggested Yakov Protazanov instead, who had experience filming the classics.

In late June Eisenstein returned from Kislovodsk and became acquainted with Pyotr Pavlenko. This was the man with whom he was supposed to collaborate on a script. At the same time, another show trial began, now against the army leadership. Like the defendants before him, General Mikhail Tukhachevsky was declared a 'German spy'. Eisenstein had met him several times in the Litvinovs' home. Eisenstein went to a sanatorium near Moscow. On July 16 his old friend Sergei Tretyakov was pulled out of his sickbed at the Kremlin Hospital and arrested as a German and Japanese spy. Shortly thereafter Tretyakov's wife was arrested too.

In August Eisenstein mulled over a script about Alexander Nevsky that was temporarily called *Russia*. The narrative of the film was supposed to be in the style of a legend, with an artificial taste of folklore. The topic was the historical battle that Prince Alexander fought against the Teutonic Knights on April 5, 1242 on the ice of Lake Peipus. The Germans had launched a crusade against Russia, but were ultimately destroyed. The expected political orientation against Fascist Germany, which was building up its armed forces, was unmistakable.

Eisenstein was only allowed to make the film in collaboration with the director Dmitry Vasiliev. He accepted this condition. In all press reports, the directors were listed alphabetically, so Vasiliev (according to the Russian alphabet) was always mentioned first. Even when Vasiliev put his name behind Eisenstein's, the order was reversed. Vasiliev had already worked as director's assistant for Mikhail Romm and Yuli Raizman and did not have ambitions to be a solo director. He had a good grasp of the situation and tried to be as *tactful* as possible towards Eisenstein. The latter was relieved that David Maryan—one of the most eager and malicious critics of *Bezhin Meadow*—had not been named his co-director, as the studio had initially planned.

One year earlier Telesheva had written Eisenstein that she had read Feuchtwanger's article about *Potemkin* in *Pravda*: 'These days people write about things so rarely.'[254] In the summer of 1937 the opera *The Battleship Potemkin* by the Ukrainian composer Oleg Chishko premiered in Leningrad and then in Moscow. The opera followed the movie closely, but Eisenstein's name was not mentioned.

That same summer, the English film critic Thorold Dickinson met Eisenstein in Moscow; the director seemed reserved and absent-minded. Marie Seton arrived in September. Markoosha Fischer told her that Eisenstein had fallen from grace—because of his last film and his relations with foreigners. If Seton did not leave immediately, he would be in great danger; he had a new partner anyway. Marie Seton should also stop writing. Seton left in shock, but Markoosha's advice was probably not the only reason for her quick departure. Genrich Yagoda, the protector of her close friends, the Afinogenovs, had just been sentenced to death for espionage.

In late September Shumyatsky appeared at the first conference of the Film Trade Union and led a massive attack against Eisenstein. The director wanted to defend himself and asked for a turn to speak, but he was told to formulate his thoughts in writing. He finished his script in this tense situation and continued working on his research. On November 13 the new screenplay was sent to the main film administration GUK and from there to Stalin. He is said to have drawn a thick black line right before the episode of Alexander's death (Alexander was poisoned by Tamerlane) and to have written: 'The screen play ends here . . . . A prince as good as that cannot die!'[255]

More friends and acquaintances were arrested, including Betal Kalmykov and Kirill Shutko, Vladimir Nilsen (Tisse's camera assistant who now worked for Alexandrov), Esfir Shub's husband Alexei Gan, the *Aerograd* actor Semyon Shagaida, Ivan Kavaleridze, and Boris Pilnyak.

Many became mentally ill. Mikhail Bulgakov suffered from fear neuroses, would not leave his apartment, and was treated with hypnosis. The writer Zoshchenko tried to save himself with self-analysis, which he described in his 1942 book *Before Sunrise*.

The times were violent. Terror and the pressure of censorship were omnipresent. How could a sensitive person survive this era?! Eisenstein envied Thomas de Quincey, because he had had opium at his disposal. One felt better, Eisenstein noted in his journal, when all sensitivity was turned off.[256] In 1937 he drew the cycles 'Despair' and 'Nothing'—tortured, flowing figures without heads that formed pyramids and circles. The captions read: 'I look into Nothingness', 'I drink Nothingness'. He was testing his old premonition, according to which art (film montage) could change consciousness and program a specific effect. The artist could gain unlimited power through his creation. Was this not a vision of horror? Had it been a coincidence that Goebbels asked his artists to make a 'National Socialist *Battleship Potemkin*'? Is art a machine of emotional and ideological enslavement and manipulation?

Eisenstein did not give up his research on ways to achieve ecstasy through art but he developed a kind of Galileo complex as an artist and researcher. He saw salvation from the brutal times in his book. In 1937, while he was studying mythological, regressive thinking, he began a book on montage that he planned as a treatise on harmonic metaphysical correspondences.

During his meeting with Joyce in Paris on November 30, 1929 Joyce had shown him the outline of *Ulysses* that he had also shared with his first commentator Stuart Gilbert. The outline was a universal map of correspondences. Every episode in the book had a connection to the real geography of Dublin, to the map of a universal city, and to the outline of a human life, the symbolism of which—birth, encounter, death—turns the singular into the universal. Every episode had its analogy in *The Odyssey*; most of the episodes corresponded to an organ of the human body—together they symbolized man.

Every episode was structured around a colored leitmotif that formally corresponded to the colors of the Catholic mass—their sum covered the entire color spectrum. Additionally, each episode had a semantic leitmotiv that could be interpreted as corresponding to a particular art form. Art, according to the medieval worldview, also encompasses science. Joyce's novel itself is a gigantic symbol, a concordance of universal knowledge and universal symbolism. Eisenstein had similar aspirations for his Moscow project; now he wanted to write that kind of book about montage. He searched for analogies between image and sound, line and music, color and music, for correspondences between different art forms. He dreamt of finding the laws of global metaphysical correspondences—between art, the human body, and the universe.

Montage projected a new concept of totality, and a new notion of a book as a reservoir of universal knowledge. Eisenstein also changed his manner of writing. In the twenties he wrote theses, notes, aphorisms, incomplete sentences that often consisted of only a verb or a noun. In the thirties his text turned into an uninterrupted flow that could keep growing and flow on and on—empirical studies escalating in correspondences.

Eisenstein's book contained an obvious paradox. Since Eisenstein was being sharply attacked for his Formalist 'montage sins', he announced in the introduction that he no longer overvalued montage as the *one* cinematic means of expression. However, in all 900 pages of his treatise he tried to prove that montage was the global structural principle of all artistic phenomena.

The idea of organic unity and the invoked synaesthestic effect now completely displaced Eisenstein's theories of the 1920s, which had focused on montage and its effect. He no longer explained montage through conflict, jump, displacement, and opposites, but through unity, synthesis, ecstasy, and organicity. He dismissed his former discoveries as incomplete solutions. Eisenstein now envisioned the problem of montage as a way of expressing the inner laws of artistic thinking that hold true for all forms of art: architecture and painting, literature and music, theater and circus, music-hall and film. Eisenstein wrote *his own* 'Laocoön', a media aesthetic that does not differentiate between poetry and painting, architecture and film, but discovers far-reaching correspondences between all forms of art. According to Eisenstein, these correspondences exist thanks to one circumstance only: each work of art aspires to create an image (*obraz*) that is absorbed in the act of perception. This image is conceived as the product of montage and establishes the foundation for corresponding relationships. The relationship between the visible and invisible emerges as the central problem of *cinematic* expression. In the conflict of two shots or two representations (*izobrazheniia*) Eisenstein no longer sought to find a specific concept, but instead looked for the image, the heart of this new theoretical system.

This new organic conception was undoubtedly related to the shift in cultural paradigms from the Constructivism of the 1920's to the universal thinking of the 1930's, when Soviet theoreticians tried to develop a systematic Marxist aesthetic and succumbed to Hegelian metaphysics.

In the late twenties Eisenstein discovered Ernst Cassirer, who had tried to renew ontology, a debunked form of systematic thinking, by turning to the notion of the symbol. In the thirties Eisenstein found his own correspondence to Cassirer's symbol in the image. With the help of this concept, conflict was transformed into organic unity. A fusion of pathos and ecstasy replaced Eisenstein's old model of stimulus-reaction. Eisenstein turned towards traditional ontological philosophies of art and joined the idea of a holistic system with the old concept of dialectics. Art was the ideal medium for this unity, which could not exist anywhere else in such a pure form. He interpreted dialectics as a cancellation of contrasts between the general and the specific, the intellectual and the emotional, a phenomenon and its representation, the subjective and the objective: art strives to dissolve these dichotomies completely. However, this dynamic abolition of opposites in a metaphysical 'organic unity' remains incomprehensible for human consciousness and can only be experienced while in an ecstatic state triggered by art. The actual experience of ecstasy involves the art recipient's recognition of the laws of nature. In this theory Eisenstein offered an idiosyncratic interpretation of the Dionysian. In Eisenstein's view, the notion of ecstasy seems mystical and far-removed from the pathos of Socialist Realism. Only the claim to universality is common to both views. In the Stalinist utopia the will of man should not only dominate history, but also subordinate natural laws: Siberia's rivers would irrigate the deserts of Central Asia, and peaches would be grown in the far north. Thus, historical and dialectical materialism would meet in a *Gesamtkunstwerk*, and then history would have to end. Eisenstein's harmonic correspondences could also lead to a *Gesamtkunstwerk*, but they would be banned to a circle joining the human body, the universe, and a work of art. History was excluded from this train of thought, which amounted to an amazing shift for the director of *Potemkin*. Eisenstein still studied the historical changes in perception and artistic techniques, but he ignored the cataclysms in society. Art was fused with the phenomenon of totality, but totality was not real. He declared that not the visible, but the invisible represented the core of film.

The book remained unfinished and was not published during Eisenstein's lifetime.

WINTER IN SUMMER. THE TWILIGHT OF THE GODS
1938-1940

On January 8, 1938 Meyerhold's theater was shut down. The ensemble sought for ways to save the company. They renamed it Mayakovsky Theater and their chief dramatist Alexander Fevralsky asked Eisenstein to take over the theater's direction. He refused. His own situation was too insecure and too complicated. He had just finished the script for *Alexander Nevsky* and was waiting for it to pass the censorship. Internally he was prepared for a conflict with Shumyatsky: 'I've got to bear the affliction. But I don't care. I'm calm. Calm like grass and cows. What could be more charming than obtuseness?'[257]

Suddenly the winds changed for Shumyatsky. The film studios were producing ever fewer films on an ever higher budget. In addition, too many 'politically harmful' films were being made. A guilty party had to be found. January 8, 1938 was also the day that Shumyatsky was removed from power. First he was sent to the provinces; he was subsequently arrested and executed. All the leaders of the film industry were arrested in one fell swoop: Mosfilm studio director Elena Sokolovskaya, director of the former Mezhrabpromfilm (now Gorky studios) Boris Babitsky, Lenfilm's artistic director Adrian Piotrovsky, studio directors in Kiev, Odessa, and Yerevan. Semyon Dukelsky was named the new chief of the Film Committee, but after a year and a half he was replaced by Ivan Bolshakov.

While working on the scenario to *Nevsky* Eisenstein read not only old Russian chronicles, but also Hitler's *Mein Kampf*. He discovered his own portrait in Prince Alexander. Nevsky had been a warrior who did great deeds in the name of the future and suffered much abuse in the present. Victorious over the Germans, he still had to bow to the Tatars. Eisenstein again made the most of tortured bodies (*his* subject) and wrote down naturalistic *guignol* details of the battle in the script: an ax splits open a head down to the teeth, a body is severed in two, a baby is thrown into the flames.

The film was not a reenactment of distant history—the focus did not really lie on the ancient Russian war of liberation against the Teutonic Knights. Instead the political present was at stake: fascists in brown uniforms were transformed into Teutons clad in white and stylized as a perfect death machine. The helmets of the Russian Knights were designed to look like Red Army headgear. Many of Eisenstein's *Nevsky* drawings are compositionally structured around the swastika, but his bodies are reminiscent of the flowing lines of his cycles 'Nothing' and 'Despair'. However, historians, not politicians, evaluated the script. They harshly criticized the 'outrageous errors' in the description of the Teutonic Knights. The debate was triggered by the script's publication in the magazine *Znamya*—Vishnevksy was the editor-in-chief. The February issue of the journal *Marxist Historian* included the essay 'Mockery of History' criticizing the screenplay's stylized speech and historical anachronisms.[258] Various attacks on the 'historically false screenplay' were published well into the summer. *Literaturnaya gazeta* printed a review on May 20; *Pravda* added its commentary on July 7. But this superficial debate had no effect. The script had already been blessed by the highest source, Stalin himself.

When Eisenstein was finally allowed to make another film, he necessarily found himself surrounded by new colleagues. He had virtually been ordered to give the lead to Nikolai Cherkasov, who had just played Gorky in *Lenin in 1918* and an old botanist turned Communist in *Baltic Deputy*. Eisenstein was allowed to keep his cameraman Tisse. He wanted Prokofiev to compose the film music, but the composer had just left for a three-month tour and postponed making a decision about the offer until his return. He hired his old acquaintance Konstantin Eliseev as set and costume designer. (Eliseev had once helped Eisenstein get a transfer from the Corps of Engineers to the Army Theater.) The film's costume needs posed a huge challenge. Under Eliseev's direction 1200 old weapons, 2000 suits of armor, and 1950 capes, furs, and jackets were made to order by Nadezhda Lamanova in the famous tailor's shop of the Moscow theaters.

In February and March Eisenstein wrote the director's script and traveled to Novgorod. He was disappointed to learn he could not film there. Most of the ancient buildings were no longer standing; their remains had sunk so deep into the ground that they were useless as film sets. The film architect Iosif Shpinel had to build models of the old cathedrals in the studio. Eisenstein demanded that he stylize Russia in the manner of Nikolai Rerikh and Utamaro. The question of how and where to film the battle on Lake Peipus was raised immediately. Winter was almost over; the ice had already melted. Would they have to postpone the film for whole year? Vasiliev suggested using artificial ice. They spent April and May looking for a suitable location in Pereslavl-Zalessky near Moscow, but finally decided to film the battle in the studio. The summer was turned into winter.

Eisenstein worked day and night. He had officially been fired from the Film Institute, but he was allowed to continue teaching since several of his students (Alexander Stolper, Alexander Andrievsky, and Isidor Annensky) were about to receive their degrees. The institute did not rehire Eisenstein until March 10, 1938, after the film studio had officially re-employed him as director of *Alexander Nevsky*. 'Order Number 22' was back-dated February 15 and designated Eisenstein an 'instructor in the field of film composition'. However, Eisenstein had had to submit a petition to the institute even for this position. During this time Eisenstein continued his book on montage by writing 'Montage 1938'. This long essay examines the psychological nature of the image, which is formed as the mind engages in its associative process.

In May Eisenstein met with Prokofiev, who still had relatively little experience with film music. He had written the score to Lieutenant Kizhe in 1933 and composed 24 fragments for Mikhail Romm's The Queen of Spades three years later. The latter film was never finished since Romm was assigned other, bigger projects for the celebration of the twentieth anniversary of the Revolution. However, after composing three operas and four ballets Prokofiev was accustomed to the visual, dramatic, vocal, and rhythmic demands of choreographing music and plot. Many people recognized his music's affinity for plastic representation. The world of film, however, was foreign to him. Prokofiev liked Chaplin, whom he had met in Biarritz in 1930 and whom he had just visited in Hollywood in 1938. He had gone to see Disney's Snow White several times while he was on tour in Denver. Disney and Prokofiev met in California, where the composer was thrilled by sound technology and by the possibilities of sound film.[259] In Hollywood Prokofiev was offered a contract for $2,500 a week. As he later told his friend Nikolai Myaskovsky, he would have stayed in America, but he had just established himself in Moscow and decided to return home to his children. Prokofiev and Eisenstein bonded over their enthusiasm for Disney. Prokofiev offered Eisenstein several musical themes in May before he left for vacation in the Caucasus.

Filming began on June 5 in the Mosfilm Studio. Eisenstein had plotted every detail of every day's work in advance. Every change, including minute cuts in the dialogue, had to be approved in writing by the studio chiefs. They filmed the central episode, the battle on the ice of Lake Peipus, during a July heat wave. On the set Eisenstein wore sunglasses and a sun helmet made of cork that he had brought back from Mexico—he made an exotic impression. To film the battle, they chopped down the studio's apple orchard. They covered 3,000 square meters with asphalt in order to build rocky cliffs. The shooting attracted reporters and was covered extensively in the press.[260] The asphalt turned to ice as if by magic: hot asphalt was covered with chalk that appeared light blue as the asphalt cooled. Before each shot the asphalt would be sprayed with liquid gas that glittered like ice. White sand, moth powder, salt and sawdust were then sprinkled on the 'ice'. With the help of orange and blue light filters, the dust turned into snow.

Forty stuntmen were used for the mounted battle. To create a dynamic effect, Tisse filmed at a speed of 8-12 frames per second. The organization was perfect. Nobody was injured and the shooting was completed in only 115 days rather than the planned 198.

Eisenstein cut the film in October. Its perfect rhythm is due partly to the interplay of image and music. Eisenstein especially valued the 'gesture' of Prokofiev's music, the way the composer grasped the inner dynamic of image and emotion. Prokofiev's ability to filter rhythm from a given image and offer a musical equivalent remained a fascinating mystery for Eisenstein. He tried to find an explanation in his literary portrait of the composer.[261] There were also tense moments. Eisenstein wanted Prokofiev to use music from the 12th century. Prokofiev considered that music unacceptable and too strange for a 20th century audience. He composed an artistic stylization instead. The two men were also unable to agree on an overture. Prokofiev wanted Eisenstein to replace the first ominous images, since they would look strange with a light overture. Eisenstein would not change the shots and Prokofiev refused to write a somber overture, so the opening credits ran silently. Prokofiev would usually compose the music from a final cut of the scene. When he could not feel the rhythm, he would ask Eisenstein to reedit the passage.

Alexander Nevsky was Eisenstein's first completed sound film. He knew that two separate stimuli—visual and acoustic—could either suppress or intensify each other. In this film, he explored a synaesthetic correspondence where the visual image acted as a sort of seeing-eye dog for the music and vice versa. The movement of the music made the movement within the image perceptible—it highlighted not only the obvious physical motion, but also the hidden emotional dynamism. The music enabled the viewer to grasp the visual structure of the image. Eisenstein did not want the music to increase the representative qualities of the image; instead, he wanted the music to intensify the reception of the image's *shape*. In this simple, narrative film, Eisenstein explored the theoretical and practical foundations for an abstract musical film. He described the counterpoint in the Lake Peipus battle scene as 'the simplest abstract case' that only hinted at the possibilities of true counterpoint.[262] However, he managed to make the visual and acoustic levels so interchangeable that British Radio played the sound track as a radio drama in 1943. The sound alone carried the entire content of the image.

According to plan, *Alexander Nevsky* was to be finished on December 31, but the crew was ordered to complete the picture by November 7, the anniversary of the Revolution. Eisenstein added the final touches to the montage on November 4. The film was shown in the studio on November 6, the Central Administration was to review it on November 9. The night before the first official screening, the film was shown to Stalin and one reel was accidentally left behind in the studio. Since the film was accepted in the form it had been delivered, one reel was missing when the film reached distribution. On November

WINTER IN SUMMER. THE TWILIGHT OF THE GODS | 1938-1940

14 Eisenstein wrote Semyon Dukelsky asking for permission to include the forgotten reel. Without the passage there was a non sequitur in the plot. The scene in which two warriors meet on the Novgorod Bridge was missing entirely. His request went unheeded. Dovzhenko publicly addressed the question of the missing reel at a conference on historical and revolutionary film. However, nobody dared admit that they had forgotten to show Stalin ten minutes of the film. They would rather live with unmotivated gaps in the plot.

Nevsky premiered on November 23. On December 1 the film began playing in movie theaters. At a showing in the House of Film Eisenstein spoke of his deep gratitude to Comrade Stalin, who had personally taken the time to edit the screenplay.[263] The premiere was very successful. Stalin allegedly told Eisenstein, 'You're a good Bolshevik after all!' Eisenstein was showered with presents and fame. After a nine-year hiatus the major papers again praised him. On November 11 reviews were published in *Izvestiya* (Ilya Bachelis), *Pravda* (Pudovkin), *Za sotsialistichesky film* (Shklovsky), and *Vechernyaya Moskva* (Khersonsky). Even Veitsman, the zealot against *Bezhin Meadow*, offered praise in *Sovetskoe iskusstvo*. The few critical comments were disregarded as 'scorn'. The Film Institute VGIK apologized for Eisenstein's dismissal by requesting that Eisenstein be awarded the degree of 'Doctor of the Arts'. He received the honorary degree on March 23, 1939 without ever having written a dissertation. On February 1, 1939 Eisenstein was awarded the Order of Lenin. During the awards ceremony in the Kremlin, Eisenstein gave a speech thanking the Party, the government, and Stalin. His share of the proceeds of the screenplay was doubled as a reward. Eisenstein bought a car and hired a chauffeur. Now he could compete with Prokofiev's blue Ford.

At the 18th Party Congress on March 13, 1939 Emelyan Yaroslavsky called *Alexander Nevsky* an 'outstanding achievement'. He used the same epithet for *Chapaev* and Romm's films about Lenin. On July 17, 1939 Eisenstein received a place in the Film Union's book of honor as a 'Stakhanovite' alongside his co-workers Dmitry Vasiliev, Iosif Shpinel, Nikolai Cherkasov, the editor Esfir Tobak and the actor Andrei Abrikosov.

The film was a box office hit too, but Eisenstein knew very well what he had sacrificed. The old Eisenstein was gone. The new Eisenstein did not fascinate everybody: Dovzhenko mockingly called *Nevsky* a daytime two-penny opera.

In April 1939 Eisenstein made a diary entry in English: 'Traumatisme d'Alexandre. It is the first film where I gave up the Eisenstein touch. Conflict had also a hand in it for sure! This is not the only case! The Novgorod Bridge as reel—You ought to be ashamed of Your self, dear Master of Art!'[264]

Eisenstein asked Jay Leyda to send him reports on the reception of *Nevsky*. He wanted to know what people thought about it and what *The Nation* or *The*

New Republic were writing about it. Unfavorable reviews interested him even more than favorable ones.[265] He was not eager to make another movie right away—he wanted to wait until summer. Instead, he started another book project about El Greco and cinema.

In January 1939 *Alexander Nevsky* was screened in England, Belgium, and Switzerland. The American premiere took place in March. On April 25 and June 8, 1939 *Pravda* reported on the film's outstanding success: the movie's clear warning against fascism had been understood and welcomed abroad. On May 29 *Vechernyaya Moskva* wrote that President Roosevelt had loved the film. However, on February 4, 1939 the Paris paper *Combat* published a review by Denis Marion, a friend of Malraux. Marion perceived *Alexander Nevsky* to be 'uncinematic and archaic'. He wrote, 'when after five years of silence, the man who was once—alongside Chaplin and Stroheim—one of the greatest directors, produces such a pitiful film, it is proof of the degeneration of Soviet cinema.' Eisenstein collected all the newspaper clippings. He put letters from the German and Japanese embassies in a separate envelope—the embassies requested tickets to the film on December 3 and 7, 1938.

Goskinoizdat published the screenplay in a separate edition as an example of how to write a proper script. They also prepared to rerelease *Potemkin* and to print an anthology about the film. That same year Gosizdat also printed Vishnevsky's 31-page biography of Eisenstein. Vishnevsky's portrayal of the past several years was telling: enemies of the people (like Shumyatsky) had rejected Eisenstein's screenplays and forced him to shoot such dubious films as *Bezhin Meadow*. They offered him material that crippled his creativity. The 'mistakes of *Bezhin Meadow*' were now blamed on saboteurs and enemies. One could only imagine what great works Eisenstein could have produced without these enemies. Luckily, Eisenstein himself had realized in time that *Bezhin Meadow* was a mistake. He then wanted to film two other movies—one on the Spanish Civil War and one the birth of the Red Army in 1917 (Vishnevsky's *We, the Russian People*), but the enemies of the people thwarted him again. 'Then the Party, the Government, and Stalin personally came to the rescue.'[266]

Eisenstein understood his change of fortune very well, and he grasped the fate he had possibly escaped. In January 1939 the NKVD chief Ezhov was fired; Isaak Babel was arrested May 15, 1939; Meyerhold was arrested on June 20. Both men were tortured and condemned to death in secret trials. Meyerhold's wife Zinaida Raikh was murdered in her apartment on July 15. The script of the 'artist plot' against Stalin included the names Ehrenburg, Eisenstein, Olesha and Shostakovich as possible conspirators, Trotskyites, and terrorists connected to André Malraux.

During this period Eisenstein made another English entry in his diary:

'Which way to go? What to do? Why is there nobody to lead me exactly the way I ought to go?'[267] At this point he had already been fully rehabilitated and was writing euphoric reviews of Mikhail Chiaureli's cult Stalin film *Great Glow* and the no less cultic film *Lenin in 1918*, directed by Mikhail Romm. He added a few words to every Party resolution, praised the heroism of Soviet pilots, and spoke at every anniversary celebration. In 1940 Eisenstein was suddenly even allowed to publish his theoretical essay 'Vertical Montage' on audiovisual counterpoint in the journal *Iskusstvo kino*. On October 16, 1940 he was named artistic director of Mosfilm.

This new appreciation gave him a sense of security, which he used to petition the NKVD on behalf of arrested acquaintances Valentin Stenich-Smetanich (who had translated Brecht, Joyce, and Dos Passos) and the Jewish actor Charles Puffy (Karl Huszar), who had wanted to reach the United States by crossing the Soviet Union and had then disappeared without a trace in Vladivostok. Paul Kohner had asked Eisenstein to help.

During the summer of 1939 Eisenstein considered filming Maupassant's *Mademoiselle Fifi*. He was probably trying to postpone the new film project so he could find more time to write. Most days, he worked on *Grundproblem* ('Fundamental Problem'). The manuscript had grown to more than a thousand pages.

At this time Marie Seton sent Eisenstein a list via Amkino of all the Mexican shots that she had just tested and viewed. This renewed his hope to finish his old film. But the newly resumed negotiations over the release of the material—at least the shots of the Day of the Dead—went nowhere.

In mid-November 1938 Eisenstein received an offer to direct a monumental epic about the defeat of Wrangel's Army in the Crimea. This time Fadeev was in charge of the screenplay. Fadeev invited Lev Nikulin to be the coauthor. They sent the script to Eisenstein via the Film Committee. Eisenstein was spending the semester break in a sanatorium near Moscow, where he was again trying to cure his heart. He thought the script was of scandalously poor quality and showed no signs of talent. It was merely a pitiful copy of *Chapaev*, sentimental, speculative, and cliché-ridden. The authors offered no philosophy of the events and none of the drama of the battle, Eisenstein wrote in his evaluation on March 26. He did not want to shoot a boring history of the Civil War. He wanted monuments on the scale of the Pyramids. Eisenstein had planned the break with Fadeev and Nikulin. He could now afford to turn down film offers.

However, when Pavlenko, who had just returned from Uzbekistan, suggested making a film about the Ferghana Canal, Eisenstein agreed. He thought he might be able to use episodes about the Golden Horde that he had had to cut from *Alexander Nevsky*. He wanted to shift the action from the time of Tamerlane to the current 240-meter canal in the desert. On June 18 Eisenstein, Tisse and Pavlenko traveled to Uzbekistan, where the local Central Committee welcomed them as guests of state.

Eisenstein tried to make up for everything he was unable to realize in Mexico and on the Moscow project in this new Asian film. The team traveled through the entire republic—Tashkent, Kokand, Samarkand, and Bukhara. Eisenstein read books about Ulugbek, the great astronomer and ruler of Samarkand. The Orient's exoticism reminded him of Mexico; he wanted to test the principles of his interrupted film on the new material. He wrote Leyda that it would be a film of architecture with two basic elements—desert and water. In that letter he did not mention the third component of the drama-turgy—death. The film was to begin with a huge massacre: Tamerlane is flood-ing a city. Eisenstein used Leonardo da Vinci's description of the visionary painting *Deluge* as a model for his dynamic film fresco. The main difference was that Leonardo's massacre was an act of God and Eisenstein's was caused by a worldly tyrant. The tyrant stood at the center of the film project, just as in the story of the black Napoleon, another idea Eisenstein never realized. The Ferghana material included elements that inspired Eisenstein's apocalyptic fantasy: mass death and destruction. But there was also a real counterpoint: the construction of a gigantic canal in the middle of the desert.

On July 12 they returned to Moscow. In Kratovo, Eisenstein and Pavlenko worked on the script. The screenplay was finished by the end of July. Eisenstein compiled the director's notes in only three days; they were full of journalistic excursions. He planned numerous flashbacks so he could jump between Tamerlane's times, the pre-Revolutionary era, and the present. He looked to dramas by J. B. Priestley for help with narrative technique, planned to intro-duce a Dzhambul-like folk singer and construct the screenplay like a folk song. His preface to the screenplay was published in the September 1939 edition of *Iskusstvo kino*. Since the Ferghana Canal was just being built, Eisenstein was in a hurry to get documentary footage. At first the main film administration agreed to everything. He traveled to Tashkent and filmed the first shots with Tisse on July 29. The Moscow team joined them on August 13. Eisenstein was even able to cut the footage in Tashkent with the help of his editor Esfir Tobak. For one month they filmed the construction work, which involved 160,000 people, and performances by Uzbek artists that were staged for the workers. Eisenstein was interviewed by *Pravda*;[268] on September 2 he even wrote an article about the construction project. In another interview in the paper *Sovetskaya Kara-Kalpakiya* he described many of the water structures he had seen in his life-time, including bridges in New York and San Francisco, the Niagara Falls, the port of the Mississippi. But only the Ferghana Canal had taken his breath away. The Suez Canal and the Panama Canal had been built on flesh and blood—this, however, was a festival of the people.[269] Unfortunately he was less thrilled by the film footage. It looked like a newsreel. He had hardly been able to shape the shots and had not choreographed the masses. So he tried to speed up preparations of the historical scenes in Tashkent instead. Prokofiev declined to participate in the film. Eisenstein sent him the screenplay and asked for two main themes—water and sand. Prokofiev was finishing an opera and wrote back that he would need a lot of time to write something like 'water' and 'sand'.[270]

The Ferghana press reported that the historical sections would be shot in October, first in Kokand and then in Choresm. Eisenstein wanted to convey the image of the ancient Orient through montage—not in cardboard sets—since the old mosques were still standing. The project was difficult to realize. The screenplay called for many long shots and mass scenes. But how could he film the storming and destruction of a historical city in the real downtown of Kokand? Where would he get the costumes and the weapons? Mosfilm wanted a new, operative film about a current, politically relevant event. The studio did not have the funds to produce a monumental historical film à la Cecil B. DeMille, especially in Central Asia, where the studios were ill-equipped for large projects. Mosfilm was overextended with other elaborate historical productions: Pudovkin had just had the studio rebuild half of 16th-century Moscow for Minin and Pozharsky. The main film administration decided that the historical section of the film was not expedient. Eisenstein despaired. The present that was depicted in the filmed material was not expressive enough, not dramatic enough, not substantial enough to carry a film. He tried to resist, wrote to Pavlenko in Moscow, and asked the Secretary of the Uzbek Central Committee Usman Yusupov for help. The latter wrote to Andrei Zhdanov describing Eisenstein's conception of the film. He added that the film would lose its monumental nature if the historical section were cut altogether. No trace has remained of Zhdanov's answer; he probably did not respond. While Eisenstein was shooting in Ferghana, Moscow was hosting the signing of the Molotov-Ribbentrop non-aggression pact between the Soviet Union and Germany. Eisenstein was still in the east when Hitler's troops attacked Poland, and Moscow decided to stop showing Alexander Nevsky in movie theaters out of consideration for the new political alliance.

The Ferghana project was canceled in October 1939, and Eisenstein returned home. The filmed material was handed over to the documentary film archive and used anonymously in numerous news programs.

October also brought about the premiere of a newly-cut version of Eisenstein's Mexican material at Hollywood's Academy of Motion Pictures and Sciences. Marie Seton and Paul Burnford had edited The Time in the Sun according to their understanding of Eisenstein's original plan. Eisenstein knew of the project, but did not voice his opinion on the matter.

In spite of the Central Asian failure, Eisenstein's position was stable, as

was the attitude of those in power. Both the Civil War and the Ferghana Canal were considered politically important, topical material. Eisenstein abandoned both projects without inner turmoil. Telesheva suggested that he direct *Oliver Twist* at the Children's Theater. That hardly interested Eisenstein.
He was writing. In 'Vertical Montage' he analyzed visual and acoustic phenomena and demonstrated how the dynamic law of perception functioned by
alternating between the two planes. In the essay 'On the Structure of Things'
Eisenstein searched for the basic principle that would explain the universal correspondences between an artwork's composition, the human body, and the cosmos.
He found the answer in the 'golden section', a compositional principle that mathematically expresses the growth pattern of plants and human bones.[271]

In 1936 Elizaveta Telesheva had taken over the management of Eisenstein's
household. This was the role that he assigned to all of his female companions.
When he was away traveling she had to pay the driver Alexei and get him to
buy gas (the studio allotted 30 liters a month to their directors). Gossip about
their relationship was all over Moscow. People said only obese women were
of any use to Eisenstein. However, popular opinion did give Telesheva credit
for having changed Eisenstein's dress: he used to run around in pajama pants
and undershirts, but now preferred well-tailored suits and Stetson hats. Only
his hair was still untamed, in spite of the bald spot. Eisenstein looked like an
aged, elegant child from a good home. He now looked as though he had never
known anything but comfort. Telesheva forced him to take part in society life
and to throw parties. The parties were usually in her apartment, but his housekeeper Aunt Pasha had to cook, serve the guests and clean up afterwards, which
led to her increasing disgruntlement. Eisenstein is said to have run away to
Pera's apartment at times, where he would hide from his social duties. On
such occasions Telesheva would allgedly send the driver to fetch him. In his
diary Eisenstein ironically called her 'Madame'.

After three years as Eisenstein's household manager Telesheva was bitter.
She wrote Eisenstein in October 1939 that she got little out of their relationship: 'Your only way of relating to me is via the telephone. In the morning I wait
for a call, since that is the only means of communicating with the beloved person.
Sometimes you need to come to town, so you ask if you can drop by. That's just
laziness, not a true desire to see me. I understand that your health is bad, I've even
agreed to live apart . . . . Our relations are abnormal. I want to take a break.'[272]

At this time, in December 1939, Eisenstein received an unexpected offer
from Samuil Samosud, the chief conductor of the Bolshoi Theater. Eisenstein
was to direct Wagner's opera *Die Walküre*.

The match had been made by Prokofiev. Earlier in the year the composer
had requested that Eisenstein direct the premiere of his opera *Semyon Kotko*

after Meyerhold, the opera's director, had been arrested during rehearsal. At that time Eisenstein had declined, and the production was completed by Serafima Birman. Eisenstein was surprised by the call from Samosud, but the two men met the next day at the theater. Eisenstein agreed to tackle the project, Samosud wrote in his memoirs, after he heard the orchestra rehearse 'Ride of the Valkyries'.

Samosud immediately emphasized the diplomatic significance of the production. However, the assignment was tricky. Eisenstein's friend Maxim Litvinov, a Jew from Bialystok, had been forced to leave the post of foreign minister so Vyacheslav Molotov could take his place and the pact would be signed by a Russian. But the Jew Eisenstein had been given the state commission to direct the 'German national' musical epic as a sign of the new political alliance!

Nevsky had stopped running in the theaters; the Teutonic Knights had been transformed into *Nibelungen*. Should Eisenstein now compare himself to Fritz Lang? Rehearsals started ten days after the phone call.

The people in power expected a new Russian-German cultural program. Schubert Lieder and recitations of Goethe's poetry replaced anti-Fascist propaganda in Radio Moscow's German-language broadcasts. Eisenstein, an artist who was well-known in Germany, was asked to compile a new program. On February 18, 1940 he spoke on a Radio Moscow show geared towards Germany. He spoke German and said that the pact had laid a solid foundation for cultural exchange, even cooperation between the two great peoples. *One* proof of his statement unexpectedly followed. The negative of *The Battleship Potemkin*, which had been sold to Germany in 1926, was returned to the State Film Archive in Moscow from the Reich Film Archive. As a sign of the new friendship, Eisenstein was to be invited to Germany to stage an opera in Berlin, possibly Modest Mussorgsky's *Boris Godunov*.

Eisenstein understood *Die Walküre* as a kind of Saturnalia of elemental drives—this was yet another source that dealt with the mythological thinking in which he was so interested. The project intrigued him as more than just a political assignment. His last film had been called a 'daytime opera'—perhaps it was not a coincidence that his next production should be an actual opera.

Eisenstein started rehearsing *Die Walküre* in December 1939; the premiere took place one year later, on November 21, 1940. That this date coincided with a second summit meeting was not accidental. One day earlier the Soviet delegation had returned from Berlin under Molotov's leadership. Molotov even mentioned the production in his Berlin talks with Ribbentrop.

In March Eisenstein wrote his Wagner essay 'The Incarnation of Myth'. In the context of the essay 'Vertical Montage', Eisenstein now looked at the artistic synthesis of Wagner's musical drama as the counterpoint of sound, image, color, and *space*, which he had to solve on the stage. He also needed to

decode Wagner's allegory. Wotan and Fricka were the rulers—he was an anarchist, and she represented the powerful structures of order. But what to do
with the Valkyrie? Should she be understood as Wotan's unconscious? Eisenstein
had to peek at Bayreuth's interpretations and make sure his own was different. He
thought Brünhilde was shaped by pity. 'What is fascistic in this play, wonder?!!!'
he wrote in English in the director's notes on December 24, 1939.[273]

In 1940, after a fifteen-year hiatus, *Die Walküre* had returned to the stage of
the Bolshoi Theater. In spite of the problematic political circumstances, the
production reawakened memories of Wagner's reception in Russia, as shaped
in the twentieth century by the Symbolists Vyacheslav Ivanov, Alexander Blok,
and Andrei Bely. On the one hand, the Bolshoi's 1913-14 production of the *Ring
Cycle* had been interpreted by Ivanov's student, the philosopher Alexei Losev,
as the expression of an approaching catastrophe. But the Symbolists had also
been the first to connect Wagner with the spiritual origins of the Russian
Revolution. The integration of artistic energy in a synthetic art form served as a
model for a social utopia that was first tested in the theater. According to Vyacheslav
Ivanov, this 'Theater of the Future' would become the locus of the artistic, prophetic self-determination of the people; the chorus would transform the drama
from an external object of contemplation to an internal object of communion, would
create political freedom, and appear as the medium of the people's will. In this
worldview, art itself was also a medium; the goal was social utopia.

Meyerhold had been heavily influenced by Ivanov's ideas; Eisenstein had
seen his Wagner productions as a student in Petrograd. In his diary Eisenstein
now legitimized his own semi-voluntary excursion into opera as the work of a
humble student. He only dared to step onto the opera stage because Meyerhold
was no longer directing. At the time when Eisenstein agreed to the production and penned these lines, Meyerhold was being held in prison. Eisenstein
could not leave the realm of art during his Wagner interpretation. Social utopia was reduced to an artistic utopia. The artistic conception was 'social' only
in the sense that the different senses communicated 'socially' in the ritual space
of the opera house.

Eisenstein illustrated the movement of the music through the gestures of
the chorus, pantomime, and a moving set. The choruses represented the movement of the individual hero's drive amplified by the collective body. (In a sense
they materialized Ivanov's ideas of the orgiastic body as an expression of the communion of the actors and the audience.) Fricka was surrounded by half-sheep,
half-humans; Hunding by the atavistic community—half-dogs and half-servants;
Wotan was accompanied by the Valkyries. The 'collective body' (the 'materialized' drive) moved like an undifferentiated mass, or the surface of the ocean.

The stage of *Die Walküre* reached far into the audience. Though Pyotr

Vilyams, a friend of Shostakovich, had been appointed stage designer, Eisenstein designed all of the sets himself. The first act showed the *Welt-Esche* (World Ash Tree) on which the singers act on three planes. Valhalla stands at the top, Hunding in the middle, Siegmund and Sieglinde at the bottom. In the second and third acts, only cliffs jutted into the vertical axis of the stage. The scene was framed in a gold oval, as if surrounded by the golden serpent. After years of experience with black and white film, the colors in *Die Walküre* seemed strange. The entire stage was shrouded in black velvet that swallowed color and created an unreal effect. White was replaced by colored red and golden light: red spotlights for the Ride of the Valkyries, golden rays for the ecstasy of love. In this manner, the black-white-gray of film was expanded only by a spectrum of black-dark blue-gold-red in the opera production.

The light was supposed to create spatial volume. During Siegmund and Sieglinde's love scene, golden rays of light moved from the stage into the hall, thus uniting the lovers with the audience; the finale was conceived as 'music of light'. Eisenstein also wanted to emphasize the audience's absorption into the play's action—the singers were to walk out into the first rows on a *hanamichi*,[274] in the tradition of the Kabuki theater. He planned to help the audience visualize the music spatially by filling the room with sound in an unusual way. Loudspeakers would be put up around the room, so that the Ride of the Valkyries would create a stereophonic effect. Light was the most mobile element of the decorations, but the set itself moved as well—in rhythmic correspondence to the music.

Eisenstein did not succeed in realizing all of his ideas. The hall of the Bolshoi Theater and the huge orchestral pit were a hindrance, so the *hanamichi* had to be abandoned. Originally Eisenstein had intended to perform the opera in the recently built Moscow Planetarium, but that suggestion was too outlandish for this high profile, state-ordered production.

The movements envisioned by Eisenstein were too dynamic and complicated. He expected the singers to jump and run as they sang, which scared the famous artists. The Bolshoi stars—Mark Reizen and Ksenia Derzhinskaya—had turned down the parts anyway. Eisenstein rehearsed the opera with young, inexperienced vocalists—Nataliya Shpiller as Sieglinde and Nikolai Shanayev as Siegmund. The theater's safety inspectors frequently interrupted rehearsals since the singers' flight through the black cliffs was life-threatening: the stairs were invisible, and the ephemeral stage sets rocked to and fro under the singers' bulky bodies.

To make the opera more dynamic and to visualize the music, Eisenstein had mimes in the background illustrate some of the arias—at first he even thought of inserting filmed material. Eisenstein was told that the pantomime was bothersome and distracted from the music. The theater's mechanics were also ill-suited to the job; the cliffs shook and squeaked at every step, and the singers did not look especially graceful as they jumped over them. The composer Yury Shaporin's critique of the premiere in *Pravda* on November 23, 1940 was nonetheless benevolent: 'The film tempi with which Eisenstein usually works and the epic development of Wagner's music are polar phenomena. Perhaps this circumstance has helped to make the static scenes in Acts I and II more dynamic.' But that same day the reviewer for *Izvestiya*, the musicologist Alexander Shaverdyan, found the pantomime and arrangements to be unconvincing. He called the production, 'a fairy play with rocking-horses'. The critic for *Sovetskaya muzyka* was even more skeptical. He wrote that Eisenstein's inventions were controversial and did little to make the music accessible. In his opinion the Valkyries looked like showgirls.[275]

While Eisenstein was rehearsing *Die Walküre*, he returned to the old idea of filming Feuchtwanger's *Der falsche Nero* ('The Pretender'). He also outlined a film biography of Pushkin. The Wagner production gave Eisenstein the opportunity to test the correspondences between light, space, color, and music. In the Pushkin screenplay *The Love of a Poet* he searched for color correspondences on the level of plot development. His efforts were influenced by Andrei Bely's *The Art of Gogol* (1934), where Bely analyzed Gogol's use of adjectives of color. Eisenstein, however, approached Pushkin's life not as a scholar but as a director. Once again his script tested his own theories—another step towards film-synaesthesia.[276] The Pushkin topic had been suggested to Eisenstein by Esfir Shub, who was preparing a documentary film about the poet. She also pointed out Tynyanov's Pushkin novel and 'Pushkin's Anonymous Love', an essay published in the summer of 1939, in which Tynyanov speculates about Pushkin's secret love of the wife of historian Nikolai Karamzin. The essay was published simultaneously in a Leningrad and a Moscow journal. Eisenstein secretly made fun of Shub, since he suspected that she envisioned herself in the role of his Ekaterina Karamzina. He spent a year collecting material for *The Love of a Poet*; in December he wrote a draft of the screenplay as a color composition. Eisenstein developed Tynyanov's approach and constructed a psychoanalytic interpretation of Pushkin's biography. He analyzed this repressed love as the crucial event of Pushkin's life and used it to explain Pushkin's Don-Juanism. Eisenstein projected Pushkin onto Chaplin, whose lover Marion Davies had been seduced by the media magnate Hearst. Chaplin had subsequently looked for Davies in each one of his numerous wives. Eisenstein met Tynyanov in February 1939 at the awards of the Order of Lenin. They, however, did not speak about Pushkin, but about Eisenstein's Mexico film. Tynyanov's doctor had seen the film in Paris and had praised it.

In the search for new material Eisenstein met the writer Lev Sheinin, who offered him several topics. On May 19 Eisenstein submitted the ideas to Ivan Bolshakov, the new chief of the main film administration. They included the Beilis Affair, an anti-Semitic trial that took place in 1913, and the story of the English spy Lawrence of Arabia. Eisenstein had read T. E. Lawrence's 1926 report *Seven Pillars of Wisdom* and interpreted it as the confessions of a nihilist, a Dostoevskian figure that attracted him. Since Eisenstein was intensely contemplating the effect of color and was especially fascinated by the combination of red-gold-black-blue, any topic was equally welcome—Lawrence of Arabia, Pushkin, Giordano Bruno, Soviet gold diggers in Siberia, or the plague. He expressed his new enthusiasm for color film as the synthesis of painting and drama, music and sculpture, architecture and dance in the essay 'Achievement', which was published in the issue 1/2 of *Iskusstvo kino*. Eisenstein delved into all of world culture to explain the phenomenon of film. He illustrated all of art via film— from Kandinsky and Malevich to Hokusai, Scriabin, Wagner, and Pushkin. His preoccupation with color was a logical continuation of his montage book of correspondences; he wanted to conclude the book with a chapter on the montage of color sound film. Yet another chapter would be dedicated to Wagner.

On November 21, 1940 the premiere of *Die Walküre* took place in the Bolshoi Theater. The event was planned as a gala of state; high-ranking members of government and the diplomatic corps had been invited to welcome the Soviet delegation after its trip to Berlin. The opera would be another opportunity to celebrate the new German-Soviet ties. Only a very few knew at this point that Molotov had achieved nothing in Berlin and that the summit had been a gigantic failure; however, the premiere could hardly be canceled. The German ambassador Count Schulenburg appeared in dress uniform nonetheless. The German diplomats thought the performance was very unusual. The pantomimic half-sheep, half-humans left an 'Asiatic' impression. They did not understand the point of the rhythmically moving cliffs. Eisenstein was called to the ambassador's box. When he was asked about his future plans, Eisenstein is said to have answered provocatively that he was making a film about Russian anti-Semitism. At least this is how the incident has since been reported. There are also claims that the hasty discontinuation of the production after only six performances was due to the efforts of the German embassy. However, today there are no documents or other factual grounds to support that assumption. The German cultural attaché at the time denied such claims in interviews as late as 1988.[277] *Die Walküre* was discontinued on February 27, 1941 after three months on the stage. Perhaps the reason is simply that the Bolshoi Theater closed for reconstruction in March and was opened only shortly before the German invasion on June 22. By that point Eisenstein's *Die Walküre* had done its duty and *Alexander Nevsky* had returned to the theaters.

STATE ASSIGNMENT
1940-1946

In 1939 Soviet cinema was ordered to orient itself towards historical personages: movies were supposed to tell history in images, like picture books, and to educate Soviet citizens in patriotism. Cinema's rendition of historical facts pragmatically followed the politics of the day. Before the war, when Stalin's military doctrine envisioned the war arena on enemy territory, the studios made Soviet science-fiction movies that depicted a future clash with Germany on German soil. The 18th-century military leader Alexander Suvorov, who had been victorious on the European battlefield, was chosen as the hero of a lavish historical film: Stalin himself edited the screenplay, which was staged by Pudovkin. During the war, which took a different territorial course, General Mikhail Kutuzov, who had abandoned Moscow to Napoleon, became history's main hero. He was joined by the defender of Sevastopol, Admiral Pavel Nakhimov, who had been forced to sink the Russian fleet so it would not fall into the hands of the British. The same actor, Alexei Diky, who at this time also impersonated Stalin, played both heroes. In 1939—after Poland's final partitioning—Pudovkin filmed *Minin and Pozharsky* and the Ukrainian director Igor Savchenko made *Bogdan Khmelnitsky*. Both films depicted the Poles as aggressive conquerors, sadists, and tricky schemers against Russia, and thus supported Stalin's new politics. In this context, a special assignment was waiting for Eisenstein.

In January 1941 Andrei Zhdanov suggested in a private conversation that Eisenstein make a film about Ivan the Terrible. He made it clear that the assignment came directly from Stalin. Eisenstein understood very well what this was all about. The glorification of Ivan—in contrast to usual Russian interpretations of the tsar—was already in full swing in many different areas (history, theater, literature). Hardly a single historian, philosopher or poet, from Lomonosov to Dostoevsky, had been able to pass up the chance to write about Ivan the Terrible, that strange, unhappy, sadistic, perverse, perhaps insane, homosexual monarch who had been married seven times. Ilya Repin had painted the tsar's murder of his son. In 1923 Conrad Veidt portrayed Ivan as a manic executioner in Paul Leni's Expressionist film *Das Wachsfigurenkabinett* ('Wax Works'). Three years later Leonid Leonidov played the tsar as a homosexual, power-obsessed sadist in a Russian film *The Wings of a Serf*, based on a script by Viktor Shklovsky.

Eisenstein recalled that as early as 1928 Stefan Zweig had given him the idea to make a film about Ivan in their conversations about father-tyrants. In

Voices of October, Eisenstein called Ivan a figure from a story by Edgar Allen Poe that could hardly interest a Soviet worker. Ivan's story could never be depicted realistically, but only as a fantasy about a devilish, bestial tsar.[278]

Now 'the times' dictated a different interpretation of this monarch. The historian Robert Vipper, whose 1922 book was reprinted more than once in a short period of time, saw Ivan as a positive figure whose great historical role had been to establish Russia's absolute monarchy and to unite the country in a centralized state. The tsar's cruelty needed to be understood as an expression of his historic refusal to compromise. This interpretation seemed tailored to Stalin's Great Terror. The writer Valentin Kostylyov was working on a new novel, and Alexei Tolstoy on a new play about Ivan IV—both depicted the ruler in this new, positive light.

Zhdanov offered Eisenstein all imaginable help and assistance. All writers would be at his disposal—Alexei Tolstoy, Leonid Leonov, Pyotr Pavlenko. He should examine the character according to the ideas of his client. Stalin wanted a mirror to justify his own terror in the name of a great idea of state. For Eisenstein personally, this met legitimizing the persecution and death of many close friends—Babel, Meyerhold, Tretyakov.

Eisenstein was given access to all historical materials, archives, the rooms of the Kremlin and the Kremlin cathedrals, but he had no freedom of interpretation. Nonetheless, Eisenstein wrote on January 21, 1941 that during the ceremony commemorating Lenin's death in the Bolshoi Theater he could not get the Ivan idea out of his mind. The topic had grabbed him. By January and February, he had already started planning the new project and had written drafts of the screenplay. However, the first scene that came to his mind was Ivan's confession and repentance after a mass execution.

As he designed the screenplay, Eisenstein jumped from drawings to scraps of dialogue. He spent a long time debating who should write the dialogue. Alexei Tolstoy, whose unbridled cynicism was too much even for Eisenstein, was not even considered. He thought of Shklovsky and conferred with him several times. On February 5, 1941 he wrote in his diary, 'Shklovsky thinks I should write the screenplay myself'.[279] He made the literary scholar Lev Indenbom his assistant. Indenbom took notes on various historical works, Ivan's tracts, Ivan's correspondence with the deserter Prince Andrei Kurbsky, and the biographies of Ivan's hangmen and lovers, Fyodor Basmanov and Malyuta Skuratov. The film was conceived as a trilogy. The first part was to deal with Ivan's youth, his ascent to the throne and his first colonial war: the conquest of Kazan. The second part focused on the formation of Ivan's personal army (the *oprichnina*), and the conspiracies of the Boyars, who poison Ivan's wife and plan to murder Ivan himself in order to put the weak-minded

Vladimir Staritsky on the throne. The third part was to show the bloody conquest of Novgorod, the execution of the inner circle, and the war against Livonia.

Eisenstein found autobiographical traits in this figure as well. The sadist Ivan grew up without his mother and without love. Eisenstein, another lonely child, was aware of his own interest in physical pain: Ivan actually tortured people, Eisenstein lived out his fascination in his art. In Eisenstein's films and drawings people often die violent deaths. Skulls are shattered; bodies are pierced by arrows; bulls bleed to death; a shot horse hangs from a raised bridge. Eisenstein even declared that Ivan was his favorite character. Since he sensed Stalin's desire to be reflected in the figure of Ivan, he himself was tempted to identify with the new father figure, the Father State. He looked into the same mirror and tried to find traits in common with the man who had taken over the role of his father figure in 1926. Since then Stalin had proposed film topics, shaped Eisenstein's movies by demanding cuts, forced Eisenstein to return home, and now expressed his most intimate trust in Eisenstein. Stalin was the type of tyrant that had attracted and repulsed Eisenstein since childhood—in this sense he was much like Eisenstein's real father or his spiritual father Meyerhold. His relationships with them had ended in classic oedipal revolt. But now he was faced not with a man, but with the state. Was he flattered by this dangerous intimacy? In retrospect he considered his work on the script to be a deciphering of the hidden pathology of self.[280]

Eisenstein wrote the script in verse that stylized Old Church Slavonic. His outline was ahistorical from the very beginning. He turned the free, democratic cities of Novgorod and Pskov into seats of reactionary Boyars and let the war over the Baltic Sea end on a victorious note, as if Ivan had actually won. Shklovsky listed all of Eisenstein's errors and made fun of the patterns Eisenstein had cribbed from *Rigoletto* and Dumas' musketeer novels: Malyuta dies in the same way as Portos, Vladimir Staritsky (like Rigoletto's daughter) dies in royal garb, stabbed by a killer hired by his own mother. Paul Leni had already made the most of that motif. It was also hard to miss the formulas borrowed from propaganda films that had been used in the fight against the opposition. However, Eisenstein idealized the hangman Malyuta Skuratov, whose brutality filled even Ivan himself with horror, as the protector of the tsar's son. Shklovsky thought that showing the baby boy in Malyuta's arms was too crass a break with historical tradition, but Eisenstein responded angrily that, 'people always know history according to films. At some point there will be a house for 'Mother and Malyuta'. Eisenstein, playing on the close proximity of *Malyuta* and *malyutka* [infant], was parodying the expression 'House of Mother and Child'. 'Incidentally,' Shklovsky writes, 'our conversation took place on the Moscow River, outside the building of a former orphanage.'[281]

Eisenstein told Shklovsky that Ivan would not execute a single person him-self: Malyuta would do all that with his hands.

On February 1 there was a special showing of *The Battleship Potemkin* to cel-ebrate the film's fifteenth anniversary. One month later, on March 15, 1941, Eisenstein received the new Stalin Prize First Class for *Alexander Nevsky*, the film that had been taken out of theaters. The prize included a sum equivalent to the money earned by an average worker over ten years.

Eisenstein spent the whole winter in Kratovo writing the screenplay for *Ivan*. On April 8, 1941 he finished the first draft. He prepared to start filming and published several statements about the forthcoming film,[282] in which he promised to depict Ivan as a thoroughly positive figure and to conduct a polemic with the portrayals of the tsar by Repin, Viktor Vasnetsov, and the sculptor Mark Antokolsky. Eisenstein laughed about the tsar's 'terrible' reputation and about the legends concerning the tsar's wives; he sought Ivan's image in folklore. Engrossed in his work, the beginning of the war on June 22 took him by surprise.

Two days after the German invasion *Alexander Nevsky* was back in movie theaters. The new film poster showed Nevsky stabbing a Teutonic Knight; the shadow of a Red Army soldier killing a Fascist loomed behind the prince.

Soon the first bombs were dropped on Moscow. During these days Eisenstein contemplated historical brutality—not only Ivan's, but the Medicis' terror on St. Bartholomew's Eve. He observed the destruction of Moscow— the Empire House built by the architect Osip Bove on the Novinsky Boulevard had burned, the Vakhtangov Theater was damaged. One bomb fell on to the stage of the Art Theater, another hit the building where the writers Pasternak, Olesha and Paustovsky lived. Eisenstein too could perish any day now: 'War entered life unexpectedly. It wasn't there yesterday. Today it's here. I was writing. Yesterday it rained. Today it's sunny. Yesterday there was no war. Now there is. It's that simple... The same holds true for the bombs. They weren't here. Now they are... If I survive, I've got to live differently.'[283] He was sur-prised that he could sleep so calmly: 'War opens your eyes. And what if I'm bombed to pieces today? How will I appear before God, if he exists? The au-tumn leaves of *Peer Gynt*—thoughts that haven't been thought through, deeds that haven't been done. That's my baggage.'[284]

In this mood Eisenstein reconsidered his screenplay, but had trouble find-ing time to work, since different—political—actions were being demanded of him. As the studio's artistic director, he had to develop a new kind of war movie: operative war almanacs that could be shown on the front, films that would mobilize the population, a 'school of hate'. In a speech to studio em-ployees, Eisenstein called upon them to make films in the style of short stories by Robert Louis Stevenson and Ambrose Bierce. The war almanacs consisted of short feature films; number six included a fragment from *Alexander Nevsky*.

In August 1941 Eisenstein joined the newly founded Anti-Fascist Jewish Committee. On August 24 Eisenstein spoke on a radio broadcast to America: 'To Brother Jews of All the World'. This radio broadcast was filmed and included in the 1942 English film *To the Jews of the World*. He also wrote several articles for the papers *Krasny voin*, *Pravda*, and *Krasny flot* about the Fascist brutality which he had seen depicted in weekly newsreels of several countries.

At this time Eisenstein was reading an English translation of Buddhist texts, *The Importance of Living* by Lin Yutang. Foreign diplomats were leaving Moscow and deposited their libraries in Moscow's second-hand bookshops on the way out. Eisenstein bought a lot of books at his usual store on Kuznetsky Most.

That same August Zinaida Raikh's daughter Tatyana Esenina asked Eisenstein to hide Meyerhold's archive, which she had managed to save from the NKVD. She had been keeping the documents at her summerhouse, but the area—next to a large factory—was bombed so often that she feared they would be destroyed. Eisenstein agreed without a moment's hesitation. The suitcases full of papers were stashed on the floor of his Kratovo dacha.[285]

He collaborated with the American war correspondent Quentin Reynolds on the film *Moscow Fights Back*. The film remained unfinished, since Reynolds was evacuated and a bomb struck the studio's film depot. Most of the material in the depot was destroyed—the negative to *Bezhin Meadow* was probably among the wreckage. On October 6 Eisenstein was finally relieved of his post as studio director so he would have time to finish the script to *Ivan the Terrible*. The real reason behind his dismissal was probably Bolshakov's bad mood: Eisenstein had used the script to *Ivan* as an excuse for missing a meeting.

On October 14 at 6 a.m., Eisenstein was evacuated from the city to Alma-Ata. He took five books along, all of them mystery novels—or so he claimed in his memoirs. In reality, the studio had allotted him a whole train car for the evacuation of his library. In such times that was an extraordinarily generous gesture.

Alma-Ata, Kazakhstan's capital at the foot of the Tienshan mountains, was known for its apple orchards. Both Mosfilm and the Leningrad studio Lenfilm were evacuated to Alma-Ata. They formed the joint studio TsOKS since film production had to continue.

Eisenstein lived in a room in the two-story building of film workers. The building was filled with artists who had been awarded the Stalin Prize. He immediately ordered bookshelves and a drop ceiling built for his books. His domestic servant Aunt Pasha lived in the entryway. He had taken his Mexican carpet, several masks and Japanese graphic art with him; he also managed to pack the photos of Chaplin and Robeson. His mother stayed in Kratovo; Elizaveta Telesheva followed the Art Theater to Kuibyshev on the Volga, where the government had also taken temporary shelter.

Eisenstein was supposed to be working on *Ivan the Terrible*—that was an order. However, he spent time thinking about his Pushkin sketches and wrote Yury Tynyanov that he would like to discuss his psychoanalysis of Pushkin. The letter was never mailed since Eisenstein did not know to which city Tynyanov had been evacuated. When he finally found out it was too late. Tynyanov died in a Moscow hospital in 1943.

In February 1942, in the midst of the battle of Stalingrad, Eisenstein polished the dialogue to *Ivan*. On February 11 he posted two letters, one to Zhdanov and one to Bolshakov. He described the changes in the script: he had given the *oprichnina* a more positive role and made Germany a more dangerous enemy.[286] He wrote Zhdanov: 'Dear Andrei Alexandrovich! Finally the work on your assignment is finished. The screenplay about Ivan the Terrible is complete. If it weren't for the war, the script would have been done months ago. I must thank you once again for the topic—the work has been captivating. I now need to know your response to the work I have already done, especially on one point: should I leave the line of Ivan's connections to England or should I alter them? I wait for your assessment of my work and for all further necessary suggestions. With friendly greetings, most sincerely yours, S. Eisenstein.'[287]

At this time Zhdanov was active in the besieged city of Leningrad and had no time to answer. By 1944 one million people died from cold and starvation in the city that was under his control. Eisenstein waited. He could not begin filming until the script had been read and affirmed by the highest powers in the state, but the situation on the front did not leave either Stalin or Zhdanov time to read the screenplay. Instead Eisenstein studied the iconography of the era—he had a huge collection of reproductions, photographs of weapons, dishes, needlework, and writings.

The role of the tsar had been given to Cherkasov. Viewers had just come to know him as the Sun Prince Alexander Nevsky, who had been sanctified by the Church, and as the repulsive, degenerate son of Peter I, who had been sentenced to death by his father for treason. Eisenstein wanted to play with merging these two roles into a third. He assigned a comic, Mikhail Zharov, to play Malyuta, since he was charming in a very negative way. The delicate prettyboy Mikhail Kuznetsov was chosen to play Fyodor Basmanov.

In the third part of Eisenstein's script, Ivan kills—in contrast to the stereotype immortalized by Repin—not his son, but his adopted son Basmanov. The latter kills his biological father on Ivan's orders when he chooses the state—Ivan—as his father. The killing of the son is transformed into an encrypted suicide of power.

Later Eisenstein wrote about his film in the paper *Literatura i iskusstvo*: 'But

I do not intend to wipe one drop of blood from the life of Ivan the Terrible. Not to whitewash, but to explain.'[288] He also spoke of the war against Hitler—a people's war against bloody, gruesome obscurantism in defense of free, democratic elections. At the same time he wrote the preface to the English edition of his writings, which Jay Leyda was preparing in New York.[289] He again called for victory over Fascism—a victory of light over darkness—a Pushkinian image usually reserved to describe the battle against state despotism.

The winter of 1942 was very harsh. The outcome of the war was being decided in Stalingrad, but remained unclear until February 1943. Vasily Grossman, who was reporting from the front, thought that he had witnessed the liberation of the enslaved spirit of the people. He experienced this as a spontaneous de-Stalinization, without which a Russian victory would have been impossible.

In Alma-Ata Eisenstein was far removed from the front. He was spared the worst of everyday hardships. He read about the man who had defeated Napoleon, the Duke of Wellington, and quoted that book in his diary in 1942: 'Those who imagine that they can govern men with pompous formulas and the promulgation of abstract principles know neither the human heart, nor the source of power.'[290]

In June 1942 Prokofiev came to Alma-Ata to work with Eisenstein on the music for *Ivan the Terrible*. Prokofiev stayed in the hotel of the House of Soviets. Eisenstein thought the building looked like a giant beehive that had been filled with dust instead of honey. The people in the rooms were like letters in a post office that nobody came to pick up—on hold, in alphabetical order.[291]

Prokofiev was composing the opera *War and Peace* and wanted Eisenstein to direct the premiere at the Bolshoi Theater. Eisenstein listened to the composer's own performance of the opera at the piano, drew thirteen pages of sketches, and started making his first director's notes. His interest in the subject was unexpectedly reinforced a year later. On June 5, 1943 the English producer Alexander Korda made Eisenstein and Pudovkin a joint offer to film Tolstoy's novel.

In July 1942 Eisenstein traveled to Moscow to give a talk on American and British film at a conference organized by VOKS. Film workers were called upon to participate on the second front. In August Leyda's volume of Eisenstein's essays *The Film Sense* came out in New York. Eisenstein only received the book by mail six months later, but it reached him exactly on his birthday: 'In memory of the saddest day of my life, my birthday, the book *Film Sense* finally arrived. I think it's the first time in my life that I am completely content with the way a book of mine has been published. They could not have done a better job. The cover is even just the way I wanted it: boulevard yellow and black, like a detective story. Against that background, my face with an absolutely indecent look in my eyes and a Mona Lisa smile.'[292] Eisenstein was also pleased that he could use his royalties—7.5% of the profit—to buy more books, which Leyda ordered at Brentano's. Leyda's translation fee, one dollar per page, was also paid out of Eisenstein's cut.

Eisenstein had plenty of free time and rewrote the manuscript to *Grundproblem*. The original manuscript had stayed in Moscow after the move, and he did not know if he would ever find it again. The second version of the book was a reconstruction completely by memory of the first book. He called the new manuscript, which was several thousand pages long, *Method*. In September 1942 he took up teaching again in Alma-Ata at the evacuated film school VGIK.

He was lost in his own book and in other, older books. He even joked about it: 'A young man from *Komsomolskaya Pravda* was sent to Eisenstein to find out what he was doing on the first day of the war year 1943. He found me reading *Quellen Shakespeares in Novellen, Märchen und Sagen* ['Shakespeare's Sources in Novellas, Fairy Tales, and Legends'], Berlin 1836.'[293] In 1943 the publishing house Goskinoizdat suggested that Eisenstein write a book about art in general and cinema in particular. During the war, such an offer was very flattering.

He read a lot of Dostoevsky and noted on January 3, 1943 that he would like to film *The Brothers Karamazov*. He was enchanted by a young woman who later married the director Alexander Zarkhi; this was the platonic infatuation of an old man, which he called 'a romance at the head of the bed'.[294] He made fun of the *Marseillaise* of 1942, Konstantin Simonov's poem 'Wait for Me!' and immediately wrote an obscene parody.

In April 1943, after the opportunity to film the winter scenes had been lost for the year, Bolshakov ordered that filming be begun immediately.

Work on the set started slowly, since Stalin had not yet read the screenplay. The script had been ready since May 14, 1942 and Bolshakov had approved of its conception as 'fundamentally correct'. However, Eisenstein and Bolshakov were both still waiting for Stalin's answer. Eisenstein continued making preparations for the film. He made drawings of the entire film—every picture, every shot, every sequence. The visual solution towards which he strove would be a complete rupture with his previous experience. He had a mental image of El Greco with the lighting effects of German Expressionis. In the twenties, films by Fritz Lang, Paul Leni, and F. W. Murnau had both attracted and repulsed him. At that time he understood his own style as an effective counterpoint to theirs. Now he relented and directed the 'Expressionist' film he had thus far avoided.

He also switched cameramen. In April 1943, after the first days of shooting, he told Tisse that he was dissatisfied with his indoor footage. In June he decided to work with Andrei Moskvin, who had complete mastery over Expressionist lighting and work with shadows. Moskvin had previously collaborated with the former FEKS members Kozintsev and Trauberg on *The Overcoat* and *New Babylon*. All of Tisse's interior shots were redone. In Eisenstein's notes to the film the visual played the larger part; sound was only secondary.

The visual direction of the film was daring. Since Soviet film tended towards sunlight and brightness, such dark images were a challenge. The complex buildings of the Kremlin halls and cathedrals created a strange environment that seemed to engulf people. This was not all caused by the darkness. The space itself dominated the people; there were no views out, no exits, just low doors, secret passageways, and tunnels. All the heroes were isolated and lonely, their glances never met. The Cubist breakdown of space was reminiscent of *The Strike*, but now had a different effect—instead of becoming dynamic and more open, the space became metaphysical and claustrophobic.

Eisenstein searched for a mask for Ivan. Sixteen masks were designed for his face, and 156 test shots made. Cherkasov was 39 years old and would have to cover the tsar from age 17 to 54. Eisenstein used Meyerhold's face as one of the prototypes. Eisenstein wrote a character sketch for each part, but he had difficulty grasping Ivan until May 1942, when he decided at which exact moment Ivan's face would have to undergo a terrible change. The transformation would occur after Ivan's return from Alexandrovskaya Sloboda, when he decides to take bloody revenge on everybody. The Sun Prince, the handsome youth, would turn into an ugly, repulsive old man with a stooped back who would rival the worst Expressionist film villain, the vampire *Nosferatu*. Ivan's transformation and his shadow kingdom, populated by black, demonic *oprichniki* wearing hooded robes reminiscent of the Ku-Klux-Klan, pointed towards an unmistakable conclusion.

A serious argument erupted over the casting of Ivan's antagonist Serafima Staritskaya. The main administration favored the beautiful actress Olga Zhizneva. Eisenstein insisted on the eccentric, ugly, smart actress Faina Ranevskaya and made forty-four screen tests of her in different masks. Bolshakov became irate and wrote Eisenstein, 'I consider your request to give the part to Ranevskaya an expression of your lack of discipline, even of your intolerable weakness of character. I suggest you follow my order immediately. I expect a telegram report of its execution.'[295] In an effort to compromise, Eisenstein chose Serafima Birman, which elicited even more amazement: how could a Jew play a Russian Boyarina? This casting decision finally sealed the strange homoerotic physiognomy of the film's ensemble. The men around Ivan appeared delicate, pretty, and feminine; the women had masculine, hard, even ugly faces. There was only one exception: the poisoned Tsarina Anastasia, a silent Madonna. At first Eisenstein wanted Galina Ulanova, the prima ballerina of the Bolshoi Theater, who had a finely chiseled face, to play the part of the tsarina. But Ulanova and the Bolshoi Theater had to return to Moscow in 1943, and she was not allowed to stay in Alma-Ata for the filming. Lyudmila

Tselikovskaya, whose name had been brought up by her husband Mikhail Zharov, took the part instead. Eisenstein was able to stylize even this happy blonde musical comedy star into an icon.

In September 1943, VGIK returned to Moscow. Eisenstein stayed behind in Alma-Ata to shoot the film, even though he had still not received official permission. Several scenes were already finished when Stalin's announcement arrived, dated September 13, 1943: 'Eisenstein has mastered his assignment. He has successfully depicted Ivan the Terrible as the progressive power of his time and the *oprichnina* as his purposeful instrument.' No critical comments, merely, 'this screenplay should be put into production at once.'[296] For Stalin, the film represented the artistic justification of all the victims and sacrifices; he had been given historical justification by the great victories in Moscow and Stalingrad. For Eisenstein this evaluation clearly indicated that he had failed to find a way out of the land of necessity into the land of (interpretative) freedom. From this point on, his work was given absolute preferential treatment. In spite of the war he got everything he wanted—people for the mass scenes, brocade for the costumes, wood for the sets. The outside shots were filmed during the day; they spent the nights shooting in the studio. The film stock was of poor quality, light was provided for only five hours, and the footage often had to be thrown out for technical reasons or they would have to re-shoot the scene. Eisenstein had trouble coping with the stress and fell ill.

In 1946 Eisenstein wrote in his memoirs that he often thought about suicide during this period: 'I decided to do it not by hanging, or smoking a stick of dynamite, or eating what my diet forbid, or with a pistol, or by poison. I decided to work myself to death.'[297] Might these words suggest that Eisenstein consciously planned to subvert the doctrine demanded of him by Stalin? This is unlikely. Eisenstein had never understood his mission in a political sense. He succumbed to the images of his future film as an artist and visionary. He wanted to find a very specific, visual, color and sound solution. From this point on he felt bound only to his artistic vision. This vision came through in the final product, more than in the screenplay that was tested and finally accepted. The (still invisible) image carried away a victory over the word.

Mikhail Nazvanov, who played Kurbsky, wrote to his wife in Moscow: 'This person is completing his life's work. This is an artistic-historical dissertation in the form of a film. He is in no hurry, since this film is clearly his final and greatest effort. He tests, experiments, films, does retakes, and clearly mocks all of us, because he enjoys the slowness and measured pace of his work. From his point of view, he is absolutely in the right. Works such as *Ivan the Terrible*, especially if you consider that he is also the scriptwriter and the set designer, are the greatest trial for any mature director. He knows that the second part

will be more polemical politically, but also stronger artistically. For that reason, he is doing everything so that the gap between the two films will be as
small as possible. As a result he has already filmed fifty percent of the second
part and keeps on working on it. The first part will have to wait, along with
us, the actors. Ever since his rough cut was enthusiastically received in Moscow, Eisenstein has become a complete boor. He yells at everybody. In the
studio he is so inaccessible and prickly that it has become unpleasant to talk
to him. But that doesn't stop him from fawning over young men.'[298]

Ivan Bolshakov arrived from Moscow to speed work on the set. All three parts
were filmed simultaneously. By late 1943 the first part was finished. In the meantime Elizaveta Telesheva had returned to Moscow. She had cancer and had to
undergo a mastectomy. Her health rapidly declined after radiation therapy. She
frequently wrote Eisenstein and sought emotional support. But he did not even
answer her short letters and telegrams. Her death was reported all over the world.
The *New York Times* published the obituary of 'Eisenstein's wife' on July 12, 1943.
However, Eisenstein did not make it to her funeral—he wrote his mother from
Alma-Ata that his heart ailments had prevented him from coming.

After Telesheva had announced the termination of their relationship in
1939, Pera reappeared and again took over the role of household manager. During the war she stayed in Moscow and took care of Eisenstein's apartment.
Since relations with the United States, the Soviet Union's main ally, were im-
proving, Atasheva compiled two volumes about Chaplin and D. W. Griffith.
She asked Eisenstein to write two of the essays.

On December 26, 1943 the footage was sent to Moscow and accepted by
the main film administration. Eisenstein kept on filming, since he did not consider his work to be complete. His intention of stretching work on the film
over the coming year met with resistance, so he wrote a letter directly to Stalin
on January 20, 1944. 'Dear Iosif Vissarionovich! Only absolute necessity al-
lows me to write to you in these tense times, which all of us—but you more
than anyone else—have to endure.' He described in great detail the production difficulties, his bad health, and that Bolshakov was driving him to work
at a pace he could no long handle. Eisenstein asked Stalin to be his advocate
and to ask Bolshakov to be more flexible in terms of deadlines. He promised
Stalin to have the film finished by the middle of the year.[299] Stalin, more generous than Upton Sinclair, gave in to all of Eisenstein's requests. Eisenstein was
allowed to finish the film according to his own vision, and was able to work
on *Ivan the Terrible* until July 1944.

The screenplay, meanwhile, was being prepared for publication. The poet
Vladimir Lugovskoi, who had already written the texts for the chorus in *Alexander
Nevsky*, helped Eisenstein with the literary adaptation. Before the screenplay came

out in book form, it was to be published in the journals *Znamya* and in *Novyi mir*.

On July 26 Eisenstein returned to Moscow and began to work on the editing and sound of part one. The work conditions were very complicated. The
army provided vehicles to transport the actors to the sound recording studio.
The rough cut was finished by August 15; they started recording the music on
September 3. Eisenstein had to remove Ivan's childhood and several other episodes from the first part, because the sets hadn't been ready in time. On October
20 he finished the first part, which was shown to the main film administration on
December 7, 1944. The film officially passed the censor on December 21, 1944.

The studio discussion of the film was typical. Most viewers expressed their
confusion and surprise. The popular actor Boris Chirkov, Molotov's nephew,
said, 'I am scared to talk about this film. I was raised on another kind of art,
and that art moves me more. I do little, insignificant things, perhaps depict
insignificant events, but out of these events I create a person. This film does
not show little things, deeds, feelings, events. Everything shown here is very
important and touches some larger question. But I have to say that the film
did not move me, but surprised me—with its ideas, its scope, its taste. This
movie has nothing to do with me.'[300] Alexei Diky harshly criticized the actors.
Konstantin Simonov said the film reminded him of a game of chess, but that
the people were missing. Alexandrov defended the movie as a textbook example of high tragedy. Bolshakov was dissatisfied with the critical response
and disagreed with everybody. He abruptly announced that the film should
be released and accepted, since it should have been in the theaters in April
1944. Presumably Bolshakov was the only person present who knew that Stalin
had already seen and blessed the film. The acceptance report signed by the
studio director Pyrev and the film minister Bolshakov stated that the first part
of *Ivan the Terrible* was a significant work of art because it interpreted the complex historical role of Ivan IV in a new way. Therein lay the film's educational
value.[301] This evaluation was already based on Stalin's opinion.

Eisenstein read the transcript of the studio discussion and underlined several passages, including the actor Diky's comment: 'Russia looks foreign here,
like Pompei.' In his diary Eisenstein took note of his phone conversation with
Bolshakov, in which the minister had given him a detailed description of the
discussion. On January 11 *Ivan the Terrible* was screened in the House of Film;
the costumes were on exhibit in the foyer. The premiere took place five days
later in the Udarnik movie theater, located across from the Kremlin, next to
the house of government.

The press started publishing euphoric reviews as early as January 8.
Vishnevsky wrote on the film's political significance in *Pravda*. Yutkevich approached the movie from an art historian's perspective in *Sovetskoe iskusstvo*

and wrote on its 'baroque drama'. Vishnevsky honored Ivan the Terrible as a warrior who had fought against the Germans for control of the Baltic Sea. The genius Ivan had guessed the enemy's plans and had been able to cut off the Germans just before they formed a coalition. In fact Vishnevsky was just describing Stalin's tactics in the last months of the war. A negative review, written by Pyotr Pavlenko, was rejected by the paper's editors.

In the meantime Eisenstein sat at his dacha writing the book *Nonindifferent Nature*, which he planned as a sequel to his study of universal correspondences.

On May 8 he learned that the war had ended.

In early June he sketched a new film project, *The World Upside Down*, in three drawings. The first sketch was titled 'Le monde à l'envers' ('The world upside down') and 'Don't ask me why'. A city has lost its normal orientation. The sky hangs at the bottom of the picture; the rain falls upwards; towers resist the laws of gravity; apples are blown horizontally by the wind; figures floating around in the middle take on various shapes without letting on which way is up and which down—each figure has its own center of gravity. This world is not only 'upside down', but lacks any center at all. The second drawing, 'City', also shows houses growing towards the bottom; a parachutist falls upwards out of a plane. The third sketch, 'La Révolte des anges' ('Revolt of the Angels') plays with the same motifs (mixing up and down) and adds two more: the buildings are transparent—there are elevators inside that travel downward in order to reach heaven; angels floating around the page add another element of insecurity. The bottom of the page reads: 'In the moment of materialization body and soul become one; the soul becomes invisible, *much trouble in transportation of souls.*' In these sketches Eisenstein returned to his old fascination with transparency, not just of one building, but even of a large city, and played with this sense of insecurity. What happens when borders are abolished between inside and outside, up and down, near and far, between material and immaterial substance, between body and soul, visible and invisible?

These enigmatic drawings betray Eisenstein's dream of cinema as a medium that is subject to none of the limitations of past art forms. Sculpture was too static and focused on the body; painting could include more surroundings, but would always remain static; literature could penetrate into inner worlds, but only offered mental images; music was dynamic, but destined to remain vague; theater could not free itself from human behavior, its material basis. Every attempt to overcome these limitations ended with the destruction of the medium itself. The only medium that did not know such boundaries was film. Its only limitation lay in people's false understanding of what film really is (namely equating it to drama, theater, or painting). In actuality film could give the inner processes of human thought and feeling a material form.

Eisenstein's film sketch *The World Upside Down* was his most radical challenge to the theory and the possibilities of the medium. But that was not why he was appointed a member of the editorial board of the film journal *Iskusstvo kino*.

Ivan the Terrible started its run abroad. The film was first screened in Sweden in April 1945, then moved to Prague and several French cities. The reaction to *Ivan's* barbaric violence, its perfect artistic conception and rich images was euphoric. After the Berlin premiere on August 8, 1945 a critic for *Neue Zeit* suggested calling the film 'Ivan, a Friend of the People'—the statement was ironic.[302] Wolfgang Staudte was assigned to make a German version, which was finished in April 1946. Chaplin sent Eisenstein an excited telegram on January 4, 1946. Orson Welles also wrote about the movie, but remained more reserved. The numerous film effects bothered him. He called them sterile exercises, interesting only to the director.[303] Mikhail Chekhov, Eisenstein's old Masonic brother, wrote a long letter from Hollywood on May 31, 1945 that included an extensive analysis of the film and was even printed in the VOKS film section bulletin! Immediately after the war, talk arose about a possible Soviet-American co-production. The idea that Eisenstein should film *War and Peace* in the USA came up again.

However, the London magazine *Today's Cinema* reported on August 21, 1945 that Eisenstein planned to film the life of Stalin as a trilogy—*Caucasus, Moscow*, and *Victory*. This report may even have been true. Eisenstein returned to his old project *Moscow* and started working out its color scheme.

The pressure on Eisenstein kept on growing. At night he would cut the second part of *Ivan*; during the day he taught at VGIK and worked on the book *Nonindifferent Nature*. He attended meetings almost daily. His income was high, five thousand rubles a month, but his health was poor.

He was forced to take a break from the work on the film. He was waiting for Prokofiev to finish the music he needed to shoot the dance scene, and for Moskvin. Prokofiev was completing the ballet *Cinderella* and did not have any free time. Moskvin had to finish a film in Central Asia with Kozintsev. During this time Eisenstein watched the German color movies that had been brought to Moscow from the Reich Film Archive as war booty, such as *Die Frau meiner Träume* ('The Woman of my Dreams'). He hated them all. He accidentally came upon a Soviet documentary on the Potsdam conference that included several color episodes filmed on Agfa.

At that point, Eisenstein decided to shoot one episode of the film in color. Color material that had been confiscated from Germany was put at his disposal in December. He used it to film the drinking orgy of the *oprichniki*. Only four, maybe three, colors interested him. The gold of the dishes and the *oprichniki* shirts slowly turn to red as the murder plans develop. The faces are lit up in red and red dancers displace all the other. Then red is swallowed up by black when the executioners don black robes over their red atlas shirts. Eisenstein used the black to return to the cathedral and the darkness of black-and-white. This color dramatization intensifies the frightening orgy of the hangmen, which is followed by the death of Vladimir, a homosexual, whose mother wanted to see him at the pinnacle of power. Eisenstein had already filmed the murder in the cathedral in February and March in Alma-Ata.

In the winter of 1944 Eisenstein returned to his intense study of ecstasy. Now he understood ecstasy as the state of being absorbed in the womb and referred to it as the 'MLB-complex', based on the German word *Mutterleib* (womb). He had taken the idea from a book by Freud's student Otto Rank, *Das Trauma der Geburt* ('The Trauma of Birth', 1924). As an interpretative model, Rank's book had a much more lasting influence on Eisenstein than Willhelm Reich's energetic and physiological interpretation.

Rank offered his model as an alternative hypothesis to the Oedipus complex, and stressed the role of the embryonic experience. Birth was the first biological trauma and the origin of many neuroses; it explained why the mother's womb determined the spatial concepts of human existence: the cathedral, the house, closed dark areas. Eisenstein modified Rank's idea and unexpectedly included it in the murder scene, which he interpreted as a return to the womb. He wanted the cameraman to light the scene the way an embryo would see it from inside. The designer Shpinel was not allowed to use corners in the set construction. Everything was to remain round, and Eisenstein wanted Prokofiev to write the music in the rhythm of birthing contractions. Eisenstein conceived of Staritsky's murder as the climax of the movie. The scene imitated the iconography of the pieta and lifted the murder out of the frame of political necessity: the murder of the least important person cannot be justified by state power.

This ending tipped the entire film. The dances of the *oprichniki*, the last scene of *Ivan* that Eisenstein was able to film, emphasized this effect even more.

On January 26, 1946 Eisenstein received the Stalin Prize for the direction of part one. Around 10:30 p.m. on February 2 he finished cutting part two and attended a party that was held for the Stalin Prize recipients. He waltzed with the actress Vera Maretskaya, the wife of the former Freemason Yury Zavadsky. Suddenly he collapsed. He was rushed from the dance floor to the Kremlin hospital, where doctors diagnosed a heart attack. The attack occurred after Eisenstein finished his film. The deed was done.

'All the facts of science dictated that I should die. For some reason, I survived. I therefore consider that everything which happens from now on is a postscript to my own life . . .'[304]

POSTSCRIPT
1946-1948

On February 7, while Eisenstein was in the hospital, the Mosfilm studio's artistic council discussed the second part of *Ivan*. The tenor of the debate on the first part had been that Eisenstein's interpretation was cold and un-Russian because it did not move the soul. The discussion of the second part stressed the captivating effect of the music, which obviously moved the participants' emotions, but criticized Eisenstein's reading of the tsar as a grave ideological error. The director Sergei Gerasimov asked straight out: 'Who is this Ivan? A clinically ill person thirsting for blood? Or a statesman who wants to free Russia from the Boyar heresy?' Eisenstein had failed to depict the *oprichnina* as a progressive force. Mikhail Romm noted that the film was so dark because there was no release of positive energy; the second part needed to include some battle scenes, for example the conquest of the Baltic Sea. Nobody believed—or at least nobody suggested out loud—that Eisenstein had intended to criticize the brutality of state terror. Pyrev only commented that since Ivan and the *oprichniki* seem so foreign, the viewer felt pity for the executed *Russian* Boyars, especially Vladimir. Ivan looked like Dostoevsky's Grand Inquisitor and the *oprichniki* like 16th-century Fascists. Pyrev thus coined the formula on which everyone else agreed: the film was not Russian, and Ivan was not a Russian tsar, but a Byzantine emperor. Grigory Alexandrov reminded the participants that the same reproaches had been uttered in regard to the first film, but that it had still received the Stalin Prize.[305]

But this time Bolshakov remained grim and refused to believe in the film's success. He found the different parts of the film to be too contradictory. A committee consisting of the actor Diky, the directors Gerasimov and Alexandrov, and the composer Tikhon Khrennikov was to come up with suggestions for improvement.

That same day Bolshakov sent Eisenstein a letter to the hospital in which he described the committee's decision gently, carefully, and with tact. However, he did not mention any of the details of the discussion.

Eisenstein's heart attack had been severe, and he recovered very slowly. In a letter to his new friend, the American theater critic Brooks Atkinson, Eisenstein reported that he was being taught how to sit up. Several days later he continued the letter—he had now taken his first steps, his 'baby performances'.[306] As his physical state made Eisenstein feel as though he had regressed back to childhood, he began writing his 'souvenirs d'enfance', his childhood memories, on May 1. Prokofiev thought he had given Eisenstein the idea of

writing his memoirs, but Eisenstein had sporadically been working on autobiographical notes since 1943. Now he wrote them down one after the other.

Eisenstein counted on receiving another Stalin Prize for part two. But on
May 18, he had to conclude: 'Well. They've passed me over for the Stalin Prize
for the second part of *The Terrible*.'[307] Only now did Bolshakov describe the
details of the film's discussion over the phone. Eisenstein took notes on the
debate in his journal. He wanted to know who had said what. At the end of
May he was transferred to a sanatorium in Barvikha near Moscow. When he
was released one month later he retreated to his dacha. He wrote his memoirs,
the chapters of which were loosely connected, held together by association.
At the same time he also put together a systematic plan for a history of Soviet film,
worked on several essays about color, and drafted an outline for his *Moscow* project.

His memoirs reconstructed the story of a good boy from Riga, the son of a
high official and a rich woman who disliked his sheltered childhood. The book
was a semi-fictional novel about himself, which the author called *Yo* ('I'), in
which he lived out his blatant narcissism. 'How does one become Eisenstein?'
his students asked.

Eisenstein himself offered several explanations. Two years earlier, he had
noted: 'Every normal child does three things: he breaks things; he gets inside
dolls or watches .... and he torments animals .... I was a bad child .... But let
him grow up and he will be irresistibly drawn towards diversions of this nature .... Watches that I failed to take apart at the right time led to my passion
for rooting around in the recesses and springs of the 'creative mechanism'.
Dinner services that were not smashed when they should have been were re-
born as respect for authority and traditions. My cruelty, which did not find an
outlet with flies, dragonflies and frogs, colored my choice of theme, method
and the credo of my work as director.'[308]

Now he restructured the guiding principles of his life. First: the slogan
that philosophy, like cocaine, kills joy but releases from pain. Second: the legend of a warrior who saves all his strength for a future deed and suffers humiliation in the meantime: 'In my personal, too personal history I have had on
several occasions to stoop to these levels of self-abasement .... to no avail.'[309]
Third: George Bernard Shaw's *The Chocolate Soldier*, which cooled his youthful
bent for pathos with irony. 'And then I spent my whole life in heroic-pathetic
drudgery, with screen 'canvases' in the heroic style!'[310]

Eisenstein strolled through the past, freed from the categories of space and
time. Though he disliked Proust, his own 'souvenirs d'enfance' also consisted
of smells, silhouettes, and spots of color, memories of taste ('I later ate such a
pear with Pirandello'), sounds, bits of melodies, screams. He built his autobiography around dissonance, simple contrasts, literary images, and eccentri-

cally transposed details. He sorted momentous events for his future biographers and gave them the literary keys to his childhood and later life: Gogol,
Pushkin, Chaplin—as projections of himself or as role models. His goal was to
explain how one becomes Eisenstein. With a wink—the best means of con-
cealing something—everything would be laid bare. He filtered the life of the
director through a sieve of clichés from graphic arts, fiction, kitsch. Art (and
especially film) had taught him to see and classify impressions, now it helped
him observe and shape his own life as a work of art. He turned the real man
into a fictional character.

He intentionally sprinkled the memoirs with inaccuracies in order to stylize the perfect Eisenstein legend. His memoirs were supposed to answer 'how
one becomes Eisenstein', but in reality Eisenstein mystified and transfigured
his own biography and adapted it to the artistic canon.

He carefully avoided mentioning his crises, his attempts at psychoanalysis
with Zalkind, and hypnosis with Kannabikh. There is no hint of his 1936
thoughts of suicide—he moved them to the year 1943. Eisenstein encoded his
own story and corrected his judgments about people who had greatly impressed him in his youth. An enormous gulf lay between his diaries and memoirs, but this gap was not caused by self-censorship or fear (he paid great hom-
age to Meyerhold, who had been executed and then forgotten), but by the
distance between the young and the old Eisenstein. None of his romances with
women made their way into Yo, and Eisenstein said nothing about his relationship with Grisha. Instead he wrote (in English!) an encoded parable about
the unhappy romance of a mute architect and a 'dollar-princess', a millionaire's
daughter. The colorful, kitschy fairy tale seemed completely fantastic, rather
than the key to a secret love, a real event beyond the ocean. The princess's
encrypted name was Katerina, the name of Pushkin's secret love Karamzina.

He wrote that tale on the day his mother died. He had been living with her
in his dacha. His mother had grown weaker and weaker, had suffered two
strokes in a short period of time, and finally passed away on August 8, 1946.
One day later Eisenstein described her death as his liberation from hate towards this 'absurd woman' who had tortured him all his life. Now he could
finally find peace in his relations with her.

In August Bolshakov screened the second part of Ivan in the Kremlin. Stalin
was highly dissatisfied. One month later, on September 4, the Central Committee resolved to ban Ivan the Terrible, Part Two along with a number of other
films. This decision was part of a new campaign that had already attacked
literature and theater in August. Accusations against very different works of
art and artists were summarized under the vague heading 'bourgeois influ-
ences on Soviet culture'. 'Sergei Eisenstein,' announced the text of the pub-

lished resolution, which dealt mostly with Leonid Lukov's film *A Great Life*, 'has revealed his ignorance in his portrayal of historical facts, by representing the progressive army of Ivan the Terrible's *oprichniki* as a gang of degenerates akin to the American Ku-Klux-Klan; and Ivan the Terrible, a strong-willed man of character, as a man of weak will and character, not unlike Hamlet.'[311]

In order to discuss the resolution, the studio's artistic council met on September 12. Eisenstein, who was still ill, was not forced to attend, but he was expected to express regret about his mistakes once more, which he did: on October 20 the paper *Kultura i zhizn* published an open letter: 'We know Ivan the Terrible as a man of strong will and character. Does that mean that we have to exclude the possibility that the tsar was occasionally plagued by doubt? It would be hard to believe that this man, who achieved such new and unprecedented deeds for his time, never thought twice about the choice of his means, that he never had doubts about how he would act in one situation or another.' However, this confession was too meager. The artistic council wanted a harmonious Ivan, not a tragic tyrant. Eisenstein promised to take out Ivan's self-doubt and to end the film with his triumphant campaign in Livonia. At this point Cherkasov entered the discussion. His relations with Eisenstein had been strained for some time. Not all of the director's decisions made sense to him, and he frequently responded in an irritated manner. Work on the set had been grinding—he had to wear an uncomfortable, elaborate mask and master complicated assignments to create the physical effect Eisenstein desired. He was insulted by Eisenstein's despotism and was now troubled by the ideas behind the film. Cherkasov said that in part two Ivan's historic dimension had been lost; he now wanted to see his historic victories.[312]

In November Eisenstein and Cherkasov sent Stalin a letter asking for a personal meeting. In spite of the criticism Eisenstein received the medal 'For Exceptional Achievements in the Great Patriotic War' on November 23. He was also promised that a four-volume set of his written works would soon be published.

Three months after the letter, the night of February 25, 1947, Cherkasov and Eisenstein were suddenly summoned to the Kremlin. They were allowed to discuss the film and the proposed changes with Stalin, Molotov, and Zhdanov. They passed through the Kremlin's Spassky Gate at 10:30 p.m. After the conversation they returned to Eisenstein's apartment and compiled a protocol of the talks from memory: '*Stalin:* 'Have you studied history?' *Eisenstein:* 'More or less.' *Stalin:* 'More or less? I too have a little knowledge of history. Your portrayal of the *oprichnina* is wrong. The *oprichnina* was a royal army . . . . You make the *oprichnina* look like the Ku-Klux-Klan.' *Eisenstein:* 'They wear white headgear; ours wore black.' *Molotov:* 'That does not constitute a difference in principle.' *Stalin:* 'Your Tsar has turned out indecisive, like Hamlet. Everyone tells him what he ought to do, he does not make decisions himself. Tsar Ivan was a great and wise ruler . . . . Ivan the Terrible's wisdom lay in his national perspective and his refusal to allow foreigners into his country, thus preserving the country from the penetration of foreign influence. In showing Ivan the Terrible the way you did, aberrations and errors have crept in.' *Zhdanov:* 'Eisenstein's Ivan the Terrible comes across as a neurasthenic.' *Stalin:* 'Historical figures should be portrayed in the correct style. In Part One, for instance, it is unlikely that the Tsar would kiss his wife for so long. That was not acceptable in those days.' *Zhdanov:* 'The picture was made with a Byzantine tendency. That was also not practiced.' *Molotov:* 'Part Two is too confined to vaults and cellars . . . . You can show the conspiracies and the repressions, but not just that.' *Stalin:* 'Ivan the Terrible was very cruel. You can depict him as a cruel man, but you have to show why he *had* to be cruel. One of Ivan the Terrible's mistakes was to stop short of cutting up the five key feudal clans. Had he destroyed these five clans, there would have been no Time of Troubles. And, when Ivan the Terrible had someone executed, he would spend a long time in repentance and prayer. God was a hindrance to him in this respect. He should have been more decisive."[313]

However, Eisenstein had not only missed the mark on his hero's psychology. The Party's reproaches also concerned the film's visual effect: 'Comrade Zhdanov said that Eisenstein's fascination with shadows distracted the viewer from the action, as did his fascination with Ivan's beard.'[314] Eisenstein promised to cut the beard. He was allowed to leave the scene of Vladimir Staritsky's murder the way it was, and to keep the episode in part three when Malyuta murders the Metropolitan.

Stalin decided not to read the revised screenplay. Eisenstein should make a new film with a new ending; only then did he want to see it. He gave Eisenstein access to all means, all production capacities in order to finish his work. Stalin promised that Eisenstein would face no limitations either of time or of money.

However, Eisenstein did not make any effort. Since the last cuts on February 2, 1946 he had changed nothing of the movie. He just constantly showed it to friends and acquaintances, asked for their opinion and speculated about the 'harmful' effects of the film. He took an ironic stance, but he was deeply worried and was looking for affirmation. The screenings for friends reversed the situation. Most were impressed by the film and at the same time shocked that such things were possible. Vishnevsky, however, was totally opposed to the film. In a fifteen-page letter to Eisenstein, he managed to say only one thing: there was no way to improve the film, since it was not *Russian*. Its style and music were influenced by El Greco and Byzantium. Malyuta made the worst impression, as something 'greasy, unwashed, sweaty, stupid, predatory.'[315]

Eisenstein found himself in an odd situation. His film had been banned, but his person enjoyed highest favor, a fact he exploited. Eisenstein viewed his work, which was not intended to be at all subversive, as complete. His expectation that he would receive another Stalin Prize confirms his own belief that the film conformed to the demands of the time. However, Eisenstein had remained more faithful to his art than to his patron. He had played out his oedipal revolt against his super-father in art; this led to conflict with Stalin. Eisenstein avoided the conflict as best he could.

As superstitious as Eisenstein was, he was afraid of his own hero. Ivan the Terrible had already managed to bring about the death of two artists. Nikolai Khmelyov, who had wanted to play the part of Ivan in Eisenstein's film, had died wearing Ivan's mask during a rehearsal at the Art Theater. Alexei Tolstoy passed away several days before the premiere of his Ivan play at the Maly Theater.

To avoid thinking about the film, Eisenstein kept busy with other things. He followed Luria's suggestion and started working on the lecture cycle 'Psychology of Art', which he was to give at Moscow University's Psychological Institute. The lectures would introduce the audience to the main ideas of his book *Method*. In March Eisenstein saw *Time in the Sun* and *Thunder over Mexico*, two versions of his Mexico material, for the first time. He wrote the essay 'Stereoscopic Film' and analyzed the color scene in *Ivan* at VGIK. In April he was interviewed by American reporters in connection with the US premiere of the first part of *Ivan the Terrible*. He talked to Leyda over the phone and told him that he planned to finish the second part by October. He sketched ballet productions, *The Queen of Spades* and *Carmen*, for young dancers, and tried his skills as a choreographer. He wrote an outline for a history of cinema that began with a survey of the close-up in literature and painting. As he approached the history of film, he simultaneously attempted to work through the development of genres—tragedy, comedy, drama. These beginnings gradually grew into plans for a seven-volume opus. On the side, he started a new study, *Pushkin and Gogol*.

On June 19, 1947 Eisenstein was named Director of the new Cinema Section of the Institute for Art History at the Academy of Sciences that had been founded in 1944 by Igor Grabar—a painter, art historian, and long-time director of the Tretyakov Gallery—with two sections: plastic arts and music. The faculty already included the architects Viktor Vesnin and Alexander Shchusev, the art historian Mikhail Alpatov, and composer Boris Asafev. Eisenstein and Nikolai Lebedev had convinced Grabar that film was also a subject worthy of the institute's research program. Thus, the cinema section was opened in June.

Now Eisenstein was working on another book, *Pathos*. This was supposed to complete the study *Nonindifferent Nature*. Then he planned to rework the 548 hours of directing class—192 hours of lecture and 356 of practical work—into the book *Film Composition*. None of these projects was ever completed.

Eisenstein had returned to an older understanding of art and the artist. He had exchanged his 1920s theories on film's influence for the idea of the viewer's complete absorption, be it by the revitalization of a Dionysian commemorative act or by stereoscopic film. He now understood art, an emotional experience, as a form of interaction, a joint sacral act of the artist and the recipient, of man and the universe, of emotional and rational thought. Towards the end of his manuscript *Nonindifferent Nature* Eisenstein cites the American philosopher and psychologist William James: man strives towards harmony, though the knowledge of contradictions remains. 'I feel as if it must mean something, something like what the Hegelian philosophy means, if one could only lay hold of it more clearly...'[316] James had religious experience in mind, but Eisenstein transposed this fictional, but actually experienced sense of harmony to art— the only area of social being other than religion that made this kind of experience possible. Art allowed for opposites—God and Satan, black and white, life and death, you and I, the collisions of which made up the inner turmoil of man—to be experienced as a unified whole. Eisenstein's solution to these contradictions was more reminiscent of mythological forms of thinking than of Hegelian philosophy. He had always considered art to be close to mythological thinking—now he no longer tried to overcome myth, but to absorb it. Ritual, drugged states, sexual orgasm (a trivial solution), religious ecstasy (his past phase) and fictional union in art: all of these had the power to abolish contradictions. This way Eisenstein could elevate art as a higher form of reality, and social reality could be negated completely.

His real life in 1948 was far removed from this vision.

A new campaign started in January—this time the enemy was cosmopolitanism and foreign influence, from which (according to Stalin) Ivan the Terrible had once so wisely freed Russia. On January 16, 1948 Eisenstein read the lead article in *Pravda* and noted in his diary: 'The battle against those who bow to the West is developing with a crescendo. No mercy is shown either the living or the dead. Yesterday the *Litgazeta* destroyed Alexander Veselovsky and the posthumous notes by Sakhnovsky [the director of the Moscow Art Theater]. The editor Gorchakov got his share too, for mentioning too many foreign names. Even . . . for mentioning Piranesi. And I'm analyzing him in *Pathos*. To include foreigners in *Pathos* wouldn't be pathos, but a *faux pas*.'[317]

The 'rootless cosmopolitans' who now came under attack were all of Jewish ancestry and were most often theater and music critics. Works by writers, such as Eduard Bagritsky, Mikhail Svetlov, and Vasily Grossman were forbidden. The list of banned books included Grossman and Ehrenburg's *The Black Book* about German extermination of Jews on Soviet territory during World War II. The cultural authorities even went so far as to remove Felix Mendelssohn-Bartholdy's portrait from the wall of the Great Hall of the Conservatory. The actor and director Solomon Mikhoëls was killed in a staged car accident in Minsk. The writers Itzik Fefer and Perez Markish were executed four years later for espionage. Others were sent to Siberia or into exile. Many of the victims of this macabre anti-Semitic campaign were members of the Anti-Fascist Jewish Committee, which was now accused of connections with the American Jewish organization JOINT, allegedly a branch of the U.S. Secret Services.

Eisenstein was ordered to be part of the organizing committee for Mikhoël's funeral. As he stood by the coffin, he whispered to his neighbor that he would be the next victim of this wave of terror. But he would not live to see that day.

In early 1948 Eisenstein received permission to travel to Prague, Paris, and London. He had to postpone his trip until March for health reasons. He celebrated his fiftieth birthday on January 23.

Two weeks later Alexandrov visited him. Eisenstein promised to write the foreword to his book.[318] On February 10 he wrote a letter to Lev Kuleshov, who was preparing a new edition of *Fundamentals of Film Direction*. Eisenstein made a few comments on *Fundamentals* and extensively discussed the problems of color film. As he was writing, he suffered a second heart attack. His pencil would not obey him. Eisenstein still managed to scribble: 'At this moment I am having a heart attack. Here, the trace in my handwriting. Feb. 10, 1948.' He dragged himself to the heating pipes and banged for help—a signal on which he and his neighbors, the family of his old critic Ilya Vaisfeld, had agreed. But they did not hear him. He died towards morning on February 11. His housekeeper found him on the floor of the hallway.

The autopsy showed that Eisenstein's heart was used up like the heart of an eighty-year-old man; his brain still looked like that of a twenty-year-old. His brain was given to his friend Luria for research purposes. Eisenstein's official wife, Pera Atasheva, inherited his library, the numerous manuscripts, and his bank account with 50,000 rubles.

On Friday, February 13 Eisenstein was laid out in the House of Film until 13:00, then buried on the Novodevichy cemetery in Moscow. Eisenstein was very superstitious; the numbers fit perfectly.

EISENSTEIN: AUTO RITRATTO REALISTA, DECEMBER 1944

CHRONOLOGY

1898   Born January 23 (10 accordinhg to the old calendar) in Riga; only child of civil engineer and architect Mikhail Eisenstein and his wife Yulia, née Konetskaya.

1906   Sees his first film in Paris: *Les 400 farces du diable* by Georges Méliès.

1908   Enters municipal *Realschule*.

1909   Parents separate; E. stays with his father.

1913   *Turandot*, performed by the Nezlobin Company, awakens E.'s passion for theater and commedia dell'arte.

1915   Graduates from *Realschule*. Begins studies at the Petrograd Institute of Civil Engineering.

1917   Meyerhold's production of *Masquerade* strengthens E.'s desire to become a professional artist.

1918   Recruited into Red Army Corps of Engineers as technical expert. North-eastern Front.

1919   Works as actor and designer in army clubs in Voshega, Dvinsk, Kholm, Velikie Luki. Intense study of theater; sketches and designs sets.

1920   Polotsk, Mogilyov, Smolensk. Reassigned to the PUZAP (Political Administration of the Western Front) theater. Joins a Rosicrucian order and later, in Moscow, a Masonic lodge. September: transferred to General Staff Academy in Moscow to study Japanese. In Moscow begins work at the Proletkult theater; designs set for *The Mexican*. Expelled from General Staff Academy. In charge of set design at the Proletkult. Studies at the Proletkult workshop as of December; students include childhood friend Maxim Strauch, Grigory Alexandrov et al.

1921   Joins leadership of Proletkult theater. Premiere of *The Mexican*. Accepted to Meyerhold's Higher Workshops in Directing (GVYRM). Costume designer in Foregger's theater MASTFOR.

1922   Trip to FEKS (Factory of the Eccentric Actor) in Petrograd. Becomes director of Proletkult's traveling theater company.

1923   Premiere of *The Wise Man* with short film *Glumov's Diary*. 'Montage of Attractions' (E.'s first theoretical manifesto) published in *LEF*. Premiere of Tretyakov's *Can You Hear Me, Moscow?* under E.'s direction.

1924   *Gas Masks* premieres in a Moscow gasworks. Reedits Fritz Lang's *Dr. Mabuse the Gambler*. July-October: *The Strike* filmed; November: editing. Break with Proletkult in December. Begins writing screenplay *The Red Cavalry*, based on short stories by Babel, for the Moscow section of the studio Sevzapkino.

1925   *The Strike* premieres on April 28 in the Moscow cinema 'Coliseum'. Begins work on film *The Year 1905*. July: filming in Moscow and Leningrad; August: Odessa. Project narrowed down to *The Battleship Potemkin*. Filming in Sevastopol. November: editing in Moscow. December 21: premiere of *The Battleship Potemkin* in the Bolshoi Theater to commemorate 20th anniversary of 1905 Revolution.

1926   March: Travels to Berlin with Tisse to study new film technology. May: begins work on the screenplay for *The General Line*. July: meets Douglas Fairbanks and Mary Pickford in Moscow; they represent United Artists and invited E. to Hollywood. First takes of *The General Line* in Rostov on the Don, Baku, and the northern Caucasus. September: the state film committee Sovkino commissions film in honor of the 10th anniversary of the October Revolution. November: E. writes screenplay for *October*.

1927   Interrupts work on *The General Line*. Continues work on script for *October*. April: filming in Leningrad. September: editing in Moscow. Contemplates making film of *Capital*. November 7: first public screening of *October*. Continues work on final cut.

1928   Breaks with the LEF-group. *October* premieres March 14. Begins teaching at GTK (State Technical College for Film). Attends Kabuki guest performance in Moscow. 'Statement on Sound' (manifesto).

1929   Finishes and submits *The General Line*. Cycle of essays for a 'spherical book'. Theory of intellectual film. August: travels to Berlin with Alexandrov and Tisse. Takes part in the Congress of Independent Film-Makers in La Sarraz (Switzerland). Codirects *Women's Misery—Women's Happiness* in Zurich for Lazar Wechsler. Lectures in Berlin and Hamburg. Spends time in Belgium, England, France, Holland.

1930   Amsterdam, Berlin, Brussels, Paris. Lectures and meetings. Coedits sound for film *Romance sentimentale* (directed by Grigory Alexandrov).

Negotiates with Paramount. Invited to Hollywood. May: arrives in USA. Lectures at Columbia, Harvard, Yale, and elsewhere. Meets Chaplin, Sinclair, Dreiser, and Disney in Hollywood. Works on screenplays to *Sutter's Gold* and *An American Tragedy*. Develops the concept of inner monologue. Leaves Paramount. Begins work on film about Mexico, financed by Upton Sinclair's Mexican Picture Trust. December: begins filming in Mexico.

1931   Films all over Mexico.

1932   February: interrupts work in Mexico. Returns to Moscow via USA and Europe. Works on screenplay for eccentric comedy *MMM*. Travels to Armenia and Georgia.

1933   Works on a theoretical and practical program of film direction, on the book *Direction*, based on his lectures at GIK (State Film Institute). Works on the scenario *Moscow*. Signs directing contract with the Moscow film studio Soyuzkino.

1934   Prepares production of play *Moscow 2* by N. Zarkhi at the Theater of the Revolution. Takes part in First All-Union Congress of Writers. Spends time in Yalta and Odessa. Marries journalist Pera Atasheva.

1935   Gives speech at All-Union Creative Conference of Workers in Soviet Cinema outlining his book project *Grundproblem* ('Fundamental Problem'). Works on script for *Bezhin Meadow*. Moves into new apartment next to Mosfilm studios. Begins shooting in Moscow and Kharkov.

1936   First version of *Bezhin Meadow* banned. Works on a new script with writer Isaak Babel. Resumes shooting in Yalta and Odessa.

1937   Appointed professor at VGIK. Terminates work on *Bezhin Meadow* on order from the main film administration. Forced to leave VGIK. Works on screenplay *Rus* (later *Alexander Nevsky*) with Pyotr Pavlenko. Book manuscript *Montage*.

1938   Collects material for *Alexander Nevsky* in Novgorod. June: films at Mosfilm studios and near Pereslavl-Zalessky. Premiere of *Alexander Nevsky*.

1939   Receives Order of Lenin and honorary degree 'Doctor of Arts'. Reinstated at VGIK. Works on film project *Ferghana Canal*. Travels to Central Asia for test shooting. Interrupts filming. Writes 'On the Structure of Things'. December: works on the production of *Die Walküre* at the Bolshoi Theater in Moscow.

1940   Outlines color film about Pushkin. Begins taking notes for his autobiography. Works on 'Vertical Montage', *Grundproblem* (first draft of the book *Method*), 'Once Again on the Structure of Things'. Begins drafting screenplay for *Ivan the Terrible* on Zhdanov's order.

1941   Evacuated to Alma-Ata. Finishes script for *Ivan the Terrible*. Works on the book projects *A History of the Close-Up* and *Method*.

1942   Script for *Ivan the Terrible* approved by State Committee for Artistic Affairs. Writes preface to *The Film Sense*, an American edition of his essays.

1943   April: begins shooting *Ivan the Terrible*. Works on the book *Method*. June: returns to Moscow. Finishes and turns in the first part of *Ivan the Terrible*. Writes the essay 'Dickens, Griffith and Ourselves'.

1945   January 20: Premiere of *Ivan the Terrible, Part I* in Moscow. Begins working on second part. Writes *Nonindifferent Nature*.

1946   Stalin Prize for *Ivan the Terrible, Part I*. Central Committee of Communist Party bans Part II. E. suffers severe heart attack and spends time in the hospital. His mother dies. E. completes his autobiographical writings.

1947   Appointed director of new Cinema Section at the Institute of Art History of the Academy of Sciences. Finishes book *Pathos*, essay 'Stereoscopic Film', plans a 'History of Cinema.'

1948   Essay 'The Question of Mise-en-scène'. February 11: dies of a heart attack. February 13: buried at the Novodevichy Cemetery in Moscow.

BIBLIOGRAPHY

Aksenov, Ivan
___ 'Iunost' khudozhnika.' *Iskusstvo Kino* 1 (1968), pp. 88-114.
___ *Sergei Eizenshtein: portret khudozhnika.* Moscow: Muzei kino, 1991.

Aleksandrov, Grigorii
___ *Epokha i kino.* Moscow: Izd. polit. literatury, 1976.

Alpers, Boris
___ 'Teatr sotsial'noi maski.' In: *Teatral'nye ocherki v 2 tomakh*, 2 vols. Moscow: Iskusstvo, 1977.

Balázs, Béla
___ *Schriften zum Film.* 2 vols. Berlin/GDR: Henschel Verlag, 1984.

Barna, Yon
___ *Eisenstein.* Bloomington IN: Indiana UP, 1973.

Behlmer, Rudy
___ (ed.). *Memo from David O. Selznick.* New York: Viking Press, 1972.

Benjamin, Walter
___ 'Surrealism.' In: *Reflections: Essays, Aphorisms, Autobiographical Writings.* New York: Schocken Books, 1978, pp. 177-192.

Bordwell, David
___ *The Cinema of Eisenstein.* Cambridge MA: Harvard UP, 1993.

Bouissounouse, Janine
___ *La Nuit d'automne.* Paris: Calmann-Lévy, 1977.

Bulgakowa, Oksana
___ (ed.). *Eisenstein und Deutschland.* Berlin: Henschel, 1998.
___ (ed.). *Herausforderung Eisenstein, Arbeitsheft 41 der Akademie der Künste der DDR.* Berlin/GDR: Akademie der Künste, 1989.
___ *Sergej Eisenstein: drei Utopien. Architekturentwürfe zur Filmtheorie.* Berlin: PotemkinPress, 1996.

Cherkasov, Nikolai
___ *Zapiski sovetskogo aktera.* Moscow: Iskusstvo, 1953.

Christie, Ian and Taylor, Richard
___ (eds). *Eisenstein Rediscovered.* London: Routledge, 1993.

Christie, Ian and Elliot, David
___ (eds). Eisenstein at Ninety. Oxford: Museum of Modern Art; London: BFI, 1988.

Cocteau, Jean
___ *Opium.* Paris: Delamain & Boutelleau, 1930.

Dreiser, Theodore
___ *Dreiser Looks at Russia.* New York: Horace Liveright, 1928.

Eastman, Max
___ *Artists in Uniform: A Study of Literature and Bureaucratism.* New York: Knopf, 1934.

Eisenstein, Sergei
___ Eisenstein Archive, RGALI (Russian State Archive for Art and Literature), Moscow. The four

numbers in the endnote citations refer to the document's location. 1: Depository (*fond*); 2: Inventory (*opis*); 3: Administrative unit (*edinitsa khraneniia*); 4: page (*list*—here p.).

___ *Eisenstein 2: A Premature Celebration of Eisenstein's Centenary.* Jay Leyda, ed. Calcutta: Seagull, 1985.

___ *Eisenstein on Disney.* Jay Leyda, ed. Calcutta: Seagull, 1986.

___ *Film essays and a Lecture.* Jay Leyda, ed. London: Dennis Dobson, 1968; New York: Praeger 1970.

___ *Film Form: Essays in Film Theory.* Jay Leyda, ed. New York: Harcourt, Brace and Co., 1949.

___ *The Film Sense.* Jay Leyda, ed. New York: Harcourt, Brace & Co., 1942; London: Faber & Faber, 1943.

___ *Immortal Memoires: An Autobiography by Sergei M. Eisenstein.* Herbert Marshall, transl. Boston: Houghton Mifflin and London: Peter Owen, 1985.

___ *Notes of a Film Director.* Moscow: Foreign Languages Publishing House, 1958; New York: Dover, 1970.

___ *On the Composition of the Short Fiction Scenario.* Allan Upchurch, transl. Calcutta: Seagull, 1984.

___ *Nonindifferent Nature.* Herbert Marshall, transl. Cambridge: Cambridge UP, 1987.

___ *The Psychology of Composition.* Allan Upchurch, transl. Calcutta: Seagull, 1987.

___ *Selected Works.* Richard Taylor, ed. 4 vols. London: BFI and Bloomington IN: Indiana UP, 1988-96.

Eisenstein, Sergej (= Eisenstein, Sergei)

___ *Das dynamische Quadrat. Schriften zum Film.* Oksana Bulgakowa and Dietmar Hochmuth, eds. Leipzig: Reclam jr., 1988.

___ *Yo—Ich Selbst.* 2 vols. Naum Klejman and Walentina Korschunowa, eds. Berlin/GDR: Henschel Verlag and Vienna: Löcker Verlag, 1984.

Eizenshtein, S. M. (= Eisenstein, Sergei)

___ *Izbrannye proizvedeniia v 6 tomakh.* 6 vols. Moscow: Iskusstvo 1964-71.

___ *Memuary.* Naum Kleiman, Valentina Korshunova, eds. Moscow: Trud/Muzei kino, 1997.

Fernandez, Dominique

___ *Eisenstein: L'arbre jusqu'aux racines.* Paris: B. Grasset, 1975.

Fevralskii, Aleksandr

___ 'Eisenstein v teatre.' In: *Voprosy teatra.* Moscow: Iskusstvo, 1967, pp. 82-102.

Freeman, Joseph

___ 'The Soviet Cinema.' In: J. Freeman, J. Munitz et al. *Voices of October: Art and Literature in Soviet Russia.* New York: Vanguard Press, 1930, pp. 217-264.

___ *An American Testament: A Narrative of Rebels and Romantics.* New York: Octagon Books, 1973.

___ 'Perepiska Eizenshteina s Frimenom.' In: Lazar Fleishman (ed.). *Materialy po istorii russkoi i sovetskoi kultury. Iz arkhiva Guverovskogo instituta.* Stanford: Stanford Slavic Studies, 1992, 220-262.

Geduld, Harry M. and Gottesman, Ronald

___ (eds). *Sergei Eisenstein and Upton Sinclair: Making and Unmaking of* Que viva Mexico!. Bloomington: Indiana UP, 1970.

Goodwin, James

___ *Eisenstein, Cinema and History.* Urbana IL: University of Illinois P, 1993.

Gert, Valeska

___ *Ich bin eine Hexe: Kaleidoskop meines Lebens.* Munich: Knaur, 1968.

Glizer, Judith

___ 'Eizenshtein i zhenshchiny.' *Kinovedcheskie zapiski* 6 (1990), pp. 119-134.

Iurenev, Rostislav
___ (ed). *Eizenshtein v vospominaniiakh sovremennikov.* Moscow: Iskusstvo, 1973.
___ *Sergei Eizenshtein: Zamysly. Filmy. Metod.* 2 vols. Moscow: Iskusstvo, 1985, 1988.

Kerr, Alfred
___ 'Der Russenfilm.' In: *Russische Filmkunst.* Berlin: Ernst Pollack, 1927.

Kleberg, Lars
___ *Starfall: A Triptych.* Evanston IL: Northwestern UP, 1997.

Kleiman, Naum, Dymshits, Nina and Troshin, Aleksandr
___ (eds) *Kinovedcheskie zapiski* 36-37 (1997-98).

Konlechner, Peter and Kubelka, Peter
___ *Sergej Michailovic Eisenstein. Eine Übersicht.* Vienna: Österreichisches Filmmuseum, 1964.

Leyda, Jay and Voynow, Zina
___ *Eisenstein at Work.* New York: Pantheon Books, 1982.

Maksimenkov, Leonid
___ *Sumbur vmesto muzyki. Stalinskaia kul'turnaia revoliutsiia 1936-38.* Moscow: Iuridicheskaia kniga, 1977.

Mierau, Fritz
___ ed. *Russen in Berlin. Literatur, Malerei, Theater, Film 1918-1933.* Leipzig: Reclam jr., 1990.

Montagu, Ivor
___ *With Eisenstein in Hollywood.* New York: International Publishers, 1967.

Moussinac, Léon
___ *Sergei Eisenstein.* New York: Crown Publishers, 1970.

Nazvanov, Mikhail
___ 'Pis'ma.' *Iskusstvo kino* 1 (1998), pp. 138-47 and 2 (1998), pp. 129-39.

Nikitin, Andrei
___ *Moskovskii debiut Sergeia Eizenshteina.* Moscow: Intergraf servis, 1996.

Nizhnii, Vladimir
___ *Lessons with Eisenstein.* I. Montagu, ed. and transl. London: Allen & Unwin and New York: Hill & Wang, 1962.

Oshibki 'Bezhina luga'. Protiv formalizma v kino. Moscow, 1937.

Prokofiev, Sergei
___ *Stat'i i materialy.* I. Nest'ev and G. Edel'man, eds. Moscow: Sovetskii kompozitor, 1965.

Richardson, William Harrison
___ *Mexico through Russian Eyes, 1806-1940.* Pittsburgh: University of Pittsburgh Press, 1988.

Richter, Hans
___ *Köpfe und Hinterköpfe.* Zurich: Verlag der Arche, 1967.

Rodenberg, Hans and Herlinghaus, Hermann
___ (eds). *Sergej Eisenstein—Künstler der Revolution.* Berlin/GDR: Henschel, 1960. *Rozhdenie zvukovogo obraza. Khudozhestvennye problemy zvukozapisi v ekrannykh iskusstvakh i na radio.* E.

M. Averbakh, ed. Moscow: Iskusstvo, 1985.

Schpiller, Natalja
___ 'Die Walküre in der Inszenierung Sergej Eisensteins.' Kunst und Literatur 28 (July 1980), pp. 773-80.

Seton, Marie
___ Sergei M. Eisenstein: A Biography. London: Dobson Books, 1952.

Shklovskii, Viktor
___ Ikh nastoiashchee. Moscow: Kinopechat', 1927.
___ Eizenshtein. Moscow: Iskusstvo, 1973.

Shub, Esfir
___ Zhizn' moia—kinematograf. Moscow: Iskusstvo, 1972.

Shumiatskii, Boris
___ Kinematografiia millionov. Moscow: Kinofotoizdat, 1935.

Sinclair, Upton
___ American Outpost: A Book of Reminiscences. New York: Farrar and Rinehart, 1932.

Sinko, Erwin
___ Roman eines Romans, Moskauer Tagebuch. Cologne: Wissenschaft und Politik, 1962.

Sudendorf, Werner
___ Sergej M. Eisenstein: Materialien zu Leben und Werk. Munich: Hanser, 1975.

Swallow, Norbert
___ Eisenstein: A Documentary Portrait. London: Allen and Unwin, 1976; New York: Dutton, 1977.

Taylor, Richard and Christie, Ian
___ (eds). Inside the Film Factory: New Approaches to Russian and Soviet Cinema. Cambridge MA: Harvard UP, 1988.
___ (eds). The Film Factory: Russian and Soviet Cinema in Documents 1896-1939. Cambridge MA: Harvard UP, 1988.

Tikhonovich, Valentin
___ 50 let v teatre i okolo teatra. Manuscript: Biblioteka VTO (Vserosiiskoe teatral'noe obshchestvo).

Vaisfeld, Ilia
___ 'Mon dernier entretien avec Eisenstein.' Cahiers du cinéma 208 (1969), pp. 19-21.

Viertel, Salka
___ The Kindness of Strangers. New York: Holt, Rinehart, and Winston, 1969.

Vishnevskii, Vsevolod
___ Eizenshtein. Moscow: Goskinoizdat, 1939.

Weise, Eckhard
___ Sergej M. Eisenstein in Selbstzeugnissen und Bilddokumenten. Reinbeck bei Hamburg: Rowohlt, 1975.

Za bol'shoe kinoiskusstvo. Moscow: Kinofotoizdat, 1935.

Zorkaia, Neia
___ 'Eizenshtein.' In: Portrety. Moscow: Iskusstvo, 1966, pp. 63-139.

LIST OF EISENSTEIN'S WORKS

Filmography
Glumov's Diary, 1923
The Strike, 1925
The Battleship Potemkin, 1925
October, 1928
The Old and the New, 1929
Women's Misery—Women's Happiness, 1930 (Switzerland; contributed)
Romance sentimentale, 1930 (France; contributed)
Earthquake in Oaxaca, 1931
Qué viva México!, 1932 (unfinished, cut by Sol Lesser 1933; Marie Seton and Paul
    Burnford 1939; Jay Leyda 1957; Grigory Alexandrov 1977)
Bezhin Meadow (1st version, interrupted, lost)
Bezhin Meadow (2nd version, interrupted, lost)
Alexander Nevsky, 1938
Ivan the Terrible (Part I, 1946; Part II banned, screened 1958; Part III unfinished)

Works for the Theater
The Mexican, 1921 (set design; costumes with Leonid Nikitin)
On the Abys, 1921 (set design and costumes with Leonid Nikitin)
Being Good to Horses, 1921 (costumes)
Dawn of the Proletkult, 1921 (set design)
Lena, 1921 (stage design and costumes with Leonid Nikitin)
Les Deux orphelines [Vorovka detei], 1922 (costumes)
Macbeth, 1922 (costumes)
The Wise Man, 1923 (direction, set design, costumes)
Can You Hear Me, Moscow?, 1923 (direction, set design, costumes)
Gas Masks, 1924 (direction, set design, costumes)
Moscow 2, 1934 (interrupted)
Walküre, 1939 (direction, sketches for set design)

Unrealized Screenplays
The Bazaar of Lust, 1925
Sutter's Gold, 1931
An American Tragedy, 1931
MMM, 1933

Notes for Screenplays
The Glass House, 1926-30
Capital, 1928-29
Moscow, 1933
The Great Ferghana Canal, 1939
The Love of a Poet, 1940

Film Projects
The Red Cavalry, 1924

Benya Krik, 1925
Zhonghua, 1926
Le chemin de Buenos Aires [The Road to Buenos Aires], 1929
The Man of Darkness, 1929 (Later The Twilight of the Gods, 1930-32)
The Life of Emile Zola, 1930
Black Majesty, 1930-31
The Black Consul, 1923
The Five Year Plan, 1932
A film about Persia, 1933
The Human Condition, 1934
We the Russian People, 1937
Spain, 1937
The Moor of Peter the Great, 1937
The Lay of Igor's Campaign, 1937
Perekop, 1938
Mademoiselle Fifi, 1939
Giordano Bruno, 1940
A film about the plague, 1940
A film about Lawrence of Arabia, 1940
The Beilis Affair, 1940-41
The World Upside Down, 1945

Theater Projects (sketches of set designs, adaptations of plays)
Puss-in-Boots (by Ludwig Tieck), 1921-22
The Golden Pot (based on E. T. A. Hoffmann), 1922
Master Martin the Cooper and his Journeymen (based on E. T. A. Hoffmann), 1922
Columbine's Garter (with Sergei Yutkevich), 1922
Heartbreak House (by George Bernard Shaw), 1922
Tales of Hoffmann (Jacques Offenbach), 1922-23
War and Peace (opera by Sergei Prokofiev), 1943
Carmen (ballet) or The Last Conversation, 1946

Bibliography of Eisenstein's texts
'Bibliografiia rabot Eisensteina, opublikovannykh na russkom iazyke'; in: S. M. Eisenstein, Izbrannye proizvedeniia v 6 tomakh. Vol. 1 (Moscow 1964), pp. 591-606
W. Sudendorf, 'Bibliographie'; in: Sergej M. Eisenstein. Materialien zu Leben und Werk (Munich 1975), pp. 241-269
F. Albera and J. Aumont, 'Bibliographie des écrits d'Eisenstein et des études, articles, critiques'; in: B. Améngual, Que viva Eisenstein! (Lausanne 1980), pp. 650-710
O. Bulgakowa, 'Bibliographie'; in: A. Hiersche and E. Kowalski (eds), Literaturtheorie und Literaturkritik in der Frühsowjetischen Diskussion. Standorte—Programme—Schulen. Dokumente, (Bern 1993), pp. 492-496
V. Zabrodin, S. M. Eizenshtein. Bibliografiia publikatsii na russkom iazyke'; in: Kinovedcheskie zapiski, 36/37 (1997/98), pp. 345-397
V. Zabrodin, 'Novye publikatsii S. M. Eizenshteina na russkom iazyke'; in: Kinovedcheskie zapiski, 46 (2000), pp. 208-218

NOTES

Notes to 'The Boy From Riga'

[1] S. Eisenstein, *Beyond the Stars: The Memoirs of Sergei Eisenstein*, ed. R. Taylor (London and Calcutta, 1995), pp. 16-18. Translator's note: Richard Taylor's edition omits the line of Eisenstein's original memoirs which I have translated as: 'You might think it about time to start feeling like a grownup.'

Notes to 'Childhood and Youth. The Betrayed Father' (1898-1918)

[2] Eisenstein, *Beyond the Stars*, p. 425.

[3] V. Tikhonovich, *50 let v teatre i okolo teatra*. Vol. 1. Unpublished and undated manuscript, Biblioteka VTO (Vserossiiskogo teatral'nogo obshchestva), p. 210.

[4] Eisenstein, *Beyond the Stars*, p. 493.

[5] Eisenstein, *Selected Works*, Vol. 3, *Writings 1934-47*, ed. R. Taylor (London, 1996) p. 284.

[6] Eisenstein, *Beyond the Stars*, p. 126.

[7] *Cinémonde*, 1929, no. 59.

Notes to 'A Young Soldier's Reading List. Freemasons and Japan' (1918-1920)

[8] *Eisenstein Archive*, 1923-1-1549, pp. 35-40.

[9] Ibid., pp. 43-45.

[10] Ibid., p. 51.

[11] Ibid., pp. 53-58.

[12] Eisenstein, *Beyond the Stars*, pp. 80-83.

[13] *Eisenstein Archive*, 1923-1-1978, pp. 3-5.

[14] *Eisenstein Archive*, 1923-2-891, pp. 3-4.

Notes to 'Anarchists in Mexico. Meyerhold – the Second Father' (1920-1923)

[15] *Eisenstein Archive*, 1923-1-1549, pp. 87-90.

[16] *Gorn*, 1922, no. 27.

[17] *Eisenstein Archive*, 1923-1-1549, pp. 83-86.

[18] N. Ensky, 'Lena V. Pletneva', *Bednota*, 1921, no. 1050 (15 October).

[19] *Eisenstein Archive*, 1923-1-1549, pp. 74-75.

[20] Ibid., pp. 76-77.

[21] Eisenstein, *Beyond the Stars*, p. 263.

[22] I. Aksenov, 'Iunost' khudozhnika', *Iskusstvo kino*, 1968, no. 1, p. 100.

[23] *Eisenstein Archive*, 1923-1-1550, p. 3.

[24] *Eisenstein Archive*, 1923-1-2062, p. 4.

[25] *Eisenstein Archive*, 1923-2-1103, p. 30.

[26] Ibid., pp. 30, 48.

[27] A. Piotrovskii, 'Kinofikatsiia teatra. (Neskol'ko obobshchenii)', *Zhizn' iskusstva*, 22 November 1927, p. 4; translated in R. Taylor and I. Christie, eds., *The Film Factory: Russian and Soviet Cinema in Documents, 1896-1939* (London and New York, 1988), pp. 178-180.

[28] Eisenstein, *Beyond the Stars*, pp. 106-107.

[29] *Kinovedcheskie zapiski*, 1997/98, no. 36/37, p. 293.

[30] Eisenstein, *Beyond the Stars*, p. 272.

Notes to 'THE WISE MAN. The Suffering of Young S.' (1923)

[31] R. Iurenev, ed., *Eizenshtein v vospominaniiakh sovremennikov* (Moscow, 1973), p. 150.

[32] Eisenstein, *Selected Works. Vol. 1: Writings 1922-34*, ed. R. Taylor (London and Bloomington IN, 1988), p. 34.

[33] *Eisenstein Archive*, 1923-2-1102, p. 2.

[34] *Zrelishcha*, 1923, no. 39, p. 3; cited in R. Iurenev, *Sergei Eizenshtein: Zamysly. Filmy. Metod. Vol. 1* (Moscow, 1985), p. 67.

[35] *Zrelishcha*, 1923, no. 40, pp. 5-6.

[36] *Eisenstein Archive*, 1923-1-1550, p. 28.

[37] A. Fevralskii, 'Eizenshtein v teatre', *Voprosy teatra* (Moscow, 1967), p. 59.

[38] *Eisenstein Archive*, 1923-2-1102, p. 1.

[39] *Eisenstein Archive*, 1923-1-1550, p. 28.

[40] Ibid., p. 7.

[41] Ibid., p. 13.

[42] Note originally in English; dated May 8, 1946; published in the Russian and German editions of Eisenstein's memoirs: S. M. Eizenshtein, *Memuary. Vol. 2* (Moscow, 1997), p. 473; S. Eisenstein, *Yo-ich selbst. Memoiren. Vol. 2*, eds., N. Klejman and W. Korschunowa, (Berlin/GDR and Vienna, 1984), pp. 1129-1130.

[43] J. Glizer, 'Eizenshtein i zhenshchiny', *Kinovedcheskie zapiski*, 1990, no. 6, p. 124.

[44] *Eisenstein Archive*, 1923-2-323, pp. 1-2.

[45] *Eisenstein Archive*, 1923-2-1102, p. 2.

[46] *Eisenstein Archive*, 1923-2-323, pp. 1-2.

[47] *Eisenstein Archive*, 1923-2-1104, p. 99.

Notes to 'The Jump into Film: THE STRIKE' (1924)

[48] B. Alpers, 'Teatr sotsial'noi maski' (Moscow 1931), in B. Alpers, *Teatral'nye ocherki v 2 tomakh* (Moscow, 1977), p. 151.

[49] L. Trotsky, 'Vodka, the Church and the Cinema', in *The Film Factory*, pp. 94-97.

[50] *Kinematograf* (Moscow 1919), p. 87.

[51] *Kinogazeta*, 25 January 1925.

[52] V. Pletnev, 'Otkrytoe pis'mo v redaktsiiu Kinonedeli', Kinonedelia, no. 6, 3 February 1925, p. 9; Engl. transl.: V. Pletnyov, 'An open letter to the editors of the journal *Kinonedelya*', in: J. Leyda, ed., *Eisenstein 2. A Premature Celebration of Eisenstein's Century* (Calcutta, 1985), pp. 3-5.

[53] *Eisenstein Archive*, 1923-1-903, pp. 3-7.

[54] Cited in R. Iurenev, *Sergei Eizenshtein: Zamysly. Filmy. Metod*, Vol. 1 (Moscow, 1985), p. 99.

[55] Pletnev, 'Otkrytoe pis'mo v redaktsiiu Kinonedeli', p. 9.

[56] *Kinonedelia*, 1925, no. 14, p. 17.

[57] *Kinogazeta*, 17 March 1925.

[58] *Kinogazeta*, 24 March 1925.

[59] Eisenstein, *Selected Works*, Vol. 1, pp. 62-64.

[60] *Kinozhurnal A R K*, 1925, no. 8, pp. 3-4.

[61] V. Shklovskii, 'Neobkhodimoe zlo', *Kinogazeta*, 10 November 1925.

Notes to 'Three Months and a Lifetime: THE BATTLESHIP POTEMKIN' (1925)

[62] *Kinogazeta*, 7 July 1925.

[63] Ibid.

[64] The film *Behind White Lines* was directed by Boris Chaikovsky and Olga Rakhmanova in 1924, but Kirill Shutko was not given any credit.

[65] G. Aleksandrov, *Epokha i kino* (Moscow, 1976), p. 84.

[66] S. Eizenshtein, *Izbrannye proizvedeniia v 6 tomakh*. Vol. 5 (Moscow, 1968), p. 178.

[67] Reprinted in *Filmwissenschaftliche Mitteilungen*, 1967, no. 3, pp. 786-793.

[68] A. Kerr, 'Der Russenfilm', *Russische Filmkunst* (Berlin, 1927), p. 14.

[69] *Berliner Tageblatt*, 7 June 1926.

[70] *Berliner Börsen Courier*, 1 May 1926.

[71] *Deutsche Allgemeine Zeitung*, 11 February 1934.

[72] *Vossische Zeitung*, 1 May 1926.

[73] *Literarische Welt*, 11 March 1927; reprinted in F. Mierau, *Russen in Berlin. Literatur, Malerei, Theater, Film 1918-1933* (Leipzig, 1990), pp. 515-524.

[74] *Völkermagazin 11*, 1927 (March), p. 55.

Notes to 'The Morning after Fame' (1926-1928)

[75] *Eisenstein Archive*, 2744-1-23, p. 1.

[76] *Eisenstein Archive*, 1923-2-1103, p. 2.

[77] *Eisenstein Archive*, 1923-2-1104, p. 86.

[78] J. Freeman, 'The Soviet Cinema', in J. Freeman and J. Munitz, eds., *Voices of October: Art and Literature in Soviet Russia* (New York, 1930), p. 541.

[79] *Eisenstein Archive*, 1923-1-765.

[80] Muir & Merrilees was one of the biggest department stores in Moscow, opened by the Scotsmen Archibald Merrilees and Andrew Muir in the 1880s. In 1892 the store moved into a building near the Bolshoi Theater and in 1922 was renamed the Central Department Store.

[81] Iurenev, *Sergei Eizenshtein*, Vol. 1, p. 201.

[82] G. Aleksandrov, *Epokha i kino* (Moscow, 1976), p. 117.

[83] Cited in D. Volkogonov, 'Stalin', *Oktiabr'*, 1988, no. 11, p. 87.

[84] *Eisenstein Archive*, 1923-2-1105, p. 62.

[85] *Pravda*, 9 February 1928.

[86] *Novyi Lef*, 1928, no. 4 (April) pp. 27-36; translated in *The Film Factory*, pp. 229-230.

[87] V. Shklovskii, *Eisenstein* (Moscow, 1973), pp. 152-158.

[88] *Eisenstein Archive*, 1923-2-1195, p. 71.

[89] *Eisenstein Archive*, 1923-2-1108, p. 8; original in German.

[90] *Eisenstein Archive*, 1923-2-1110, p. 72.

[91] *Eisenstein Archive*, 1923-2-1109, p. 29; italicized passage originally in German.

[92] *Eisenstein Archive*, 1923-2-1110, p. 8; original in English.

[93] Eizenshtein, *Izbrannye proizvedeniia v 6 tomakh*, Vol. 5, p.441.

[94] *Eisenstein Archive*, 1923-2-1110, p. 36-37; original in German.

[95] *Eisenstein Archive*, 1923-2-1114, p. 97.

[96] *Eisenstein Archive*, 1923-2-1110, pp. 37-39.

[97] J. Freeman, *An American Testament: A Narrative of Rebels and Romantics* (New York, 1973), p. 589.

[98] *Eisenstein Archive*, 1923-2-1105, p. 77.

[99] *Eisenstein Archive*, 1923-2-1107, p. 44.

[100] Eisenstein, *Selected Works*, Vol. 1, pp. 113-4.

[101] Ibid., pp. 117-119.

[102] Ibid., p. 118.

[103] *Eisenstein Archive*, 1923-2-1110, p. 4; original in English.

[104] *Eisenstein Archive*, 1923-2-1744, p. 11.

Notes to 'The Pilgrims. The Search for a World Language' (1928-1929)

[105] T. Dreiser, *Dreiser Looks at Russia* (New York, 1928), p. 206.

[106] S. Eisenstein, 'Mass Movies', interview with Louis Fischer, *The Nation*, 9 November 1927.

[107] Freeman, *An American Testament: A Narrative of Rebels and Romantics*, p. 589.

[108] Eisenstein, *Selected Works*, Vol. 1, p. 77.

[109] V. S., 'Novaia klientura gospodina Korb'usie [Corbusier]' *Sovetskii ekran* no. 46, 1928, p. 5.

[110] V. Gert, *Ich bin eine Hexe* (Munich, 1968), p. 53.

[111] *Eisenstein Archive*, 1923-1-973, p. 2.

[112] *Licht-Bild-Bühne*, no. 185, 2 August 1928.

[113] *Eisenstein Archive*, 1923-1-1030; excerpts printed and translated in S. Eisenstein, *Das dynamische Quadrat: Schriften zum Film*, ed. O. Bulgakowa and D. Hochmuth, (Leipzig, 1988), p. 344.

[114] Published as 'I. A. 28' in *Kinovedcheskie zapiski*, 1997/98, no. 36/37, pp. 39-48.

[115] First published in Russian in 1985; English in Eisenstein, *Selected Works*, Vol. 1, pp. 39-58.

[116] 'Beyond the Shot'; in Eisenstein, *Selected Works*, Vol. 1, pp. 138-150.

[117] See S. Eizenshtein, 'Predislovie [k knige Gvido Zebera] *Tekhnika kinotriuka*', *Izbrannye proizvedeniia v 6 tomakh*, Vol. 5, pp. 36-38.

[118] This last group of essays are published and translated in Eisenstein, *Selected Works*, Vol. 1, pp. 33-38, 115-123, 151-195.

[119] *Eisenstein Archive*, 1923-2-1105, p. 134.

[120] Eisenstein, 'The Dramaturgy of Film Form'; in *Selected Works*, Vol. 1, pp. 161-80.

[121] S. Eisenstein, 'A Statement', *Close Up*, Vol. 3, 1928, no. 4 (October), pp. 10-13 and 'The New Language of Cinematography', *Close Up*, Vol. 4, 1929, no. 5 (May), pp. 10-13.

[122] M. Seton, *Sergei M. Eisenstein: A Biography*, (London, 1952), p. 218.

[123] *Eisenstein Archive*, 1923-2-1105, pp. 77-8.

[124] S. Eisenstein, 'Notes for a Film of *Capital*', *October* 1976, no.2, pp. 3-26.

[125] Eisenstein, *Selected Works*, Vol. 1, p. 105.

[126] *Eisenstein Archive*, 1923-2-1112, p. 66.

[127] *Eisenstein Archive*, 1923-2-1105, p. 69.

[128] Ibid., p. 128.

[129] B. Shumiatskii, *Kinematografiia millionov* (Moscow 1935), p. 78.

[130] *Sovetskii ekran*, 1929, no. 40. Cited in R. Iurenev, *Sergei Eizenshtein*, Vol. 1, p. 276.

Notes to 'The Journey' (1929-1930)

[131] K. Malevich, 'And Images Triumph on the Screen' (1925); in *Essays on Art*, Vol. 1 (Copenhagen, 1968), pp. 226-232.

[132] S. Eisenstein, 'Imitation as Mastery'; in I. Christie and R. Taylor, eds., *Eisenstein Rediscovered* (London, 1993), pp. 66-71.

[133] B. Balázs, *Schriften zum Film*, Vol. 2 (Berlin/GDR, 1984), p. 202.

[134] *Eisenstein Archive*, 1923-1-1908, p. 1.

[135] *Eisenstein Archive*, 1923-1-972, pp. 13-4.

[136] *Kinovedcheskie zapiski*, 1997/98, no. 36/37, p. 221.

[137] E. Averbakh, ed., *Rozhdenie zvukovogo obraza. Khudozhestvennye problemy zvukozapisi v ekrannykh iskusstvakh i na radio* (Moscow, 1985), pp. 190-191.

[138] 'Eisenstein freut sich', *Film-Kurier*, no. 103, 30 April 1930; in W. Sudendorf, ed., *Sergei M. Eisenstein: Materialien zu Leben und Werk* (Munich, 1975), p. 109.

[139] Gert, *Ich bin eine Hexe*, p. 59.

[140] *Kinovedcheskie zapiski*, 1997/98, no. 36/37, pp. 222-223.

Notes to 'America' (1930)

[141] *Eisenstein Archive*, 1923-2-1745, pp. 5, 10.

[142] *Eisenstein Archive*, 1923-1-1458, p. 30.

[143] Eisenstein, *Beyond the Stars*, p. 4.

[144] *Motion Picture Herald*, 28 April 1930; Reprinted in: M. Seton, *Sergei M. Eisenstein*, p. 167.

[145] 'Perepiska Eizenshteina s Frimenom'; in: L. Fleishman, ed., *Materialy po istorii russkoi i sovetskoi kul'tury: Iz arkhiva Guverovskogo Instituta* (Stanford, 1992), p. 245.

[146] Seton, p. 166.

[147] *Kinovedcheskie zapiski*, 1997/98, no. 36/37, p. 231.

[148] L. Moussinac, *Sergei Eisenstein* (Paris, 1964), p. 50.

[149] S. Eisenstein, 'The Cinema in America', *International Literature*, 1933, no. 3, p. 103.

[150] Aleksandrov, *Epokha i kino*, p. 151.

[151] Eisenstein, *Beyond the Stars*, pp. 332-333.

[152] *Kinovedcheskie zapiski*, 1997/98, no. 36/37, p. 229.

[153] W. Benjamin, 'Surrealism'; in: *Reflections: Essays Aphorisms, Autobiographical Writings*, ed., P. Demetz (New York, 1986), p. 180.

[154] Moussinac, p. 52.

[155] W. Sudendorf (ed.), Sergej M. Eisenstein: Materialien zu Leben und Werk (Munich 1975), p. 116.

[156] R. Behlmer, *Memo from David O. Selznick* (New York, 1972), pp. 26-27.

[157] C. Seiler, 'Redmongers Go West', *New Republic*, 12 November 1930, pp. 347-348.

[158] *Eisenstein Collection*, Museum of Modern Art; cited in Seton, p. 184.

[159] Seton, p. 186.

[160] 'Perepiska Eizenshteina s Frimenom', pp. 243-8.

[161] *Eisenstein Archive*, 1923-2-1551, p. 45.

[162] I. Montagu, *With Eisenstein in Hollywood* (New York, 1967), p. 131.

[163] H. M. Geduld and R. Gottesmann, eds., *Sergei Eisenstein and Upton Sinclair: Making and Unmaking of Que viva Mexico!* (Bloomington, 1970), p. 22.

[164] Seton, p. 190.

Notes to 'Mexico' (1931-1932)

[165] Geduld and Gottesmann, p. 48.

[166] *Eisenstein Archive*, 1923-1-1621, p. 55.

[167] *Kinovedcheskie zapiski*, 1997/98, no. 36/37, pp. 234-235.

[168] Eisenstein, *Beyond the Stars*, p. 505.

[169] Geduld and Gottesmann, p. 110.

[170] Ibid., pp. 125-6.

[171] Ibid., p. 128.

[172] Ibid., p. 132.

[173] *Prometei*, 1972, no. 9, p. 196.

[174] Geduld and Gottesmann, p. 173.

[175] Ibid., pp. 173-82.

[176] Ibid., pp. 201-2.

[177] H. G. Weinberg, 'The 'Lesser' of Two Devils. Concerning the Case of Que viva Mexico!' *The Modern Monthly*, Vol. VII, 1933, no. 5, p. 300.

[178] Letter to Stern, 7 January 1932; cited in Seton, *Sergei M. Eisenstein*, pp. 211-2.

[179] Cited in Geduld and Gottesmann, p. 212.

[180] Ibid., pp. 212-214.

[181] *Eisenstein Archive*, 1923-2-1116.

[182] *Eisenstein Archive*, 1923-2-2259, p. 9.

[183] *Eisenstein Archive*, 1923-2-1551, p. 50.

[184] *Eisenstein Archive*, 1923-1-1622, pp. 11-2.

[185] *Film-Kurier*, 30 November 1931, no. 280.

[186] *Eisenstein Archive*, 1923-1-524, 997 a, pp. 7-8.

[187] Seton, p. 230.

[188] Ibid., p. 266.

[189] Geduld and Gottesmann, p. 274.

[190] Ibid., p. 279.

[191] S. Viertel, *The Kindness of Strangers* (New York, 1969), pp. 156-7.

[192] J. Leyda and Z. Voynow, *Eisenstein at Work* (New York, 1982), pp. 70-71.

[193] Seton, p. 516.

[194] Letter to Seton, 5 April 1950; in Seton, p. 515.

[195] Ibid., 235.

[196] Ibid., 231-232.

[197] Geduld and Gottesmann, p. 293.

[198] Ibid., pp. 307-310.

Notes to 'Return' (1932-1934)

[199] Shumiatskii, *Kinematografiia millionov*, pp. 33-34; cited in R. Taylor, 'Ideology as Mass Entertainment: Boris Shumyatsky and Soviet Cinema in the 1930s'; in R. Taylor and I. Christie, eds., *Inside the Film Factory: New Approaches to Russian and Soviet Cinema* (Cambridge MA, 1988), pp. 193-216.

[200] *Literaturnaia gazeta*, 20 November 1930.

[201] Geduld and Gottesmann, p. 343.

[202] Ibid., pp. 347-349.

[203] *Eizenshtein v vospominaniiakh sovremennikov*, p. 75.

[204] Iurenev, S. *Eizenshtein*, Vol. 2, p. 72.

[205] Seton, pp. 250, 276, 516.

[206] Ibid., p. 275.

[207] Ibid., p. 276.

[208] Eizenshtein, *Memuary*, Vol. 2, p. 287.

[209] Eisenstein, *Selected Works*, Vol. 1, , pp. 280-284.

[210] M. Eastman, *Artists in Uniform: A Study of Literature and Bureaucratism* (New York, 1934).

[211] *Eisenstein Archive*, 1923-1-2172-1.

[212] First publication: *Sergei Eizenshtein: portret khudozhnika* (Moscow 1991).

[213] M. Kalatozov, S. Bartenev, 'Obraz i dramaturgiia v tvorchestve S. Eizenshteina', *Kino*, 16 June 1933, p. 3.

[214] *Krasnaia gazeta*, 22 August 1934, evening edition.

[215] Seton, p. 305.

[216] Ibid., p. 134.

[217] *Eisenstein Archive*, 1923-2-268, p. 20: 'At this time Alexandrov and I were in love (and more!) with Yanukova, and her number was a Sunday 'shock': We both feared for her (the risk of falling, and if she had fallen, the chance of knocking herself to pieces was truly enormous).'

[218] *Eisenstein Archive*, 1923-2-1179, p. 6: 'The auto-biographical element in Ivan. Kurbsky as Grisha. Even so in the choice of the type. Nazvanov's eyebrow over the cross exactly Grisha's. The betrayal of the principles we have been fostering together

(or so it seemed) in film aesthetics. His betrayal of these (in Happy Guys), his betrayal of me personally (par excellence, of Bor[is] Zakh[arevich] [Shumyatsky]) on the eve of our anniversary in 1935). Even more profound: the completely forced scene of [Kurbsky's] love affair with Anastasia now (for the first time) appears to be a reproduction of the situation with him [Alexandrov] and Irina H [Hold = Meyerhold] whom he won over from me.'

[219] Ibid.

[220] *Screen*, Vol. 22, no. 4, 1981, pp. 79-86; W. Reich, *Die Funktion des Orgasmus. Zur Psychopathologie und zur Soziologie des Geschlechtslebens* (Vienna, Leipzig 1927).

[221] *Screen*, Vol. 22, no. 4, 1981, p. 81.

Notes to 'Inside the Ivory Tower' (1935)

[222] Seton, pp. 298-299.

[223] S. Eisenstein, *Selected Works*, Vol. 3, pp. 16-46.

[224] Ibid., p. 38.

[225] Za bol'shoe kinoiskusstvo (Moscow 1935), p. 55.

[226] Ibid., pp. 72-73.

[227] Ibid., p. 109.

[228] Ibid., pp. 112-113.

[229] Ibid., p. 141.

[230] Ibid., p. 121; this excerpt is translated in *The Film Factory*, p. 355.

Notes to 'BEZHIN MEADOW: Father and Son' (1935-1937)

[231] *Eizenshtein v vospominaniiakh sovremennikov*, p. 267.

[232] *Eisenstein Archive*, 1923-1-1152, p. 1.

[233] *Krest'ianskaia gazeta*, 18 March 1936.

[234] *Eisenstein Archive*, 1923-2-1151, pp. 9-10.

[235] Ibid., p. 10.

[236] Eizenshtein, *Izbrannye proizvedeniia v 6 tomakh*, Vol. 5, p. 259.

[237] *Eisenstein Archive*, 1923-2-1151, pp. 0-11; original English.

[238] E. Sinko, *Roman eines Romans: Moskauer Tagebuch* (Cologne, 1962), p. 354.

[239] Ibid., p. 357.

[240] *Eisenstein Archive*, 1923-2-1152, p. 9.

[241] *Eisenstein Archive*, 1923-1-1489, p. 1.

[242] L. Maksimenkov, *Sumbur vmesto muzyki. Stalinskaia kul'turnaia revoliutsiia 1936-38* (Moscow, 1997), pp. 252-253

[243] *Oshibki Bezhina Luga: Protiv formalizma v kino* (Moscow, 1937), pp. 15-16; Maksimenkov, p. 242

[244] *Kino*, 24 March 1937.

[245] *Oshibki Bezhina Luga*, p. 40.

[246] Ibid., p. 50.

[247] Ibid., pp. 60-61.

[248] *Eisenstein Archive*, 1923-2-1152, p. 29.

[249] Ibid.; original in English.

[250] Shumyatsky's letter is reprinted in its entirety in Maksimenkov, pp. 245-246.

[251] Ibid., p.246.

[252] *Kinovedcheskie zapiski*, 1997/98, no. 36/37, p. 240.

[253] *Eisenstein Archive*, 1923-1-1517.

[254] *Eisenstein Archive*, 1923-1-2139, p. 13.

[255] Eisenstein, *Beyond the Stars*, p. 740.

[256] *Eisenstein Archive*, 1923-2-1153, p. 10.

Notes to 'Winter in Summer. The Twilight of the Gods' (1936-1940)

[257] *Eisenstein Archive*, 1923-2-1152, p. 10.

[258] M. Tikhomirov, 'Izdevka nad istoriei', *Istorik Marksist*, 1938, no. 2, pp. 92-96.

[259] S. Prokofiev, *Statii i materialy*, eds., I. Nest'ev and G. Edel'man (Moscow, 1965), pp. 222-223.

[260] *Izvestiia*, 9 August 1938; *Internatsional'naia literatura*, 1938, no. 9; *Pioner*, 1938, no. 16.

[261] S. Eisenstein, 'P-R-K-F-V'; in *Notes of a Film Director* (Moscow, 1958), pp. 149-167.

[262] S. Eisenstein, *Selected Works, Vol. 2, Towards a Theory of Montage*, eds., M. Glenny and R. Taylor (London, 1991), pp. 378-399.

[263] N. Cherkasov, *Zapiski sovetskogo aktera* (Moscow, 1953), p. 128.

[264] *Eisenstein Archive*, 1923-2-1152, p. 11, original English.

[265] Seton, p. 388.

[266] V. Vishnevskii, *Eizenshtein* (Moscow, 1939), p. 20.

[267] *Eisenstein Archive*, 1923-2-1152, p. 11; original English.

[268] *Pravda*, 13 August 1939.

[269] *Sovetskaia Kara-Kalpakiia*, 9 September 1939.

[270] *Iskusstvo kino*, 1958, no. 1, p. 96.

[271] S. Eisenstein, *Nonindifferent Nature* (Cambridge, 1987), pp. 3-37.

[272] *Eisenstein Archive*, 1923-2-1837, p. 2.

[273] O. Bulgakowa, *Eisenstein und Deutschland* (Berlin, 1998), p. 56.

[274] Hanamichi: in Kabuki theater, the runway that passes from the rear of the theater to the stage at the level of the spectators' heads.

275 *Sovetskaia muzyka*, 1941, no. 2, pp. 72-6.

276 Eisenstein, *Beyond the Stars*, pp. 712-24.

277 B. Schafgans, "If ever the whole Ring should be produced..." Eisensteins Walküre, eine deutsch-sowjetische Beziehung'; in *Eisenstein und Deutschland*, pp. 171-196

Notes to 'State Assignment' (1940-1946)

278 Freeman, 'The Soviet Cinema', *Voices of October*, p. 233.

279 R. Iurenev, *Sergei Eizenshtein*, p. 213.

280 S. Eisenstein, *Beyond the Stars*, pp. 23-24.

281 Shklovskii, *Eisenstein*, p. 267.

282 *Izvestiia*, 30 April 1941; *Vecherniaia Moskva*, 14 June 1941.

283 *Eisenstein Archive*, 1923-2-1166, p. 10.

284 Ibid.

285 Eizenshtein, *Memuary*, Vol. 2, pp. 224-227.

286 *Eisenstein Archive*, 2456-1-644, p. 2

287 Ibid., p. 2; cited in R. Iurenev, *Sergei Eizenshtein*, Vol. 2, p. 223.

288 Eisenstein, *Selected Works*, Vol. 3, p. 191.

289 S. Eisenstein, *The Film Sense*, ed. and transl., J. Leyda (New York, 1942)

290 Eisenstein Archive, 1923-2-1170, p. 5.

291 Ibid., p. 7.

292 Ibid., p. 9.

293 *Eisenstein Archive*, 1923-2-1179, p. 5.

294 Ibid., p. 6.

295 *Eisenstein Archive*, 2456-1-644, p. 17.

296 O. Bulgakowa, *Herausforderung Eisenstein, Arbeitsheft 41 der Akademie der Künste der DDR* (Berlin/GDR, 1989), p. 66.

297 S. Eisenstein, Selected Works. Vol. 4, p. 381.

298 M. Nazvanov, 'Prokliataia kartina. Pis'ma k Ol'ge Viklandt so s'emok fil'ma 'Ivan Groznyi", *Iskusstvo kino*, 1998, no. 1, p. 129.

299 *Eisenstein Archive*, 2456-1-657, pp. 3-4; cited in full in R. Iurenev, *Sergei Eisenstein.*, Vol. 2, pp. 234-235.

300 *Eisenstein Archive*, 2456-1-956, pp. 1-51.

301 Ibid., p. 51.

302 *Neue Zeit*, 14 August 1945.

303 *Post* (New York), 23 May 1945; 25 May 1945.

304 Eisenstein, *Beyond the Stars*, Vol. 4, p. 797.

Notes to 'Postscript' (1946-1948)

[305] *Eisenstein Archive*, 2456-1-1278, pp. 1-30.

[306] Seton, p. 455.

[307] *Eisenstein Archive*, 1923-2-1179, pp. 12-14.

[308] Eisenstein, *Beyond the Stars*, p. 23.

[309] Ibid., pp. 740-741.

[310] Ibid., p. 741.

[311] Eisenstein, *Selected Works*, Vol. 3, p. 297.

[312] Cherkasov, *Zapiski sovetskogo aktera*, pp. 136, 138.

[313] Eisenstein, *Selected Works*, Vol. 3, pp. 299-304.

[314] Ibid., p. 302.

[315] *Eisenstein Archive*, 1923-1-670.

[316] Eisenstein, *Nonindifferent Nature*, p. 370.

[317] *Eisenstein Archive*, 1923-2-1156.

[318] V. Pudovkin, G. Alexandrov, I. Pyrev, *Soviet Films: Principal Stages of Development* (Bombay, 1951).

INDEX OF NAMES

on 20th century theatrical production. *29*

Arensky, Anton (1861-1906). Russian composer and teacher. *14*

Arensky, Pavel (1887-1941). Russian poet and mystic, son of Anton Arensky. *14-19, 24, 33*

Arnheim, Rudolf (b. 1904). German film critic and psychologist, lives in the USA. *81*

Aroseev, Alexander (1890-1938). Soviet administrator and diplomat, head of Society for Cultural Ties with Foreign Countries (1934-1937), victim of Stalin's repressions. *178*

Artaud, Antonin (1896-1948). French dramatist, poet, actor, and theoretician of the Surrealist movement. *104*

Artsybashev, Mikhail (1878-1927). Russian writer. *3*

Arvatov, Boris (1896-1940). Soviet art historian, theoretician of production art. *21, 23, 32, 33, 39, 43, 44, 54*

Arzhanov, Pyotr (1901-1978). Soviet stage and film actor, role in *Bezhin Meadow*. *183*

Asafev, Boris (1884-1949). Soviet composer and musicologist. *230*

Asari. Japanese Kabuki actor. *81*

Asquith, Anthony (1902-1968). British screenwriter and film director, son of British Prime Minister. *101*

Atasheva (Fogelman), Pera (1900-1965). Soviet journalist, Eisenstein's wife. *82, 90, 102, 147, 157, 165, 179, 180, 232*

Atkinson, Brooks (1894-1984). Drama critic of the *New York Times*. In 1947, he won a Pulitzer prize for a series of articles he had written in Moscow in 1945. *225*

Auriol, Jean-Georges (1907-1950). French screenwriter and critic. *96*

Averbakh, Leopold (1903-1938). Soviet literary critic, arrested and shot. *186*

Averchenko, Arkady (1881-1925). Russian humorist, editor of the magazines *Satirikon* and *Novy Satirikon* from 1908 to 1917; emigrated. *8, 13*

Avramov, Arseny (1886-1944). Soviet avant-garde composer. *45*

Axyonov [Aksenov], Ivan (1884-1935). Soviet poet, translator, rector of Meyerhold's Higher Workshops in Directing (GVYRM). *5, 25, 27, 28, 39, 52, 160*

*B*abanova, Maria (1900-1983). Soviet stage actress, worked in Meyerhold's theater 1920-1927. *26*

Babel, Isaak (1894-1940). Soviet Jewish writer. *xi, 31, 33, 55, 57, 71, 72, 157, 163, 182-186, 200, 211*

Babitsky, Boris (1901-1938). Soviet film administrator, executive manager of the Moscow film studios Mezhrabpomfilm and Mosfilm, victim of Stalin's repressions. *195*

Bachelis, Ilya. Soviet literary critic. *199*

Bagritsky, Eduard (1895-1934). Soviet poet. *232*

Bakhtin, Mikhail (1895-1975). Russian literary theorist and philosopher of language. *88*

Balázs, Béla (1884-1949). Hungarian film critic and screenwriter, worked in Austria, Germany and the Soviet Union. *95, 96, 104*

Balderas, Félix. Mexican peasant, actor in Eisenstein's Mexican film. *133*

Balzac, Honoré de (1799-1850). French novelist. *82, 163*

Bancroft, George (1882-1956). American film actor, famous in gangster roles. *100*

Baranovskaya, Vera (1885-1935). Soviet stage and film actress, emigrated in 1928. *99*

Barbey d'Aurevilly, Jules Amédée (1808-1889). French novelist and critic. *19*

Barbusse, Henri (1873-1935). French novelist. *22, 91, 106*

Barkov, Ivan (1732-1768). Russian writer, known for his pornographic poems. *172*

Barnet, Boris (1902-1965). Soviet film actor and director. *35, 75, 76, 190*

Barnsdall, Aline (1882-1946). Oil heiress; close friend of the Sinclairs, patroness of the arts. *124*

Barsky, Vladimir (1889-1936). Soviet film director, role in *The Battleship Potemkin*. *59*

Bartenev, Sergei (1900-1966). Soviet film director. *161*

Barthelmess, Richard (1895-1963). American film actor. *87*

Basmanov, Fyodor. Favorite of Ivan the Terrible, executed his own father in Ivan's presence to prove his fealty. *211, 215*

Bassalygo, Dmitry (1884-1969). Russian and Soviet actor and film director. *47*

Baudelaire, Charles (1821-1867). French poet, literary and art critic. *19*

Bauer, Evgeny (1865-1917). Russian pre-Revolutionary film director. *34*

Baum, Vicki (1888-1960). Austrian novelist and screenwriter. *106*

Bazhanov [Bajanov], *Boris*. Stalin's secretary 1923-1924. *131*

Beach, Sylvia (1887-1962). American publisher and founder of the bookshop 'Shakespeare and Company', first publisher of Joyce's *Ulysses*. *103*

Bebutov, Valery (1885-1961). Soviet stage director, teacher at Meyerhold's Higher Workshops in Directing (GVYRM). *25*

Becker, John. Gallery owner in New York. *141*

Beckett, Samuel (1906-1989). Irish author and playwright. *158*

Beethoven, Ludwig van (1770-1827). German composer. *60, 156*

Beetson, Fred W. Treasurer and secretary of the Motion Picture Producers' Association on the West Coast. *119, 120*

Beilis, Menahem Mendel (1874-1934). Ukrainian Jew, accused of ritual murder in a trial in Kiev 1911-1913. *209*

Bekhterev, Vladimir (1857-1927). Russian physiologist and psychiatrist who studied the formations of the brain and investigated conditioned reflexes. *88*

Bella, Stefano della (1610-1664). Florentine Baroque printmaker noted for his engravings of military events. *9*

Belsky. Russian provincial stage actor. *15*

Bely, Andrei (1880-1934). Russian Symbolist poet, novelist, and critic. *150, 154, 155, 206, 208*

Bergson, Henri (1859-1941). French philosopher. *15*

Berkeley, George (1685-1753). Anglo-Irish Anglican bishop, philosopher, and scientist. *88*

Berna, Emil (1907-2000). Swiss cinematographer. *97*

Bernhardt, Sarah (1844-1923). French actress. *41*

Bernstein, Nikolai (1896-1966). Russian scientist and physiologist. *26*

Bertels, Alexei. Eisenstein's childhood friend. *3*

Bertels, Ostap. Russian general, city commandant in Riga. *3*

Best-Maugard, Adolfo (1892-1964). Mexican painter and film director; employed by the Mexican Ministry of Education; became Eisenstein's advisor on cultural and historical questions in Mexico. *125, 126*

Bierce, Ambrose Gwinnett (1842-1914). American newspaperman, satirist,

early Surrealist films. *95, 101, 103, 113*

Burlyuk, David (1882-1967). Russian Futurist poet and painter, founder of Russian Futurism; emigrated. *145*

Burnford, Paul. Editorial supervisor for Marie Seton's film *The Time in the Sun*. *203*

Burov, Andrei (1900-1957). Soviet architect, set designer for *The Old and The New*. *68, 84*

Butovskaya, Anna. Eisenstein's aunt. *7*

Butovskaya, Nita. Eisenstein's cousin. *9*

Caesar, Julius (100?BC-44BC). Roman General and statesman who had launched a series of political and social reforms when he was assassinated. *144*

Calderón de la Barca, Pedro (1600-1681). Spanish playwright of the Golden Age. *7*

Calles, Plutarco Elías (1877-1945). Military and political leader who modernized the revolutionary armies and later became president of Mexico; between 1928-1934 he was the real power behind three puppet presidents, forced to exile in 1934. *134, 136*

Callot, Jacques (1592/3-1635). French printmaker. *9*

Cañedo, Jorge Palomino y (1980-1994). Mexican writer. *129*

Capek, Karel (1890-1938). Czech novelist and playwright. *106, 109, 159*

Capone, Al (1899–1947). American gangster. *106, 109, 159*

Carroll, Lewis (1832-1898). English author of *Alice in Wonderland*. *162*

Cassirer, Ernst (1874-1945). German Jewish philosopher. *194*

Catherine II [byname Catherine the Great] (1729-1795). German-born Russian Empress. *9, 102, 153*

Cavalcanti, Alberto (1897-1982). Brazilian-born film director, worked in France and Great Britain. *95*

Cendrars, Blaise (1887-1961). Swiss French-speaking poet and essayist. *106, 114, 117*

Chaliapin, Feodor [Shalyapin, Fyodor] (1873-1938). Russian operatic *basso profundo*, best known singer of his time. *102, 156*

Chaplin, Charlie (1889-1977). British comedian and director, one of the most important figures in motion picture history. *ix, 66, 69, 81, 113, 114, 117, 122, 124-126, 142, 156, 184, 197, 200, 208, 214, 220, 223, 227*

Chardynin, Pyotr (1878-1934). Russian film director. *47*

Charlot, Jean (1898-1979). French-born Mexican painter. *126, 145*

Chekhov, Mikhail (1891-1955). Russian stage actor, emigrated in 1927. *17, 24, 86, 223*

Cherkasov, Nikolai (1903-1966). Soviet stage and film actor, played the leads in *Alexander Nevsky* and *Ivan the Terrible*. *196, 199, 215, 218, 228*

Chevalier, Maurice (1888-1972). French actor and singer, worked in Hollywood. *108*

Chiaureli, Mikhail (1894-1974). Soviet film director whose films were instrumental in creating the cult of Stalin. *201*

Chirkov, Boris (1901-1982). Soviet film and stage actor. *221*

Chkheidze, Nikolai (1844-1926). Menshevik leader, chairman of the Petrograd (St. Petersburg) Soviet of Workers' and Soldiers' Deputies in 1917. *73*

Chomette, Henri (1896-1941) French film director, brother of René Clair. *84*

Christophe, Henri (1767-1820). Haitian revolutionary leader. A freed black slave, he aided Toussaint L'Ouverture in the liberation of Haiti and was army chief under Dessalines. *155*

Chukhnovsky, Boris (1898-1975). Soviet Arctic pilot. *86*

Cocteau, Jean (1889-1963). French poet, novelist, film director, and painter. *95, 103, 105*

Colette (1873-1954). Pseudonym of Colette, Sidonie-Gabrielle, French novelist. *105, 106*

Conan Doyle, Arthur (1859-1930). Scottish writer, best known for his creation of the detective Sherlock Holmes. *42*

Conway, Jack (1887-1952). American film director. *178*

Cook, Proctor (Ted). American newspaper columnist. *110, 121*

Cooper, Gary (1901-1961). American film actor. *111*

Cowan, Lester (1907-1990). American producer, Secretary of the Academy of Motion Picture Arts and Sciences in Hollywood.

Craig, Edward Gordon (1872-1966). English actor, stage director, designer, and influential theorist. *14*

Crommelynck, Fernand (1886-1970). Belgian playwright. *27, 52*

Cromwell, John (1887-1979). American film director. *119*

Dalcroze (see Jaques-Dalcroze)

Dali, Salvador (1904-1989). Spanish surrealist painter, and printmaker. *85, 95, 103*

Dana, Henry Wadsforth Longfellow (1881-1950). American theater historian and critic. *83, 109, 120, 142, 157*

Danashev [Danashevsky], Anatoly. Russian émigré, worked in Hollywood as a film technician, returned to the Soviet Union, denounced as saboteur and arrested. *136, 137*

Danashev, Fred. Film technician who supervised the development of the Mexican film stock in Hollywood, son of Anatoly Danashev. *136, 137*

D'Annunzio, Gabriele (1863-1938). Italian writer, military hero, and political leader. *27*

Dante, Alighieri (1265-1321). Italian poet. *139, 182*

Daragan, Josef. Head of the Riga-Orlovsk railways. *3*

Daumier, Honoré (1808-1879). French caricaturist, painter, and sculptor. *5*

Davies, Marion (1897-1961). American actress. *208*

De Quincey, Thomas (1785-1859). English essayist and critic, best known for his Confessions of an English Opium-Eater. *192*

Deborin, Abram (1881-1963). Soviet Marxist philosopher. *88*

Delsarte, François (1811-1871). French teacher of acting and singing. *189*

Dembo, Tamara (1902-1993). Russian-born American psychologist, student and assistant of Kurt Lewin. *98*

DeMille, Cecil B. (1881-1959). American film producer and director. *72, 73, 142, 178, 203*

Denikin, Anton (1872-1947). Russian General who led the White Army. *12*

Derzhinskaya, Ksenia (1884-1951). Soviet operatic singer (soprano) at the Bolshoi Theater. *207*

Descartes, René (1596-1650). French mathematician, scientist, and philosopher. *60*

Desnos, Robert (1900-1945). French Surrealist poet. *103*

Dessalines, Jean-Jacques (1758-1806). Em-

...can writer. *117*

Grabar, Igor (1871-1960). Soviet painter and art historian, director of Tretyakov-Gallery. *230*

Granach, Alexander (1893-1945). Film and stage actor of Jewish origin, emigrated in 1928, worked in Germany, the Soviet Union, and the United States. *94*

Granet, Marcel (1884-1940). French Sinologist and sociologist. *167, 170*

Granovsky, Alexei (1890-1937). Soviet stage and film director, emigrated to France. *58, 86*

Griboedov, Alexander (1795-1829). Russian diplomat and playwright. *149*

Grierson, John (1898-1972). British film director and producer. *101*

Griffith, David Wark (1875-1948). American actor and director, a great pioneer of American film. *ix, 51, 53, 69, 87, 121, 220*

Gris, Mara. Russian émigré, role in *Romance sentimentale*. *102*

Gropius, Walter (1883-1969). German architect and educator, director of the Bauhaus school of design 1919–1928. *96, 152*

Grossman, Vasily (1905-1964). Soviet Jewish writer. *216, 232*

Grosz, George (1893-1959). German artist. *97*

Guilbert, Yvette (1867-1944). French singer and actress. *102*

Gulbransson, Olaf (1873-1958). Illustrator of Norwegian origin, noted for his portrait caricature style that used a minimum number of lines. Worked for the famous Munich magazine *Simplicissimus*. *5*

*H*arbou, *Thea von* (1888-1954). German author and screenwriter, Fritz Lang's wife and collaborator in the 1920s. *63, 114*

Harte, Bret (1836-1902). Popular American writer. *117*

Hauptmann, Gerhart (1862-1946). German playwright, poet, and novelist; recipient of the Nobel Prize for Literature in 1912. *9*

Hay, Will H. (1879-1954). Prominent American political figure, president of the Motion Picture Producers and Distributors of America 1922 to 1945. Because of his pervasive influence on the association's censorship office, it was known as the Hays Office. *117, 119*

Hearst, William Randolph (1863-1951). American newspaper publisher who built up the nation's largest newspaper chain. *113, 130, 208*

Hegel, Georg Wilhelm Friedrich (1770-1831). German philosopher who developed a dialectical scheme that emphasized the progress of history and of ideas from thesis to antithesis and thence to a synthesis. *104, 174, 194, 231*

Henselmann, Hermann (1905-1995). German architect. *98*

Hillkowitz, S. Wholesale produce distributor with radical and Socialist sympathies; investor in Mexican film enterprise. *123, 138*

Hirschfeld, Magnus (1868-1935). German physician, pioneer in sexology, led a thirty-year campaign to repeal paragraph 175 of the Imperial Penal Code according to which male homosexuality had been a criminal offence. *104, 131*

Hitchcock, Alfred (1899-1980). English-born American film director. *95*

Hoffmann, Ernst Theodor Amadeus (1776-1822). German Romantic writer, composer, and painter. *20, 24, 118*

Hogarth, William (1697-1764). English artist, known for his moral and satirical engravings and paintings. *9*

Hokusai, Katsushika (1760-1849). Japa-

novative stage director and designer, immigrated to England in
1919, then lived in the United
States. 5

Konetskaya, Iraida. Mother of Yulia
Konetskaya, grandmother of Sergei
Eisenstein. 1

Konetsky, Grigory. Iraida Konetskaya's
brother-in-law, owner of the Neva
cargo shipping company. 1, 18

Korda, Alexander (1893-1956). Hungar-
ian-born British producer and director. 178, 216

Kornilov, Konstantin (1879-1957). Soviet
psychologist. 88

Kosterlitz, Hermann (Koster, Henry)
(1905-1988). German film director,
worked in Hollywood. 178

Kostylyov, Valentin (1884-1950). Soviet
novelist. 211

Kozintsev, Grigory (1905-1973). Soviet
film director, cofounder of Factory
of the Eccentric Actor (FEKS). 29,
72, 168, 172, 217, 223

Kramer. Eisenstein's physician. 79

Krasin, Leonid (1870-1926). Soviet diplomat. 56, 71

Krauss, Werner (1884-1959). German
stage and film actor. 185

Kravchunovsky, Ivan (1898-1957). Soviet
film director, coauthor of The Strike.
48

Krestinsky, Nikolai (1883-1938). Soviet
politician, ambassador in Berlin in
the 1920s, shot after a show trial.
64

Kreuger, Ivan (1880-1932). Swedish
'match king', committed suicide at
the onset of the Great Depression.
102

Krinitsky, Alexander (1894-1937). Soviet
Party activist, deputy head of Party
Agitprop Department 1926-29, later
Deputy's People's Commissar for

Rabkrin (Deputy People's Commissar for Worker Peasant Inspection), arrested and shot. 77, 90, 92,
149, 150

Krull, Germaine (1897-1985). French photographer. 101

Krumgold. Worked in Paramount's publicity department. 112

Krupp, Gustav (1879-1950). German industrialist and weapons manufac-
turer. 90

Krupskaya, Nadezhda (1869–1939). Russian revolutionary and educator,
Lenin's wife. 71, 73, 76

Kulbin, Nikolai (1868-1917). Russian physician, painter, and promoter of Futurism. 7

Kuleshov, Lev (1899-1970). Soviet film
director, know for his montage
experiments. 34-36, 46, 47, 53,
54, 62, 63, 70, 86, 87, 94, 171, 172,
232

Küppers, Sophie (1891-1978). German
graphic artist, El Lissitzky's wife.
87

Kurbsky, Andrei, Prince (c. 1528–1583).
Russian statesman and publicist
who deserted to the Poles. 163, 211,
219

Kushnir, Boris (1888-1937). Soviet journalist and writer. 33

Kustodiev, Boris (1878-1927). Russian Soviet painter and graphic artist. 174

Kutepov, Alexander. Russian General,
head of the military organization of
the Russian White Army in exile,
kidnapped by the NKVD. 105

Kutuzov, Mikhail (1745-1813). Russian
field marshal. 210

Kuzminichna. The Strauch family housekeeper. 23

Kuznetsov, Mikhail (1918-1986). Soviet actor, played Fyodor Basmanov in
Ivan the Terrible. 215

painter. *79, 119*

Raskolnikov, Fyodor (1892-1939). Soviet revolutionary, arts administrator and diplomat, defected from Bulgaria in 1937, where he was ambassador; wrote a letter to Stalin denouncing his regime and the purges of Bolsheviks. *77, 90, 150*

Rasputin, Grigory (1872-1916). Siberian peasant and mystic, an influential favorite at the court of Emperor Nicholas II. *85*

Ray, Man (1890-1976). American photographer, painter, and filmmaker of the Dada and Surrealist movements, worked in Paris. *95, 101, 104*

Razin, Stepan (1630-1671). Russian leader of a major Cossack and peasant rebellion in 1670–1671. *176*

Redslob, Erwin (1884-1973). German art historian and cultural politician of the Weimar Republic. *94*

Reed, John (1887-1920). American poet, revolutionary writer, and activist; was eyewitness to the 1917 Bolshevik Revolution in Russia and recording this event in his book *Ten Days That Shook the World* (1919). *70, 126*

Regler, Gustav (1898-1963). German novelist. *65*

Reich, Wilhelm (1897-1957). Viennese psychologist, psychoanalyst, and Marxist. *166, 224*

Reizen, Mark (1895-1993). Soviet operatic basso at the Bolshoi Theater. *207*

Rembrandt [Rembrandt Harmenszoon van Rijn] (1606-1699). Dutch painter, draftsman, and etcher, master of chiaroscuro. *109*

Repin, Ilya (1844-1930). Russian realist painter. *174, 210, 213, 215*

Rerberg, Ivan (1869-1932). Russian architect, engineer, and teacher. *173*

Rerikh, Nikolai [Roerich, Nicholas]

(1874-1947). Russian painter and set designer. *14, 196*

Reynolds, Quentin (1902-1965). American war correspondent in Moscow, worked with Eisenstein on a documentary film *Moscow Fights Back* (unfinished). *214*

Richter, Hans (1888-1976). German artist and experimental filmmaker. *65, 94-96, 100, 101, 103, 104*

Rittau, Gunther. (1893-1971). German cinematographer, worked with Fritz Lang. *63*

Rivera, Diego (1886-1957). Mexican painter and muralist. *84, 125, 126, 187*

Robeson, Paul (1898-1976). American singer, actor, and black activist. *98, 113, 114, 155, 167, 186, 190, 214*

Robespierre, Maximilien-François-Marie-Isidore de (1758-1794). Radical Jacobin leader and one of the principal figures in the French Revolution. *155*

Rodchenko, Alexander (1891-1956). Russian painter, designer, photographer, cofounder of Constructivism. *23, 33, 62, 69*

Rolland, Romain (1866-1944). French novelist, dramatist, and essayist, deeply involved with pacifism; awarded the Nobel Prize for Literature in 1915. *85, 185*

Romanov (royal family)

Romm, Mikhail (1901-1971). Soviet film director. *190, 191, 197, 199, 201, 225*

Room, Abram (1894-1976). Soviet film director. *62, 83, 188*

Roosevelt, Franklin Delano (1882-1945). 32nd president of the United States; only president elected to office four times. *ix, 200*

Rosenfeld, Mikhail. Soviet journalist. *180*

Rosenthal, Léonhard. French millionaire, pearl trader, wrote books *Faisons*

sionist dramatist, poet, and political activist; prominent exponent of Marxism and pacifism. *97, 104, 106*

Tolstoy, Alexei (1883-1945). Russian and Soviet novelist and playwright. *85, 186, 211, 230*

Tolstoy, Alexei K. (1817-1875). Russian poet, novelist, and dramatist.

Tolstoy, Leo (1828-1910). Russian novelist. *3, 46, 65, 85, 169, 216*

Tomsky, Mikhail (1886-1936). Soviet politician, leader of the Soviet trade unions; committed suicide during the 1936 Moscow trial. *184*

Toulouse-Lautrec, Henri de (1864-1901). French artist, predecessor of fauvism and art nouveau. *101*

Toussaint-L'Ouverture, François Dominique (c. 1744-1803). Haitian patriot. A self-educated slave, he joined the black rebellion to liberate the slaves and became its organizational genius. *155*

Trauberg, Leonid (1902-1990). Soviet film director, cofounder of Factory of the Eccentric Actor (FEKS). *29, 72, 168, 170, 172, 217*

Tretyakov, Sergei (1834-1892). Russian merchant and collector of Western European paintings, brother of Pavel Tretyakov (1832-1898), art collector of Russian painting and founder of the Tretyakov-Gallery. *35, 230*

Tretyakov, Sergei (1892-1939). Soviet Futurist poet, playwright and theoretician, editor of *Novy lef*. Chairman of the artistic council of the Goskino studio 1 in 1925; worked closely with Eisenstein in the 1920s. *33, 34, 36, 37, 39, 40, 44, 45, 50, 52, 58, 67, 69, 72, 78, 84, 85, 120, 146, 162, 191, 211*

Trotsky, Leon (1879-1940). Bolshevik leader, commissar of foreign affairs and of war 1917-1924; his rivalry

with Stalin led to his exile and assassination. *8, 10, 47, 49, 51, 68, 71, 75, 76, 79, 88, 91, 93, 98, 102, 113, 126, 131, 136, 138, 141, 159, 187, 200*

Tselikovskaya, Lyudmila (b.1919). Soviet stage and film actress, role in *Ivan the Terrible*. *219*

Tukhachevsky, Mikhail (1893-1937). Soviet military chief, arrested and shot. *191*

Turgenev, Ivan (1818-1883). Russian novelist, poet, and playwright. *178*

Tvardovsky von. One of Mikhail Eisenstein's clients in Riga. *6*

Tynyanov, Yury (1894-1943). Soviet literary historian and novelist, one of the leading theoreticians of Formalism, a Russian school of literary criticism. *33, 71, 86, 149, 186, 208, 215*

Tyrsa, Nikolai (1887-1942). Russian painter and watercolorist of Armenian origin, a professor at the Academy of Fine Arts in St. Petersburg; after 1917 designer, book and magazine illustrator, especially of children's literature. *7*

Ulanova, Galina (1910-1998). Soviet prima ballerina of the Bolshoi Theater. *218*

Ulugbek (1394-1449). Tamerlane's grandson, ruler of Samarkand, scientist and astronomer. *202*

Ulyanova, Maria (1878-1937). Lenin's younger sister, professional revolutionary, Bolshevik. member of the *Pravda* editorial board and its secretary. *73*

Utamaro (1753-1806). Japanese printmaker and painter. *196*

Vaillant-Couturier, Paul (1892-1937). French politician and journalist, chief editor of L'Humanité. *84, 106*

Vaisfeld, Ilya (b. 1909). Soviet film critic.

ILLUSTRATIONS

Front Cover: Eisenstein in Mexico, 1931 *(Photo by Agustín Jiménez)*

Page viii: To touch or not to touch..? *(Sergei Eisenstein, early 1940's)*
Page 233: Auto Ritratto Realista *(Sergei Eisenstein, December 1944)*

Back Cover: Eisenstein shooting *Ivan the Terrible* in Alma-Ata, 1944

ACKNOWLEDGMENTS

Thanks to Richard Taylor, who encouraged the English edition and worked on the translation as editor, whose knowledge contributed immensely to this work; to my colleagues and friends François Albera, Olivier Debroise, Grisha Freidin, Ekaterina Khokhlova, Anna Muza, Andrei Nikitin, Valérie Posener, Susana Sosa, and Eduardo de la Vega Alfaro, who helped me with advice and information.

Special gratitude to the Russian State Archive for Literature and Art in Moscow, that made my work in the archive possible; to Janis Ekdhall at the Museum of Modern Art, New York for giving me access to the Jay Leyda Collection; and to the archive of the Academy of Motion Pictures and Sciences, Los Angeles.

Without the help of Dietmar Hochmuth, my husband, first reader, and strictest editor, this book would never have become what it is.

Oksana Bulgakowa, Stanford, Summer 2001

OKSANA BULGAKOWA

was born in 1954 and graduated from the Moscow Film Institute. She has been living in Berlin since 1977, and received her doctoral degree from Humboldt Universität in 1982. She works as an author, editor, and translator. Since 1998 she has been a visiting professor at Stanford University.

Publications:

Books: *Sergej Eisenstein: Das dynamische Quadrat. Schriften zum Film* (Leipzig 1988, with Dietmar Hochmuth); *FilmAugeFaustSprache. Stummfilmdebatten im Sowjetrußland der 20er Jahre* (Berlin 1992); *Die ungewöhnlichen Abenteuer des Dr. Mabuse im Lande der Bolschewiki. Das Buch zur Filmreihe Moskau-Berlin* (Berlin 1995); *Sergej Eisenstein—drei Utopien. Architekturentwürfe zur Filmtheorie* (Berlin 1996); *FEKS. Die Fabrik des Exzentrischen Schauspielers* (Berlin 1996); *Kazimir Malevich: Das weiße Rechteck. Schriften zum Film*, ed. (Berlin 1997); *Eisenstein und Deutschland*, ed. (Berlin 1998); et al.

Films: *Stalin—eine Mosfilmproduktion* (WDR 1993, with Enno Patalas); *Jewgeni Bauer. Das Kino des Zaren* (NDR 1995, with Dietmar Hochmuth); *Die verschiedenen Gesichter des Sergej Eisenstein* (arte 1998, with Dietmar Hochmuth); *America made in Russia* (2000); et al.